Theodore D. Strickler

When and Where we Met Each Other on Shore and Afloat

battles, engagements, actions, skirmishes, and expeditions during the Civil War,

1861-1866

Theodore D. Strickler

When and Where we Met Each Other on Shore and Afloat
battles, engagements, actions, skirmishes, and expeditions during the Civil War, 1861-1866

ISBN/EAN: 9783337224837

Printed in Europe, USA, Canada, Australia, Japan

Cover: Foto ©Andreas Hilbeck / pixelio.de

More available books at **www.hansebooks.com**

WHEN AND WHERE WE MET EACH OTHER

ON SHORE AND AFLOAT

BATTLES, ENGAGEMENTS, ACTIONS, SKIRMISHES, AND EXPEDITIONS DURING THE CIVIL WAR
1861—1866

TO WHICH IS ADDED CONCISE DATA CONCERNING THE ARMY CORPS AND LEGENDS OF THE ARMY CORPS BADGES

COMPILED FROM OFFICIAL AND OTHER AUTHENTIC SOURCES BY

THEODORE D. STRICKLER

Published by
THE NATIONAL TRIBUNE
Washington, D. C.

TO THE BOYS WHO WERE THERE.

The publisher of this book has been creditably informed that during General Grant's administration, the Secretary of War detailed a corps of clerks to compile a list of battles, engagements, combats, and skirmishes of the Civil War. After the expenditure of thousands of dollars in its compilation, ten copies were printed for use in the various bureaus of the War Department.

The Adjutant-General, taking one of these copies, said, "Mr. Secretary, here is the book. What do you think of it?" After a careful examination he commended the neat appearance, the quality of paper, and excellent execution displayed. "Now, General, I am going to see if your book is complete." After a little searching, he said, "Your book is not complete." The Adjutant-General answered with surprise, "Why so?" The Secretary replied, "I do not find any mention of a little affair in which I was interested. Let me tell you. At the breaking out of the war I had the honor to command a small body of troops, and one night, while in camp near the State line, a colored man reported that the enemy had a recruiting station at or near Athens, Missouri. I marched my men nearly all night with the colored man as a guide, and toward morning we surprised, attacked, and cleaned out their camp, having a few of my men wounded. Your book does not mention it."

To the question, "Did you report this to the Department?" the Secretary answered, "No. I was a lawyer at the time, and did not know that such small affairs had to be reported." "Well! your failure to do your duty as the commander of those troops is the only excuse that we have for not having it in our book. This is the first time I ever heard of it."

The compiler of this book was fortunate enough to have one of the few copies of the book referred to, and, with this for a

TO THE BOYS WHO WERE THERE.

nucleus, has been for more than ten years adding to it from authentic as well as additional official sources.

Many histories of the war have been published, and special attention is given to the story of the great battles, Shiloh, Antietam, Fredericksburg, Stone's River, Chancellorsville, Gettysburg, Chickamauga, Chattanooga, Charleston, Fort Fisher, and Mobile, and then call it a history of the war.

The hundreds of so-called minor affairs, the hurried scout by day and night into the enemy's territory, the sharp skirmish where the regiment suffered severely, while perhaps the same regiment held its place in some of the great battles without loss, the dangerous raids on lines of communication, these are the things lacking in many publications.

The Departments recognize only data received through official channels. In this book facts are given, whether official or not, and we submit it unhesitatingly as the most complete compilation in existence to the "Boys Who Were There."

This book is dedicated to every man, woman, or child who suffered that the Union might be preserved, and that "a government of the people, by the people, and for the people, might not perish from the earth."

CONTENTS

	Page
Alabama	7
Arizona Territory	15
Arkansas	16
Army Corps	205
California	29
Colorado	31
Dakota	32
Ditsrict of Columbia	33
Florida	33
Georgia	37
Idaho Territory	46
Illinois	47
Indiana	47
Indian Territory	47
Kansas	49
Kentucky	50
Louisiana	60
Maine	73
Maryland	73
Massachusetts	76
Mexico	76
Minnesota	77
Miscellaneous	77
Mississippi	77
Mississippi River	90
Missouri	90
Montana	111
Naval Engagements will be found under the Heading of each State.	
Naval Squadrons	217

CONTENTS.

Nebraska 111
Nevada 112
New Mexico 112
New York 114
North Carolina 115
Ohio 124
Oregon 125
Pennsylvania 125
South Carolina 126
Tennessee 133
Texas 156
Utah 159
Vermont 159
Virginia 159
Washington 194
West Virginia 194

ALABAMA.

Seceded Jan. 11, 1861.

ANTIOCH CHURCH, Skirmish near, Aug. 18-19, 1864.
ASHBYVILLE, Occupied by Union troops, March 31, 1865.
ATHENS, Operations in the vicinity of, May 1-2, 1862.—Skirmish at, May 8, 1862.—Reconnoissance to, from Fayetteville, Tenn., Aug. 7-8, 1863.—Scout from, March 30, 1864.—Skirmish at, Sept. 23, 1864.—Action at, and surrender of, Sept. 24, 1864.—Skirmish at, Oct. 1-2, 1864.
AUBURN, Skirmish near, July 18, 1864.
BAINBRIDGE FERRY, Skirmish at, Jan. 25, 1864.
BARTON'S STATION, Skirmish at, April 17, 1863.—Skirmishes at, Oct. 20, 26, and 31, 1863.
BEAR CREEK, Expedition to, April 12-13, 1862.
BENTON, Skirmish near, April 10, 1865.
BIG COVE VALLEY, Skirmish in, June 27, 1864.
BLACK CREEK, Skirmish at, near Gadsden, May 2, 1863.
BLAKELY, Skirmish near, April 1, 1865.
BLAKELY, FORT, Siege of, April 2-9, 1865.
BLOUNT'S PLANTATION, Action at, May 2, 1863.
BLOUNTSVILLE, Skirmish at, May 1, 1863.
BLUE POND, Skirmish at, Oct. 20, 1864.
BOLIVAR, Skirmish at, April 28, 1862.
BONSECOURS RIVER, Expedition from Mobile Bay to, Sept. 9-11, 1864.
BOYD'S STATION, Skirmish near, March 10, 1865.—Skirmishes at, March 15-18, 1865.
BRADDOCK'S FARM, Action at, near Welaka, Fla., Feb. 5, 1865.
BRIDGEPORT, Skirmish at, April 23, 1862.—Skirmish at, April 27, 1862.—Skirmish at, Aug. 27, 1862.—Skirmish near, July 29, 1863.—Reconnoissance from, towards Trenton, Oct. 20, 1863.—Reconnoissance from, to vicinity of Triana, April 12-16, 1864.
BROOMTOWN VALLEY, Reconnoissance into, from Winston's Gap. Sept. 5, 1863.
BROWN'S FERRY, Operations about, Feb. 19, 1864.
BUCKTHORN TAVERN, Skirmish at, near New Market, Oct. 12, 1863.
CAHAWBA RIVER (See Fike's Ferry, April 7, 1865).
CANE CREEK, Skirmish at, Oct. 20, 1863.—Skirmish near, Oct. 26, 1863.

ALABAMA.

CANOE STATION, Steele's column reached, March 27, 1865.
CAPERTON'S FERRY, Skirmish at, Aug. 29, 1863.—Scout to, March 28, 1864.—Affair at, March 29, 1864.—Scout from Bridgeport to, March 31-April 2, 1864.—Scout from Stevenson to, April 11, 1864.
CEDAR BLUFF, Skirmish near, May 3, 1863.—Scout from Rome, Ga., to, July 28-29, 1864.
CENTRE, Skirmish near, May 2, 1863.—Scout from Rome, Ga., to, July 11-13, 1864.
CENTRE STAR, Skirmish at, May 15, 1864.
CENTREVILLE, Skirmish at, April 1, 1865.—Skirmish near, April 2, 1865.
CHEHAW, Skirmish near, July 18, 1864.
CHEROKEE STATION, Skirmish at, Dec. 12, 1862.—Skirmish at, April 17, 1863.—Action at, Oct. 21, 1863.—Skirmish at, Oct. 29, 1863.
CHICKASAW, Expedition from Pittsburg Landing, Tenn., to, April 1, 1862.
CHICKASAW, Naval reconnoissance to, March 7-12, 1862.—Naval action at, Dec. 27, 1864.—Reconnoissance from Savannah, Tenn., to, April 3, 1862.—Raid from, to Selma, Ala., and Macon, Ga., March 22 to April 24, 1865.
CITRONELLE, Surrender of Confederate forces at, May 4, 1865.
CLAIBORNE, Expedition from Blakely to, April 9-17, 1865.
CLAYSVILLE, Skirmish at, March 14, 1864.
CLEAR SPRING VALLEY, Scout in, July 18-21, 1864.
COLUMBUS ROAD, Skirmish on, near Montgomery, April 12, 1865.—Skirmish on, near Tuskegee, April 14, 1865.
COOSA RIVER, Skirmish near, July 13, 1864.
COURTLAND, Skirmish at, July 25, 1862.—Expedition from Corinth, Miss., to, April 15-May 8, 1863.—Affair at, March 8, 1864.—Expedition from Decatur to, July 25-28, 1864, and skirmishes.
CRAWFORD, Skirmish at, April 16, 1865.
CROOKED CREEK, Action at, April 30, 1863.
CROSS ISLAND, At mouth of Crow Creek, Reconnoissance from Stevenson to, August, 1863.
CURTIS WELLS, Skirmish at, June 24, 1864.
DANNELLY'S MILLS, Skirmish near, March 23-24, 1865.
DANVILLE ROAD, Affair on, near Decatur, July 28, 1864.
DAUPHIN ISLAND, Landing of Union forces on, Aug. 3, 1864.
DAVIS GAP, Skirmish near, July 12, 1862.—Skirmish at, Sept. 1, 1863.
DAY'S GAP, Action at, April 30, 1863.
DECATUR, Occupation of, by Union forces, April 13, 1862.—Expedition from, July 12-16, 1862.—Attack on convalescent train near, Aug. 7, 1862.—Expedition from Maysville to, Nov. 14-17, 1863.—Skirmish at, March 7, 1864.—Skirmish

ALABAMA.

near, April 13, 1864.—Skirmish near, April 18, 1864.—Affair near, April 24, 1864.—Swirnish near, April 27, 1864.—Skirmish at, April 30, 1864.—Skirmish at, May 8, 1864.—Expedition from, to Courtland, July 25-28, 1864, and skirmishes.—Affair on Somerville Road near, Aug. 6, 1864.—Expedition from, to Moulton, Aug. 17-20, 1864.—Demonstrations against, Oct. 26-29, 1864.—Skirmishes near, Dec. 27-28, 1864. —Skirmish at, March 3, 1865.
DEER PARK ROAD, Skirmish on, March 25, 1865.
DE KALB COUNTY (See Elrod's Tan-Yard, Jan. 27, 1865).
DICKSON STATION, Skirmish at, April 19, 1863.—Skirmish at, April 23, 1863.—Skirmish at, Oct. 20, 1863.
DUCKETT'S PLANTATION, Skirmish at, near Paint Rock River, Nov. 19, 1864.
EAST BRANCH, Big Warrior River, Skirmish on, May 1, 1863.
EBENEZER CHURCH, Action at, near Maplesville, April 1, 1865.
EIGHT-MILE CREEK BRIDGE (See Whistler, April 13, 1865).
ELK RIVER, Operations in the vicinity of, May 1-2, 1862.
ELROD'S TAN-YARD, Skirmish at, in De Kalb County, Jan. 27, 1865.
ELYTON, Skirmish at, March 7, 1865.—Skirmish near, March 28, 1865.
EVERGREEN, Affair near, March 24, 1865.
FEARN'S FERRY, Expedition from Whitesburg to, Feb. 17-18, 1865.
FIKE'S FERRY, Skirmish at, April 7, 1865. (Cahawba River.)
FISH RIVER, Expedition from Mobile Bay to, Sept. 9-11, 1864.
FLETCHER'S FERRY, Skirmish at, May 18, 1864.
FLINT RIVER. Affair at, April 17, 1864.
FLORENCE, Expedition to, Feb. 6-10, 1862.—Affair near, March 25, 1863.—Skirmish at, April 23, 1863.—Expedition from Corinth, Miss., to, May 26-31, 1863.—Skirmish near, May 28, 1863.—Scout from Pulaski, Tenn., to, Dec. 11-17, 1863.—Skirmish near, April 12, 1864.—Skirmish near, May 7, 1864.—Scout from Pulaski, Tenn., to July 20-25, 1864.—Skirmishes at, Oct. 6-7, 1864.—Skirmish at Muscle Shoals, or Raccoon Ford, near, Oct. 30, 1864.—Skirmish at, Nov. 9, 1864.—Expedition from Gravelly Springs to, March 1-6, 1865.
FOWL RIVER NARROWS, Expedition from Dauphin Island, to, March 18-22, 1865, and skirmishes.
GADSDEN, Skirmish at Black Creek, near, May 2, 1863.
GADSDEN ROAD, Skirmish on, Oct. 25, 1864.
GAINES, FORT, Seizure of by State Troops, Jan. 5, 1861.—Naval reconnoissance of, Jan. 20, 1864.—Investment of, by Union forces, Aug. 3, 1864.—Surrender of, Aug. 8, 1864.
GIRARD, Skirmish at, April 16, 1865.
GOSHEN, Skirmish at, Oct. 28, 1864.

ALABAMA.

GOURD NECK, Expedition from Larkins's Landing to, March 2-3, 1864.
GREAT BEAR CREEK, Skirmish at, April 17, 1863.
GREENPOINT, Skirmish near, July 14, 1864.
GUNTER'S LANDING, Skirmish at, Aug. 24, 1863.—Scout from, to Warrenton, July 11, 1864, and skirmish.
GUNTERSVILLE, Expedition from Woodville to, July 27-30, 1862.—Skirmish at, July 28, 1862.—Reconnoissance to, Aug. 5-7, 1862.—Scout from Woodville to, and vicinity, Aug. 19-20, 1862.—Expedition from Larkins's Landing to, March 2-3, 1864.
GURLEY'S TANK, Skirmish near, Feb. 16, 1865.
HALLOWELL'S LANDING (See Jackson's Ferry, May 12, 1864).
HARRISON'S GAP, Affair at, April 21, 1864.
HILLSBOROUGH, Skirmish at, Dec. 29, 1864.
HOG JAW VALLEY (See Ladd's House, Feb. 3-4, 1865).
HOG MOUNTAIN, Action at, April 30, 1863.
HUGER BATTERY, Bombardment and capture of, April 9-11, 1865.
HUNT'S MILL, Skirmish at, Sept. 26, 1863.
HUNTSVILLE, Occupation of, by Union forces, April 11, 1862.—Skirmishes at, June 4-5, 1862.—Skirmish at, July 2, 1862.—Skirmish at, Aug. 31-Sept. 1, 1862.—Expedition to, July 13-22, 1863.—Skirmish near, Oct. 1, 1864.—Skirmish near, Oct. 18, 1864.
ISABELLA, SLOOP, Seizure of, at Mobile, March 20, 1861.
JACKSON'S FERRY (Hallowell's Landing), Skirmish at, May 12, 1864.
JACKSONVILLE, Expedition from Rome, Ga., to, Aug. 11-13, 1864.
JONESBOROUGH, Action near, July 26, 1862.
KELLY'S PLANTATION, Affair near, April 11, 1864.
KING'S HILL, Skirmish at, Oct. 23, 1864.
KING'S STORE, Skirmish at, April 6, 1865.
LADD'S HOUSE (Hog Jaw Valley), Skirmish at, Feb. 3-4, 1865.
LADIGA, Skirmish at, Oct. 28, 1864.
LAMB'S FERRY, Skirmish at, May 10, 1862.—Skirmish at, May 14, 1862.
LANIER'S MILLS (Sipsey Creek), Skirmish near, April 6, 1865.
LARKINSVILLE, Skirmish near, Aug. 30, 1862.—Skirmish, near, Sept. 26, 1863.—Affair near, Feb. 14, 1864.
LAWRENCE COUNTY, Scout in, July, 1864.
LAW'S LANDING, Skirmish at, July 28, 1862.
LEBANON, Skirmish at, Sept. 5, 1863.
LEESBURG, Skirmish at, Oct. 21, 1864.
LEIGHTON, Skirmish at, April 23, 1863.—Skirmish near, Dec. 30, 1864.

ALABAMA.

LIMESTONE BRIDGE, Operations in the vicinity of, May 1-2, 1862.
LITTLE BEAR CREEK, Skirmish at, Dec. 12, 1862.—Skirmish at, Oct. 27, 1863.
LITTLE RIVER, Skirmish at, Oct. 20, 1864.
LOWNDESBOROUGH, Skirmish at, April 10, 1865.
LUNDY'S LANE, Action at, April 17, 1863.
MADISON COUNTY, Operations in, Aug. 12-14, 1864.
MADISON STATION, Affair at, May 17, 1864.
MAPLESVILLE, Action near, April 1, 1865.
MARION COUNTY, Operations against Unionists in, April 19, 1864.
MAYSVILLE, Skirmish at, Aug. 21 1863.—Skirmish at, Oct. 13, 1863.—Skirmish at, Nov. 4, 1863.—Skirmish near, Nov. 17, 1864.—Scout from Huntsville to, April 5-7, 1865.
MOBILE, Operations about, Feb. 16-March 27, 1864.—Seizure of the sloop Isabella at, March 20, 1861.—Evacuation of, by Confederate forces, April 11, 1865.—Occupation of, by Union forces, April 12, 1865.—Explosion of ordnance depot at, May 25, 1865.—Campaign, March 17 to May 4, 1865.
MOBILE BAY, Naval reconnoissance of Forts Morgan and Gaines, Jan. 20, 1864.—Operations in, Aug. 2-23, 1864.—Capture of C. S. S. Selma in, Aug. 5, 1864.—Boat reconnoissance into, July 6, 1864.—Naval engagement in, Dec. 24, 1861.—Naval battle of, Aug. 5, 1864.—Naval reconnoissance in, Aug. 15, 1864.—Attack on U. S. S. Sebago in, Oct. 9, 1864.—Attack on U. S. S. Octoraro in, Jan. 28, 1865.
MONTEVALLO, Skirmish at, March 30, 1865.—Action near, March 31, 1865.
MONTGOMERY, Occupation of, by Union forces, April 12, 1865.
MONTPELIER SPRINGS, Skirmish at, April 20, 1865.
MOORESVILLE, Operations in the vicinity of, May 1-2, 1862.
MORGAN, FORT, Seizure of, by State Troops, Jan. 5, 1861.—Attack on blockade runner under the guns of, Oct. 12, 1863.—Naval reconnoissance of, Jan. 20, 1864.—Capture of Confederate picket near, July 22, 1864.—Passage of, by the Union fleet, and engagement in Mobile Bay, Aug. 5, 1864.—Siege of, Aug. 9-22, 1864.—Bombardment of, by Union naval forces, Aug. 22-23, 1864.—Surrender of (by Confederate forces), Aug. 23, 1864.
MOULTON, Affair at, March 8, 1864.—Skirmish near, March 21, 1864.—Action at, May 29, 1864.—Expedition from Decatur to, Aug. 17-20, 1864.
MOUNT PLEASANT, Skirmish near, April 11, 1865.
MOUNT VERNON ARSENAL, Seizure of, by State Troops, Jan. 4, 1861.
MUDDY CREEK, Skirmish at, March 26, 1865.
MUNFORD'S STATION, Action at, April 23, 1865.
MUSCLE SHOALS (See Florence, Oct. 30, 1864).

ALABAMA.

NASHVILLE, Expedition from Decherd, Tenn., to, Aug. 5-9, 1863.
NEAL'S GAP, Skirmish at, Sept. 1, 1863.—Skirmish at, Sept. 17, 1863.
NEW MARKET, Skirmish near, Aug. 5, 1862.—Skirmish near, Oct. 12, 1863.—Skirmish near, Nov. 17, 1864.—Scout from Huntsville to, April 5-7, 1865.—Expedition from Pulaski, Tenn., to, May 5-13, 1865.
NORTHPORT, Action at, April 3, 1865.
OLD DEPOSIT FERRY, Skirmish at, July 29, 1862.
OPELIKA, Skirmish near, April 16, 1865.
PAINT ROCK, Skirmish at, Jan. 26, 1865.
PAINT ROCK BRIDGE, Skirmish at, April 28, 1862.—Skirmish at, April 8, 1864.—Skirmish near, Dec. 7, 1864.—Affair at, Dec. 31, 1864.
PAINT ROCK RIVER, Skirmish near, Nov. 19, 1864.
PAINT ROCK STATION, Skirmish at, July 30, 1864.
PETER'S BLUFF, Naval action at, Sept. 11, 1864.
PLANTERSVILLE, Skirmish at, April 1, 1865.
POLLARD, Expedition from Barrancas, Fla., toward, July 21-25, 1864.—Expedition from Barrancas, Fla., to, Dec. 13-19, 1864, and skirmishes.—Occupation of, by Union forces, March 26, 1865.
POND SPRINGS, Skirmish at, May 27, 1864.—Affair at, June 29, 1864.—Skirmish at, Dec. 29, 1864.
PORT DEPOSIT, Skirmish near, Aug. 24, 1863.
POWELL, FORT, Evacuation of, by Confederate forces, Aug. 5, 1864.
RACCOON FORD (See Florence, Oct. 30, 1864).
RANDOLPH, Skirmish near, April 1, 1865.
RAWLINGSVILLE, Destruction of salt-works near, Sept. 5, 1863.
ROCK CUT, Action at, April 22, 1863.
RODDEY'S RAID (See Wheeler and Roddey's Raid, Sept. 30-Oct. 17, 1863).
ROGERSVILLE, Occupation of, May 13-14, 1862.—Scout from Pulaski, Tenn., to, April 23-26, 1865.
ROSECRANS'S COMMUNICATIONS, Raid on, Sept. 30-Oct. 17, 1863.
ROUND MOUNTAIN, Skirmish near, Oct. 25, 1864.
RUSSELLVILLE, Skirmish near, July 3, 1862.—Skirmish at, Dec. 31, 1864.—Expedition from Eastport, Miss., to, Feb. 19-23, 1865.—Sand Mountain, Action at, April 30, 1863.—Skirmish at, Dec. 26, 1863.
SCOTTSVILLE, Skirmish near, April 2, 1865.
SEBAGO, U. S. S., Attack on, in Mobile Bay, Oct. 9, 1864.
SELMA, C. S. S., Capture of, in Mobile Bay, Aug. 5, 1864.
SELMA, Raid from Chickasaw to, March 22-April 24, 1865.
SHOAL CREEK, Skirmish at, Jan. 14, 1864.—Skirmish near, Oct. 31, 1864.—Skirmishes at, Nov. 5-6, 1864.—Skirmish at,

ALABAMA.

Nov. 9, 1864.—Skirmish at, Nov. 11, 1864.—Skirmishes on the line of, Nov. 16-20, 1864.
SINK SPRING VALLEY, Scout in, July 18-21, 1864.
SIPSEY CREEK (See Lanier's Mills, April 6, 1865).
SIX-MILE CREEK, Action at, March 31, 1865.
SOMERVILLE, Scout from Triana to, July 29, 1864.
SOMERVILLE ROAD, Affair on, Aug. 6, 1864.
SPANGLER'S MILL, Action near, July 26, 1862.
SPANISH FORT, Skirmish near, March 26, 1865.—Siege of, March 27-April 8, 1865.
STEVENSON, Skirmish at, July 28, 1862.—Skirmish at, Aug. 31, 1862.—Skirmish at, Sept. 7, 1863.—Scout from, to Caperton's Ferry and vicinity, April 11, 1864.
STEVENSON'S GAP, Skirmishes at, March 15-18, 1865.
STOCKTON, Steele's column reached, March 31, 1865.—Scout from near Blakely toward, April 7, 1865.
STREIGHT'S RAID from Tuscumbia, Ala., toward Rome, Ga., April 26-May 3, 1863.
SULPHUR BRANCH TRESTLE, Action at, and surrender of, Sept. 25, 1864.
SULPHUR SPRINGS ROAD (See Kelly's Plantation, April 11, 1864).
SUMMERFIELD, Skirmish at, April 2, 1865.
TALLADEGA, Occupation of, by Union troops, April 22, 1865.
TAP'S GAP, Skirmish at, Sept. 1, 1863.
TECUMSEH, U. S. S., Sunk near Fort Morgan, Aug. 5, 1864.
TEN ISLAND FORD, Skirmish at, July 14, 1864.
TENNESSEE, C. S. S., Capture of, in Mobile Bay, Aug. 5, 1864.
TENNESSEE RIVER, Reconnoissance down, April 12-16, 1864.
THORN HILL, Skirmish near, Jan. 4, 1865.
TOWN CREEK, Skirmish at, April 6, 1863.—Skirmish at, April 27, 1863.—Action at, April 28, 1863.
TRACY, BATTERY, Bombardment and capture of, April 9-11, 1865.
TRENTON, Reconnoissance from Bridgeport toward, Oct. 20, 1863.
TRIANA, Reconnoissance from Bridgeport to the vicinity of, April 12-16, 1864.—Scout from, to Somerville, July 29, 1864.
TRINITY, Skirmishes at and near, July 25, 1862.—Skirmish at, Aug. 22, 1862.—Affair near, Aug. 23, 1862.
TRION, Skirmish at, April 1, 1865.
TURKEYTOWN, Skirmish at, Oct. 25, 1864.
TUSCALOOSA, Action near, April 3, 1865.—Occupation of, by Union forces, April 4, 1865.
TUSCUMBIA, Occupation of, by Union forces, April 16, 1862.—Skirmishes at, April 24-25, 1862.—Reconnoissance from Corinth, Miss., toward, Dec. 9-14, 1862.—Attack on,

ALABAMA—ARIZONA TERRITORY.

Feb. 22, 1863.—Skirmish at, April 23, 1863.—Raid from, toward Rome, Ga., April 26-May 3, 1863.—Skirmishes at, Oct. 24-25, 1863.—Skirmishes near, Feb. 20, 1865.
TUSKEGEE, Skirmish near, April 14, 1865.
UNION SPRINGS, Expedition from Blakely to, April 17-30, 1865.
VALHERMOSO SPRINGS, Scout from Triana to, Aug. 15, 1864.
VIENNA, Skirmish near, July 8, 1864.—Scout from Huntsville to near, April 3-4, 1865.
WARRENTON, Scout from Gunter's Landing to, July 11, 1864, and skirmish.
WATERLOO, Skirmish at, Feb. 12, 1865.
WATKINS'S PLANTATION, Affair near, July 31, 1864.
WEATHERFORD, Steele's column reached, March 29, 1865.
WEST BRIDGE, Action at, April 29, 1862.
WETUMPKA, Skirmish at, April 13, 1865.—Skirmish at, May 4, 1865.
WHEELER AND RODDEY'S RAID on Rosecrans's communications, Sept. 30-Oct. 17, 1863.
WHISTLER (or Eight-Mile Creek Bridge), Skirmish at, April 13, 1865.
WHITESBURG, Skirmish at, May 29, 1862.—Expedition from Maysville to, Nov. 14-17, 1863.—Operations about, Feb. 2, 1864.—Expedition from, to Fearn's Ferry, Feb. 17-18, 1865.
WILL'S CREEK, Skirmish at, Sept. 1, 1863.
WILL'S VALLEY, Skirmish in, Aug. 31, 1863.
WILSON'S RAID from Chickasaw to Selma, Ala., and Macon, Ga., March 22-April 24, 1865.
WINSTON'S GAP, Reconnoissance from, into Broomtown Valley, Sept. 5, 1863.—Skirmish at, Sept. 8, 1863.
WOODALL'S BRIDGE, Skirmish at, April 7, 1864.
WOODVILLE, Attack on Union pickets near, Aug. 4, 1862.—Reconnoissance from, to Guntersville, Aug. 5-7, 1862.—Affair near, Jan. 23, 1864.—Scout from, March 30, 1864.

ARIZONA TERRITORY.

BOWIE, FORT, Skirmish near, April 25, 1863.—Affair at, Aug. 27, 1863.
BUCHANAN, FORT, Skirmish at, Feb. 17, 1865.
CAVALRY CANON, Skirmish at, July 4, 1865.
CHIRICAHUA MOUNTAINS, Skirmishes in, Sept. 8-9, 1863.
COTTONWOOD CREEK, Skirmish on, July 3, 1865.
GILA RIVER, Expedition to, May 9-June 3, 1864.—Expedition from Fort Wingate, N. M., to, May 25-July 13, 1864.—Expedition from Fort Bowie to, June 26-July 6, 1865.

ARIZONA TERRITORY—ARKANSAS.

GOODWIN, FORT, Expedition from Fort Craig, N. M., to May 16-Aug. 2, 1864.—Expedition from Fort Craig to, Oct. 1-Nov. 27, 1864.
HASSAYAMPA CREEK, Skirmish on, Dec. 15, 1864.
MARICOPA WELLS, Expedition from Fort Bowie to, July 10-21, 1865.
MOJAVE, FORT, Expedition from Fort Crittenden, Utah Territory, to, May 9-June 22, 1864.
PICACHO PASS, Skirmish at, April 15, 1862.
PINAL MOUNTAINS, Expedition to, July 18-Aug. 7, 1864.
PINOS ALTOS, Skirmish at, Feb. 27, 1864.
SAN CARLOS RIVER, Skirmishes on, June 7-8, 1864.
SAN PEDRO CROSSING, Affair at, Sept. 21, 1862.—Affair at, Aug. 22, 1863.
SOUTHEASTERN ARIZONA, Scout from Fort Goodwin, into, July 6-24, 1864.
SYCAMORE SPRINGS, Skirmish at, Jan. 1, 1865.
TUCSON, Occupied by Union forces, May 20, 1862.

ARKANSAS.

Seceded May 6, 1861.

ADAMS' BLUFF, Skirmish at, June 30, 1862.
ALLIGATOR BAYOU, Scout from Helena to, Sept. 9-14, 1864.—Scout from Helena to, Sept. 22-28, 1864.—Scout from Helena to, Oct. 1-4, 1864.
ANTOINE CREEK (or Terre Noir Creek), Skirmish at, April 2, 1864.
ARKADELPHIA, Skirmish near, Feb. 15, 1863.—Skirmish at, March 20, 1864.—Skirmish at, March 29, 1864.—Skirmish near, March 31, 1864.—Skirmish at, April 1, 1864.
ARKANSAS POST, Expedition from Helena against, Nov. 16-21, 1862.—Expedition against, and operations in that vicinity, Jan. 4-17, 1863.
ARKANSAS RIVER, Scout from Fayetteville to, Feb. 5-12, 1863, and skirmish at Threlkeld's Ferry.—Skirmishes on, April 6-7, 1864.—Operations north of, May 13-31, 1864.—Scout on, Aug. 27-28, 1864, with skirmishes.—Operations on the, Jan. 28-Feb. 9, 1865.—Scout from Pine Bluff to, Feb. 17-18, 1865.
ASHLEY'S MILLS, or Ferry Landing, Skirmish at, Sept. 7, 1863.
ASHLEY'S STATION, Action at, Aug. 24, 1864.
AUGUSTA, Reconnoissance from Jacksonport toward, May 26-29, 1862.—Reconnoissance toward, June 23, 1862.—Action near, April 1, 1864.—Expedition from Jacksonport to, April 22-24, 1864, and skirmish near Jacksonport.—Skirmish near,

ARKANSAS.

Aug. 10, 1864.—Expeditions from Little Rock and Devall's Bluff to, Aug. 27-Sept. 6, 1864.—Scout from Devall's Bluff to, Nov. 22-24, 1864.—Expedition from Devall's Bluff to, Dec. 7-8, 1864.—Expedition from Brownsville to, Jan. 4-27, 1865.

BACKBONE MOUNTAIN, or Devil's Backbone, Action at, Sept. 1, 1863.

BAILEY'S, Affair at, Jan. 23, 1864.

BAKER'S SPRINGS, Scout from Waldron to, Jan. 21-25, 1864, and skirmish.

BARTHOLOMEW BAYOU, Scout from Pine Bluff to, April 1-4, 1865.

BASS'S PLANTATION, Expedition from Pine Bluff to, March 17-20, 1865.

BATES TOWNSHIP, Skirmish in, Nov. 2, 1863.

BATESVILLE, Skirmish at, May 3, 1862.—Scout from, June 16-17, 1862.—Skirmish at, July 14, 1862.—Skirmish at, Feb. 4, 1863.—Scout from Forsyth, Mo., to, Dec. 26, 1863-Jan. 2, 1864.—Expedition from, Feb. 12-20, 1864.—Expedition from Rolla, Mo., to, Feb. 29-March 13, 1864.—Expedition from Rolling Prairie to, March 19-April 4, 1864, with skirmishes.

BAYOU METOE, Skirmish near, Aug. 26, 1863.—Action at (or Reed's Bridge), Aug. 27, 1863.—Skirmish near, Feb. 17, 1865.—Scout from Pine Bluff to, Feb. 22-24, 1865.—Skirmish at, Feb. 24, 1865.—Scout from Little Rock to, May 6-11, 1865.

BAYOU METOE BRIDGE, Skirmish near, Sept. 23, 1863.

BEALER'S FERRY, Little Red River, Skirmish at, June 6, 1864.

BEATTY'S MILL, Skirmish near, Sept. 1, 1864.

BELLEFONTE, Scouts from, March 28-April 1, 1864.

BENNET'S BAYOU, Skirmish near, March 2, 1864.—Operations about, Feb. 16-18, 1865.

BENTON, Skirmish near, Dec. 1, 1863.—Scout from Little Rock to, March 27-31, 1864.—Skirmish near, July 6, 1864.—Affair at, July 25, 1864.—Skirmish at, Aug. 18, 1864.—Scout from Little Rock to, Sept. 6-7, 1864.—Scout from Little Rock to, Nov. 27-30, 1864.

BENTON COUNTY, Expedition in, Aug. 21-27, 1864, and skirmishes.—Skirmish in, Oct. 20, 1864.

BENTON ROAD, Skirmishes on, March 23-24, 1864.—Skirmish on, July 19, 1864.—Skirmish on, Jan. 22, 1865.

BENTONVILLE, Action at, Feb. 18, 1862.—Skirmish at, May 22, 1863.—Skirmish at, Aug. 15, 1863.—Skirmishes at, Sept. 4-5, 1863.—Skirmish at, Jan. 1, 1865.

BERRYVILLE, Reconnoissance to, March 3-7, 1862.—Scout from Elk Horn to, Jan. 8-10, 1863.—Scout from Cassville, Mo., to, July 18-26, 1863.—Expedition from Springfield, Mo., to, Nov. 10-18, 1863.

ARKANSAS.

BIG CREEK, Expedition from Helena to, March 6-10, 1863.—Pursuit of Confederates to, March 30, 1864.—Action at, July 26, 1864.
BIG INDIAN CREEK, Skirmish at, May 27, 1862.
BIG LAKE, Expedition to, Sept. 7-30, 1863.
BLACK'S MILL, Skirmish at, Feb. 17, 1864.
BLUE MOUNTAINS, Expedition to, June 19, 1862.
BOGGS' MILLS, Skirmish at, Jan. 24, 1865.
BOONESBOROUGH, Skirmish at, Nov. 7, 1862.
BOSTON MOUNTAINS, Skirmish at, Nov. 9, 1862. (See Cane Hill, Nov. 28, 1862.)
BRANCHVILLE, Skirmish at, Jan. 19, 1864.—Affair at, March 27, 1864.
BREWER'S LANE, Skirmish at, Sept. 11, 1864.
BROOK'S MILL, Skirmish at, March 27, 1864.
BROWNSVILLE, Skirmish at, July 25, 1863.—Skirmish near, Sept. 12, 1863.—Affair at, Sept. 16, 1863.—Skirmish at, Aug. 25, 1863.—Scouts from, Jan. 17-19, 1864.—Scout from, June 27-29, 1864.—Skirmish near, July 13, 1864.—Skirmish near, July 30, 1864.—Skirmish at, Sept. 4, 1864.
BUCK HORN, Skirmish at, May 25, 1864.
BUCKSKULL, Skirmish at, Nov. 20, 1864.
BUFFALO CITY, Skirmish near, March 1, 1864.
BUFFALO MOUNTAINS, Skirmish at, Oct. 24, 1863.
BUFFALO RIVER, Expedition from Huntsville to, Jan. 9-12, 1863.—Skirmish at, Dec. 25, 1863.—Scouts from Yellville to, March 13-26, 1864.
BULL BAYOU, Skirmish at, Aug. 7, 1864.
BURROWSVILLE, Skirmishes near, Jan. 23, 1864.
BUSH'S FORD, Scout from Batesville to, June 16, 1862.
CACHE BAYOU, Skirmish at, July 6, 1862.
CACHE RIVER BRIDGE, Skirmish at, May 28, 1862.
CADDO GAP, Skirmish at, Nov. 11, 1863.—Scouts from Waldron to, Dec. 2-7, 1863.—Skirmish at, Jan. 26, 1864.—Skirmish at, Feb. 12, 1864.—Skirmish at, Feb. 16, 1864.
CADDO MILL, Skirmish at, Dec. 14, 1863.
CALICO ROCK, Skirmish at, May 26, 1862.
CAMDEN, Skirmishes about, April 15-18, 1864.—Skirmish near, April 20, 1864.—Confederate demonstrations on, April 23, 1864.—Skirmish near, April 24, 1864.—Expedition, March 23-May 3, 1864.—Scout from Pine Bluff toward, Jan. 26-31, 1865, with skirmishes.
CANE HILL, Skirmish near, Nov. 9, 1862.—Skirmish near, Nov. 25, 1862.—Engagement at, Nov. 28, 1862. (Boston Mountains.)—Operations about, Dec. 4-6, 1862.—Skirmish at, Dec. 20, 1862.—Skirmish at, Jan. 2, 1863.—Skirmish at, Nov. 6, 1864.
CARROLLTON, Skirmish at, Jan. 10, 1863.—Expedition from Springfield, Mo., to, Nov. 10-18, 1863.—Skirmish at, March 13, 1864.—Skirmish at, Aug. 15, 1864.

17

ARKANSAS.

CEDAR GLADE, Skirmish at, March 1, 1864.
CHALK BLUFF, Skirmish at, May 15, 1862.—Expedition from Bloomfield, Mo., to, March 9-19, 1863.—Skirmish at, April 1, 1863.—Expedition from Lake Springs, Mo., to, April 21-May 2, 1863.—Skirmishes at, May 1-2, 1863. (Saint Francis River.)
CHARLESTOWN, Skirmish at, April 4, 1864.
CHEROKEE BAY, Scout from Patterson, Mo., to, Jan. 23-27, 1864.—Skirmish at, May 8, 1864.—Expeditions from Cape Girardeau and Dallas, Mo., to, Dec. 20, 1864,-Jan. 4, 1865, with skirmishes.
CHICOT, LAKE, Engagement at, June 6, 1864. (Old River Lake.)
CINCINNATI, Skirmishes near, Nov. 6, 1864.
CLAPPER'S SAW-MILL, Skirmish at, March 31, 1863. (Crooked Creek.)
CLARENDON, Expedition from Helena to, Aug. 4-17, 1862.—Skirmish near, April 1, 1863.—Naval expedition to, Aug. 15-16, 1863.—Skirmish at, March 15, 1864.—Naval action at, June 24, 1864.—Skirmish near, June 26, 1864.—Attack on steamer J. D. Perry at, Sept. 9, 1864.—Attack on steamer Resolute near, Oct. 11, 1864.—Expedition from Devall's Bluff toward, Oct. 16-17, 1864.
CLARKE'S STORE, Scout from Helena to, Feb. 24, 1865.
CLARKSVILLE, Skirmish at, Oct. 28, 1863.—Skirmish at, Nov. 24, 1863.—Affair near, April 3, 1864.—Skirmish at, May 18, 1864.—Skirmish at, Sept. 28, 1864.—Skirmish at, Oct. 9, 1864.—Skirmish at, Jan. 18, 1865.
CLEAR CREEK, Skirmish at, Jan. 22, 1864.—Skirmish at, Feb. 11, 1865.
CLEAR LAKE, Scout from Little Rock to, March 10-13, 1865.
CLINTON, Scouts from, June 4-17, 1864.—Scout from Devall's Bluff to, Nov. 9-15, 1864.
COLUMBIA, Naval actions near, June 1-2, 1864.
COMMERCIAL, STEAMER, Attack on, at Gregory's Landing, White River, Sept. 4, 1864.
COON CREEK, Expedition from Batesville to, March 24-31, 1864.
COTTON PLANT, Skirmish at, May 14, 1862.—Affair at, April 21, 1864.—Affair near, April 22, 1864.
COVE CREEK, Skirmish at, Nov. 8, 1862.
CRAIGHEAD COUNTY, Scout in, May 5-9, 1864.
CRAWFORD COUNTY, Skirmish in, Nov. 25, 1863.—Skirmish in, Aug. 11, 1864.—Skirmish in, Oct. 19, 1864.
CROOKED CREEK, Affair on, Jan. 23, 1864.—Skirmish on, Feb. 5, 1864.
CROSS HOLLOW, Skirmish at, Oct. 18, 1862.—Skirmish at, March 30, 1863.—Scout from Cassville, Mo., to, June 9-14, 1864.—Scouts from Cassville, Mo., to, June 20-24, 1864.
CROSS-ROADS, Skirmish near, March 27, 1864.

ARKANSAS.

CROWLEY'S RIDGE (See Taylor's Creek, May 11, 1863).
CYPRESS BEND, Expedition to, Feb. 14-26, 1863.
CYPRESS CREEK, Skirmish at, May 13, 1864.—Skirmish near, Dec. 1, 1864.
DALLAS, Scout from Waldron to, Dec. 2-7, 1863.—Scout from Waldron to, Dec. 11-13, 1863.—Skirmish at, Jan. 28, 1864.
DANVILLE, Skirmish at, March 28, 1864.
DARDANELLE, Skirmish at, Sept. 12, 1863.—Skirmish at, May 10, 1864.—Skirmish near, May 15, 1864.—Capture of, May 17, 1864.—Skirmish near, Aug. 30, 1864.—Attack on the steamer Alamo near, Nov. 29, 1864.—Action at, Jan. 14, 1865.
DAVIS, FORT, Capture and destruction of, by Union forces, Dec. —, 1862.
DENMARK, Scout from Batesville to, June 16, 1862.
DES ARC, Reconnoissance from Jacksonport toward, May 26-29, 1862.—Capture of, Jan. 17, 1863.
DES ARC BAYOU, Expedition from Searcy Landing to, May 27, 1862.—Action at, July 14, 1864.
DEVALL'S BLUFF, Skirmish near, July 6, 1862.—Capture of, Jan. 17, 1863.—Naval action with and capture of batteries at, July 16, 1863.—Skirmish near, Dec. 1, 1863.—Skirmish at, Dec. 12, 1863.—Affair near, May 22, 1864.—Action near, Aug. 24, 1864.—Affair near, Nov. 2, 1864.—Affair near, Dec. 13, 1864.—Scout from Pine Bluff to, Feb. 9-19, 1865, and skirmish.
DE VIEW BAYOU, Skirmish at, July 7, 1862.—Pursuit of Confederates to, June 26-28, 1864.
DEVIL'S BACKBONE (See Backbone Mountain, Sept. 1, 1863).
DEVIL'S FORK OF RED RIVER, Expedition from Batesville to, March 24-31, 1864.
DITCH BAYOU (See Old River Lake, or Lake Chicot, La., June 6, 1864).
DOUGLAS'S PLANTATION, Scout from Pine Bluff to, Feb. 21-22, 1865, and skirmish (22).
DOVER, Skirmish at, March 25, 1864.
DRIPPING SPRINGS, Skirmish at, Dec. 28, 1862.
DUBUQUE, Scout from Ozark, Mo., to, Jan. 4-6, 1863.
DUBUQUE CROSSING, Scout from Ozark, Mo., to, Aug. 23-26, 1864.
DUTCH CREEK, Scouts from Waldron down, Dec. 9-14, 1863.
DUTCH MILLS, Skirmish at, April 14, 1864.
EASTERN ARKANSAS, Operations in, Aug. 1-5, 1864.
ELEVEN POINTS RIVER, Expedition from Cape Girardeau, Mo., to, Jan. 24-Feb. 22, 1865.
ELGIN, Scout from Batesville to, Jan. 15-17, 1864.
ELIZABETHTOWN, Skirmish at, Oct. 1, 1863.
ELKHORN TAVERN (See Pea Ridge, March 6-8, 1862). Skirmish at, Oct. 16, 1862.

ARKANSAS.

ELKIN'S FERRY, Little Missouri River, Engagement at, April 3-4, 1864.
ELM SPRINGS, Skirmish at, April 26, 1863.—Skirmish near, July 30, 1863.
EUDORA CHURCH, Skirmish at, May 9, 1864.
EUNICE, Expedition from Helena to, Aug. 28-Sept. 3, 1862.
EVENING SHADE, Skirmish at, Oct. 7, 1863.
FAIRVIEW, Skirmish at, June 7, 1862.—Scout from Batesville to, June 16-17, 1862.—Scout from Batesville to, March 25-26, 1864.—Expeditions from Little Rock and Devall's Bluff to, Aug. 27.-Sept. 6, 1864.
FAYETTEVILLE, Occupation of, by Union forces, Feb. 23, 1862.—Action near, July 15, 1862.—Skirmish near, Oct. 24, 1862.—Skirmish at, Oct. 27, 1862.—Skirmish near, Nov. 9, 1862.—Battle of, Dec. 7, 1862.—Scouts from, March 29-April 5, 1863.—Action at, April 18, 1863.—Skirmish at, June 4, 1863.—Skirmish at, Aug. 23, 1863.—Demonstrations against, Oct. 11-14, 1863.—Scout from, Dec. 16-31, 1863.—Scout from Springfield, Mo., toward, April 28-May 7, 1864.—Skirmish at, May 19, 1864.—Affair near, June 24, 1864.—Expedition from Cassville, Mo., to, Aug. 23-28, 1864.—Operations about, Oct. 25-Nov. 4, 1864.—Skirmish at, Jan. 24, 1865.
FERRY LANDING (See Ashley's Mills, Sept. 7, 1863).
FERRY'S FORD, Skirmish at, Oct. 7, 1863.
FISH BAYOU (See Old River Lake, or Lake Chicot, June 6, 1864).
FITZHUGH'S WOODS, Action at, April 1, 1864.
FLINT CREEK, Skirmishes at, Sept. 4-5, 1863.—Skirmish at, March 6, 1864.
FOUCHE-LE-FAIX MOUNTAINS, Skirmish at, Nov. 11, 1863.
FOURCHE BAYOU, Engagement at, Sept. 10, 1863.
FROG BAYOU, Skirmish near, Feb. 12, 1863.—Skirmish on, March 19, 1863.—Expedition from Fayetteville to, Nov. 7-13, 1863.
GAINES' LANDING, Skirmish at, July 20, 1862.—Skirmish near, June 28, 1863.—Expedition from Vicksburg, Miss., to, Nov. 6-8, 1864.
GAINESVILLE, Scout from Pilot Knob, Mo., to, May 10-25, 1864.
GALLOWAY'S FARM, Affair at, June 2, 1862.
GERALD MOUNTAIN, Skirmish at, Aug. 24, 1864.
GLASS VILLAGE, Skirmish near, Sept. 8, 1864.
GRAND GLAIZE, Scout to, May 14, 1862.—Expedition to, May 31, 1862.—Scout from Batesville to, March 15-21, 1864.
GRAND LAKE (See Old River, or Lake Chicot, June 6, 1864).
GRAND PRAIRIE, Skirmish at, July 6, 1862.—Skirmish at, Aug. 17, 1863.
GREEN'S FARM, Skirmish at, Nov. 19, 1863.

ARKANSAS.

GREGORY'S LANDING, White River, Attack on the steamers Celeste and Commercial at, Sept. 4, 1864.
HAHN'S FARM, Skirmish at, June 19, 1864.
HARRISON'S LANDING, Skirmish at, Aug. 16, 1863.
HATCH'S FERRY, Skirmish at, Aug. 9, 1864.
HAY STATION No. 3, Skirmish at, July 30, 1864.
HAZEN'S FARM, Affair at, Nov. 2, 1864.
HELENA, Skirmish near, July 14, 1862.—Skirmish near, Aug. 11, 1862.—Skirmishes near, Sept. 19-20, 1862.—Skirmish at, Oct. 11, 1862.—Skirmish near, Oct. 18, 1862.—Skirmish near, Oct. 20, 1862.—Skirmish near, Oct. 22, 1862.—Skirmish near, Oct. 25, 1862.—Affair near, Dec. 14, 1862.—Skirmish near, Dec. 23, 1862.—Affair near, Jan. 1, 1863.—Skirmish near, Jan. 12, 1863.—Skirmish near, May 25, 1863.—Attack on, July 4, 1863.—Expedition to, July —, 1863.—Expedition from, Nov. 14-17, 1863.
HICKORY PLAINS, Skirmish at, Aug. 7, 1864.
HICKORY STATION, Skirmish near, April 2, 1865.
HILCHER'S FERRY, Scout from Batesville to, June 16-17, 1862.
HILL'S PLANTATION, Cache River, Action at, July 7, 1862.
HINDMAN, FORT (See Arkansas Post).
HOG EYE, Skirmishes at, Sept. 4-5, 1863.
HOPEFIELD, Burning of, Feb. 19, 1863.—Skirmish at, March 14, 1864.
HORSEHEAD CREEK, Skirmish at, Feb. 17, 1864.
HOT SPRINGS, Skirmish at, Feb. 4, 1864.
HUNTERSVILLE, Scouts from, June 4-17, 1864.—Skirmish near, July 8, 1864.
HUNTSVILLE, Skirmish at, Oct. 22, 1862.—Expedition from Fayetteville to, Dec. 21-23, 1862.—Scout from Cassville, Mo., to, July 18-26, 1863.—Expedition from Springfield, Mo., to, Nov. 10-18, 1863.—Scout from Fayetteville to, Sept. 12-15, 1864.—Scout from Springfield, Mo., to, Nov. 11-12, 1864, and skirmishes.—Skirmish at, Jan. 6, 1865.
ILLINOIS CREEK (See Prairie Grove, Dec. 7, 1862).
INDIAN BAY, Skirmish at, Feb. 16, 1864.—Skirmish at, April 13, 1864.
IVEY'S FORD, Skirmish near, Jan. 8, 1865.—Action at, Jan. 17, 1865.
JACKSON, Skirmish at, Aug. 3, 1862.
JACKSONPORT, Affair near, June 2, 1862.—Skirmish near, June 12, 1862.—Scout to, June 11, 1863.—Affair at, Nov. 21, 1863.—Skirmish at, Dec. 23, 1863.—Attack on, April 20, 1864.—Skirmish near, April 24, 1864.
JEFFERSONVILLE, Expedition from Helena to, Sept. 26, 1862.
JENKINS' FERRY, Engagement at, April 30, 1864.
JENNY LIND, Skirmish at, Sept. 1, 1863.

ARKANSAS.

JOHNSON COUNTY, Skirmish in, Oct. 26, 1863.—Skirmish in, Jan. 7, 1865.
JOHNSON'S FARM, Scout from Pine Bluff to, May 15-17, 1865.
JONESBOROUGH, Skirmish at, Aug. 2, 1862.
JONES' STATION, Action at, Aug. 24, 1864.
KENDAL'S GRIST-MILL, Affair at, Sept. 3, 1864.
KENT'S LANDING, Expedition from Helena to, Aug. 11-13, 1864.
KICKAPOO BOTTOM, Skirmish at, May 29, 1862.
KIMBALL'S PLANTATION, Expedition from Fort Pinney to, Jan. 27, 1865.
KING'S RIVER, Skirmish at, Jan. 10, 1864.—Skirmish on, April 19, 1864.
KINGSTON, Skirmish near, Nov. 10, 1863.
KNIGHT'S COVE, Skirmish near, June 19, 1862.
LA GRANGE, Skirmish at, Sept. 6, 1862.—Expedition from Helena to, Sept. 26, 1862.—Skirmish at, Nov. 1, 1862.—Skirmish at, Nov. 8, 1862.—Skirmish at, Dec. 30, 1862.—Skirmish at, May 1, 1863.
LAKE VILLAGE, Skirmish at, Feb. 10, 1864.—Skirmish near, June 6, 1864.
LAMB'S PLANTATION, Skirmish at, Aug. 1, 1864.
L'ANGUILLE FERRY, Skirmish at, Aug. 3, 1862.
LAWRENCE COUNTY, Scout in, May 5-9, 1864.
LAWRENCEVILLE, Expedition from Clarendon to, Sept. 11-13, 1862.—Skirmish near, Nov. 19, 1863.
LEE'S CREEK, Skirmish at, May 1, 1864.
LEWISBURG, Skirmish at, Jan. 17, 1864.—Skirmish at, June 10, 1864.—Scouts from, June 20-23, 1864.—Operations in the vicinity of, Sept. 6-8, 1864.—Skirmish near, Dec. 5, 1864.—Skirmish at, Dec. 6, 1864.—Skirmish near, Feb. 12, 1865.
LIBERTY POST OFFICE, Skirmish at, April 16, 1864.
LICK. CREEK, Skirmish at, Jan. 12, 1863.—Expedition from Helena to, March 6-10, 1863.
LIMESTONE VALLEY, Skirmish in, April 17, 1864.
LITCHFIELD, Skirmish at, May 2, 1862.
LITTLE BAYOU, Scout from Little Rock to, May 6-11, 1865.
LITTLE MISSOURI RIVER, Skirmish on, Jan. 25, 1864.—Skirmish on, April 6, 1864.
LITTLE RED RIVER, Skirmish on, May 17, 1862.—Expedition to mouth of, May 31, 1862.—Skirmish at, June 5, 1862.—Skirmish at June 7, 1862.—Expedition up, Aug. 13-16, 1863.—Skirmish at, June 6, 1864.—Expedition from Little Rock to, Aug. 6-16, 1864.
LITTLE RIVER, Expedition from Helena up, March 5-12, 1863.—Skirmishes in the swamps of, April 5-9, 1864.
LITTLE ROCK, Advance of Union forces upon, Aug. 1-Sept. 14, 1863.—Reconnoissance from, Dec. 5-13, 1863.—Skirmish near, April 26, 1864.—Skirmish near, May 24, 1864.—Skir-

ARKANSAS.

mish near, May 28, 1864.—Skirmish near, July 10, 1864.—Skirmish near, July 19, 1864.—Skirmish near, Sept. 2, 1864.—Skirmish near, Jan. 22, 1865.—Expedition on the Arkansas River near. Feb. 8-9, 1865.
LITTLE ROCK ARSENAL, Seizure of, Feb. 8, 1861.
LITTLE ROCK ROAD, Skirmish on, April 2, 1863.
LONG VIEW, Expedition from Pine Bluff to, March 27-31, 1864.
LUNA LANDING, Skirmish at, Feb. 22, 1864.
LUNENBURG, Skirmish at, Jan. 20, 1864.
McGUIRE'S, Action at, Oct. 28, 1862.—Affair at, Oct. 12, 1863.
McGUIRE'S FERRY, Skirmish at, Sept. 23, 1862.
McMILLEY'S FARM, Expedition from Pine Bluff to, Feb. 26-28, 1865.
MADISON, Skirmish at, March, 1863.—Skirmish at, June 25, 1863.—Scout from Helena to, Feb. 8-13, 1865.
MADISON COUNTY, Skirmish in, Jan. 15, 1865.
MARIANNA, Expedition from Helena to, July 24-26, 1862.—Expedition from Helena to, Sept. 26, 1862.—Skirmish at, Nov. 8, 1862.
MARION, Expedition from Memphis, Tenn., to, Jan. 19-22, 1865.
MARION COUNTY, Expedition from Ozark, Mo., into, Dec. 9-15, 1862.—Scout in, Feb. 16-20, 1865.
MARK'S MILLS, Skirmish at, April 5, 1864.—Action at, April 25, 1864.
MARTIN'S CREEK, Skirmish at, Jan. 7, 1864.
MASSARD PRAIRIE, Action at, July 27, 1864.
MAYSVILLE, Skirmish near, Jan. —, 1863.—Skirmish at, Sept. 5, 1863.—Skirmish near, May 8, 1864.—Skirmish near, July 20, 1864.
MEFFLETON LODGE, Skirmish at, June 29, 1864.
MERRIWETHER'S FERRY, Bayou Boeuf, Skirmish at, Dec. 13, 1863.
MOFFAT'S STATION, Franklin County, Skirmish at, Sept. 27, 1863.
MONTICELLO, Scout from Pine Bluff to, Jan. 13-14, 1864.—Skirmish at, March 18, 1864.—Expedition from Pine Bluff toward, Sept. 9-11, 1864.—Scout from Pine Bluff toward, Jan. 26-31, 1865, with skirmishes.—Scout from Pine Bluff to, March 21-23, 1865.—Scout from Pine Bluff to, May 23-27, 1865.
MONTICELLO ROAD, Skirmish on, June 17, 1864.—Skirmish on, May 16, 1865.
MORGAN'S MILL, Spring River, Skirmish at, Feb. 9, 1864.
MORO, Expedition from Helena to, Nov. 5-8, 1862.
MORO BOTTOM, Skirmishes in, April 25-26, 1864.
MOSCOW, Action at, April 13, 1864.
MOUND CITY, Burning of, Jan. 15, 1863.
MOUNTAIN FORK, Skirmish at, Feb. 4, 1864.

ARKANSAS.

MOUNTAIN HOME, Skirmish at, Oct. 17, 1862.
MOUNT ELBA, Expedition from Pine Bluff to, March 27-31, 1864.—Expedition from Little Rock to, Jan. 22-Feb. 4, 1865.
MOUNT IDA, Expedition from Benton to, Nov. 10-18, 1863.— Scout from Waldron to, Dec. 2-7, 1863.
MOUNT VERNON, Skirmish at, May 11, 1863.—Scout from Helena to, Aug. 22-25, 1864.
MUD TOWN, Skirmish at, Dec. 9, 1862.—Skirmish at, Aug. 24, 1864.
MULBERRY RIVER, Skirmish near mouth of, Feb. 3, 1863.
MULBERRY SPRINGS, Skirmish at, Jan. 26, 1863.
NAPOLEON, Seizure of U. S. ordnance stores at, Feb. 12, 1861.—Expedition from Helena to, May 23-26, 1863.
NEWTON COUNTY, Skirmish in, Nov. 15, 1863.
NOBLE'S FARM, Scout from Pine Bluff to, May 4-6, 1865.
NORRISTOWN, Skirmish near, May 19, 1864.—Skirmish at, Sept. 6, 1864.—Scout from Lewisburg to, Sept. 9-12, 1864.
NORTHEASTERN ARKANSAS, Operations in, Jan. 1-30, 1864.—Operations in, July 18-Aug. 6, 1864.
NORTHERN ARKANSAS, Scout from Springfield, Mo., into, Feb. 23-March 9, 1864.
NORTHWESTERN ARKANSAS, Scout from Cassville through, May 21-30, 1863.—Operations in, Jan. 16-Feb. 15, 1864.—Operations in, Aug. 15-24, 1864.
OIL TROUGH BOTTOM, Skirmish at, March 24, 1864.—Skirmish near, March 27, 1864.
OKOLONA, Skirmishes at, April 2-3, 1864.
OLD RIVER LAKE (or Lake Chicot), Engagement at, June 6, 1864.
OLD TOWN, Expedition from Helena to, July 28-31, 1862.
OSAGE BRANCH OF KING'S RIVER, Affair on, April 16, 1864.
OSAGE SPRINGS, Affair at, Feb. 28, 1862.
OSCEOLA, Skirmishes near, April 5-9, 1864.—Skirmish at, Aug. 2, 1864.
OUACHITA RIVER, Skirmish at, April 29, 1864.
OXFORD BEND, White River, Action at, Oct. 28, 1862.
OZARK, Skirmish at, Oct. 29, 1863.
PEA RIDGE (or Elkhorn Tavern), Battle of, March 6-8, 1862.
PEMISCOT BAYOU, Skirmish on, April 6, 1864.
PERRY COUNTY, Skirmish in, Dec. 3, 1864.
PETIT JEAN, Skirmish near, July 10, 1864.
PINE BLUFF, Seizure of U. S. subsistence stores at, April 18, 1861.—Action at, Oct. 25, 1863.—Skirmish at, May 1, 1864.— Skirmish at, May 21, 1864.—Skirmish near, June 17, 1864.— Reconnoissance from, July 13, 1864.—Skirmish near, July 22, 1864.—Skirmish near, July 30, 1864.—Capture of the steamer Miller near, Aug. 17, 1864.—Skirmish near, Aug. 18, 1864.—Scout near, Aug. 27-28, 1864, and skirmishes.—

ARKANSAS.

Expedition from, Jan. 7-9, 1865.—Expeditions from, Jan. 15-18, 1865.—Skirmish near, Feb. 11, 1865.—Affair near, March 4, 1865.
PINEY MOUNTAIN, Skirmish at, April 6, 1864.
PITMAN'S FERRY, Skirmish at, Oct. 27, 1862.—Skirmish at, Nov. 25, 1862.
POCAHONTAS, Skirmish at, Oct. 27, 1862.—Expeditions from Cape Girardeau and Pilot Knob, Mo., to, Aug. 17-26, 1863.—Expeditions from Pilot Knob, Mo., to, Sept. 29-Nov. 12, 1863.—Skirmish at, Feb. 10, 1864.
POISON SPRING, Engagement at, April 18, 1864.
POLK'S PLANTATION, Skirmish at, May 25, 1863.
POPE COUNTY, Skirmish in, Feb. 5, 1863.
POTT'S HILL, Action at, Feb. 16, 1862.
PRAIRIE D'ANE, Skirmishes on, April 9-12, 1864.
PRAIRIE GROVE, Battle of, Dec. 7, 1862.—Skirmishes near, April 6-7, 1864.
PRINCETON, Skirmish at, Dec. 8, 1863.—Skirmish near, April 28, 1864.
QUITMAN, Skirmish near, March 26, 1864.—Skirmish near, Sept. 2, 1864.
RECTOR'S FARM, Skirmish at, Dec. 19, 1864.
RED MOUND, Skirmish at, April 17, 1864.
REED'S BRIDGE, Action at, Aug. 27, 1863.
REED'S MOUNTAIN, Skirmish at, Dec. 6, 1862.
REMOUNT CAMP, Skirmish near, Aug. 5, 1864.
RESOLUTE, STEAMER, Attack on, Oct. 11, 1864.
RHEA'S MILLS, Skirmish at, Nov. 7, 1862.—Skirmish at, April 7, 1864.
RICHLAND, Skirmish at, Sept. 6, 1864.—Scout from Pine Bluff to, Dec. 24-25, 1864.
RICHLAND CREEK, Skirmish at, April 11, 1864.—Skirmishes at and near, April 13-14, 1864.—Skirmishes near mouth of, May 3 and 5, 1864.—Skirmish on, Aug. 16, 1864.
ROCKPORT, Skirmish at, March 25, 1864.
RODGERS'S CROSSING, White River, Skirmish at, Sept. 14, 1864.
RODGERS' PLANTATION, Scout from Pine Buff to, and skirmish at, April 25, 1865.
ROLLING PRAIRIE, Skirmish on, Jan. 23, 1864.—Skirmish at, Feb. 4, 1864.
ROSEVILLE, Skirmish at, Nov. 12, 1863.—Skirmish at, March 29, 1864.—Skirmishes at, April 4-5, 1864.—Skirmish at, April 15, 1864.
ROSEVILLE CREEK, Skirmish at, March 20, 1864.
ROSS' LANDING, Skirmish at, Feb. 14, 1864.
ROUND HILL, Skirmish at, July 7, 1862.
ROUND PRAIRIE, Skirmishes at, Sept. 4-5, 1863.
RUSSELLVILLE, Scout from Lewisburg to, Sept. 9-12, 1864.

ARKANSAS.

SAINT CHARLES, Engagement at, June 17, 1862.—Expedition from Clarendon to, Sept. 11-13, 1862.—Capture of, Jan. 13, 1863.—Attack on Union transport on White River near, Oct. 22, 1864.—Skirmish at, April 11, 1865.
SAINT FRANCIS COUNTY, Skirmish in, April 8, 1863.
SAINT FRANCIS RIVER, Expedition from Helena up, March 5-12, 1863.—Scout near, May 6-15, 1863.—Expedition from Helena up, Feb. 13-14, 1864.
SAINT FRANCIS ROAD, Skirmish on, Dec. 23, 1862.
SALEM, Capture of wagon train at, May 29, 1864.
SALINE BOTTOM, Skirmish near, April 29, 1864.
SALINE RIVER, Skirmish at, Feb. 15, 1864.—Skirmish at, Jan. —, 1865.—Scout from Little Rock to, April 26-29, 1865.
SCATTERVILLE, Skirmish at, Aug. 3, 1862.—Scout from Bloomfield to, March 24-April 1, 1863.—Skirmish at, July 28, 1864.
SCOTT'S FARM, Washita Cove, Skirmish at, Feb. 14, 1864.
SEARCY, Expedition from Searcy Landing to, May 27, 1862.—Affair near, May 18, 1864.—Skirmish at, June 3, 1864.—Scout to, July 26-28, 1864.—Skirmish near, Aug. 13, 1864.—Expeditions from Little Rock and Devall's Bluff to, Aug. 27-Sept. 6, 1864.—Skirmish near, Sept. 13, 1864.—Scout from Devall's Bluff to, Nov. 9-15, 1864.
SEARCY COUNTY, Skirmish in, Dec. 31, 1863.—Skirmish in, July 4, 1864.—Scout from Lewisburg into, March 12-23, 1865.
SEARCY LANDING, Skirmish at, May 19, 1862.—Expedition from Batesville to near, Jan. 30-Feb. 3, 1864.—Scout from Batesville to, March 15-21, 1864.
SHALLOW FORD, Bayou Metoe, Skirmish at, Aug. 30, 1863.—Skirmish near, Sept. 2, 1863.
SHELBY'S RAID in Arkansas and Missouri, Sept. 22-Oct. 26, 1863.
SMITH, FORT, Seizure of, April 23, 1861.—Reconnoissance toward, Nov. 20-23, 1862.—Skirmish opposite, March 5, 1863.—Skirmish at, May 15, 1863.—Occupation of by Union forces, Sept. 1, 1863.—Action near, July 27, 1864.—Action near, July 31, 1864.—Skirmish at, Sept. 1, 1864.—Skirmish near, Sept. 11, 1864.—Affair near, Sept. 23, 1864.—Expedition from Little Rock to, Sept. 25-Oct. 13, 1864.—Skirmish near, Oct. 14, 1864.—Expedition from Lewisburg to, Nov. 5-23, 1864, and skirmishes.—Skirmish near, Dec. 24, 1864.
SMITHVILLE, Skirmish near, June 17, 1862.—Skirmish near, April 13, 1864.
SNAKE CREEK, Skirmish on, April 23, 1865.
SOUTH BEND, Arkansas River, Expedition to, Jan. 14-15, 1863.
SOUTHEASTERN ARKANSAS, Expedition from Memphis, Tenn., into, Jan. 26-Feb. 11, 1865.
SPAVINAW, Skirmish at, May 13, 1864.

ARKANSAS.

SPRING CREEK, Affair on, March 18, 1864.
SPRING RIVER, Action at, March 13, 1862.—Skirmish on, April 13, 1864.
SPRING RIVER COUNTY, Scout in, Oct. 7-10, 1863.
SPRING RIVER MILLS, Scout from Houston to, Aug. 6-11, 1863, and skirmishes.—Scouts from Licking and Salem, Mo., to, Feb. 23-March 2, 1865, and skirmishes.
STEWART'S PLANTATION, Skirmish at, June 27, 1862.
STONY POINT, Skirmish at, May 20, 1864.
STRAWBERRY CREEK, Expedition from Batesville to, March 10-12, 1864.
STROUD'S STORE, Skirmish at, Dec. 23, 1863.
SUGAR CREEK, Action at, Feb. 17, 1862.—Skirmish at, Oct. 17, 1862.
SUGAR LOAF PRAIRIE, Scout from Ozark, Mo., to, Aug. 23-26, 1864.—Affair near, Jan. 12, 1865.
SULPHUR SPRINGS, Skirmish at, Jan. 25, 1864.
SUNNYSIDE LANDING, Expedition from Vicksburg, Miss., to, Jan. 10-16, 1864.—Skirmish at, June 7, 1864.
SWAN LAKE, Affair at, April 23, 1864.
SYLAMORE, Skirmish near, May 29, 1862.
SYLAMORE CREEK, Skirmishes near, Jan. —, 1864.
TALBOT'S FERRY, Skirmish at, April 19, 1862.—Skirmish at, March 20, 1865.
TAYLOR'S CREEK, Skirmish at, May 11, 1863. (Crowley's Ridge.)
TERRE NOIR CREEK, Skirmish at, April 2, 1864.
THRELKELD'S FERRY, Skirmish at, Feb. —, 1863.
TOLBERT'S MILL, Operations about, Feb. 16-18, 1865.
TOMAHAWK, Skirmish at, Jan. 22, 1864.
TOMAHAWK GAP, Skirmish at, Feb. 9, 1864.
TRENTON, Expedition from Helena to, July 28-31, 1862.—Skirmish at, Oct. 14, 1862.
TULIP, Skirmish at, Oct. 10, 1863.—Skirmish at, Oct, 12, 1863.—Skirmish at, Oct. 27, 1863.
TYLER, U. S. S., Engagement with Shelby's forces on White River, June 24-25, 1864.
UPPER ARKANSAS RIVER, Operations on, Jan. 28-Feb. 9, 1865.
VACHE GRASS, Skirmish at, Sept. 26, 1864.
VAN BUREN, Reconnoissance toward, Nov. 20-23, 1862.—Skirmish at, Dec. 21, 1862.—Capture of, Dec. 28, 1862.—Scout from Fayetteville to, Jan. 23-27, 1863.—Skirmish near, Feb. 10, 1863.—Skirmish at, April 12, 1864.—Skirmish at, July 7, 1864.—Skirmish at, Aug. 12, 1864.—Skirmish near, April 2, 1865.
VAN BUREN COUNTY, Skirmish in, March 25, 1864.
VANCE'S STORE, Skirmish at, Oct. 2, 1863.
VILLAGE CREEK, Skirmish at, May 21, 1862.—Skirmish near, June 12, 1862.

ARKANSAS

VINE PRAIRIE, Skirmishes at, Feb. 2, 1865.
VOCHE'S, MRS., Skirmish near, Feb. 23, 1865.
WADDELL'S FARM, Skirmish at, June 12, 1862.
WALDRON, Skirmish at, Sept. 11, 1863.—Skirmish at, Oct. 6, 1863.—Scout from, to Mount Ida, Caddo Gap, and Dallas, Dec. 27, 1863.—Attack on, Dec. 29, 1863.—Scout from, to Baker's Springs, Jan. 21-25, 1864, and skirmish.—Skirmish at, Feb. 1, 1864.—Skirmish near, June 10, 1864.
WALLACE'S FERRY, Big Creek, Action at, July 26, 1864.
WASHINGTON, Skirmish at, Aug. 30, 1863.—Skirmish at, May 28, 1864.—Skirmish at, March 11, 1865.
WASHINGTON COUNTY, Expedition into, Aug. 21-27, 1864, and skirmishes.—Skirmish in, Feb. 17, 1865.
WASHITA COVE, Skirmish at, Feb. 14, 1864.
WAUGH'S FARM, near Batesville, Capture of wagon train at, Feb. 19, 1864.
WEST POINT, Expedition from Searcy Landing to, May 27, 1862.—Skirmish at, Aug. 14, 1863.—Scout from Batesville to, March 15-21, 1864.—Skirmish at, June 16, 1864.—Scout to, July 20-28, 1864.—Scout from Devall's Bluff to, Nov. 10-18, 1864, and skirmishes.
WHITE COUNTY, Skirmish in, Feb. 9, 1864.
WHITELEY'S MILL, Skirmish at, April 5, 1864.
WHITE OAK CREEK, Skirmish at, April 14, 1864.—Skirmish on, Aug. 11, 1864.—Skirmish at, Sept. 20, 1864.
WHITE RIVER, Skirmish on, May 6, 1862.—Operations on, June 10-July 14, 1862.—Expedition from Helena to mouth of, Aug. 5-8, 1862.—Expedition from Helena up, Jan. 13-19, 1863, and capture of Clarendon.—Skirmish on, March 6, 1863.—Skirmish near the head of, March 22, 1863.—Skirmish on, April 9, 1863.—Scout near, May 9-15, 1863.—Expedition up, Aug. 13-16, 1863.—Expedition from Helena up, Feb. 4-8, 1864.—Expedition from Helena up, Feb. 20-29, 1864.—Skirmish near, March 25, 1864.—Operations on, June 20-29, 1864.—Operations, July 10-25, 1864.—Expeditions from Helena up, Aug. 29-Sept. 3, 1864.—Attack on steamers Celeste and Commercial on, Sept. 4, 1864.—Skirmish at, Sept. 11, 1864.—Attack on the steamer on, Oct. 11, 1864.—Attack on Union transport on, Oct. 22, 1864.—Expedition from Devall's Bluff up, Dec. 13-15, 1864.
WHITE RIVER STATION, Skirmish at, June 22, 1864.
WHITE SPRINGS, Skirmish at, Jan. 2, 1863.
WHITMORE'S MILLS, Skirmish at, April 30, 1864.
WILD HAWS, Strawberry Creek, Expedition from Batesville to, March 10-15, 1864.
WOLF CREEK, Skirmish on, April 2, 1864.
WORTHINGTON'S LANDING, Skirmish at, June 5, 1864.
YELL COUNTY, Scout in, July 25-Aug. 11, 1864, and skirmishes.—Skirmish in, Aug. 22, 1864.—Scout from Lewisburg into, March 12-23, 1865.

ARKANSAS—CALIFORNIA.

YELLVILLE, Skirmish at, June 25, 1862.—Expedition from Ozark, Mo., toward, Oct. 12-19, 1862.—Expedition to, Nov. 25-29, 1862.—Scout from Carrollton to, April 3-8, 1863, and skirmishes.—Skirmish near, March 13, 1864—Skirmish near, March 26, 1864—Scout from Springfield, Mo., to, Nov. 11-21, 1864, and skirmishes.

CALIFORNIA.

ALBEE'S RANCH, Skirmish near, July 29, 1862.
ANDERSON, FORT, Skirmish near, April 6, 1862.—Action near, July 28, 1862.
ANGEL'S RANCH, Skirmish at, May 14, 1862.
ANTELOPE CREEK, Expedition from Camp Bidwell to, April 5-18, 1865.
ARCATA, Skirmish near, April 8, 1862.—Skirmishes near, June 6-7, 1862.—Skirmish near, Aug. 21, 1862.
BAKER, FORT, Skirmish near, April 26, 1862.
BALD MOUNTAIN, Scout from Camp Anderson to, Aug 8-12, 1864.
BALD SPRING CANON, Eel River, Skirmish at, March 22, 1864.
BELL SPRING, Skirmish opposite, June 4, 1861.
BIG BAR, Skirmishes near, Nov. 13-14, 1863.
BIG BEND of the Eel River, Skirmish on, April 28, 1864.
BIG FLAT, Skirmish at, May 28, 1864.
BISHOP'S CREEK, Skirmish near, April 9, 1862.
BLUE ROCK STATION, Skirmish near, March 17, 1864.
BOOTH'S RUN, Affair at, May 1, 1864.
BOYNTON'S PRAIRIE, Skirmish near, May 6, 1864.
CROGHAN'S RANCH, Skirmish at, May 7, 1862.
CROOK, FORT, Affair near, Sept. 21. 1862.
CUTTERBACK'S HOUSE, Attack on, July 2. 1862.
DALEY'S FERRY, Skirmishes at, June 6-7, 1862.
EEL RIVER, Skirmish on, May 26, 1861.—Skirmish on the South Fork of, May 28, 1861.—Skirmish on, June 4, 1861.—Skirmish on the South Fork of, June 14, 1861.—Skirmish on the South Fork of, June 16, 1861.—Skirmish on the South Fork of, July 21, 1861.—Skirmish on, April 26, 1862.—Skirmish on, May 31, 1862.—Skirmish on, March 21, 1863—Skirmish on, March 24, 1863.—Skirmish on, March 19, 1864.—Skirmish on, March 22, 1864.—Skirmish on, March 27, 1864.—Engagement on, March 23, 1864.—Skirmish on the Big Bend of, April 28, 1864.—Scout from Camp Grant to the North Fork of, Sept. 1-29, 1864.
ELK CAMP, Affair near, July 30, 1862.
FAWN PRAIRIE, Skirmish at, June 8, 1862.
GASTON, FORT, Skirmish near, Aug. 6, 1862.—Skirmish near, Dec. 25, 1863.—Skirmish near, Dec. 26, 1863.

CALIFORNIA.

GROUSE CREEK, Skirmish at, May 23, 1864.
HONEY LAKE VALLEY, Scouts from Fort Crook, Cal., and Fort Churchill, Nev., to, Nov. 3-29, 1862.
HOOPA VALLEY, Skirmish in, Sept. 3, 1863.
HUMBOLDT DISTRICT, Operations in, March 23-Aug. 31, 1862.—Operations in, March 10-July 10, 1863.—Operations in, Sept. 3, 1863-Jan. 28, 1864.—Operations in, Feb. 1-June 30, 1864.
HUMBOLDT, FORT, Operations in the vicinity of, Jan. 16-May 18, 1861.
HYDESVILLE, Skirmish near, Oct. 21, 1862.
KEATUCK CREEK, Skirmish on, May 30, 1861.
KELLOGG'S LAKE, Skirmish near, Aug. 19, 1861.
KETTENSHAW, Skirmish near, June 17, 1861.
KEYSVILLE, Expedition from Camp Babbitt to, April 12-24, 1863.
KNEELAND'S PRAIRIE, Skirmish on, May 2, 1864.
LARRABEE'S HOUSE, Skirmish near, June 2, 1861.—Skirmish near, June 8, 1861.
LARRABEE'S RANCH, Skirmish near, May 23, 1861.
LIGHT PRAIRIE, Skirmish at, Aug. 21, 1862.
LISCOMBE'S HILL, Skirmish near, June 8, 1862.
LITTLE RIVER, Affair on Aug. 23, 1862.
MAD RIVER, Skirmishes near, April 14-15, 1861.—Operations on, May 23-June 17, 1861.—Skirmish on, May 14, 1862.—Skirmishes on, June 6-7, 1862.—Skirmish on, June 11, 1862.—Affair at, July 9, 1862.
MATTOLE VALLEY, Skirmish in, June 7, 1862.
MILLER'S RANCH, Affair at, July 30, 1862.
NORTH FORK, Eel River (see Eel River, Sept. 1-29, 1864).
OAK CAMP, Attack near, April 30, 1863.—Skirmish at, June 6, 1863.
OAK GROVE, Expedition from San Bernardino to, Sept. 25-Oct. 5, 1861.
OWEN'S LAKE, Skirmish at, June 24, 1862.
OWEN'S RIVER, Expedition from Camp Latham to, March 19-April 28, 1862.—Expedition from Camp Latham to, June 11-Oct. 8, 1862.—Operations at and near, April 24-May 26, 1863.
PITT RIVER, Expedition from Fort Crook to, Aug. 15-22, 1861.
PITT RIVER VALLEY, Skirmish in the Upper, Aug. 5, 1861.
RED MOUNTAIN, Skirmish on, March 17, 1864.
REDWOOD CREEK, Skirmish on, Sept. 8, 1862.—Attack on, July 9, 1863.—Skirmish on, Feb. 29, 1864.
REDWOOD MOUNTAINS, Skirmish in, March 1, 1864.
ROUND VALLEY, Scout from Fort Crook to, Aug. 3-12, 1861.—Operations in, July 20-26, 1863.
SAN JOSE VALLEY, Pursuit and capture of the Showalter Party at Warner's Ranch in, Nov. 20-29, 1861.

CALIFORNIA—COLORADO.

SANTA ANA CANON, Skirmish near, Sept. 7, 1861.
SANTA CATALINA ISLAND, Occupation of, Jan. 2, 1864.
SHELTER COVE, Skirmish at, May 9, 1863.
SHOWALTER PARTY, Pursuit and capture of, at Warner's Ranch, in the San Jose Valley, Nov. 20-29, 1861.
SIMMON'S RANCH, Skirmish near, Oct. 21, 1862.
SOUTH FORK OF EEL RIVER (See Eel River).
SOUTH FORK OF TRINITY RIVER, Skirmishes near, Nov. 13-14, 1863.
TABLE BLUFF, Affair at, April 4, 1862.
TEMECULA RANCH, Expedition from San Bernardino to the, Sept. 25-Oct. 5, 1861.
THOMAS'S HOUSE, Trinity River, Skirmish at, May 27, 1864.
TRINITY RIVER, Skirmishes near South Fork of, Nov. 13-14, 1863.
TRINITY RIVER VALLEY, Operations in, Sept. 1-Dec. 3, 1864.—Skirmish on, Nov. 17, 1863.—Skirmish on, May 27, 1864.
VAN DUSEN'S CREEK, Skirmishes on, April 14-15, 1861.—Skirmish near, May 31, 1862.—Skirmish at, July 2, 1862.
WARNER'S RANCH (See San Jose Valley, Nov. 20-29, 1861).
WEAVERVILLE CROSSING, Mad River, Affair at, July 9, 1862.
WHITNEY'S RANCH, Attack on, July 28, 1862.
WILLIAMS'S VALLEY, Expedition from Fort Wright to, April 7-11, 1863.
WILLOW CREEK, Skirmish near, Nov. 17, 1863.
WRIGHT, FORT, Expedition from, to Williams's Valley, April 7-11, 1863.
YREKA ROAD, Affair on the, Sept. 21, 1862.

COLORADO.

AMERICAN RANCH, Skirmish at, Jan. 15, 1865.
CEDAR BLUFFS, Skirmish at, May 3, 1864.—Scout from American Ranch to, May 9-10, 1864.
COLLINS, FORT, Operations against Indians near, June 4-10, 1865.
DAN SMITH'S RANCH, Skirmish at, May 13, 1865.
DENVER, Operations on the Overland Stage Road near, Jan. 14-28, 1865.
FORT UNION ROAD, Scout on the, Aug. 12-16, 1864.
FREMONT'S ORCHARD, Skirmish near, April 12, 1864.
GARLAND, FORT, Scout from, Oct. 12-16, 1863, and killing of outlaw Epanoza.—Scout on the Fort Union Road near, Aug. 12-16, 1864.—Affair near, April 1, 1865.
GITTRELL'S RANCH, Skirmish at, Jan. 25, 1865.
GODFREY'S RANCH, Skirmish at, Jan. 14, 1865.

COLORADO—DAKOTA.

JULESBURG, Skirmish at, Jan. 7, 1865.—Operations on the Overland Stage Road near, Jan. 14-29, 1865.—Affair at, Feb. 2, 1865.—Skirmish near, May 13, 1865.
LILLIAN SPRINGS RANCH, Skirmish at, Jan. 27, 1865.
LYON, FORT, Affair near, Aug. 7, 1864.—Affairs near, Nov. 6-16, 1864.
MOORE'S RANCH, Skirmish at, Jan. 26, 1865.
MORRISON'S RANCH, Skirmish at, Jan. 15, 1865.
OVERLAND STAGE ROAD, Operations on the, between Julesburg and Denver, Jan. 14-29, 1865.
OVERLAND STAGE STATION at Julesburg, Attack on, Feb. 2, 1865.
SAGE CREEK, Skirmish at, June 8, 1865.
SAND CREEK, Skirmish near, Aug. 11, 1864.—Engagement on, Nov. 29, 1864.
SOUTH PLATTE RIVER, Scout on, July 17-28, 1864.
SQUIRREL CREEK CROSSING, Skirmish near, April 11, 1863.
VALLEY STATION, Skirmish near, Oct. 10, 1864.—Skirmish at, Jan. 7, 1865.—Skirmish near, Jan. 15, 1865.—Skirmish near, Jan. 28, 1865.
WISCONSIN RANCH, Skirmish at, Jan. 15, 1865.

DAKOTA.

ABERCROMBIE, FORT, Action with Indians at, Sept. 3, 1862.—Skirmish with Indians at, Sept. 6, 1862.—Action with Indians at, Sept. 23, 1862.—Skirmish with Indians at, Sept. 26, 1862.
BIG LARAMIE, Affair at, Aug. 1, 1865.
BIG MOUND, Action at the, July 24, 1863.
DAKOTA CITY, Affair with Indians at, Dec. 1, 1863.
DEAD BUFFALO LAKE, Action at, July 26, 1863.
DEAD MAN'S FORK, Skirmish at, June 17, 1865.
DEER CREEK, Scout from, to Sage Creek, April 22-23, 1865.—Skirmishes on, May 20, 1865.
DEER CREEK STATION, Skirmish at, May 20, 1865.
DRY CREEK, Skirmish with Indians at, June 3, 1865.
HALLECK, FORT, Skirmish near, Feb. 20, 1863.—Expedition from Denver, Colo., to, June 17-19, 1865.
HORSE CREEK, Action with Indians at, June 14, 1865.
LARAMIE, FORT, Operations against Indians west of, April 1-May 27, 1865.
LITTLE LARAMIE, Affair at, Aug. 1, 1865.
LITTLE MISSOURI RIVER, Action on, Aug. 8-9, 1864.
PLATTE BRIDGE, Skirmish with Indians at, June 3, 1865.—Skirmish at, July 26, 1865.
PLUM, CAMP, Scout from, May 20-22, 1865.

DISTRICT OF COLUMBIA—FLORIDA.

POWDER RIVER, Skirmish near, Aug. 13, 1865.—Skirmish at, Aug. 16, 1865.
POWDER RIVER INDIAN EXPEDITION, June 20-Oct. 7, 1865.
RICE, FORT, Expedition from, to relieve Captain Fiske's emigrant train, Sept. 11-30, 1864.—Affair near, April 26, 1865.—Operations about, June 2, 1865.
ROCK CREEK STATION, Operations about, June 24-30, 1865.
SAGE CREEK, Scout from Deer Creek to, April 22-23, 1865.
SEVEN MILE CREEK, Operations about, June 24-30, 1865.
SIOUX EXPEDITIONS, June 16-Sept. 13, 1863; July 25-Oct. 8, 1864.
STONY LAKE, Action at, July 28, 1863.
TAHKAHOKUTY MOUNTAIN, Action at the, July 28, 1864.
THREE CROSSINGS STATION, Operations about, May 20-22, 1865.
TONGUE RIVER, Action at, Aug. 28, 1865.
WHISKEY GAP, Scout from Sweetwater Bridge to, May 19-20, 1865.
WHITE STONE HILL, Action near, Sept. 3, 1863.—Skirmish at, Sept. 5, 1863.
WIND RIVER, Expedition from Fort Laramie to, May 3-21, 1865.

DISTRICT OF COLUMBIA.

STEVENS, FORT, Skirmish near, July 11, 1864.—Action near, July 12, 1864, and skirmishes along the northern defenses of Washington.

FLORIDA.

Seceded June 10, 1861.

ALLIGATOR BAY, Naval action in, July 1-2, 1863.
ALVARADO, BARK, Destruction of, in Saint Mary's River, Aug. 6, 1861.
AMELIA ISLAND, Evacuation of, by Confederate forces, March 3, 1862.—Occupation of, by Union forces, March 4, 1862.
APALACHICOLA, Naval expedition to, March 24, 1862.—Capture of, by Union naval forces, April 3, 1862.—Expedition from Barrancas to, May 21-June 6, 1865.
APALACHICOLA ARSENAL, Seizure of, by State troops, Jan. 6 1861.
BAGDAD, Reconnoissances from Pensacola to, Aug. 7-10, 1862.
BALDWIN, Union raid from Jacksonville on, July 23-28, 1864, and skirmishes.—Skirmishes at, Aug. 10 and 12, 1864.
BARBER'S FORD, Skirmish at, Feb. 10, 1864.

FLORIDA.*

BARRANCAS BARRACKS, Transfer of U. S. troops from, to Fort Pickens, Jan. 10, 1861.
BARRANCAS, FORT, Bombardment of, Jan. 1, 1862.—Expedition from, Aug. 13-14, 1864.
BAY PORT, Boat expedition to, March 27-April 4, 1863.—Naval engagement at, April 4, 1863.
BERESFORD, LAKE, Expedition from Jacksonville to, Oct. 6-9, 1862.
BLACK CREEK, Skirmish at, July 27, 1864.
BLACKWATER BAY, Expedition up, Oct. 25-28, 1864.
BLUFF SPRINGS, Action at, March 25, 1865.
BROOKE, FORT, Engagement at, Oct. 16, 1863.—Engagement at, Dec. 25, 1863.
BRYANT'S PLANTATION, Skirmish at, Oct. 21, 1864.
CANOE CREEK, Action at, March 25, 1865.
CEDAR CREEK, Skirmishes at, March 1, and April 2, 1864.
CEDAR KEYS, Naval descent upon, Jan. 16, 1862.—Boat expedition from Sea Horse Key to, Feb. 23-24, 1862.—Boat expedition to, Oct. 6, 1862.—Skirmish near, Feb. 16, 1865.
CHARLOTTE HARBOR, Boat expedition from, to Pease Creek, Dec. 25-31, 1863.—Naval expedition to, Jan. 5-9, 1864.
CHOCTAWHATCHIE BAY, Descent upon Confederate saltworks in, Dec. 10-19, 1863.
CLAY'S LANDING, Boat expedition to, near, July 6-8, 1864.
COOPER, CAMP, Capture of, by Union forces, Feb. 10, 1864.
COTTON CREEK, Skirmish at, March 25, 1865.
COW FORD CREEK, Skirmish at, April 2, 1864.
CROOKED RIVER, Affair on, May 20, 1862.
EASTERN FLORIDA, Expedition along the coast of, Nov. 3-10, 1862.
EAST RIVER BRIDGE, Skirmishes at, March 4-5, 1865.
ESCAMBIA RIVER, Skirmish at, March 25, 1865.
EUCHEE ANNA COURT-HOUSE, Affair at, Sept. 23, 1864.
FERNANDINA, Naval expedition from Port Royal, S. C., to, Feb. 28-March 4, 1862.—Capture of, by Union naval forces, March 4, 1862.—Skirmish near, April 10, 1862.
FINEGAN, CAMP, Skirmish near, Feb. 8, 1864.—Skirmish near, May 25, 1864.
FLORIDA EXPEDITION, Feb. 5-22, 1864.
FLORIDA RAILROAD, Union raid on, Aug. 15-19, 1864.
GADSDEN, FORT, Naval expedition to, Jan. 26-30, 1865.
GADSDEN'S POINT, Shelling of, by Union naval forces, March 27, 1863.
GAINESVILLE, Skirmish at, Feb. 14, 1864.—Action at, Aug. 17, 1864.
GATES, FORT, Expedition from Palatka to, April 1, 1864.—Naval expedition to, April 26-28, 1864.
GONZALES, CAMP, Skirmish at, July 22, 1864.
GRAND BAYOU, Affairs at, Jan. 25 and Aug. 7, 1864.

FLORIDA.

HORSE LANDING, Naval action at, April 23, 1864.
INDIAN RIVER, Naval reconnoissance in, Feb. 20-28, 1863.
JACKSON'S BRIDGE, Affair at, May 25, 1864.
JACKSONVILLE, Occupation of, by Union forces, March 12, 1862.—Evacuation of, by Union forces, April 9, 1862.—Recapture of, by Union forces, Oct. 5, 1862.—Reoccupation of, by Union forces, March 10, 1863.—Operations near, March 23-31, 1863.—Occupation of, by Union forces, Feb. 7, 1864.—Skirmish near, May 28, 1864.—Expedition from, July 15-20, 1864.—Expedition from, into Marion County, March 7-12, 1865.
JEFFERSON, FORT, Occupation of, by U. S. troops, Jan. 18, 1861.
KING'S FERRY MILLS, Expedition from Fernandina to, Feb. 15-23, 1864.
LAKE CITY, Skirmish at, Feb. 11, 1864.
LAKE GEORGE, Capture of C. S. S. Sumter in, March 13, 1864.
McGIRT'S CREEK, Skirmish at, March 1, 1864.
McREE, FORT, Seizure of, by State troops, Jan. 12, 1861.—Naval attack on, Nov. 22, 1861.—Bombardment of, Jan. 1, 1862.
MAGNOLIA, Skirmish at, Sept. 24, 1864.—Skirmish near, Oct. 24, 1864.
MARIANNA, Expedition from Barrancas to, Sept. 18-Oct. 4, 1864.—Action at, Sept. 27, 1864.
MARION COUNTY, Expedition from Jacksonville into, March 7-12, 1865.
MARION, FORT, Seizure of, by State troops, Jan. 7, 1861.—Capture of, by Union naval forces, March 11, 1862.
MAYPORT MILLS, Boat expedition to, June 8, 1862.—Skirmishes near, Oct. 2, 1862.—Naval engagement at, March 29, 1864.
MILTON, Expedition from Pensacola to, June 14-15, 1862.—Reconnoissance from Pensacola to, Aug. 7-10, 1862.—Skirmishes at, Aug. 29 and Oct. 26, 1864.—Skirmish near, Oct. 18, 1864.—Expeditions from Barrancas to, Feb. 19 and 22-25, 1865.
MILTON, CAMP, Expedition from Jacksonville to, May 31-June 3, 1864.—Capture of, by Union forces, June 2, 1864.
MITCHELL'S CREEK, Skirmish at, March 25, 1865.
MONROE, LAKE, Expedition from Jacksonville to, April 26-May 6, 1864.
MOSQUITO INLET (See Smyrna).
MYERS, FORT, Attack on, Feb. 20, 1865.
NASSAU RIVER, Expedition from Fernandina up, Feb. 9-10, 1864.—Naval expedition into, Jan. 10-17, 1865.
NATURAL BRIDGE, Action at, March 6, 1865.
NEWPORT BRIDGE, Skirmish at, March 5-6, 1865.
NEW SMYRNA, Affair at, March 23, 1862.

FLORIDA.*

NORTH BAY, Destruction of the C. S. S. Florida in, April 5, 1862.
OCEAN POND (or Olustee), Engagement at, Feb. 20, 1864.
OCKLOCKONNEE BAY, Affair in, March 24, 1863.
OCKLOCKONNEE RIVER, Naval action in, March 27, 1863.—Boat expedition into, and operations at Marsh Island, Oct. 18-19, 1864.
OLUSTEE (or Ocean Pond), Engagement at, Feb. 20, 1864.
PALATKA, Skirmishes at, March 27, 1863, March 31, and Aug. 13, 1864.—Skirmish near, March 16, 1864.—Naval actions at, March 21 and 29, 1864.
PEASE CREEK, Skirmishes at, Feb. 13, 14, and 20, 1864.
PENSACOLA, Bombardment of Confederate lines about, Nov. 22-23, 1861.—Evacuation of, by Confederate forces, and occupation of, by Union forces, May 9-12, 1862.—Skirmishes near, June 25, 1862; April 2, 1864.—Reconnoissance from, to Bagdad and Milton, Aug. 7-10, 1862.—Evacuation of, by Union forces, March 20-24, 1863.—Affair near, May 25, 1864.
PENSACOLA BAR, Naval affair at, Nov. 14, 1863.
PENSACOLA NAVY-YARD, Descent on, by boats from the U. S. squadron, Sept. 14, 1861.
PICKENS, FORT, Re-enforcement of, by Union forces, April 12, 1861.
PINE BARREN BRIDGE, Expedition from Barrancas to, Nov. 16-17, 1864.
POINT WASHINGTON, Skirmish near, Feb. 9, 1864.
SAINT ANDREW'S BAY, Affair at, April 7, 1862.—Naval operations in, Nov. 14-Dec. 9, 1862.—Affair in, March 20, 1863.—Boat expeditions in, Feb. 17-18 and Oct. 5-6, 1864.—Naval operations in, Nov. 30-Dec. 1, 1864.—Naval expedition from, to Lake Ocala, and destruction of salt-works, Dec. 2-3, 1864.—Boat expedition into, Jan. 16-29, 1865.
SAINT AUGUSTINE, Occupation of, by Union naval forces, March 11, 1862.—Skirmishes near, March 9 and Dec. 30, 1863.
SAINT JOHN'S BLUFF, Engagements at, Sept. 11 and 17, 1862.—Expedition from Hilton Head, S. C., to, Sept. 30-Oct 13, 1862.—Capture of batteries at, by Union naval forces, Oct. 5, 1862.
SAINT JOHN'S MILL, Capture of signal station at, Aug. 19, 1863.
SAINT JOHN'S RIVER, Naval expedition from Port Royal, S. C., up, Sept. 30-Oct. 5, 1862.—Boat expedition into, Aug. 19, 1863.—Destruction of the U. S. Transport Harriet A. Weed in, May 9, 1864.
SAINT JOSEPH'S BAY, Naval operations in, Jan. 9, 1863.
SAINT MARKS, Naval descent upon, June 15, 1862.—Naval expeditions to the vicinity of, and destruction of salt-works near, Feb. 17-18 and 27-28, 1864.—Operations in the vicinity of, Feb. 21-March 7, 1865.

FLORIDA—GEORGIA.

SAINT MARYS, Occupation of, by Union naval forces, March 3, 1862.—Skirmish at, March 6, 1862.
SAINT MARY'S RIVER, Destruction of the bark Alvarado in, Aug. 6, 1861.—Boat expedition into, and destruction of salt-works on Marsh Island, July 12-13, 1863.
SANTA ROSA ISLAND, Action on, Oct. 9, 1861.—Reconnoissance on, March 27-31, 1862.
SAUNDERS, Affair at, May 19, 1864.—Skirmish at, March 19, 1865.
SMYRNA, Affair at, March 23, 1862.—Naval engagement at, March 2, 1863.
STATION FOUR, Naval expeditions to, Oct. 4 and 6, 1862.—Action at, Feb. 13, 1865.
SUMTER, C. S. S., Capture of, in Lake George, March 31, 1864.
SUWANEE RIVER, Boat expedition up, to near Clay's Landing, July 6-8, 1864.
TAMPA, Bombardment of, June 30-July 1, 1862.—Affair at, May 6, 1864.
TAMPA BAY, Boat expedition into, Oct. 16-17, 1863.—Naval expeditions from, and destruction of salt-works, July 11, 16, Aug. 2-4, 1864.
TAYLOR, FORT, Garrisoned by U. S. troops, Jan. 14, 1861.
TEN MILE RUN, near Camp Finegan, Skirmish at, Feb. 8, 1864.
TROUT CREEK, Skirmish at, July 15, 1864.
WEED, HARRIET A., U. S. Transport, Destruction of, in Saint John's River, May 9, 1864.
WELAKA, Affair at, May 19, 1864.—Action at Braddock's Farm, Ala., near, Feb. 5, 1865.—Skirmish at, March 19, 1865.
WEST BAY, Naval expedition from Saint Andrew's Bay into, Dec. 10-12, 1863.—Naval expedition into, Feb. 12-14, 1865.
WHITESIDE, BLACK CREEK, Skirmish at, July 27, 1864.
WHITESVILLE, Skirmish at, July 24, 1864.
WOODSTOCK, Expedition from Fernandina to, Feb. 15-23, 1864.
YELLOW RIVER, Operations on, June 25, 1864.

GEORGIA.

Seceded, Jan. 19, 1861.

ACKWORTH, Skirmish at, Oct. 4, 1864.
ADAIRSVILLE, Engagement at, May 17, 1864.
ALEXANDER'S BRIDGE, Skirmish at, Sept. 18, 1863.
ALLATOONA, Engagement at, Oct. 5, 1864.
ALPINE, Skirmishes near, Sept. 3 and 5, 1863.—Skirmishes at, Sept. 8 to 12, 1863.—Scout from Chattanooga, Tenn., to, May —, 1864.

GEORGIA.

ALTAMAHA RIVER, Boat reconnoissance in, Sept. 19, 1863.
—Boat expedition up, to Troop's Plantation, Dec. 20, 1864.
ARGYLE ISLAND, Naval affair at, Dec. 12, 1864.
ARMUCHEE CREEK, Skirmish at, May 15, 1864.
ATLANTA, Battle of, July 22, 1864.—Operations about, July 23-Aug. 25, 1864.—Occupation of, by Union forces, Sept. 2, 1864.—Skirmishes near, Nov. 6 and 9, 1864.
ATLANTA CAMPAIGN, May 1-Sept. 8, 1864.
ATLANTA AND WEST POINT RAILROAD, Union raid on, July 27-31, 1864.
AUGUSTA ARSENAL, Seizure of, by State troops, Jan 24, 1861.
BALD HILL (or Leggett's Hill), Engagement at, July 21, 1864.
BALL'S FERRY, Skirmishes at, Nov. 23-25, 1864.
BARNESVILLE, Skirmish near, April 19, 1865.
BEAR CREEK STATION, Skirmish at, Nov. 16, 1864.
BEAR'S BLUFF, Naval reconnoissance to, Feb. 24, 1862.
BEAULIEU, FORT, Naval attack on, Dec. 14-21, 1864.
BIG SHANTY, Skirmish near, June 9, 1864.—Skirmish at, Oct. 3, 1864.
BLUE BIRD GAP, Skirmish near, Sept. 11, 1863.
BRUNSWICK, Occupation of, by Union naval forces, March 8, 1862.—Attack on Union boat's crew near, March 11, 1862.—Naval reconnoissance from, to Darien, March 13-15, 1862.—Affair near, June 8, 1863.
BRUSH MOUNTAIN, Combat at, June —, 1864.
BRYAN COURT-HOUSE, Skirmish near, Dec. 8, 1864.
BUCK CREEK, Skirmish at, Dec. 7, 1864.
BUCK HEAD, Skirmish at, July 18, 1864.
BUCK HEAD CHURCH, Skirmish at, Nov. 28, 1864 (Reynolds's Plantation).—Skirmish at, Dec. 2, 1864.
BUCK HEAD STATION, Skirmish at, Nov. 19, 1864.
BURKE'S MILL, Scout from Ooltewah, Tenn., to, Feb. 18-19, 1864.
BURNT HICKORY (or Huntsville), Skirmish at, May 24, 1864.
BUZZARD ROOST, Skirmishes at, Feb. 24-25, 1864; April 22, 1865.
BUZZARD ROOST GAP, Combats at, May 8-11 and Oct 13-14, 1864.
CALHOUN, Skirmish near, May 16, 1864.—Skirmish at, June 10, 1864.
CAMPBELLTON, Skirmish near, July 28, 1864.—Affair at, Sept. 10, 1864.
CAMP CREEK, Combat at, Aug. 18, 1864.—Skirmish at, Sept. 30, 1864.
CARTERSVILLE, Skirmish near, May 20, 1864.—Skirmish near, July 24, 1864.—Skirmish at, Sept. 20, 1864.
CASS STATION, Skirmish at, May 24, 1864.

GEORGIA.

CASSVILLE, Combats near, May 18-19, 1864.—Skirmish at, May 24, 1864.
CATLETT'S GAP, Pigeon Mountain, Skirmishes at, Sept. 15-18, 1863.
CATOOSA PLATFORM, Skirmish near, Feb. 27, 1864.
CATOOSA SPRINGS, Skirmish at, May 3, 1864.
CATOOSA STATION, Skirmish at, Feb. 23, 1864.
CAVE SPRINGS ROAD, Reconnoissance from Rome on, Oct. 13, 1864.
CHATTAHOOCHEE RAILROAD BRIDGE, Operations at, Aug. 26-Sept. 1, 1864.
CHATTAHOOCHEE RIVER, Operations on the line of, July 5-17, 1864.
CHATTOOGA RIVER, Skirmish near, Sept. 12, 1863.
CHENEY'S FARM, Combat at, June 22-27, 1864.
CHICKAMAUGA, Battle of, Sept. 19-20, 1863.
CHICKAMAUGA CAMPAIGN, Aug. 16-Sept. 22, 1863.
CHICKAMAUGA CREEK, Skirmish at, Jan. 30, 1864.—Skirmish at, May 3, 1864.
CLEAR CREEK, Skirmish at, July 30, 1864.
CLINTON, Combat at, July 30, 1864.—Skirmish near, Nov. 20, 1864.—Skirmishes at, Nov. 21-23, 1864.
COLUMBUS, Action at, April 16, 1865.—Occupation of, by Union forces, April 16, 1865.
COOSAVILLE ROAD, Skirmishes on, Oct. 12-13, 1864.
COOSAWATTEE RIVER, Expedition from Dalton to the, April 1-4, 1865.
COTTON RIVER BRIDGE, Skirmish at, Nov. 16, 1864.
COVINGTON, Union raid to, July 22-24, 1864.
CROW'S VALLEY, Skirmishes at, Feb. 24-25, 1864.
CUMBERLAND ISLAND, Occupation of, by Union naval forces, March 2, 1862.
CUYLER'S PLANTATION, Skirmish at, Dec. 9, 1864.
CYPRESS SWAMP, Skirmish at, Dec. 7, 1864.
DALLAS, Skirmish near, May 24, 1864.—Combats at and about, May 26-June 1, 1864.—Skirmish at, Oct. 7, 1864.
DALLAS LINE (See Pumpkin Vine Creek, May 25-June 5, 1864).
DALTON, Skirmish at, Jan. 6, 1864.—Scout from Rossville toward, Jan. 21-23, 1864.—Demonstration on, Feb. 22-27, 1864.—Combat at, May 13, 1864.—Combats at, Aug. 14-15, 1864.—Surrender of, Oct. 13, 1864.—Skirmish near, Nov. 30, 1864.—Skirmish near, Dec. 5, 1864.—Skirmishes near, March 13-14, 1865.
DARIEN, Attack on, June 11, 1863.—Naval reconnoissance from Brunswick to, March 13-15, 1862.—Destruction of Hudson Place Salt-Works near, Sept. 22, 1863.
DAVISBOROUGH, Skirmish near, Nov. 28, 1864.
DAVIS CROSS ROADS, Skirmish at, Sept. 11, 1863. (Davis's House.)

GEORGIA.

DECATUR, Skirmish near, Sept. 28, 1864.
DEDMON'S TRACE, Scout to, April 10, 1864.
DEER HEAD COVE, Scout from Lookout Valley to, March 29-31, 1864.
DIRT TOWN, Skirmish at, Sept. 13, 1863.
DOBOY RIVER, Expedition from Beaufort to, Nov. 13-18, 1862.
DOUBLE BRIDGES, Flint River, Skirmish at, April 18, 1865.
DRY VALLEY, Skirmish at, Sept. 21, 1863.
DUCKTOWN ROAD, Skirmish on, April 3, 1864.
DUG GAP, Skirmish near, Sept. 11, 1863.—Combats at, May 8-11, 1864.
DYER'S FORD, Skirmish at, Sept. 18, 1863.
EAST MACON, Skirmish at, Nov. 20, 1864.
EAST POINT, Skirmish near, Aug. 30, 1864.—Skirmish near, Nov. 15, 1864.
EAST TENNESSEE AND GEORGIA RAILROAD, Raid on, Nov. 24-27, 1863.
EATONTON, Skirmish near, Nov. 21, 1864.
EBENEZER CREEK, Skirmish at, Dec. 8, 1864.
EDEN STATION, Skirmish near, Dec. 9, 1864.
ELBA ISLAND, Reconnoissance to, March 7-11, 1862.
ELLIDGE'S MILL, Scout from Ooltewah, Tenn., to, Feb. 18-19, 1864.
ETOWAH RIVER, Skirmish at, May 20, 1864.
EZRA CHURCH, Battle of, July 28, 1864.
FAIRBURN, Skirmish at, Aug. 15, 1864.—Skirmish near, Oct. 2, 1864.
FLAT CREEK, Expedition from Atlanta to, Oct. 11-14, 1864, and skirmishes.
FLAT ROCK BRIDGE, Skirmish at, July 28, 1864.
FLAT ROCK ROAD, Skirmish on, Oct. 2, 1864.
FLINT RIVER, Combat at, Aug. 19, 1864.—Skirmish at, April 18, 1865.
FLINT RIVER BRIDGE, Action at Aug. 30, 1864.
FLOYD'S SPRING, Skirmish at, May 16, 1864.
FRICK'S GAP, Scout from Whiteside's, Tenn., to, Feb. 25-26, 1864.
GEORGETOWN, Expedition from Blakely, Ala., to, April 17-30, 1865.
GEORGIA CENTRAL RAILROAD BRIDGE, Skirmish at, Nov. —, 1864.
GILGAL CHURCH (See Marietta, June 10-July 3, 1864).
GORDON, Skirmish at, Nov. 21, 1864.
GRAYSVILLE, Skirmish near, Sept. 10, 1863.—Skirmish near, Nov. 26, 1863.
GRISWOLDVILLE, Skirmishes at, Nov. 20-21, 1864.—Engagement at, Nov. 22, 1864.
HILLSBOROUGH, Combats at, July 30-31, 1864.
HINESVILLE, Skirmish at, March 1, 1865.

GEORGIA.

HOLLY CREEK, Skirmish at, March 1, 1865.
HOWELL'S FERRY, Skirmish at, July 5, 1864.—Skirmish near, Oct. 19, 1864.
HUDSON PLACE SALT-WORKS, Destruction of, Sept. 22, 1863.
HUNTSVILLE, Skirmish at, May 24, 1864.
ISHAM'S FORD, Skirmish at, July —, 1864.
JACKSON, FORT, Seizure of, by State troops, Jan. 26, 1861.—Occupation of, by Union troops, Dec. 21, 1864.
JASPER, Expedition to, Aug. 14-15, 1864.
JEKYL ISLAND, Occupation of, by Union naval forces, March 8, 1862.
JENKS'S BRIDGE, Ogeechee River, Skirmish at, Dec. 7, 1864.
JOHNSON'S CROOK, Skirmish on, Feb. 10, 1865.
JONESBOROUGH, Combat at, Aug. 19, 1864.—Battle of, Aug. 31-Sept. 1, 1864.—Skirmish at, Nov. 15, 1864.
JUG TAVERN, Skirmish at, Aug. 3, 1864.
KENESAW MOUNTAIN (See Marietta, June 10-July 3 1864).
KENESAW WATER-TANK, Skirmish at, Oct. 3, 1864.
KINGSTON, Combats near, May 18-19, 1864.—Scout from, Nov. 10-11, 1864.
KOLB'S FARM, Combat at, June 22, 1864.
LA FAYETTE, Reconnoissance from Alpine toward, Sept. 10, 1863.—Reconnoissance from Lee and Gordon's Mills toward, Sept. 13, 1863, and skirmish.—Skirmish near, Sept. 14, 1863.—Skirmish at, Dec. 12, 1863.—Reconnoissance from Rossville to, Dec. 14, 1863.—Scout from Rossville to, Dec. 21-23, 1863.—Reconnoissance from Rossville to, April 11-13, 1864.—Scout from Ringgold to, April 24-25, 1864.—Action at, June 24, 1864.—Skirmish at, Oct. 12, 1864.
LA FAYETTE ROAD, Skirmish on, Sept. 12, 1863.
LAWRENCEVILLE, Skirmish near, Oct. 27, 1864.
LEE AND GORDON'S MILLS, Skirmishes near, Sept. 11-13, 1863.—Skirmishes near, Sept. 16-18, 1863.
LEE'S CROSS ROADS, Skirmish at, May 2, 1864.
LEET'S TAN-YARD, Skirmish near, Sept. 12, 1863.—Skirmish at, March 5, 1864.
LEGGETT'S HILL, Engagement at, July 21, 1864.
LITHONIA, Skirmish at, July 28, 1864.
LITTLE OGEECHEE RIVER, Skirmishes at, Dec. 4-5, 1864.
LOOKOUT CHURCH, Skirmish at, Sept. 21, 1863.
LOOKOUT CREEK, Destruction of bridges on, May 3, 1862.
LOOKOUT MOUNTAIN, Skirmish at, Sept. 9, 1863.
LOST MOUNTAIN (See Marietta, June 10-July 3, 1864).—Skirmishes near, Oct. 4-7, 1864.
LOUISVILLE, Skirmish near, Nov. 29, 1864.—Skirmish at, Nov. 30, 1864.

GEORGIA.

LOVEJOY'S STATION, Skirmish near, July 29, 1864.—Raid from Sandtown to, Aug. 18-22, 1864.—Actions at, Sept. 2-5, 1864.—Action at, Nov. 16, 1864.
LUMPKIN COUNTY, Skirmish in, Sept. 15, 1864.
LUMPKIN'S STATION, Skirmish near, Dec. 4, 1864.
McAFEE'S CROSS ROADS, Combat at, June 11, 1864.
MACON, Combat at, July 30, 1864.—Skirmish near, Nov. 21, 1864.—Raid from Chickasaw, Ala., to, March 22-April 24, 1865.
McALLISTER, FORT, Naval attack on, Jan. 27, 1863.—Engagement at, Feb. 28, 1863.—Destruction of C. S. Privateer Nashville near, Feb. 28, 1863.—Affair at, March 9, 1863.—Naval attack on, Feb. 1, 1863.—Naval attack on, March 3, 1863.—Engagement at, Dec. 13, 1864.
McDONOUGH ROAD, Skirmish at, Oct. 2, 1864.—Skirmish on, Nov. 6, 1864.
McINTOSH COUNTY, Naval expedition to, Aug. 2-4, 1864.
McLEMORE'S COVE, Skirmish at, Sept. 11, 1863.—Reconnoissance from Lookout Valley, Tenn., to, March 30-April 1, 1864.—Skirmish at, Feb. 1, 1865.
MARIETTA, Operations about, June 10-July 3, 1864, with combats at Pine Hill, Lost Mountain, Brush Mountain, Gilgal Church, Noonday Creek, McAfee's Cross Roads, Kenesaw Mountain, Powder Springs, Cheney's Farm, Kolb's Farm, Olley's Creek, Nickajack Creek, Noyes's Creek, and other points.
MILL CREEK GAP, Combats at, May 8-11, 1864.
MILLEDGEVILLE, Skirmish near, Nov. 23, 1864.
MILLEN'S GROVE, Skirmish at, Dec. 1, 1864.
MIMM'S MILLS, Tobesofkee Creek, Skirmish at, April 20, 1865.
MONTEITH SWAMP, Skirmish at, Dec. 9, 1864.
MOON'S STATION, Skirmish at, Oct. 4, 1864.
MULBERRY CREEK, Skirmish at, Aug. 3, 1864.
NEAL DOW STATION, Skirmish at, July 4, 1864.
NEW HOPE CHURCH (See Pumpkin Vine Creek, May 25-June 5, 1864).—Skirmish near, Oct. 5, 1864.
NEWNAN, Action near, July 30, 1864.
NICKAJACK CREEK (See Marietta, June 10-July 3, 1864).
NICKAJACK GAP, Skirmish near, March 9, 1864.—Skirmish near, May 7, 1864.
NICKAJACK TRACE, Attack on Union pickets at, April 23, 1864.
NOONDAY CREEK (See Marietta, June 10-July 3, 1864).
NOYES'S CREEK (See Marietta, June 10-July 3, 1864).—Skirmishes at, Oct. 2-3, 1864.
OCONEE RIVER, Skirmishes at, Nov. 23-25, 1864.
OGEECHEE CANAL, Skirmish at, Dec. 9, 1864.
OGEECHEE RIVER, Skirmish at, Dec. 7, 1864.—Naval action with batteries in, Feb. 1, 1863.

GEORGIA.

OGLETHORPE BARRACKS, Seizure of, by State troops, Jan. 26, 1861.
OLLEY'S CREEK (See Marietta, June 10-July 3, 1864).
OSSABAW ISLAND, Expedition to, July 3, 1863.
OSSABAW SOUND, Capture of U. S. Gun-boat Water Witch in, June 3, 1864.
OWEN'S FORD, West Chickamauga Creek, Skirmish at, Sept. 17, 1863.
PACE'S FERRY, Skirmishes at, July 5-17, 1864.—Operations at, Aug. 26-Sept. 1, 1864.
PARKER'S CROSS ROADS, Action at, May 16, 1864.
PEACH-TREE CREEK, Skirmishes on, July 19, 1864.—Battle of, July 20, 1864.
PEA VINE CREEK, Skirmish at, Sept. 10, 1863.
PEA VINE RIDGE, Skirmish at, Sept. 18, 1863.
PICKENS COUNTY, Expedition to, July —, 1864.
PICKETT'S MILLS (See Pumpkin Vine Creek, May 25-June 5, 1864).
PIGEON MOUNTAIN, Skirmishes at, Sept. 15-18, 1863.
PINE HILL (See Marietta, June 10-July 3, 1864).
PINE LOG CREEK, Skirmish at, May 18, 1864.
PLEASANT HILL, Skirmish at, April 18, 1865.
POOLER STATION, Skirmish near, Dec. 9, 1864.
POWDER SPRINGS (See Marietta, June 10-July 3, 1864).—Skirmishes near, Oct. 2-3, 1864.
PULASKI, FORT, Seizure of, by State troops, Jan. 3, 1861.
PUMPKIN VINE CREEK, Operations on the line of, May 25-June 5, 1864, with combats at New Hope Church, Pickett's Mills, and other points.—Bombardment and capture of, April 10-11, 1862.
RED CLAY, Skirmish at, May 3, 1864.
RED OAK, Combat at, Aug. 19, 1864.—Skirmish near, Aug. 29, 1864.
REED'S BRIDGE, Skirmish at, Sept. 18, 1863.
RESACA, Demonstrations against, May 8-13, 1864, with combats at Snake Creek Gap, Sugar Valley, and near Resaca.—Battle of, May 14-15, 1864.—Skirmishes near, Oct. 12-13, 1864.
REYNOLD'S PLANTATION, Engagement at, Nov. 28, 1864.
RINGGOLD, Skirmish near, Sept. 11, 1863.—Skirmish at, Sept. 17, 1863.—Reconnoissance from Rossville to, Dec. 5, 1963.—Skirmish at, Dec. 13, 1863.—Skirmish at, Feb. 8, 1864.—Skirmish at, Feb. 18, 1864.—Attack on Union pickets near, April 27, 1864.—Skirmish at, March 20, 1865.
RINGGOLD GAP, Engagement at, Nov. 27, 1863.—Skirmish near, May 2, 1864.
ROCK SPRINGS, Skirmish near, Sept. 12, 1863.
ROCKY CREEK BRIDGE, Skirmish at, April 20, 1865.
ROCKY CREEK CHURCH, Skirmish at, Dec. 2, 1864.

GEORGIA.

ROCKY FACE RIDGE, Skirmishes at, Feb. 24-25, 1864.—Demonstrations against, May 8-11, 1864, with combats at Buzzard Roost, or Mill Creek Gap, and Dug Gap.
ROME, Raid from Tuscumbia, Ala., towards, April 26-May 3, 1863.—Reconnoissance from Alpine toward, Sept. 10, 1863.—Reconnoissance toward, Sept. 11, 1863.—Expedition from Scottsborough, Ala., toward, Jan. 25-Feb. 5, 1864.—Skirmish near, May 15, 1864.—Action at, May 17, 1864.—Scout from, July 11-13, 1864.—Scout from, to Cedar Bluff, Ala., July 28-29, 1864.—Expedition from, to Jacksonville, Ala., Aug. 11-15, 1864.—Skirmishes near, Oct. 10-11, 1864.—Skirmishes near, Oct. 12-13, 1864.—Reconnoissance from, on the Cave Springs Road, Oct. 13, 1864, and skirmishes.
ROME CROSS ROADS, Action at, May 16, 1864.
ROSEDEW, FORT, Naval attack on, Dec. 14-21, 1864.
ROSSVILLE, Skirmish near, Sept. 11, 1863.—Reconnoissance from, Sept. 17, 1863.—Skirmish at, Sept. 21, 1863.—Reconnoissance from, to Ringgold, Dec. 5, 1863.—Reconnoissance from, to La Fayette, Dec. 14, 1863.
ROSWELL, Skirmish near, Sept. 26, 1864.
ROTTENWOOD CREEK, Skirmish at, July 4, 1864.
ROUGH AND READY, Skirmish near, Nov. 15, 1864.
ROUGH AND READY STATION, Skirmish near, Aug. 31, 1864.
RUFF'S MILLS, Skirmish at, July 4, 1864.
RUFF'S STATION, Skirmish at, Oct. 19, 1864.
SAINT AUGUSTINE CREEK, Reconnoissance near mouth of, March 28, 1862.
SAINT SIMON'S ISLAND, Occupation of, by Union naval forces, March 8, 1862.
SALT SPRINGS, Skirmish at, Oct. 1, 1864.
SANDERSVILLE, Skirmish near, Nov. 25, 1864.—Skirmish at, Nov. 26, 1864.
SAND MOUNTAIN, Skirmish near, Oct. 2, 1864.
SANDTOWN, Skirmish at, Aug. 15, 1864.
SAVANNAH, Skirmish near, Dec. 10, 1864.—Investment of, Dec. 11-21, 1864.
SAVANNAH CAMPAIGN, Nov. 15-Dec. 21, 1864.
SAVANNAH RIVER, Reconnoissance up, March 7-11, 1862.—Naval reconnoissance up, Jan. 26-29, 1862.—Naval engagement in, Jan. 28, 1862.—Reconnoissances on, Sept. 30-Oct. 3, 1862.
SHADNA CHURCH, Skirmish at, Oct. 2, 1864.
SHADY GROVE, Skirmish at, Dec. 1, 1864.
SHIP'S GAP, Skirmish at, Oct. 16, 1864.
SISTER'S FERRY, Skirmish near, Dec. 7, 1864.
SKIDDAWAY BATTERIES, Wilmington River, Naval reconnoissance to, March 25, 1862.
SNAKE CREEK GAP (See Resaca, May 8-13, 1864).—Skirmish at, Sept. 15, 1864.—Skirmish at, Oct. 15, 1864.

GEORGIA.

SNAPFINGER CREEK, Skirmish at, July 27, 1864.
SOUTH NEWPORT, Skirmish at, Aug. 17, 1864.
SOUTH RIVER, Raid to, July 27-31, 1864.—Skirmish near, Oct. 24, 1864.
SPAULDING'S, Skirmish at, Nov. 7, 1862.
SPRING CREEK, Skirmish at, Sept. 18, 1863.
SPRINGFIELD, Skirmish near, Dec. 10, 1864.
SPRING HILL, Skirmish near, April 20, 1865.
SPRING PLACE, Skirmish at, Feb. 27, 1865.—Expedition from Dalton to, April 1-4, 1865, with skirmishes.
STATESBOROUGH, Skirmish near, Dec. 4, 1864.
STATION No. 5, Georgia Central Railroad, Skirmish at, Dec. 4, 1864.
STEVENS'S GAP, Skirmish at, Sept. 6, 1863.—Skirmish near, Sept. 18, 1863.—Scout from Whiteside's, Tenn., to, Feb. 25-26, 1864.
STILESBOROUGH, Action at, May 23, 1864.—Skirmish near, June 9, 1864.
STOCKBRIDGE, Skirmish near, Nov. 15, 1864.
STONE CHURCH, Skirmish at, Feb. 27, 1864.—Skirmish at, May 1, 1864.
STONEMAN'S RAID to Macon, July 27-Aug. 6, 1864.
STREIGHT'S RAID from Tuscumbia, Ala., toward Rome, Ga., April 26-May 3, 1863.
SUBLIGNA, Affair at, Jan. 22, 1864.
SUGAR VALLEY (See Resaca, May 8-13, 1864).
SULPHUR SPRINGS, Scout from Whiteside's Tenn., to, Sept. 2-5, 1864.
SUMMERVILLE, Skirmishes at, Sept. 6-7, 1863.—Reconnoissance from Alpine toward, and skirmish at, Sept. 10, 1863.—Skirmish near, Sept. 13, 1863.—Skirmish at, Sept. 15, 1863.—Scout from Chattanooga, Tenn., to, July —, 1864.—Skirmish near, Oct. 18, 1864.—Skirmish at, May 5, 1865.
SWEET WATER CREEK, Skirmishes at, Oct. 2-3, 1864.
SYLVAN GROVE, Skirmish at, Nov. 27, 1864.
TAYLOR'S RIDGE, Engagement at, Nov. 27, 1863.—Skirmish at, April 14, 1864.—Attack on Union pickets on, April 27, 1864.
THOMAS'S STATION, Skirmish at, Dec. 3, 1864.
TILTON, Skirmish at, May 13, 1864.—Surrender of, Oct. 13, 1864.
TOBESOFKEE CREEK, Skirmish on, April 20, 1865.
TOWALIGA BRIDGE, Affair at, Nov. 17, 1864.
TRENTON, Reconnoissance from Stevenson, Ala., to, Aug. 28-31, 1863.—Skirmish at, Nov. 18, 1863.
TRICKUM'S CROSS ROADS, Expedition from Atlanta to, Oct. 26-29, 1864.
TRION FACTORY, Skirmish at, Sept. 15, 1863.
TROOP'S PLANTATION, Boat expedition to, Dec. 20, 1864.

GEORGIA—IDAHO TERRITORY.

TUNNEL HILL, Skirmish at, Sept. 11, 1863.—Skirmishes at, Feb. 23-24, 1864.—Reconnoissance from Ringgold toward, April 29, 1864.—Skirmish near, May 2, 1864.—Skirmish near, May 5, 1864.—Skirmishes at, May 6-7, 1864.—Skirmishes near, March 3, 1865.

TURNER'S FERRY, Skirmishes at and near, July 5-17, 1864.—Skirmish at, Aug. 26, 1864.—Skirmish near, Oct. 19, 1864.

TURTLE RIVER, Naval expedition from Brunswick up, March 11, 1862.

TYBEE ISLAND, Occupation of, by Union forces, Nov. 24, 1861.

TYLER, FORT, Attack on, April 16, 1865.

UTOY CREEK, Assault at, Aug. 6, 1864.

VAN WERT, Skirmishes near, Oct. 9-10, 1864.

VARNELL'S STATION, Skirmish at, May 7, 1864.—Combat near, May 9, 1864.—Combat near, May 12, 1864.

VARNELL'S STATION ROAD, Skirmish on, May 4, 1864.

VENUS POINT, Action at, Feb. 15, 1862.

VERNON RIVER, Naval Attack on Forts Rosedew and Beaulieu on, Dec. 15-21, 1864.

WALNUT CREEK, Skirmish at, Nov. 20, 1864.

WARSAW ISLAND, Naval expedition to, Dec. 4-5, 1861.

WARSAW SOUND, Capture of C. S. S. Atlanta (Fingal) in, June 17, 1863.

WATER WITCH, U. S. Gunboat, Capture of, in Ossabaw Sound, June 3, 1864.

WATKINS'S FERRY, Skirmish at, May 3, 1862.

WAYNESBOROUGH, Action at, Nov. 27-28, 1864.—Engagement at, Dec. 4, 1864.

WESTBROOK'S Skirmish at, Oct. 2, 1864.

WEST CHICKAMAUGA CREEK, Skirmish at, Sept. 17, 1863.

WEST POINT, Attack on and occupation of, by Union forces, April 16, 1865.

WHEELER'S RAID in North Georgia and East Tennessee, Aug. 10-Sept. 9, 1864.

WHITEMARSH ISLAND, Affairs on, March 30-31, 1862.—Skirmish on, April 16, 1862.—Skirmish at, Feb. 22, 1864.

WHITE OAK RIVER, Boat expedition into, Oct. 13-14, 1864.

WILMINGTON ISLAND, Affairs on, March 30-31, 1862.

WILMINGTON NARROWS, Reconnoissance to, Jan. 26-28, 1862; naval engagement.

IDAHO TERRITORY.

BEAR RIVER, Expedition from Camp Douglass, Utah T., to Soda Springs on, May 5-30, 1863.

BOISE, FORT, Operations about, Feb. 1-20, 1865.

BOONEVILLE, Expedition from Fort Boise to, July 20-Aug. 17, 1864.

ILLINOIS—INDIANA—INDIAN TERRITORY.

BRUNEAU VALLEY, Skirmish near, Feb. 15, 1865.
GRAND PASS, Skirmish with Indians at, July 7, 1863.
LAPWAI, FORT, Expedition from, to The Meadows, Aug. 22-Sept. 20, 1863.
LYON, CAMP, Expedition from, to the Malheur River, Ore., July 2-13, 1865, with skirmish.
MEADOWS, THE, Expedition from Fort Lapwai to, Aug. 22-Sept. 20, 1863.
OWYHEE RIVER, Skirmish on, July 17, 1865.
POISON CREEK, Skirmish at, March 8, 1865.
SALMON FALLS, Expedition from Fort Boise to, Aug. 27-Oct. 5, 1864, with skirmishes.
SNAKE INDIANS, Expeditions against, Aug. 19-Oct. 11, 1862; and May 4-Oct. 26, 1863.
SODA SPRINGS, on Bear River, Expedition from Camp Douglass, Utah T., to, May 5-30, 1863.
THE MEADOWS, Expedition from Fort Lapwai to, Aug. 22-Sept. 20, 1863.

ILLINOIS.

CHARLESTON, Coles County, Riot in, March 28, 1864.
PRAIRIE DU ROCHER, Affair at, April 6, 1864.
SHAWNEETOWN, Operations about, Aug. 13, 1864.

INDIANA.

CORYDON, Skirmish at, July 9, 1863.
HINES'S RAID into, June 17, 1863.
MORGAN'S RAID into, July 9-13, 1863.
MOUNT VERNON, Expedition from, into Kentucky, Aug. 16-22, 1864.
NEWBURG, Raid on, July 18, 1862.
PEKIN, Skirmish at, July 11, 1863.
SALEM, Skirmish at, July 10, 1863.

INDIAN TERRITORY.

ARBUCKLE, FORT, Abandoned May 5, 1861.
BEATTIE'S PRAIRIE, Action at, Oct. 22, 1862.
BERNARD, BAYOU, Skirmish at, July 27, 1862.
BOGGY DEPOT, Skirmish near, April 24, 1865.
BRAZIL CREEK, Skirmish at, Oct. 11, 1863.
CABIN CREEK, Engagement at, July 1-2, 1863—Skirmish at, July 20, 1863.—Action at, Sept. 19, 1864.
CHEROKEE COUNTY, Operations in, Dec. 4-12, 1862.—Skirmish in, Jan. 18, 1863.
CHEROKEE NATION, Operations in, Sept. 11-25, 1864.
CHOCTAW NATION, Skirmish in, Oct. 7, 1863.—Skirmish in, Oct. 11, 1863.—Skirmish in, Nov. 9, 1863.

INDIAN TERRITORY.

CHUSTENAHLAH, Engagement at, Dec. 26, 1861.
CHUSTO-TALASAH, Engagement at, Dec. 9, 1861. (Bird Creek, or High Shoal.)
COBB, FORT, Abandoned May 5, 1861.
CREEK AGENCY, Scout from, to Jasper County, Mo., May 6-19, 1863.—Skirmish on, Oct. 15, 1863.
ELK CREEK, Engagement at, July 17, 1863.
FOURTEEN MILE CREEK, Skirmish at, Oct. 30, 1863.
GIBSON, FORT, Reconnoissances from Grand River to, July 14-17, 1862.—Skirmish near, July 27, 1862.—Skirmish at, Oct. 15, 1862.—Expedition toward, Dec. —, 1862.—Skirmish near, Feb. 28, 1863.—Skirmish at, April 30, 1863.—Skirmish at, May 14, 1863.—Action near, May 20, 1863.—Skirmish at, May 22, 1863.—Skirmish near, May 28, 1863.—Operations about, June 6-20, 1863.—Demonstrations on, Dec. 16, 1863.—Skirmish near, Dec. 26, 1863.—Skirmish near, April 3, 1864.—Action at Hay Station, near, Sept. 16, 1864.
GRAND RIVER, Skirmish at, June 6, 1864.—Reconnoissances from, to Fort Gibson, Tahlequah, and Park Hill, July 14-17, 1862.
GREENLEAF PRAIRIE, Skirmish on, June 16, 1863.—Skirmish at, Nov. 11, 1863.—Skirmish at, Nov. 12, 1863.
GUNTER'S RUN, Skirmish on, Aug. 24, 1863.
HAY STATION, Action at, Sept. 16, 1864.
HIGH SHOAL, Engagement at, Dec. 9, 1861.
HILLABEE, Expedition from Fort Gibson to, March 18-30, 1865.
HONEY SPRINGS, Engagement near, July 17, 1863.
HOPOEITHLEYOHOLA, Scout in Indian Territory after, Dec. 29, 1861, to Jan. 4, 1862.
HUDSON'S CROSSING, or Ford, Neosho River, Skirmish near, June 30, 1863.—Affair at, June 4, 1864.
IRON BRIDGE, Skirmish at, June 19, 1864.
LITTLE RIVER, Expedition from Fort Gibson to, March 18-30, 1865.
LOCUST GROVE, Skirmish at, July 3, 1862.
MARTIN'S HOUSE, Skirmish at, May 8, 1863.
NEOSHO RIVER, Skirmish near, June 30, 1863.—Affair at, June 4, 1864.
OLD FORT WAYNE, Action at, Oct. 22, 1862.
PARK HILL, Reconnoissances from Grand River to, July 14-17, 1862.
PERRYVILLE, Skirmish at, Aug. 26, 1863.
PRYOR'S CREEK, Action at, Sept. 19, 1864.
ROUND GROVE, Skirmish at, June 5, 1862.
ROUND MOUNTAIN, Engagement at, Nov. 19, 1861.
SALINE, Skirmish at, Dec. 2, 1862.
SAN BOIS CREEK, Skirmish at, June 15-16, 1864.
SCULLYVILLE, Skirmishes at and near, Aug. 30-31, 1863.

INDIAN TERRITORY—KANSAS.

SHELDON'S PLACE, Barren Fork, Skirmish near, Dec. 18, 1863.
TAHLEQUAH, Reconnoissances from Grand River to, July 14-17, 1862.—Skirmishes at, March 30, 1863.
TALLAHASSA MISSION, Scout from, April 12-13, 1865.
WASHITA, FORT, Abandoned April 16, 1861.
WEBBER'S FALLS, Skirmish at, April 11, 1863.—Skirmish at, Sept. 9, 1863.—Skirmish at, Oct. 12, 1863.—Skirmish at, April 25, 1863.

KANSAS.

ASH CREEK, Skirmish with Indians at, Nov. 13, 1864.
ATCHISON, Operations in and about, Jan. 20-24, 1862.
AUBREY, Skirmish near, March 12, 1862.
BAXTER SPRINGS, Action at, Oct. 6, 1863.—Scout to and skirmish, Aug. 1, 1864.
BEAVER CREEK, Expedition from Camp Sanborn, Colo., to, April 14-18, 1864.
BIG BUSHES, Action at, May 16, 1864.
BOOTH'S RANCH, Arkansas River, Scout from Fort Larned to, Sept. 13-21, 1863.
BROOKLYN, Skirmish near, Aug. 21, 1863.
BUCKNER'S RANCH, Scout from Fort Larned to, Feb. 3-8, 1865.
CATO, Skirmish near, Nov. 8, 1862.
CHAVIS CREEK, Skirmish at, June 9, 1865.
COTTONWOOD, Expedition from Humboldt to, April 10, 1863.
COUNCIL GROVE, Affair near, Sept. 21, 1864.
COW CREEK, Skirmish on, Nov. 28, 1864.—Skirmish with Indians on, Dec. 4, 1864.
COW CREEK STATION, Skirmish near, June 9, 1865.—Skirmish near, June 12, 1865.
CROOKED CREEK, Scout from Fort Larned to, March 9-15, 1865.
DODGE, FORT, Skirmish at, June 8, 1865.—Skirmish at, June 12, 1865.—Skirmish with Indians near, June 29, 1865.
ELLSWORTH, FORT, Scout from, Jan. 7-11, 1865.
GRAND RIVER, Expedition from Baxter Springs to, July 27-29, 1863.
HUMBOLDT, Expedition from, to Cottonwood, April 10, 1863.
LARNED, FORT, Scout from Fort Lyon, Colo., to, Sept. 4-24, 1863.—Scout from, to Booth's Ranch, Arkansas River, Sept. 13-21, 1863.—Skirmish with Indians near, Nov. 13, 1864.—Skirmish near, Jan. 20, 1865.—Scout from, to South Fork of Pawnee Creek and Buckner's Branch, Feb. 3-8, 1865.—Operations about, Feb. 12-21, 1865.—Skirmish with Indians eighty miles west of, March 7, 1865.—Scout from, to Crooked Creek, March 9-15, 1865.
LAWRENCE, Massacre at, Aug. 21, 1863.

KANSAS—KENTUCKY.

LINCOLN, FORT, Skirmish at, Oct. 25, 1864.
LITTLE OSAGE RIVER, Engagement on, Oct. 25, 1864.
MARIAS DES CYGNES, Skirmish on, Aug. 31, 1863.—Engagement at, Oct. 25, 1864.
MINE CREEK, Engagement on, Oct. 25, 1864.
MOUND CITY, Skirmish at, Oct. 25, 1864.
MULBERRY CREEK, Scout from Salina to, Aug. 8-11, 1864.
NINE MILE BRIDGE, Skirmish at, Jan. 20, 1865.
OSAGE MISSION, Skirmish at, Sept. 26, 1864.
OXFORD, Skirmish near, Jan. 31, 1865.
PAOLA, Skirmish near, Aug. 21, 1863.
PAWNEE CREEK, Scout from Fort Larned to South Fork of, Feb. 3-8, 1865.
PAWNEE FORK, Scout from Fort Larned to, Jan. 15-21, 1865.
PAWNEE ROCK, Affair near, May 20, 1865.—Skirmish at, June 12, 1865.
PLUM BUTTE, Skirmish at, June 12, 1865.
POINT OF ROCKS, Skirmish at, Jan. 20, 1865.
QUANTRILL'S RAID into Kansas, Aug. 20-28, 1863, and pursuit by Union forces.
REPUBLICAN RIVER, Expedition from Denver, Colo., to, April 8-23, 1864.—Scout on, Aug. 19-24, 1864.
RILEY, FORT, Operations about, Feb. 12-20, 1865.
SALINA, Scout from, to Mulberry Creek, Aug. 8-11, 1864.
SCOTT, FORT, Skirmish near, Sept. 1, 1861.—Expedition from, and, skirmishes, Nov. 6-11, 1862.—Affair near, June 8, 1863.
SHAWNEETOWN, Skirmish near, June 6, 1863.
SMOKY HILL, Action near, May 16, 1864.
SMOKY HILL CROSSING, Skirmish with Indians near, Aug. 16, 1864.
SMOKY HILL FORK, Scout on, Aug. 1-5, 1864.
SMOKY HILL RIVER, Scout from Fort Larned to, Jan. 15-21, 1865.
WALNUT CREEK, Skirmish at, Sept. 25, 1864.—Scout from Fort Larned to, Jan. 15-21, 1865.
ZARAH, FORT, Skirmish with Indians near, Nov. 20, 1864.—Skirmish with Indians near, Dec. 4, 1864.—Skirmish at, Feb. 1, 1865.—Affair near, April 23, 1865.

KENTUCKY.

ALBANY, Affair at, Sept. 23, 1861.—Affair at, Sept. 29, 1861.—Skirmish near, Aug. 18, 1863.
ALCORN'S DISTILLERY, Skirmish at, May 9, 1863.
ASHBYSBURG, Skirmish at, Sept. 25, 1862.
ATHENS, Affair at, Feb. 23, 1863.
AUGUSTA, Skirmish at, Sept. 27, 1862.
BACON CREEK, Skirmish at, Dec. 26, 1862.

KENTUCKY.

BACON CREEK BRIDGE, Expedition to, and destruction of, Dec. 4-7, 1861.
BARBOURSVILLE, Action at, Sept. 19, 1861.—Skirmish at, Sept. 8, 1862.—Skirmish at, April 27, 1863.—Skirmish at, Feb. 8, 1864.
BARDSTOWN, Skirmish near, Oct. 3, 1862.—Skirmish near, Oct. 4, 1862.—Skirmish at, Oct. 19, 1862.—Skirmish at, July 5, 1863.—Skirmish near, Aug. 1, 1864.
BARDSTOWN PIKE, Skirmish on, Oct. 1, 1862.—Action on, Oct. 4, 1862.
BARDSTOWN ROAD, Skirmish on, Oct. 9, 1862.
BARREN MOUND, Skirmish at, Oct. 15, 1862.
BATH COUNTY, Operations in, Oct. 16-25, 1862.—Skirmish in, March 26, 1865.
BEACH FORK, Skirmish at, Oct. 6, 1862.
BEAR WALLOW, Skirmish at, Sept. 19, 1862.—Skirmish at, Dec. 25, 1862.
BEAUREGARD, CAMP, Expedition to, Dec. 28-31, 1861.
BEAVER, FORKS OF, Skirmish at, March 31, 1864.
BELL MINES, Skirmish at, July 13, 1864.
BENSON'S BRIDGE, Affair near, June 10, 1864.
BIG HILL, Action at, Aug. 23, 1862.—Skirmish at, Oct. 18, 1862.—Skirmish near, Aug. 29, 1862.—Expedition from Crab Orchard to, Oct. 21, 1862.
BIG PIGEON RIVER, Skirmishes at, Nov 5-6, 1864.
BIG ROCK CASTLE CREEK, Skirmish at, Oct. 16, 1862.
BIG SPRING, Scout from Munfordville to, July 13-15, 1864.
BLACKWATER RIVER, Skirmish at, March 29, 1865.
BLOOMFIELD, Skirmish at, Oct. 18, 1862.—Skirmish at, Nov. 5, 1864.
BOONEVILLE, Affair near, April 14, 1864.
BOSTON, Capture of stockade at, Dec. 29, 1862.
BOURBON COUNTY, Operations in, Oct. 16-25, 1862.
BOWLING GREEN, Occupation of, by Confederate forces, Sept. 18, 1861.—Evacuation of, by Confederate forces, Feb. 14, 1862.—Occupation of, by Union forces, Feb. 15, 1862.
BOWLING GREEN ROAD, Skirmish on, Sept. 17, 1862.
BRADFORDSVILLE, Skirmish at, Feb. 8, 1865.
BRANDENBURG, Skirmish at, Sept. 12, 1862.—Skirmish at, July 9, 1863.
BRECKINRIDGE COUNTY, Scout in, May 5, 1864.
BRIMSTONE CREEK, Skirmish at, Sept. 10, 1863.
BROOKVILLE, Skirmish at, Sept. 28, 1862.
BROWN HILL, Skirmish at, Oct. 7, 1862.
BROWNSVILLE, Skirmish at, Nov. 20, 1861.
BURKESVILLE, Skirmish at, Nov. 8, 1862.—Expedition from Glasgow to, June 8-10, 1863.
BURKESVILLE ROAD, Skirmish on, Dec. 25, 1862.
BURNT CROSS ROADS, Skirmish at, Oct. 6, 1862.
BUSHY CREEK, Skirmish on, April 7, 1864.

51

KENTUCKY.

CALHOUN, Skirmish at, Nov. 25, 1862.
CANTON, Skirmish at, Aug. 22, 1864.
CARTER COUNTY, Skirmish in, Aug. 27, 1863.
CASEYVILLE, Forrest's expedition to, Nov. 24-Dec. 5, 1861.—Naval expedition to, Dec. 1, 1861.
CAVE CITY, Affair at, May 11, 1862.—Skirmish near, Sept. 18, 1862.
CEDAR CHURCH, Skirmish at, Oct. 3, 1862.
CELINA, Skirmish at, April 19, 1863.—Expedition to, April 26-29, 1863.
CERRO GORDO, Naval action at, June 19, 1863.
CHAPLIN HILLS, Battle of, Oct. 8, 1862.
CHAPLINTOWN, Skirmish near, Jan. 30, 1865.
CHESSER'S STORE, Action at, Oct. 9, 1862.
CHRISTIANSBURG, Affair at, July 1, 1863.
CLARK COUNTY, Operations in, Oct. 16-25, 1862.
CLARK'S NECK, Skirmish at, Aug. 27, 1863.
CLAY VILLAGE, Skirmish at, Oct. 4, 1862.
CLINTON, Expedition from, July 22-27, 1863.—Guerrilla raid on, March 10, 1864.—Scout from Columbus to, March 30, 1864.—Skirmish at, July 10, 1864.
COAL RUN, Skirmish at the mouth of, July 2, 1863.
COLESBURG, Attack on Fort Jones near, Feb. 18, 1865.
COLUMBIA, Skirmish at, June 29, 1863.—Skirmish at, July 3, 1863.—Scouts from, Dec. 5-10, 1863.
COLUMBUS, Occupation of, by Confederate forces, Sept. 3, 1861.—Engagement at, Sept. 4, 1861.—Reconnoissance towards, Sept. 21-22, 1861.—Demonstration from Paducah upon, Nov. 7, 1861.—Naval action near, Jan. 7-11, 1862.—Naval reconnoissance to, Feb. 23, 1862.—Gunboat reconnoissance to, Jan. 14, 1862.—Evacuation of, by Confederate forces, March 2, 1862.—Occupation of, by Union forces, March 3, 1862.—Expedition from, to Covington, Durhamville, and Fort Randolph, Tenn., Sept. 28-Oct. 5, 1862.—Skirmish near, Dec. 15, 1862.—Skirmish near, Jan. 3, 1863.—Attack on Union pickets at, March 6, 1864.—Skirmish at, March 27, 1864.—Scout from, to Clinton and Moscow, March 30, 1864.—Skirmish at, April 11, 1864.—Skirmish at, April 13, 1864.
COOMB'S FERRY, Skirmish at, Feb. 22, 1863.
COVINGTON, Skirmish near, Sept. 10, 1862.
CRAB ORCHARD, Skirmish at, Oct. 15, 1862.—Skirmish at, Aug. 18, 1863.
CRAB ORCHARD ROAD, Skirmish on, Oct. 14, 1862.
CREEK HEAD, Skirmish near, April 24, 1863.
CREELSBOROUGH, Skirmish at, April 19, 1863.—Skirmish at, June 29, 1863.—Expedition from Nashville, Tenn., to, Dec. 28, 1863-Jan. 4, 1864.
CRITTENDEN, Affair at, June 27, 1864.
CROSS ROADS, Skirmish at, Oct. 18, 1862.

KENTUCKY.

CUMBERLAND FORD, Expedition from, Sept. 26-30, 1861, including skirmish at Laurel Bridge, Laurel County, and capture of salt-works in Clay County.
CUMBERLAND RIVER, Affair on, Jan. 27, 1864.—Skirmish on, March 19, 1864.
CUMMINGS'S FERRY, Skirmish near, July 7, 1863.—Skirmish near, July 8, 1863.
CYNTHIANA, Capture of, July 17, 1862.—Capture of, June 11, 1864.—Action at, June 12, 1864.
DANVILLE, Skirmish at, Oct. 11, 1862.—Skirmishes at, March 24-26, 1863.—Skirmish at, March 28, 1863.—Affair at, Jan. 29, 1865.
DANVILLE CROSS ROADS, Skirmish at, Oct. 10, 1862.
DICK'S FORD, Skirmish at, Oct. 12, 1862.
DOG WALK, Action at, Oct. 9, 1862.
DRY RIDGE, Action at, Oct. 9, 1862.
DUTTON'S HILL, Action at, March 30, 1863.
EDDYVILLE, Expedition to, Oct. 26, 1861.—Expedition to, Nov. 24-Dec. 5, 1861.—Skirmish at, Oct. 17, 1864.
EDMONTON, Skirmish near, June 7, 1863.
ELIZABETHTOWN, Capture of Union forces at, Dec. 27, 1862.
ELIZABETHTOWN ROAD, Skirmish on, Sept. 29, 1862.
ESTILL COUNTY, Operations in, Oct. 16-25, 1862.
FAIR GROUNDS, Skirmish at, Oct. 6, 1862.
FALMOUTH, Skirmish near, Sept. 17, 1862.
FANCY FARMS, Affair at, March 22, 1864.
FERN CREEK, Skirmish on, Oct. 1, 1862.
FISHING CREEK, Skirmish at, Dec. 8, 1861.—Skirmish at, Jan. 8, 1862.—Engagement at, Jan. 19, 1862.
FLAT LICK, Skirmish at, Aug. 17, 1862.
FLORENCE, Skirmish near, Sept. 18, 1862.
FLOYD COUNTY, Skirmish in, Dec. 4, 1862.
FORKS OF BEAVER, Skirmish at, March 31, 1864.
FOX SPRINGS, Skirmish at, June 16, 1863.
FRANKFORT, Demonstrations on, June 10-12, 1864.
FRANKFORT AND LOUISVILLE ROAD, Skirmish at, Oct. 1, 1862.
FRANKLIN, Skirmish at, July 5, 1863.
FRANKLIN ROAD, Skirmish on, Sept. 9, 1862.
GALLATIN COUNTY, Operations in, Oct. 15-20, 1862.
GARRETTSBURG, Skirmish at, Nov. 6, 1862.
GEIGER'S LAKE, Skirmish at, Sept. 3, 1862.—Skirmish at, July 15, 1864.—Skirmish at, Aug. 18, 1864.
GHENT, Skirmish near, Aug. 29, 1864.
GLASGOW, Occupation of, by Confederate forces, Sept. 12, 1862.—Affair at, Sept. 18, 1862.—Skirmish at, Sept. 30, 1862.—Skirmish at, Dec. 24, 1862.—Expedition from, to Burkesville and Tennessee State Line, June 8-10, 1863.—Skirmish at, Oct. 6, 1863.—Skirmish near, March 25, 1865.

KENTUCKY.

GOGGIN, CAMP, Skirmishes near, Dec. 1-2, 1861.
GOOSE CREEK SALT WORKS, Destruction of, Oct. 23-24, 1862.
GRADYVILLE, Skirmish at, Dec. 12, 1861.
GRASSY MOUND, Skirmish at, Oct. 6, 1862.
GREEN RIVER BRIDGE, Engagement at, July 4, 1863.
GREENSBURG, Operations near, Jan. 28-Feb. 2, 1862.
GREEN'S CHAPEL, Skirmish near, Dec. 25, 1862.
GREENVILLE, Skirmish near, Sept. 11, 1863.—Skirmish at, Dec. 3, 1863.
GRIDER'S FERRY, Cumberland River, Skirmish at, Dec. 28, 1861.
GRUBB'S CROSS ROADS, Skirmish at, Aug. 21, 1864.
HADDIX'S FERRY, Expedition from Paducah to, July 26-27, 1864, and skirmish.
HALF MOUNTAIN, Action at, April 14, 1864.
HAMILTON'S FORD, Skirmish near, Dec. 29, 1862.
HARRODSBURG, Reoccupation of, by Union forces, Oct. 11, 1862.—Skirmish at, Oct. 13, 1862.—Skirmish at, Oct. 21, 1864.—Skirmish near, Jan. 29, 1865.
HAZEL GREEN, Skirmish at, March 9, 1863.—Skirmish at, March 19, 1863.
HEIMAN, FORT, Skirmish near, Feb. 13, 1862.—Scout from, into Tennessee, May 26-June 2, 1863.—Capture of gunboat Undine (No. 55) and transports near, Oct. 30, 1864.
HENDERSON, Skirmish at, June 30, 1862.—Raid on, July 18, 1862.—Skirmish at, Sept. 14, 1862.—Skirmish near, Sept. 25, 1864.
HENDERSON COUNTY, Skirmish in, Nov. 1, 1862.
HENRY COUNTY, Operations in, Oct. 15-20, 1862.
HICKMAN, Occupation of, by Confederate forces, Sept. 3, 1861.—Engagement at, Sept. 4, 1861.—Occupation of, July 15-16, 1863.—Expedition from Columbus to, Aug. 1, 1863.—Scout from Columbus to, July 17-18, 1864.
HICKMAN'S BRIDGE, Skirmish at, March 28, 1863.
HODGENSVILLE, Skirmish near, Oct. 23, 1861.
HOLT, FORT, Gunboat demonstration on, Dec. 1, 1861.
HOPKINSVILLE, Skirmish at, Sept. 29, 1861.—Raid from Paris, Tenn., to, Dec. 6, 1864, to Jan. 15, 1865, and skirmishes.
HORSE CAVE, Skirmish at, Sept. 19, 1862.
HORSESHOE BOTTOM, Cumberland River, Action at, May 10, 1863.
HOWARD'S MILLS, Skirmish at, June 13, 1863.—Skirmish at, March 9, 1865.
HUSTONVILLE, Skirmish at, Feb. 9, 1865.
IRVINE, Skirmish at, July 30, 1863.
IVY MOUNTAIN, Engagement at, Nov. 8, 1861.
JACKSON, Affairs at, Dec. 1-10, 1863.
JAMESTOWN, Skirmish at, June 2, 1863.
JENNIE'S CREEK, Skirmish at, Jan. 7, 1862.

KENTUCKY.

JOE UNDERWOOD, CAMP, Attack on, Oct. 24, 1861.
JOHNSON'S FERRY, Skirmish near, Dec. 29, 1862.
JONES, FORT, Attack on, Feb. 18, 1865.
KELLER'S BRIDGE, Action at, June 11, 1864.
KENTUCKY LINE, Affair at, Sept. 8, 1862.
KENTUCKY RIVER, Skirmish on, Aug. 31, 1862.—Skirmish near, July 8, 1863.
KETTLE CREEK, Skirmish at, June 9, 1863.
LAFAYETTE, Skirmish at, Nov. 27, 1863.
LANCASTER, Skirmish at, Oct. 14, 1862.—Skirmish at, July 31, 1863.
LANCASTER ROAD, Skirmish on, Oct. 13, 1862.
LAUREL BRIDGE, Laurel County, Skirmish at, Sept. —, 1861.
LAWRENCEBURG, Skirmish at, Oct. 8, 1862.—Skirmish at, Oct. 11, 1862.—Skirmish at, Oct. 25, 1862.
LAWRENCE COUNTY, Skirmish in, Aug. 27, 1863.
LEBANON, Operations near, Jan. 28-Feb. 2, 1862.—Skirmish near and capture of, July 12, 1862.—Skirmish at, July 5, 1863.
LEBANON JUNCTION, Skirmish near, Sept. 28, 1862.
LEXINGTON, Occupation of, by Confederate forces, Sept. 2, 1862.—Action at, Oct. 18, 1862.—Capture of, June 10, 1864.—Scouts about, April 13-16, 1865.
LICKING RIVER, Action on, April 14, 1864.
LITTLE ROCKCASTLE RIVER, Skirmish at, Oct. 18, 1862.
LITTLE SANDY, Expedition to, Jan. 24-30, 1862.
LOGAN'S CROSS ROADS, Engagement at, Jan. 19, 1862.
LOG CHURCH, Skirmish at, Sept. 10, 1862.
LONDON, Action at, Aug. 17, 1862.—Skirmish at, July 26, 1863.
LOUISA, Skirmish at, March 12, 1863.—Skirmishes near, March 25-26, 1863.
LOUISVILLE, Skirmish near, Sept. 30, 1862.
LOUISVILLE AND FRANKFORT ROAD, Skirmish on, Oct. 1, 1862.
LOUISVILLE PIKE, Skirmish on, Oct. 1, 1862.
LUSBY'S MILL, Skirmish near, June 20, 1862.
LYON COUNTY, Skirmish in, April 29, 1865.
McCORMICK'S GAP, Skirmish at, Sept. 20, 1864.
MACKVILLE, Skirmish near, July 14, 1862.
MACKVILLE PIKE, Skirmish on, Oct. 9, 1862.
MADISON ROAD, Reconnoissance on, Oct. 19, 1862.
MADISONVILLE, Skirmish at, Aug. 25, 1862.—Skirmish near, Sept. 5, 1862.—Skirmish at, March —, 1863.
MAMMOTH CAVE, Skirmish near, Aug. 17, 1862.
MANCHESTER, Skirmish at, Oct. 14, 1862.—Destruction of salt-works near, Oct. 23-24, 1862.
MARROWBONE, Skirmish at, July 2, 1863.
MARROWBONE CREEK, Skirmish at, Sept. 22, 1863.
MARSHALL, Skirmish at, Jan. 12, 1864.
MARTIN CREEK, Skirmish at, July 10, 1863.

KENTUCKY..

MAYFIELD, Raid on, Feb. 22, 1864.—Guerrilla raid on, March 10, 1864.—Skirmish near, May 20, 1864.—Scout from, Aug. 14-15, 1864, and skirmish.
MAYFIELD CREEK, Skirmish on, Sept. 22, 1861.
MAYSVILLE, Skirmish at, June 16, 1863.
MEADE COUNTY, Scout in, May 5, 1864.
MERRY OAKS, Skirmish at, Sept. 17, 1862.
MIDDLE CREEK, Engagement at, Jan. 10, 1862.
MILL SPRINGS, Operations about, Dec. 1-13, 1861.—Reconnoissance from Somerset to, Dec. 18, 1861.—Engagement near, Jan. 19, 1862.—Skirmish near, May 29, 1863.
MITCHEL, FORT, Skirmish at, Sept. 10, 1862.
MONTEREY, Skirmish near, June 11, 1862.
MONTGOMERY COUNTY, Operations in, Oct. 16-25, 1862.
MONTICELLO, Expedition to, and operations in Southeastern Kentucky, April 26-May 12, 1863.—Skirmish near, May 9, 1863.—Affair at, June 9, 1863.—Skirmish at, Nov. 27, 1863.
MORGAN COUNTY, Skirmish in, Oct. 6, 1863.
MORGANFIELD, Skirmish at, Aug. 3, 1862.—Skirmish at, Sept. 1, 1862.—Skirmish near, May 6, 1864.—Skirmish at, June 25, 1864.—Skirmish at, July 14, 1864.
MORGANTOWN, Skirmish near, Oct. 31, 1861.
MOSCOW, Scout from Columbus to, March 30, 1864.
MOUNTAIN GAP, Skirmishes near, Oct. 14-16, 1862.
MOUNTAIN SIDE, Skirmish at, Oct. 18, 1862.
MOUNT CARMEL, Skirmish at, June 16, 1863.
MOUNT STERLING, Skirmish near, March 2, 1863.—Skirmish at, March 19, 1863.—Capture of, March 22, 1863.—Affairs at, Dec. 1-10, 1863.—Capture of, June 8, 1864.—Action at, June 9, 1864.—Scouts about, Jan. 9-Feb. 15, 1865.
MOUNT VERNON, Skirmish near, Oct. 16, 1863.
MOUNT WASHINGTON, Skirmish near, Oct. 1, 1862.
MOUNT ZION CHURCH, Engagement at, Aug. 30, 1862.
MUDDY RIVER, Destruction of lock at mouth of, Sept. 26, 1861.
MUD LICK SPRINGS, Bath County, Skirmish near, June 13, 1863.
MULDRAUGH'S HILL, Skirmish at, Dec. 28, 1862.—Affair at, Dec. 31, 1862.
MUNFORDVILLE, Siege of, Sept. 14-17, 1862.—Actions near, Sept. 20-21, 1862.—Skirmish near, Dec. 26, 1862.—Scout from, to Big Spring, July 13-15, 1864.
NEGRO HEAD CUT, Skirmish at, April 27, 1863.
NELSON'S CROSS ROADS, Skirmish at, Oct. 18, 1862.
NEW HAVEN, Capture of the Third Georgia Cavalry near, Sept. 29, 1862.—Skirmish at, Dec. 30, 1862.—Skirmish near, Aug. 2, 1864.
NEW HOPE STATION, Skirmish near, July 25, 1863.
NEW MARKET, Affair near, Dec. 31, 1862.—Affair at, Feb. 8, 1865.

KENTUCKY.

NOLIN, Capture of stockade at, Dec. 26, 1862.
OAKLAND STATION, Skirmish near, Sept. 16, 1862.
OLYMPIAN SPRINGS, Reconnoissance to, Oct. 8-11, 1863.
OWEN COUNTY, Affairs in, June 20-23, 1862.—Operations in, Oct. 15-20, 1862.
OWENSBOROUGH, Skirmish at, Sept. 18, 1862.—Skirmish at, Aug. 27, 1864.—Guerrilla raid on, Sept. 2, 1864.
PADUCAH, Occupation of, by Union forces, Sept. 6, 1861.—Affair at, Aug. 22, 1861.—Demonstration from, upon Columbus, Nov. 7, 1861.—Threatened attack on, July 16-18, 1863.—Attack on, March 25, 1864.—Skirmish at, April 14, 1864.—Naval action near, Oct. 30, 1864.—Expedition from, to Haddix's Ferry, July 26-27, 1864, and skirmish.
PAINT LICK BRIDGE, Skirmish at, July 31, 1863.
PAINTSVILLE, Skirmish at, April 13, 1864.
PARIS, Skirmish near, July 19, 1862.—Affair near, March 11, 1863.—Skirmish at, April 16, 1863.—Skirmish at, July 29, 1863.
PERRYVILLE, Skirmish at, Oct. 7, 1862.—Battle of, Oct. 8, 1862.—Pursuit of Confederate forces from, to Loudon, Oct. 10-22, 1862.—Morgan's retreat from, Oct. 17-Nov. 4, 1862.
PHILLIPS' FORK, Skirmish at, May 10, 1863.
PIKE COUNTY, Skirmish in, July 2, 1863.—Skirmish in, May 16, 1864.—Skirmish in, May 18, 1864.
PIKETON, Skirmish at, Nov. 9, 1861.—Expedition to, Jan. 24-30, 1862.—Affair near, Nov. 5, 1862.—Skirmish at, April 15, 1863.—Skirmish at, Feb. 25, 1865.
PITMAN'S CROSS ROADS, Skirmishes at, Oct. 19-21, 1862.
PLEASUREVILLE, Affair near, June 9, 1864.
POND CREEK, Pike County, Skirmish at, May 16, 1864.
POND CREEK, Union County, Skirmish at, July 6, 1863.
POUND GAP, Action at, March 16, 1862.—Skirmish near, May 9, 1864.—Skirmish near, June 1, 1864.
POWELL COUNTY, Operations in, Oct. 16-25, 1862.—Capture of guerrilla camp in, Dec. 26, 1862.
PRESTONBURG, Engagement near, Jan. 10, 1862.—Capture of transports and skirmishes near, Dec. 4-5, 1862.
QUICKSAND CREEK, Skirmish on, April 5, 1864.
RAGLAND MILLS, Bath County, Skirmish at, Jan. 13, 1864.
RED BIRD CREEK, Skirmish at, Aug. 25, 1862.—Skirmish at, May 10, 1863.
RICHMOND, Skirmish near, Aug. 29, 1862.—Battle of, Aug. 30, 1862.—Expedition from Crab Orchard to, Oct. 21, 1862.—Action at, July 28, 1863.
ROARING SPRING, Skirmish at, Aug. 22, 1864.
ROCKCASTLE HILLS, Skirmish near, Oct. 18, 1861.—Action at, Oct. 21, 1861.
ROCKCASTLE RIVER, Skirmish at, Oct. 18, 1862.
ROCKHOUSE CREEK, Expedition from Louisa to, May 9-13, 1864.

KENTUCKY.

ROCKY GAP, Affair at, June 9, 1863.
ROCKY HILL, Skirmish at, Oct. 17, 1862.
ROCKY HILL STATION, Burning of depot at, July 4, 1863.
ROGERSVILLE, Skirmish near, July 27, 1863.
ROLLING FORK, Skirmish near, Dec. 29, 1862.
ROWLETT'S STATION, Action at, Dec. 17, 1861.
RUSSELLVILLE, Scout in the vicinity of, Dec. 5-8, 1861.—Skirmish at, July 29, 1862.—Skirmish at, Sept. 30, 1862.—Skirmish at, June 28, 1863.
SACRAMENTO, Action at, Dec. 28, 1861.
SALEM, Skirmish at, Aug. 8, 1864.
SALT RIVER, Action near, Oct. 9, 1862.
SALT WORKS, in Clay County, Capture of, Sept. —, 1861.
SALYERSVILLE, Skirmish at, Oct. 10, 1863, Skirmish at, Oct. 30, 1863.—Skirmish at, Nov. 30, 1863.—Skirmish at, Dec. 1, 1863.—Skirmish at, April 16, 1864.
SARATOGA, Skirmish at, Oct. 26, 1861.
SCOTTSVILLE, Affair at, June 11, 1863.—Skirmish near, Dec. 8, 1863.
SCOTTSVILLE ROAD, Skirmish on, Sept. 9, 1862.
SHARPSBURG, Skirmish at, Dec. 31, 1864.
SHELBY COUNTY, Skirmish in, Sept. 3, 1864.
SHELBYVILLE, Skirmish at, Sept. 4, 1862.
SHEPHERDSVILLE, Surrender of outpost near, Sept. 7, 1862.—Skirmish near, Oct. 3, 1862.—Skirmish at, July 7, 1863.
SHEPHERDSVILLE ROAD, Skirmish on, Oct. 2, 1862.
SIMPSONVILLE, Skirmish near, Jan. 25, 1865.
SLATE CREEK, Skirmish at, March 2, 1863.
SMITH'S, Skirmish at, Sept. 11, 1862.
SMITH'S MILL, Skirmish at, Aug. 19, 1864.
SMITH'S SHOALS, Cumberland River, Skirmish at, Aug. 1, 1863.
SNOW'S POND, Skirmish near, Sept. 25, 1862.
SOMERSET, Operations about, Dec. 1-13, 1861.—Skirmish near, Dec. 8, 1861.—Reconnoissance from, to Mill Springs, Dec. 18, 1861.—Action near, March 30, 1863.
SOUTHERLAND'S FARM, Skirmish at, Sept. 19, 1862.
SOUTH UNION, Skirmish near, May 13, 1863.
SPRINGFIELD, Skirmish at, Oct. 6, 1862.—Skirmish at, Dec. 30, 1862.
STANFORD, Skirmish at, Oct. 14, 1862.—Skirmish at, July 31, 1863.
STONER BRIDGE, Skirmish at, Feb. 24, 1863.
TAIT'S FERRY, Kentucky River, Skirmish at, Sept. 1, 1862.
TAYLORSVILLE, Skirmish at, April 18, 1865.
TEBB'S BEND, Engagement at, July 4, 1863.
TERMAN'S FERRY, Skirmish at, Jan. 9, 1864.

KENTUCKY.

TOMPKINSVILLE, Skirmish near, June 6, 1862.—Capture of, July 9, 1862.—Skirmish near, Nov. 19, 1862.—Skirmish near, Nov. 24, 1862.
TRIPLETT'S BRIDGE, Rowan County, Action at, June 16, 1863.
TROUBLESOME CREEK, Skirmish on, April 27, 1864.
TUNNEL HILL, Skirmish at, Nov. 19, 1862.
UNDINE, U. S. Gunboat, Capture of, near Fort Heiman, Oct. 30, 1864.
UNION CITY, Skirmishes at and near, Sept. 2, 1864.
UNION COUNTY, Skirmish in, July 6, 1863.—Operations in, July 14-18, 1864.—Confederate raid in, Aug. 7, 1864.
UNIONTOWN, Skirmish at, Sept. 1, 1862.
UPTON'S HILL, Skirmish near, Oct. 12, 1861.
VALLEY WOODS, Skirmish at, Oct. 17, 1862.
VANCEBURG, Attack on, Oct. 29, 1864.
VINEGAR HILL, Skirmish at, Sept. 22, 1862.
VIOLA, Expedition to, Dec. 28-31, 1861.
VOLNEY, Skirmish near, Oct. 22, 1863.
WAITSBOROUGH, Accident at, May 6, 1863.—Skirmish at, June 6, 1863.
WEBSTER COUNTY, Operations in, July 14-18, 1864.
WEST LIBERTY, Skirmish at, Oct. 23, 1861.—Action at, Sept. 26, 1862.—Skirmish at, Oct. 12, 1863.
WESTON, Affair near, Sept. 14, 1864.
WHIPPOORWILL CREEK, Skirmish at, Dec. 1, 1861.
WHITE OAK SPRINGS, Skirmish at, Aug. 17, 1864.
WHITE'S FARM, Engagement at, Aug. 30, 1862.
WILD CAT, Skirmish at, Oct. 19, 1862.—Skirmish near, Oct. 20, 1862.
WILD CAT CAMP, Action at, Oct. 21, 1861.—Skirmishes about, Oct. 17, 1862.
WILD CAT MOUNTAIN, Skirmish at, Oct. 16, 1862.
WILLIAMSBURG, Skirmish at, July 25, 1863.
WINCHESTER, Skirmish near, July 29, 1863.
WOLF RIVER, Skirmish at, May 18, 1864.
WOODBURN, Skirmish at, Sept. 10, 1862.—Skirmish near, Sept. 12, 1862.—Skirmish near, April 27, 1863.—Skirmish near, May 13, 1863.—Skirmish at, July 5, 1863.
WOODBURY, Skirmishes at and near, Oct. 29, 1861.
WOODSONVILLE, Action at, Dec. 17, 1861.—Siege of, Sept. 14-17, 1862.

LOUISIANA.

LOUISIANA.

Seceded Jan. 26, 1861.

ALABAMA BAYOU, Skirmish at, Sept. 20, 1864.
ALEXANDER'S CREEK, Skirmish at, Oct. 5, 1864.
ALEXANDRIA, Taken possession of by Union naval forces, May 6, 1863.—Occupation of, by Union naval forces, March 16, 1864.—Skirmishes about, April 26-May 13, 1864.
AMITE RIVER, Reconnoissance to, June 27-29, 1862, and skirmish.—Skirmish on, July 24, 1862.—Naval action at mouth of, April 7, 1863.—Expedition from Bonnet Carre to, March 21-29, 1863.—Operations on, May 9-18, 1863.—Affair on, April 12, 1863.—Skirmish on, April 17, 1863.—Expeditions from Carrollton and Baton Rouge to, Sept. 24-29, 1863.—Skirmish on, July 25, 1864.—Expeditions to, Oct. 2-8, 1864.—Skirmish on, Dec. 12, 1864.—Skirmish on, March 18, 1865.—Expedition from Bonnet Carre to, March 26-29, 1865.—Expedition from Bonnet Carre to, March 21-29, 1863.—Operations on, May 9-18, 1863.
ANGLO-AMERICAN, U. S. S., Engagement between, and batteries at Port Hudson, Aug. 29, 1862.
ARKANSAS, C. S. S., Destruction of near Baton Rouge, Aug. 6, 1862.
ASHTON, Skirmish at, May 1, 1864.
ASHWOOD LANDING, Skirmish at, May 1, 1864.—Skirmish at, May 4, 1864.
ATCHAFALAYA, Skirmish at, July 21, 1864.—Skirmish at, Oct. 5, 1864.
ATCHAFALAYA RIVER (See Cornay Bridge, Nov. 2, 1862). Operations on, Feb. 12-28, 1863.—Skirmish at, June 4, 1863.—Skirmishes on, Sept. 7-9, 1863.—Skirmish on, Sept. 20, 1863.—Expedition from Morganza to, May 30-June 5, 1864, and skirmishes near Livonia and Morganza.—Naval action on, near Simsport, June 8, 1864.—Skirmish on, Aug. 25, 1864.—Skirmish at, Sept. 17, 1864.—Expedition from Morganza to, Dec. 16-19, 1864.
AVOYELLES PRAIRIE, Skirmish at, May 15, 1864.
BARRE'S LANDING, Expedition from Opelousas to, and capture of the steamer Ellen, April 21, 1863.—Operations on the Teche Road near, May 21-26, 1863.—Attack on the steamer Louisiana Belle near, May 22, 1863.—Skirmish at, Oct. 21, 1863.
BATON ROUGE, Seizure of U. S. Arsenal and Barracks at, Jan. 10, 1861.—Occupation of, by Union forces, May 9, 1862 (naval).—Naval actions at, May 29 and Aug. 2, 1862.—Expedition from, June 7-9, 1862.—Operations about, July 27-Aug. 6, 1862.—Engagement at, Aug. 5, 1862.—Skirmish at, Aug. 20, 1862.—Evacuation of, by Union forces, Aug. 21,

LOUISIANA.

1862.—Re-occupation of, by Union forces, Dec. 17, 1862.—Burning of State House at, Dec. 28, 1862.—Raid from La Grange, Tenn., to, April 27-May 2, 1863.—Skirmish near, Sept. 19, 1863.—Expeditions from, to New and Amite Rivers, Sept. 24-29, 1863.—Operations in the vicinity of, Sept. 25, 1863.—Skirmish near, March 3, 1864.—Skirmish near, March 8, 1864.—Skirmish near, April 15, 1864.—Skirmish near, May 3, 1864.—Operations in the vicinity of, July 3-25, 1864.—Expedition from, to Davis's Ford, near Clinton, July 17-18, 1864.—Expedition from, to Clinton, Greensburg, Osyka, and Camp Moore, Oct. 5-9, 1864.—Expedition from, to Clinton, Dec. 23-24, 1864.—Expedition from, to Jackson and Clinton, March 1-12, 1865.—Expeditions from, to Clinton and Amite River, March 30-April 2, 1865.—Affair near, July 29, 1864.—Expedition from Spring Hill, Ala., to, May 8-22, 1865.

BAYOU GOULA, Raid on, June 19, 1863.—Skirmish near, Jan. 24, 1865.—Scouts from, to Grand River, Jan. 29-Feb. 7, 1865.—Expedition from Donaldsonville to, Feb. 14-18, 1865.—Scout from Donaldsonville to, March 23-24, 1865.—Expedition from Donaldsonville to, April 21-22, 1865.—Skirmish at, May 9, 1865.

BAYOU SARA, Affair at, Aug. 10, 1862.—Affair at, Aug. 23, 1862.—Skirmish near, Nov. 9, 1863.—Expedition from Morganza to, Sept. 6-7, 1864.—Expedition from Morganza to, Oct. 3-6, 1864, and skirmishes.—Skirmishes at and near, Oct. 4, 1864.—Skirmishes near, Oct. 9-10, 1864.

BAYOU SARA ROAD, Operations on, May 18-19, 1863.

BAYOU TUNICA, Skirmish at, Nov. 8, 1863.

BEAUREGARD, FORT, Attack on, May 10, 1863.—Capture of, Sept. 4, 1863.

BELLE PRAIRIE, Engagement at, May 16, 1864.

BELLE RIVER, Expedition from Brashear City to, Oct. 22-24, 1864.

BENTON'S FERRY, Amite River, Skirmish near, July 25, 1864.

BERWICK, Operations on the Teche Road near, May 21-26, 1863.—Naval action at, April 18, 1863.—Skirmish at, June 1, 1863.—Skirmish at, April 26, 1864.—Affair at, May 1, 1864.—Reconnoissance from, to Pattersonville, Aug. 2, 1864.—Capture of U. S. S. Diana in, March 28, 1863.

BERWICK BAY, Naval operations in, Nov. 1-6, 1862.—Action at, June 23, 1863.—Expedition into, March 21-22, 1865.

BETHEL PLACE, Engagement at, April 12-13, 1863.

BISLAND, FORT, Engagement at, April 12-13, 1863.—Skirmish at, April 12, 1864.

BLACK BAYOU, Skirmish at, March 19, 1864.—Skirmish at, May 4, 1865.

BLACK RIVER, Operations on, Feb. 10-14, 1863.—Skirmish near, May 5, 1863.

LOUISIANA.

BLAIR'S LANDING, Engagement at, April 12-13, 1864.
BOEUF, BAYOU, Expeditions from Opelousas to, April 29-30, 1863.—Skirmish at, May 7, 1864.—Scout from, to Bayou Chemise, March 24, 1865.—Expeditions from, to Lake Verret, Grand Bayou, and The Park, April 2-10, 1865.—Expedition from, to Bayou De Large, May 25-27, 1865.
BOEUF, BAYOU, CROSSING, Capture of Union forces at, June 24, 1863.
BOEUF, BAYOU, ROAD, Skirmish on, April 22, 1863.
BONFOUCA BAYOU, Skirmish at, Nov. 21, 1862.—Expedition from Fort Pike to, Jan. 31-Feb. 1, 1865, and skirmish, Jan. 31.
BONNET CARRE, Skirmish at, Oct. 19, 1862.—Expedition from, to the Jackson Railroad and Amite River, March 21-29, 1863.—Expedition from, to Amite River, March 26-29, 1865.
BORGNE, LAKE, Affair at, Nov. 22, 1863.
BOURBEAU BAYOU, Skirmish at, Nov. 2, 1863.—Engagement at, Nov. 3, 1863.
BOUTTE STATION, Affair at, Sept. 5, 1862.
BOYCE'S BRIDGE, Cotile Bayou, Skirmish at, May 14, 1863.
BOYCE'S PLANTATION, Skirmish at, May 6, 1864.
BRASHEAR CITY, Naval action at, Nov. 1, 1862.—Skirmish at, June 21, 1863.—Capture of, June 23, 1863.—Re-occupation of, by Union forces, July 22, 1863.—Expedition from, Feb. 3-6, 1864.—Expedition from, to Belle River, Oct. 22-24, 1864.—Expedition from, to Bayou Portage, Nov. 17-19, 1864.—Expedition from, to Whiskey Bayou, Jan. 16-18, 1865.—Expedition from, to Bayou Sorrel, Jan. 21-22, 1865.—Expedition from, to Bayou Pigeon, March 20-22, 1865.—Expedition from, to Indian Bend, March 25-27, 1865.—Expedition from, to near Oyster Bayou, March 25-28, 1865.—Expedition from, to Lake Verret, Feb. 10-11, 1865.—Expedition from, to Lake Verret, Grand Bayou, and The Park, April 2-10, 1865.—Expedition from, to Ratliff's Plantation, May 14-16, 1865.—Operations in the vicinity of, April 30-May 12, 1865.
BREAUX BRIDGE, Expedition from Saint Martinsville to, April 17-21, 1863.
BROWN'S PLANTATION, Skirmish at, May 11, 1865.
BRUIN, LAKE, Skirmish at, April 28, 1863.
BUENA VISTA (See Donaldsonville, July 7, 1863).
BULLIT'S BAYOU, Skirmish at, Aug. 25, 1864.—Skirmish at, Sept. 14, 1864.
BUTTE-A-LA-ROSE, Capture of, by Union fleet, April 20, 1863.
BUZZARD'S PRAIRIE (See Bourbeau Bayou).
CALCASIEU PASS, Operations in, May 6-10, 1864.
CALEDONIA, Skirmish at, May 10, 1863.

LOUISIANA.

CAMPTI, Skirmish at, March 26, 1864.—Skirmish at, April 4, 1864.
CANE RIVER, Engagement at the junction of, with Red River, April 26-27, 1864.
CANE RIVER CROSSING, Engagement at, April 23, 1864.
CARRION CROW BAYOU, Skirmishes at, Oct. 14-15, 1863.—Skirmish at, Oct. 18, 1863.—Skirmish at, Nov. 3, 1863.—Skirmish at, Nov. 11, 1863.—Skirmish at, Nov. 18, 1863.
CARROLLTON, Expeditions from, to New and Amite Rivers, Sept. 24-29, 1863.
CENTREVILLE, Engagement near, April 12-13, 1863.—Skirmish at, May 25, 1863.
CHACAHOULA, Skirmish at, May 3, 1865.
CHACAHOULA STATION, Skirmish at, June 24, 1863.
CHALMETTE BATTERIES, Naval engagement with, April 25, 1862.
CHEFUNCTA RIVER, Naval action in, May 16, 1864.
CHEMISE BAYOU, Scout from Bayou Boeuf to, March 24, 1865.
CHENEYVILLE, Affair near, May 18, 1863.—Skirmish near, May 20, 1863.
CHICOTVILLE, Expeditions from Opelousas to, April 29-30, 1863.
CHOCTAW BAYOU, Skirmish at, April 28, 1863.
CLARK'S BAYOU, Skirmish at, April 26, 1863.
CLINTON, Expedition to, June 3-8, 1863.—Skirmish at, May 1, 1864.—Expedition from Baton Rouge to near, July 17-18, 1864.—Expedition to, Aug. 23-29, 1864.—Expedition from Baton Rouge to, Oct. 5-9, 1864.—Skirmish at, Nov. 15, 1864.—Expedition from Baton Rouge to, Dec. 23-24, 1864.—Expedition from Baton Rouge to, March 1-12, 1865.—Expeditions from Baton Rouge to, March 30-April 2, 1865.
CLINTON ROAD, Scouts from Merritt's Plantation on, May 14, 1863.
CLOUTIERVILLE, Skirmishes about, March 29-30, 1864.—Skirmishes at and near, April 22-24, 1864.
COLUMBIA, Skirmish at, Feb. 4, 1864, and skirmish near, June 1-2, 1864.
COMITE RIVER, Skirmishes on, March 9-10, 1863.—Skirmish on, May 2, 1863.—Skirmish on, Aug. 25, 1864.—Expeditions from Baton Rouge to, March 30-April 2, 1865.
COMO LANDING, Attack on Union gunboats at, June 15-16, 1864. (Tunica Bend.)
CONCORDIA, Skirmish at, July 22, 1864.
CONCORDIA BAYOU, Skirmish at, Aug. 5, 1864.
CORNAY BRIDGE, Atchafalaya River, Naval action at, Nov. 2, 1862.
COTILE BAYOU, Skirmish at, May 14, 1863.
COTILE LANDING, Skirmish at, April 25, 1864.
COTTON, C. S. S. (See Teche Bayou, Jan. 14, 1863).

LOUISIANA.

COURTABLEU BAYOU, Skirmish at, May 22, 1863.
COUSHATTEE, Naval action at, April —, 1864.
COVINGTON, Skirmish near, July 27, 1862.
COX'S PLANTATION, Engagement at, July 12-13, 1863.
CROSS BAYOU, Skirmish at, July 4, 1864.
CRUMP'S HILL, Skirmish at, April 2, 1864.
CYPRESS CREEK, Skirmish at, March 8, 1864.
DALLAS STATION, Expedition from Milliken's Bend to, Dec. 25-26, 1862.
DAVID'S FERRY, Red River, Capture of U. S. Transport Emma at, May 1, 1864.—Engagement at, May 4-5, 1864. destruction of the U. S. Steamer Covington and capture of the U. S. Steamers Signal and Warner.
DAVIS'S BEND, Skirmish at, June 29, 1864.
DAVISON'S FORD, Expedition from Baton Rouge to, July 17-18, 1864.
DE GLAIZE BAYOU, Skirmish near, May 17, 1864.—Engagement at, May 18, 1864.
DE LARGE BAYOU, Expedition from Bayou Boeuf to, May 25-27, 1865.
DELHI, Expedition from Milliken's Bend to, Dec. 25-26, 1862.
DELOACH'S BLUFF, Engagement at, April 26, 1864.
DE PAUL BAYOU, Skirmish at, April 8, 1864.
DE RUSSY, FORT, Evacuation of, by Confederate forces, April 23-25, 1863.—Engagement at and capture of, by Union forces, May 4, 1863.—Capture of, by Union forces, March 14, 1864.
DES ALLEMANDS, Skirmish at, July 18, 1863.
DES ALLEMANDS BAYOU, Skirmish at, June 20, 1862.—Skirmish at, June 22, 1862.—Affair at, Sept. 4, 1862.
DESERTED STATION, Skirmish at, Dec. 10, 1862.
DONALDSONVILLE, Bombardment of, Aug. 9, 1862.—Expedition from Carrollton to, Sept. 21-25, 1862, and skirmish.—Naval action near, Oct. 4, 1862.—Capture of, Oct. 25, 1862.—Attack on, June 28, 1863.—Naval engagement with batteries near, July 7, 1863.—Engagement near, July 12-13, 1863.—Affair opposite, Sept. 23, 1863.—Skirmish at, Feb. 8, 1864.—Affair near, Sept. 4, 1864.—Scout from, Jan. 19-20, 1865.—Expedition from, to Grand Bayou and Bayou Goula, Feb. 14-18, 1865.—Scout from, to Bayou Goula, March 23-24, 1865.—Expedition from, to Bayou Goula, April 21-22, 1865.
DOYAL'S PLANTATION, Affair at, Aug. 5, 1864.—Skirmish at, Nov. 29, 1864.
DUNBAR'S PLANTATION, Skirmish near, April 7, 1863.—Action near, April 15, 1863.
DUNN'S BAYOU, Engagement at, May 5, 1864.
EASTERN LOUISIANA, Operations in, Oct. 2-11, 1864.
ELLEN, Steamer, Capture of, April 21, 1863.
EMMA, U. S. Transport, Capture of, at David's Ferry, May 1, 1864.
FALSE RIVER, Reconnoissance to, March 19, 1863.

LOUISIANA.

FAUSSE POINTE, LAKE, Expeditions to, Sept. 7-11, 1864.—Skirmish at, Nov. 18, 1864.
FAUSSE RIVER, Expedition from Morganza to, Sept. 13-17, 1864.—Scouts from Morganza to, Feb. 7-10, 1865.
FLOYD, Skirmish at, Aug. 24, 1863.
FORDOCHE BAYOU ROAD, Skirmish on, May 29, 1864.
FRANKLINTON, Expedition from Madisonville to, Feb. 1-3, 1864.
FRENCH SETTLEMENT, Expedition from the Hermitage to the, April 2-5, 1865.
GENTILLY'S PLANTATION, Skirmish near, Sept. 1, 1864.
GEORGIA LANDING, Action at, Oct. 27, 1862.
GILLESPIE'S PLANTATION, Expedition from Natchez, Miss., to, Aug. 4-6, 1864, and skirmish.
GOODRICH'S LANDING, Attack on, June 30, 1863.—Skirmish near, March 24, 1864.—Expedition from, to Bayou Macon, Aug. 28-31, 1864.
GOVERNOR MOORE'S PLANTATION, Skirmishes at, May 1-4, 1864.
GRAHAM'S PLANTATION, Skirmish at, May 5, 1864.
GRAND BAYOU, Expedition from Donaldsonville to, Feb. 14-18, 1865.—Expeditions from Thibodeaux, Bayou Boeuf, and Brashear City to, April 2-10, 1865.
GRAND CAILLOU, Expedition from Terre Bonne to, April 19-25, 1865.
GRAND CAILLOU BAYOU, Capture of blockade-runner in, May 8, 1862.—Expedition from Terre Bonne to, Nov. 19-27, 1864.
GRAND COTEAU, Skirmish at, Oct. 16, 1863.—Skirmish at, Oct. 19, 1863.—Engagement near, Nov. 3, 1863.
GRAND ECORE, Skirmish at, April 3, 1864.—Retreat of Union forces to, April 10-11, 1864.—Skirmish at, April 16, 1864.—Skirmish at, April 29, 1864.
GRAND LAKE, Expeditions to, Sept. 7-11, 1864.
GRAND RIVER, Skirmish on, Aug. —, 1864.—Expeditions to, Sept. 7-11, 1864.—Expedition from Napoleonville to, Sept. 26-30, 1864.—Expedition from Napoleonville to, Jan. 18-19, 1865.—Scouts from Bayou Goula to, Jan. 29-Feb. 7, 1865.
GREENSBURG, Skirmish near, May 1, 1863.—Expedition from Baton Rouge to, Oct. 5-9, 1864.
GREENWELL SPRINGS ROAD, Skirmish on, Sept. 19, 1863.—Skirmish on, Oct. 5, 1863.
GROSSETTE, Skirmish at, Feb. 19, 1864.
GROSSETTE, BAYOU, Skirmish at, April 2, 1864.—Affair at, June 19, 1864.—Scouts from Morganza to, Feb. 7-10, 1865.
HARD TIMES LANDING, Expedition to, April 25-29, 1863.
HARRISONBURG, Expedition from Natchez, Miss., to, Sept. 1-7, 1863.—Skirmish near, Sept. 4, 1863.—Action at, March —, 1864.
HENDERSON'S HILL, Affair at, March 21, 1864.

65

LOUISIANA.

HERMITAGE, THE, Expedition from, to the French Settlement, April 2-5, 1865.
HERMITAGE LANDING, Expedition to, March 24, 1863.
HERMITAGE PLANTATION, Operations in the vicinity of, Dec. 14, 1864-Jan. 5, 1865.
HIGHLAND' STOCKADE, Affair at, July 29, 1864.
HODGE'S PLANTATION, Skirmish at, Sept. 11, 1864.
HOG POINT, Mississippi River, Operations against Union gunboats and transports near, Nov. 18-21, 1863.
HOUMA, Operations about, May 11-18, 1862.
HUBBARD, CAMP, Mutiny at, Aug. 29-30, 1863.
INDEPENDENCE STATION, Skirmish at, May 15, 1863.
INDIAN BAYOU, Skirmish near, Nov. 9, 1863.
INDIAN BEND, Skirmish at, April 13, 1863.—Expedition from Brashear City to, March 25-27, 1865.
INDIAN VILLAGE, Skirmish at, Jan. 28, 1863.—Skirmish at, Aug. 6, 1864.
IRISH BEND, Engagement at, April 14, 1863.
JACKSON, Skirmish at, Aug. 3, 1863.—Skirmish at, March 3, 1864.—Skirmish near, Oct. 5, 1864.—Expedition from Baton Rouge to, March 1-12, 1865.—Expedition from Port Hudson to, April 12-13, 1865.
JACKSON, FORT, Seizure of, Jan. 11, 1861.—Bombardment of, April 18-28, 1862.—Surrender of, by Confederate forces, April 28, 1862.—Mutiny at, Dec. 9, 1863.
JACKSON RAILROAD, Expedition from Bonnet Carre to, March 21-29, 1863.—Operations on, May 9-18, 1863.
JAMES'S PLANTATION, Skirmish at, April 6, 1863.—Skirmish at, April 8, 1863.
JEANERETTE, Skirmish at, April 14, 1863.
KITTREDGE'S SUGAR HOUSE, Skirmish at, Feb. 10, 1865.
LABADIEVILLE, Action near, Oct. 27, 1862.—Affair at, Sept. 8, 1864.
LA FOURCHE, Engagement on the, July 12-13, 1863.
LA FOURCHE CROSSING, Engagement at, June 20-21, 1863.
LA FOURCHE DISTRICT, Operations in the, Oct. 24-Nov. 6, 1862.
LAKE PROVIDENCE. Skirmish near, May 24, 1863.—Skirmish near, May 9, 1863.—Skirmish at, June 28, 1863.—Skirmish near, May 27, 1863.—Action near, June 9, 1863.—Skirmish near, June 24, 1863.
LAKE SAINT JOSEPH, Expedition to, April 24, 1863.—Affair at, June 4, 1863.
LAMOURIE BAYOU, Skirmishes at, May 6-7, 1864.—Skirmish at, May 12, 1864.
LIDDELL BAYOU, Skirmish at, Oct. 15, 1864.
LIVINGSTON, FORT, Abandoned by Confederate forces, April 26, 1862.—Recapture of, by Union forces, April 27, 1862.
LIVONIA, Skirmish near, May 31, 1864.

LOUISIANA.

LOUISIANA BELLE, Steamer, Attack on, near Barre's Landing, Bayou Teche, May 22, 1863.
McNUTT'S HILL, Skirmish near, April 26, 1864.
MACOMB, FORT, Seizure of, Jan. 28, 1861.
MACON BAYOU, Skirmish at, May 10, 1863.—Skirmish at, Aug. 24, 1863.—Expedition from Goodrich's Landing to, Sept. 27-29, 1863.—Expedition from Goodrich's Landing to, Aug. 28-31, 1864.—Expedition from Vicksburg, Miss., to Nov. 6-8, 1864.
McWILLIAMS'S PLANTATION, Skirmish at, April 13, 1863.
MADISONVILLE, Skirmish at, July 27, 1862.—Expedition from, to Franklinton, and vicinity, Feb. 1-3, 1864.—Skirmishes near, Feb. 11, 1864.
MAGNOLIA LANDING, Attack on Union gunboats at, June 16, 1864.
MANCHAC BAYOU, Expeditions to, Oct. 2-8, 1864.
MANDEVILLE, Expedition from New Orleans to, Jan. 15-17, 1865.
MANSFIELD, Battle of, April 8, 1864.
MANSURA, Engagement at, May 16, 1864.
MARAUPAS, LAKE, Naval action in, April 7, 1863.
MARINGOUIN BAYOU, Skirmish near, Sept. 13, 1864.—Skirmish near, Sept. 16, 1864.
MARKSVILLE PRAIRIE, Skirmish at, March 15, 1864.—Skirmish at, May 15, 1864.
MARTIN'S LANE, Skirmish at, Feb. 15, 1865.
MERRITT'S PLANTATION, Scouts from, on the Clinton Road, May 14, 1863.—Operations about, May 18-19, 1863.
MILLIKEN'S BEND, Affair at, and capture of the steamer Fair Play, Aug. 18, 1862.—Expedition from, to Dallas and Delhi, Dec. 25-26, 1862.—Naval action at, June 4, 1863.—Attack on, June 7, 1863.—Skirmish at, June 25, 1863.
MISSISSIPPI RIVER, Battle of the, April 24, 1862.
MONETT'S FERRY, Skirmishes about, March 29-30, 1864.—Engagement at, April 23, 1864.
MONROE, Expedition from Vicksburg, Miss., to, Aug. 20-Sept. 2, 1863.
MOORE, CAMP, Expedition from Baton Rouge to, Oct. 5-9, 1864.
MOORE'S PLANTATION, Skirmishes at, May 1-4, 1864.
MOREAUVILLE, Action near, May 17, 1864.
MORGAN'S FERRY, Skirmish at, Sept. 7, 1863.—Skirmish at, Sept. 20, 1863.—Skirmish at, Aug. 25, 1864.—Skirmish at, Sept. 20, 1864.—Expedition from Morganza to and beyond, Dec. 13-14, 1864.
MORGAN'S FERRY ROAD, Skirmish on, July 28, 1864.
MORGANZA, Skirmish near, Sept. 12, 1863.—Naval engagement with batteries at, Dec. 8, 1863.—Skirmish at, May 24, 1864.—Expedition from, to the Atchafalaya, May 30-June 5, 1864, and skirmishes near Livonia and Morganza.—Skirmish near,

LOUISIANA.

June 4, 1864.—Skirmish near, July 28, 1864.—Scouts from, Aug. 10-12, and skirmishes.—Expedition from, to Bayou Sara, Sept. 6-7, 1864.—Expedition from, to Fausse River, Sept. 13-17, 1864.—Operations in the vicinity of, Sept. 16-25, 1864.—Expedition from, to Bayou Sara, Oct. 3-6, 1864, and skirmishes.—Skirmish near, Oct. 16, 1864.—Skirmishes at, Nov. 23, 1864.—Skirmish near, Dec. 4, 1864.—Expedition from, to beyond Morgan's Ferry, Dec. 13-14, 1864.—Operations in the vicinity of, Dec. 14, 1864-Jan. 5, 1865.—Expedition from, to the Atchafalaya River, Dec. 16-19, 1864.—Expedition from, Jan. 12-15, 1865, with skirmishes.—Scouts from, to Fausse River and Grossette Bayou, Feb. 7-10, 1865.

MORGANZA BEND, Skirmish at, March 12, 1865.

MOUND PLANTATION, Skirmish at, May 24, 1863.—Skirmish at, June 24, 1863.—Skirmish at, June 29, 1863.

MOUNT PLEASANT LANDING, Attack on, May 15, 1864.

NAPOLEONVILLE, Raid on, May 6, 1864.—Skirmishes near, July 29, 1864.—Expedition from, to Grand River and Bayou Pigeon, Sept. 26-30, 1864.—Expedition from, to Grand River, Jan. 18-19, 1865.—Skirmish near, Feb. 10, 1865.

NATCHEZ, LAKE, Expedition from Paincourtville to, Aug. 15-21, 1864, and skirmish on Grand River.—Expeditions to, Sept. 7-11, 1864.

NATCHEZ, BAYOU, Expedition to, Aug. 30-Sept. 2, 1864.

NATCHITOCHES, Skirmish at, March 31, 1864.—Skirmish at, April 5, 1864.—Skirmishes about, April 20-21, 1864.—Skirmish at, May 5, 1864.

NELSON'S BRIDGE, Affair at, Oct. 4, 1863.

NEW CARTHAGE, Operations from Milliken's Bend to, March 31-April 17, 1863.—Skirmish near, April 6, 1863.—Skirmish near, April 8, 1863.

NEW IBERIA, Destruction of salt-works near, April 18, 1863.—Affair near, Oct. 4, 1863.

NEW ORLEANS, Seizure of U. S. Paymaster's office at, Feb. 19, 1861.—Operations against, April 18-May 1, 1862.—Capture of, by Union naval forces, April 25, 1862.—Occupation of, by Union forces, May 1, 1862.—Expedition from, to Mandeville, Jan. 15-17, 1865.—Destruction of C. S. S. Webb below, April 24, 1865.

NEW ORLEANS AND JACKSON RAILROAD, Raid on, May 11, 1863.

NEWPORT CROSS ROADS, Skirmish at, June 17, 1864.

NEW RIVER, Expedition from Carrollton and Baton Rouge to, Sept. 24-29, 1863.—Skirmish at, Feb. 9, 1864.—Expedition to, Oct. 2-8, 1864.

NEW ROADS, Expedition from Morganza to, Jan. 31, 1865.

NEW TEXAS ROAD, Skirmish on, Dec. 4, 1864.

NEWTOWN, Skirmish at, April 16, 1863.

NIBLETT'S BLUFF, Expedition to, May 26-29, 1863.

LOUISIANA.

NORTHEASTERN LOUISIANA, Expedition from Memphis, Tenn., into, Jan. 26-Feb. 11, 1865.
NORWOOD'S PLANTATION, Engagement at, May 18, 1864.
OLD OAKS, Skirmish at, May 17, 1864.—Engagement at, May 18, 1864.
OLD RIVER, Skirmish at, Feb. 10, 1863.
OLIVE BRANCH, Skirmish at, Aug. 5, 1864.—Skirmish at, Aug. 25, 1864.
OLIVE BRANCH BAYOU, Skirmish near, May 3, 1864.
OPELOUSAS, Expedition from Saint Martinville to, April 17-21, 1863.—Expedition from, to Barre's Landing, and capture of the steamer Ellen, April 21, 1863.—Expeditions from, to Chicotville and Bayou Boeuf, April 29-30, 1863.—Reconnoisance toward, Oct. 20, 1863.—Skirmish at, Oct. 21, 1863.—Affair near, Oct. 30, 1863.—Union forces retired from, to New Iberia, Nov. 1-17, 1863.
ORANGE GROVE, Affair at, July 31, 1864.
OUCHITA RIVER, Operations on, March 1-4, 1864, including actions at Trinity and Harrisonburg.
OYSKA, Expedition from Baton Rouge to, Oct. 5-9, 1864.
OYSTER BAYOU, Expedition from Brashear City to near, March 25-28, 1865.
PAINCOURTVILLE, Expedition from, to Lake Natchez, Aug. 15-21, 1864, and skirmish on Grand River.
PARK, THE, Expedition from Plaquemine to, Jan. 26-Feb. 4, 1865.—Expedition from Plaquemine to, Feb. 17-22, 1865.—Expeditions from Thibodeaux, Bayou, and Brashear City to, April 2-10, 1865.
PASS MANCHAC, Skirmish at, June 17, 1862.—Expedition to, July 25-Aug. 2, 1862.—Expedition to, Sept. 13-15, 1862.—Scout to, and operations about, Feb. 8-11, 1863.
PATTERSONVILLE, Skirmish near, April 11, 1863.—Reconnoissance from Berwick to, Aug. 2, 1864.
PEARL RIVER, Expedition up, July 25-Aug. 2, 1862.—Expedition from Fort Pike to, Sept. 9-12, 1864.
PEARL RIVER EXPEDITION, April 1-10, 1864.
PELTON'S PLANTATION, Expedition from Terre Bonne to, April 19-25, 1865.
PEST HOUSE, opposite Port Hudson, Attack on, May 28, 1864.
PETITE ANSE ISLAND, Affairs at, Nov. 21-22, 1862.
PHELPS' BAYOU, Skirmish at, April 26, 1863.
PIERRE BAYOU, Skirmishes at, May 2-3, 1864.
PIGEON BAYOU, Expeditions to, Sept. 7-11, 1864.—Expedition from Napoleonville to, Sept. 26-30, 1864.—Expedition from Brashear City to, March 20-22, 1865.
PIKE, FORT, Seizure of, Jan. 14, 1861.—Recapture of, by Union forces, April 27, 1862.—Expedition from, to Bayou Bonfouca, Jan. 31-Feb. 1, 1865.
PINEVILLE, Skirmish at, April 24, 1864.

LOUISIANA.

PIN HOOK, Skirmish at, May 10, 1863.
PLAINS STORE, Action at, May 21, 1863.
PLAINS STORE ROAD, Skirmish on, May 23, 1863.
PLANTON BAYOU, Expedition from Thibodeaux to, Jan. 30-31, 1865.
PLAQUEMINE, Affair near, Dec. 29, 1862.—Affairs at, Dec. 31, 1862-Jan. 3, 1863.—Affair near, April 18, 1863.—Skirmish at, June 18, 1863.—Skirmish at, Aug. 6, 1864.—Expedition from, to The Park, Jan. 26-Feb. 4, 1865.—Expedition from, to The Park, Feb. 17-22, 1865.
PLAQUEMINE BAYOU, Operations on, Feb. 12-28, 1863.—Expedition to, April 22-23, 1863.
PLEASANT GROVE, Battle of, April 8, 1864.
PLEASANT HILL, Skirmish near, April 7, 1864.—Skirmish near, April 8, 1864.—Engagement at, April 9, 1864.
PLEASANT HILL LANDING, Engagement at, April 12-13, 1864.
POINT PLEASANT, Affair at, June 25, 1864.
PONCHATOULA, Expedition to, July 5-8, 1862.—Expedition to, Sept. 13-15, 1862.—Expedition from New Orleans to, March 21-30, 1863, with skirmishes.—Skirmish at, May 13, 1863.
PONTCHARTRAIN, LAKE, Expedition to, July 25-Aug. 2, 1862, with skirmishes.—Scouting near, Sept. 13-Oct. 2, 1863.
PORTAGE, BAYOU, Affair at, Nov. 23, 1863.—Expedition from Brashear City to, Nov. 17-19, 1864.
PORTER'S PLANTATION, Skirmish at, April 13, 1863.
PORT HUDSON, Occupation of, by Confederate forces, Aug. 15, 1862.—Engagement between U. S. S. Anglo-American and the batteries at, Aug. 29, 1862.—Engagement between U. S. S. Essex and the batteries at, Sept. 7, 1862.—Demonstrations against and naval attack on, March 14-15, 1863.—Expedition from Montesano Bayou toward, March 17, 1865.—Operations against, March 7-27, 1863.—Siege of, May 21-July 8, 1863.—Surrender of, by Confederate forces, July 8, 1863.—Skirmish near, Nov. 30, 1863.—Skirmishes near, April 7, 1864.—Attack on Pest House, opposite, May 28, 1864.—Attack on the steamer White Cloud near, Aug. 29, 1864.—Expedition from, to Jackson, April 12-13, 1865.
PRATT, CAMP, Skirmish at, Nov. 20, 1863.—Affair at, Nov. 25, 1863.
PROVIDENCE, Naval action at, April 8, 1863.
QUITMAN, FORT, Abandoned by Confederate forces, April 27, 1862.
RACCOURCI, Affair at, Nov. 25, 1864.
RAPIDES BAYOU, Skirmish at, March 20, 1864.
RAPIDES BAYOU BRIDGE, Skirmish at, April 26, 1864.
RATLIFF'S LANDING, Attack on Union gunboats at, June 15, 1864.

LOUISIANA.

RATLIFF'S PLANTATION, Expedition from Brashear City to, May 14-16, 1865.
RED RIVER, Operations on, Feb. 10-14, 1863.—Naval expedition up, July 10-17, 1863.—Expeditions from Natchez and Fort Adams, Miss., to, Oct. 14-20, 1863.—Engagement at junction of, with Cane River, April 26-27, 1864.—Capture of U. S. Transport Emma on, May 1, 1864.—Surrender of Confederate naval forces in, June 3, 1865.—Naval affair at mouth of, April 23, 1865.—Passage of dam in, at Alexandria, by Union fleet, May 9-12, 1864.
RED RIVER CAMPAIGN, March 10-May 22, 1864.
REDWOOD BAYOU, Skirmish near, May 3, 1864.
RICHLAND PLANTATION, Skirmish at, Jan. 30, 1865.
RICHMOND, Skirmish near, Jan. 29, 1863.—Skirmish at, March 31, 1863.—Skirmish at, April 4, 1863.—Skirmish near, June 6, 1863.—Action near, June 15, 1863.—Reconnoissance from Young's Point to, June 20, 1863.
ROBERT BAYOU, Skirmish at, May 8, 1864.
ROBERTS'S FORD, Comite River, Skirmish at, May 2, 1863.
ROSEDALE, Expedition from Indian Village to, Feb. 19, 1863.—Skirmish near, Sept. 15, 1864.
SABINE CROSS ROADS, Engagement at, April 8, 1864.
SAINT CHARLES COURT HOUSE, Skirmish near, Aug. 29, 1862.—Expedition from Carrollton to vicinity of, Sept. 7-8, 1862, and skirmish.—Skirmish at, Oct. 5, 1864.
SAINT FRANCISVILLE, Skirmish near, Oct. 5, 1864.
SAINT JOHN BAPTIST PARISH, Skirmish in, Oct. 19, 1862.
SAINT JOSEPH, Capture of Confederate mail and recapture of Union flags near, Oct. 8, 1864.
SAINT MARTINSVILLE, Expedition from, to Breaux Bridge and Opelousas, April 17-21, 1863.—Operations about, Nov. 12, 1863.—Affair at, Dec. 3, 1863.
SAINT PHILIP, FORT, Seizure of, Jan. 11, 1861.—Bombardment of, April 18-28, 1862.—Surrender of, by Confederate forces, April 28, 1862.
SAINT VINCENT BAYOU, Scout from Napoleonville to, May 24, 1865.
SALINE BAYOU, Skirmish at, April 14, 1864.
SICILY ISLAND, Expedition from Natchez, Miss., to, Sept. 26-30, 1864.
SIGNAL, U. S. S., Capture of, at David's Ferry, May 4, 1864.
SIMSPORT, Engagement near, June 3, 1863.—Capture of, by Union naval forces, March 12, 1864.—Engagement at, June 8, 1864.—Expedition from Morganza to, July 5-7, 1864.
SMITH'S PLANTATION, Engagement at, May 16, 1864.
SORREL BAYOU, Expedition from Brashear City to, Jan. 21-22, 1865.
SPRINGFIELD LANDING, Affair at, July 2, 1863.
SPRINGFIELD ROAD, Skirmish on, May 23, 1863.

LOUISIANA.

STERLING'S PLANTATION, Skirmish at, Sept. 12, 1863.—Action at, Sept. 29, 1863.
TALLULAH, Skirmish at, Aug. 19, 1862.
TCHEFUNCTA RIVER, Expedition up, July 25-Aug. 2, 1862, and naval action in, May 16, 1864.
TECHE BAYOU, Engagement on, and destruction of C. S. Gunboat Cotton, Jan. 14. 1863.—Engagement at, April 12-13, 1863.—Atack on steamer Louisiana Belle in, May 22, 1863.—Naval engagement on, July 26, 1863.—Skirmish on, Oct 3, 1863.—Skirmish at, March 21, 1865.
TECHE COUNTRY, Operations in the, Oct. 3-Nov. 30, 1863.
TECHE ROAD, Operations on, May 21-26, 1863.
TENSAS BAYOU, Skirmish at, May 9, 1863.—Skirmish at, Aug. 10, 1863.—Skirmish at, July 30, 1864.—Skirmish near, Aug. 26, 1864.
TERRE BONNE, Expedition from, to Bayou Grand Caillou, Nov. 19-27, 1864.—Expedition from, to Pelton's Plantation and Grand Caillou, April 19-25, 1865.
THIBODEAUX, Capture of, June 20, 1863.—Mutiny at, Aug. 29-30, 1863.—Expeditions from, to Lake Verret, Grand Bayou, and The Park, April 2-10, 1865.
THOMPSON'S CREEK. Capture of the Confederate steamers Starlight and Red Chief in, May 25, 1863.—Skirmish at, Oct. 5, 1864.
THOMPSON'S PLANTATION, Skirmish at, Jan. 23, 1865.
TICKFAW BRIDGE, Skirmish at. May 16, 1863.
TRINITY, Skirmish at, Sept. 2. 1863.—Expedition from Vidalia to, Nov. 15-16, 1863.—Action at, March —, 1864.—Expedition from Natchez, Miss., to, March 20-28, 1865.
TUNICA BAYOU, or Bend, Skirmish at, Nov. 8, 1863.—Affair at, April 21, 1864.—Naval action at, June 16, 1864 (Como Landing).—Boat expedition to, and skirmish at, Jan. 13, 1865.
VERMILION BAYOU, Action at, April 17, 1863.—Skirmishes at, Oct. 9-10, 1863.—Skirmish at, Nov. 11, 1863.—Skirmish near, Nov. 25, 1863.—Skirmish at. Nov. 30, 1863.
VERMILIONVILLE, Skirmish at, Nov. 5, 1863.—Skirmish at, Nov. 8, 1863.
VERRET, LAKE, Expedition from Thibodeaux to, Jan. 30-31, 1865.—Expedition from Brashear City to, Feb. 10-11, 1865.—Expedition from Thibodeaux to, Feb. 10-13, 1865.—Expeditions from Thibodeaux, Bayou Boeuf, and Brashear City to, April 2-10, 1865.—Scout from Thibodeaux to, May 23, 1865.
VIDAL BAYOU, Skirmish near, April 7, 1863.—Action near, April 15, 1863.
VIDALIA, Attack on, Sept. 14, 1863.—Expedition from, to Trinity, Nov. 15-16, 1863.—Skirmish at, Feb. 7. 1864.—Skirmish near, July 22, 1864.—Scout from, to the York Plantation, Oct. 26-27, 1864.

LOUISIANA—MAINE—MARYLAND.

WALL'S BRIDGE, Tickfaw River, Skirmish at, May 1, 1863.
WARNER, U. S. S., Capture of, at David's Ferry, May 4, 1864.
WASHINGTON, Skirmish near, April 22, 1863.
WATERLOO, Demonstrations on, June 16, 1863.—Naval actions at, Feb. 14-16, 1864.—Skirmish near, Oct. 20, 1864.
WATERPROOF, Expedition from Vicksburg, Miss., to, Jan. 29-Feb. 23, 1864.—Attack on the U. S. S. Welcome at, Nov. 21, 1863.—Skirmish at, April 20, 1864.—Expedition from Natchez, Miss., to, Sept. 26-30, 1864.
WELLS'S PLANTATION, Skirmish at, May 2, 1864.—Skirmish at, May 6, 1864.
WESTERN LOUISIANA, Operations in, April 9-May 14, 1863.
WHISKEY BAYOU, Expedition from Brashear City to, Jan. 16-18, 1865.
WHITE CLOUD, STEAMER, Attack on, near Port Hudson, Aug. 29, 1864.
WHITE HALL POINT, Naval action with batteries at, July 10, 1863.
WILLIAMS'S BRIDGE, Skirmish at, May 1, 1863.
WILLIAMSPORT, Skirmish at, Sept. 16, 1864.—Affair near, Nov. 25, 1864.
WILSON'S LANDING, Skirmish at, May 2, 1864.—Skirmish at, May 14, 1864.
WILSON'S PLANTATION, Skirmish at, April 7, 1864, and naval action at, May 4, 1864.
WOOD, FORT, Recapture of, by Union troops, April 27, 1862.
YELLOW BAYOU, Skirmish at, May 17, 1864.—Engagement at, May 18, 1864.
YORK PLANTATION, Scout from Vidalia to, Oct. 26-27, 1864.
YOUNG'S POINT, Attack on, June 7, 1863.—Reconnoissance from, to Richmond, June 20, 1863.

MAINE.

PORTLAND HARBOR, Descent on, June 26-27, 1863.

MARYLAND.

ADAMSTOWN, Skirmish at, Oct. 14, 1864.
ALTAMONT, Affair at, April 26, 1863.
ANNAPOLIS, Naval preparation for defence of, July 11-13, 1864.
ANTIETAM, Battle of, Sept. 16-17, 1862.—Affair at, July 6, 1864.
ANTIETAM BRIDGE, Skirmish at, July 8, 1864.
ANTIETAM CREEK, Skirmish on, Sept. 15, 1862.
ANTIETAM FORD, Skirmish at, Aug. 4, 1864.
ANTIETAM IRON-WORKS, Skirmish at, Aug. 27, 1861.
BALTIMORE, Conflict between U. S. troops and mob in, April 19, 1861.

MARYLAND.

BARNESVILLE, Skirmish at, Sept. 9, 1862.
BEAVER CREEK, Skirmish at, July 9, 1863.
BENEVOLA, Skirmish at, July 9, 1863.
BERLIN, Skirmish near, Sept. 18, 1861.—Skirmish at, Sept. 29, 1861.—Skirmishes at, Sept. 4-5, 1862.
BOONSBOROUGH, Battle of, Sept. 14, 1862.—Skirmish at, Sept. 15, 1862.—Action at, July 8, 1863.
BOONSBOROUGH GAP, Battle of, Sept. 14, 1862.
BROWNSVILLE, Affair at, July 7, 1864.
BUDD'S FERRY, Affairs around, Oct. 22-Nov. 12, 1861.—Skirmish near, Oct. 28, 1861.
BUSH BRIDGE, Naval reconnoissance to, July 11, 1864.
CARROLL, FORT, Occupation of, by Union forces, April 21, 1861.
CATOCTIN CREEK, Skirmish at, June 17, 1863.
CATOCTIN MOUNTAIN, Skirmish at, Sept. 13, 1862.—Affair at, July 7, 1864.
CHOPTANK CREEK, Boat expedition into, March 3, 1862.
CLEAR SPRING, Skirmish near, July 10, 1863.—Skirmish at, July 29, 1864.
CONRAD'S FERRY, Potomac River, Skirmish at, June 17, 1861.—Reconnoissance from, into Virginia, Oct. 4, 1862.
COVE POINT, Affair at, Aug. 22, 1864.
CRAMPTON'S PASS, South Mountain, Battle of, Sept. 14, 1862.
CRANBERRY SUMMIT, Affair at, April 26, 1863.
CUMBERLAND, Occupation of, by Union forces, June 11, 1861.—Attack on, Aug. 1, 1864.—Raid on, Feb. 21, 1865.
DOWNSVILLE, Skirmish at, July 7, 1863.
EDWARDS FERRY, Skirmish at, June 18, 1861.—Skirmishes at, Sept. 3-4, 1862.—Skirmish at, Aug. 27, 1863.
EMMITSBURG, Skirmish near, July 4, 1863.—Affair at, July 30, 1864.
FAIR HAVEN, Chesapeake Bay, Capture of the steamer Harriet De Ford near, April 4, 1865.
FAIRVIEW HEIGHTS, Capture of signal station on, Oct. 10, 1862.
FALLING WATERS, Action at, July 14, 1863.
FLINTSTONE CREEK, Affair at, Aug. 1, 1864.
FOUR LOCKS, Skirmish at, Oct. 9, 1862.
FREDERICK, Evacuation of, by Union forces, Sept. 6, 1862.—Skirmishes at, Sept. 12, 1862.—Skirmish at, June 21, 1863.—Skirmish at, July 7, 1864.—Skirmish at, July 8, 1864.—Skirmish at, July 11, 1864.
FREDERICK, FORT, Skirmish at, Dec. 25, 1861.
FUNKSTOWN, Skirmish at, July 7, 1863.—Skirmishes at and near, July 10-13, 1863.
GREAT FALLS, Skirmish at, July 7, 1861.—Scout from, into Virginia, Aug. 25, 1861.—Skirmish at, Sept. 4, 1861.
GREEN SPRING FURNACE, Skirmish near, Oct. 10, 1862.

MARYLAND.

GUNPOWDER BRIDGE, Burning of, July 10, 1864.
GUNPOWDER RIVER, Naval reconnoissance up, July 11, 1864.
HAGER'S MOUNTAIN, Affair at, July 7, 1864.
HAGERSTOWN, Skirmish near, Sept. 20, 1862.—Skirmish at, July 6, 1863.—Skirmishes at and near, July 10-13, 1863.—Skirmish at, July 5, 1864.—Capture of, July 6, 1864.—Skirmish at, July 29, 1864.—Skirmish at, Aug. 5, 1864.—Skirmish at, Aug. 15, 1864.
HANCOCK, Bombardment of, July 5-6, 1862.—Skirmish at, July 31, 1864.—Skirmish at, Aug. 2, 1864.
HAVRE DE GRACE, Naval reconnoissance to, July 11, 1864.
JEFFERSON, Skirmish at, Sept. 13, 1862.
JONES' CROSS ROADS, near Williamsport, Skirmishes at, July 10-13, 1863.
KEEDYSVILLE, Skirmish near, Sept. 15, 1862.—Affair at, July 5, 1864.—Skirmish at, Aug. 5, 1864.
KINSELL'S FERRY, Skirmish at, Oct. 10, 1862.
LEITERSBURG, Skirmish near, July 10, 1863.
LISBON, Affair at, June 29, 1863.
MAGNOLIA, Capture of trains at, July 11, 1864.
MARYLAND CAMPAIGN, Sept. 3-20, 1862.
MARYLAND HEIGHTS, Action on, Sept. 12-13, 1862.—Evacuation of, June 30, 1863.—Reoccupation of, July 7, 1863.
MATTAWOMAN CREEK, Affair at mouth of, Nov. 14, 1861.
McCOY'S FERRY, Skirmish at, Oct. 10, 1862.
MIDDLETOWN, Skirmish at, Sept. 13, 1862.—Skirmish at, June 20, 1863.—Skirmish at, July 7, 1864.
MONOCACY, Skirmish near mouth of, Oct. 12, 1862.—Battle of, July 9, 1864.—Skirmish near, July 10, 1864.
MONOCACY AQUEDUCT, Skirmish at, Sept. 4, 1862.
MONOCACY CHURCH, Skirmish at, Sept. 9, 1862.
MONOCACY JUNCTION, Skirmish at, July 30, 1864.
MONTGOMERY COUNTY, Operations in, Oct. 7-11, 1864.
MUDDY BRANCH, Skirmish at, June 29, 1863.
NOLAND'S FERRY, Affair at, July 5, 1864.
OAKLAND, Skirmish at, April 26, 1863.
OFFUTT'S CROSS ROADS, Skirmish near, June 28, 1863.
OLD ANTIETAM FORGE, Skirmish at, July 10, 1863.
OLD TOWN, Skirmish at, Aug. 2, 1864.
PASPATANSY CREEK, Boat expedition into, March 5, 1862.
PETERSVILLE, Skirmish near, Sept. 14, 1862.
POINT OF ROCKS, Skirmish opposite, Aug. 5, 1861.—Skirmish near, Sept. 17, 1861.—Skirmish at, Sept. 24, 1861.—Skirmish at, Dec. 19, 1861.—Skirmishes at, Sept. 4-5, 1862.—Skirmish at, Sept. 7, 1862.—Skirmish at, June 17, 1863.—Skirmish at, July 5, 1864.
POOLESVILLE, Skirmishes at, Sept. 4-5, 1862.—Skirmish at, Sept. 8, 1862.—Raid on, Nov. 25, 1862.—Raid on, Dec. 14, 1862.—Affair at, July 14, 1864.

MARYLAND—MASSACHUSETTS—MEXICO.

POPLAR SPRINGS, Affair at, June 29, 1863.
RELAY HOUSE, Occupation of, by Union troops, May 6, 1861.
ROCKVILLE, Skirmish near, June 28, 1863.—Skirmish at, Sept. 22, 1863.—Skirmish at, July 10, 1864.—Affair at, July 13, 1864.
ROCKVILLE EXPEDITION, June 10-July 7, 1861.
SANDY HOOK, Skirmish at, Aug. 18, 1861.—Skirmish at, July 8, 1864.
SENECA, Skirmish near, June 28, 1863.
SENECA CREEK, Skirmish opposite, Sept. 16, 1861.—Skirmish opposite, Sept. 20, 1861.
SENECA MILLS, Skirmish near, June 14, 1861.—Skirmish at, June 10, 1863.
SHARPSBURG, Battle of, Sept. 16-17, 1862.—Skirmish at, Sept. 19, 1862.—Reconnoissance from, to Shepardstown and Martinsburg, W. Va., Oct. 1, 1862, and skirmishes.—Skirmish at, June 24, 1863.
SLAUGHTER'S GAP, Battle of, Sept. 14, 1862.
SMITHSBURG, Skirmish at, July 5, 1863.
SOLOMON'S GAP, Affair at, July 5, 1864.—Affair at, July 7, 1864.
SOUTH MOUNTAIN, Skirmish at, Sept. 13, 1862.—Battle of, Sept. 14, 1862.
SOUTH RIVER, Boat expedition into, July 13, 1864.
SUGAR LOAF MOUNTAIN, Skirmishes at, Sept. 10-11, 1862.
TURNER'S PASS, Battle of, Sept. 14, 1862.
URBANA, Skirmish at, July 9, 1864.
WESTMINSTER, Skirmishes, June 29-30, 1863.
WHITE'S FORD, Skirmish at, Oct. 12, 1862.
WILLIAMSPORT, Skirmish near, Sept. 11, 1862.—Skirmish near, Sept. 19, 1862.—Skirmish near, Sept. 20, 1862.—Capture of Confederate pickets opposite, Oct 29, 1862.—Skirmish near, June 15, 1863.—Action at, July 6, 1863.—Skirmish near, July 8, 1863.—Skirmish near, July 14, 1863.—Skirmish at, July 25, 1864.—Skirmish at, Aug. 5, 1864.—Affair at, Aug. 26, 1864.

MASSACHUSETTS.

BOSTON, Draft riots in, July 13-16, 1863.

MEXICO.

MATAMORAS, Affair at, Jan. 12-13, 1864.
MIER, Affair with Zapata's banditti near, Sept. 2, 1863.
PRESIDIO DEL NORTE, Skirmish near, April 7, 1864.—Skirmishes at and near, April 15, 1864.—Affair near, Jan. 21, 1865.

MINNESOTA—MISCELLANEOUS—MISSISSIPPI.

MINNESOTA.

ACTON, Action with Indians at, Sept. 2, 1862.
BIRCH COOLEY, Action with Indians at, Sept. 2, 1862.
BLUE EARTH RIVER, Affair near, May 2, 1865.
COTEAU, Skirmish with Indians on the, May 18, 1865.
HUTCHINSON, Skirmish with Indians at, Sept. 4, 1862.
MANKATO, Attack by citizens on Indian prisoners at, Dec. 4, 1862.
MINNESOTA, DISTRICT OF, Operations against Indians in, July 1-Oct. 1, 1864.
RIDGELY, Fort, Action with Indians at, Aug. 20, 1862.—Action with Indians at, Aug. 22, 1862.
SAUK CENTRE, Skirmish with Indians at, Sept. 10, 1862.
SPIRIT LAKE, Affair at, May 16, 1864.
WOOD LAKE, Action with Indians at, Sept. 23, 1862.
YELLOW MEDICINE, Action with Indians near, Sept. 23, 1862.

MISCELLANEOUS.

ERIE, LAKE, Attempt to capture the U. S. S. Michigan on, Sept. 19, 1864.
FRANCE, Naval engagement between the U. S. S. Kearsarge and C. S. S. Alabama, off Cherbourg, June 19, 1864.
JAPAN, Naval engagement at Simonoseki, July 16, 1863.
MASON, JAMES M. (See Old Bahama Channel.)
NEW GRANADA, Capture of piratical party on the steamer Salvador off the coast of, Nov. 11, 1864.
OLD BAHAMA CHANNEL, Capture of the Confederate Commissioners, James M. Mason and John Slidell, in, Nov. 8, 1861.
PORTUGAL, Capture of the C. S. S. Georgia off the coast of, Aug. 15, 1864.
SLIDELL, JOHN. (See Old Bahama Channel.)

MISSISSIPPI.

Seceded Jan. 9, 1861.

ABBEVILLE, Skirmish at, Aug. 23, 1864.
ABERDEEN, Skirmish at, Feb. 18, 1864.
ADAMS, FORT, Expedition from, to Red River, La., Oct. 14-20, 1863.—Expedition from Tunica Landing to, Oct. 5-8, 1864.—Operations about, May 3-6, 1865.
ANDERSON'S HILL, Battle of, May 1, 1863.
ASHWOOD, Skirmish at, June 25, 1864.
AUSTIN, Skirmish at, Aug. 2, 1862.—Skirmish near, May 24, 1863.—Skirmish near, May 28, 1863.

MISSISSIPPI.

BAKER'S CREEK, Battle of, May 16, 1863.—Skirmish near, July 7, 1863.—Skirmish at, Feb. 5, 1864.
BALDWIN'S FERRY, Skirmish at, May 13, 1863.—Skirmish at, Sept. 11, 1863.—Scout from Bovina Station to, Nov. 1, 1863.—Scout to, Jan. 14, 1864.
BALDWYN, Reconnoissance toward, June 3, 1862.—Reconnoissance from Booneville toward, and skirmish, June 6, 1862.—Reconnoissance to, June 9, 1862.—Skirmish near, June 14, 1862.—Skirmish at, Oct. 2, 1862.
BARNETT'S CORNERS, Skirmish at, Sept. 19, 1862.
BATH SPRINGS, Skirmish at, Jan. 1, 1863.
BAY SAINT LOUIS, Skirmish at, Nov. 17, 1863.—Expedition from Fort Pike, La., to, March 28-30, 1865.
BAY SPRINGS, Reconnoissance from Jacinto to, Aug. 4-7, 1862, and skirmish.—Expedition from Rienzi to, Aug. 19-21, 1862, and skirmishes.—Skirmish near, Oct. 26, 1863.
BEAR BLUFF, Expedition to, April 15-May 2, 1863.
BEAR CREEK, Action near, June 22, 1863.—Skirmish at, July 17, 1863.
BELMONT, Skirmish at, June 18, 1863.
BENTON, Skirmish near, Sept. 29, 1863.—Skirmish at, May 7, 1864.—Skirmish at, May 9, 1864.
BIG BLACK BRIDGE, M. C. R. R., Skirmish at, Nov. 27, 1864.
BIG BLACK RIVER, Skirmishes at, May 3-4, 1863.—Affair at, June 18, 1863.—Skirmish on, June 22, 1863.—Skirmish at, June 29-30, 1863.—Skirmish at, July 1, 1863.—Skirmish at, July 3-4, 1863.—Expedition from, to Grenada, Aug. 10-23, 1863.
BIG BLACK RIVER BRIDGE, So. Miss. R.R., Engagement at, May 17, 1863.—Skirmish at, Aug. 12, 1863.
BIG SANDY CREEK, Skirmish at, May 5, 1863.—Skirmish at, May 8, 1863.—Skirmish near, May 9, 1863.
BIG SUNFLOWER RIVER, Expedition up, May 24-31, 1863.
BILOXI, Expedition from Ship Island to, April 3-4, 1862.
BIRDSONG FERRY, Skirmish at, June 12, 1863.—Affair at, June 18, 1863.—Skirmish near, June 22, 1863.—Skirmish near, July 5, 1863.
BIRMINGHAM, Skirmish at, April 24, 1863.
BLACK BAYOU, Expedition through (See Steele's Bayou Expedition, March 14-27, 1863).—Expedition to, April 2-14, 1863.
BLACKLAND, Skirmish at, June 3, 1862.—Skirmish at, June 7, 1862.—Skirmishes at and near, June 28, 1862.—Action near, May 5, 1863.
BOGUE CHITTO CREEK, Action at, Oct. 17, 1863.
BOLIVAR, Skirmish at, Aug. 25, 1862.—Attack on the Queen of the West near, Sept. 19, 1862.—Skirmish near, July 6, 1864.
BOLTON DEPOT, Skirmish near, Feb. 4, 1864.

MISSISSIPPI.

BOLTON STATION, Skirmish at, and capture of, May 15, 1863.—Skirmish near, July 8, 1863.—Skirmish at, July 16, 1863.
BOONEVILLE, Skirmish near, May 29, 1862.—Capture of, May 30, 1862.—Skirmish near, June 11, 1862.—Action near, July 1, 1862.—Expedition to, March — to April 1, 1863.
BOX FORD, Hatchie River, Skirmish near, Oct. 7, 1862.
BRANDON, Action at, July 19, 1863.—Skirmish at, Feb. 7, 1864.
BRICE'S CROSS ROADS, Engagement at, June 10, 1864.
BRIDGEPORT, Skirmish at, May 17, 1863.
BROOKHAVEN, Skirmish at, April 29, 1863.—Union raid on, June 23-26, 1863.—Skirmish at, July 18, 1863.—Expedition from Baton Rouge, La., to, Nov. 14-21, 1864, and skirmishes.
BROWN'S PLANTATION, Skirmish at, Aug. 11, 1862.
BROWNSVILLE, Skirmishes at, Sept. 28, Oct. 15 and 22, 1863.—Skirmishes near, Oct. 15-16, 1863.—Skirmish at, March 3, 1864.—Skirmishes at, March 7-8, 1864.—Skirmish at, Sept. 28, 1864.—Expedition from Memphis, Tenn., to, April 19-23, 1865.
BRUINSBURG, Naval affair opposite, Nov. 21, 1864.
BRUINSBURG LANDING, Skirmish near, May 6, 1863.
BUCK'S FERRY, Expedition from Natchez to, Sept. 19-21, 1864.
BURNSVILLE, Reconnoissance to, May 22-23, 1862.—Skirmish at, Sept. 14, 1862.—Skirmish at, Jan. 3, 1863.—Skirmish at, June 11, 1863.
BYHALIA, Skirmish near, Oct. 12, 1863.—Affair near, Feb. 11, 1864.
BYHALIA ROAD, Skirmish on, July 2, 1864.
CAMARGO CROSS ROADS, Action near, July 13, 1864.
CANTON, Skirmish near, July 12, 1863.—Skirmish near, July 17, 1863.—Expedition from Messenger's Ferry toward, Oct. 14-20, 1863.—Skirmish at, Feb. 24, 1864.—Skirmish near, Feb. 26, 1864.—Skirmish near, Feb. 29, 1864.—Skirmish at, March 2, 1864.
CANTON ROAD, Skirmishes on, Oct. 15-16, 1863.
CARROLLSVILLE, Reconnoissance toward, June 3, 1862.
CATFISH POINT, Expedition from Goodrich's Landing, La., to, Oct. 24-Nov. 10, 1863.
CHAMPION'S HILL, Battle of, May 16, 1863.—Skirmish at, Feb. 4, 1864.
CHERRY CREEK, Skirmish at, July 10, 1864.
CHICKASAW BAYOU, Skirmishes at, Dec. 27-28, 1862.
CHICKASAW BLUFFS, Assault on, Dec. 29, 1862.
CHICKASAWHA BRIDGE, Skirmish at, Dec. 10, 1864.
CHULAHOMA, Skirmish at, Nov. 30, 1862.—Scout from Germantown, Tenn., to, Oct. 22-24, 1863.
CHUNKY CREEK, Skirmishes near, Feb. 13-14, 1864.
CLEAR CREEK, Skirmish at, June 14, 1862.

MISSISSIPPI.

CLINTON, Skirmish near, June 8, 1863.—Skirmish near, July 9, 1863.—Skirmish at, July 16, 1863.—Skirmish near, Oct. 18, 1863.—Skirmish at, Feb. 5, 1864.—Skirmish at, March 26, 1864.—Skirmish at, April 3, 1864.
CLINTON AND VERNON CROSS ROADS, Skirmish near, Oct. 16, 1863.
COCKRUM'S CROSS ROADS, Skirmish at, Sept. 9, 1862.
COFFEEVILLE, Engagement at, Dec. 5, 1862.
COLDWATER, Expedition from Helena, Ark., to, July 23-25, 1862.—Expedition to the, Sept. 8-13, 1862.—Skirmish at, Dec. 20, 1862.—Skirmish at the, Aug. 21, 1863.—Skirmish at, Dec. 29, 1863.
COLDWATER BRIDGE, Skirmish at, June 18, 1863.
COLDWATER FERRY, Affair at, Feb. 8, 1864.
COLDWATER RAILROAD BRIDGE, Skirmish at, Sept. 12, 1862.
COLDWATER RIVER, Skirmish at, Nov. 28, 1862.—Skirmish near, Feb. 19, 1863.—Expedition from Memphis, Tenn., to, April 18-24, 1863.—Skirmish at, May 11, 1863.—Skirmish on, June 16, 1863.—Action on, June 19, 1863.—Skirmish on, June 20, 1863.—Skirmish on, Oct. 6, 1863.—Skirmish at, July 22, 1864.
COLDWATER STATION, Skirmish at, June 21, 1862.
COLE'S CREEK (See Rodney, June 25, 1862), Naval engagements at, Feb. 18 and May 7, 1865.
COMMERCE, Attack on transports near, June 17, 1863.
CONCORD CHURCH, Action at, Dec. 1, 1864.
CORINTH, Siege of, April 30-May 30, 1862.—Reconnoissance towards, May 8, 1862.—Skirmish near, May 9, 1862.—Raid on Memphis and Charleston Railroad near, May 13, 1862.—Skirmish on Memphis and Charleston Railroad near, May 14, 1862.—Action at Russell's House near, May 17, 1862.—Skirmish at Widow Serratt's near, May 21, 1862.—Skirmish near, May 24, 1862.—Skirmish on Bridge Creek near, May 27, 1862.—Skirmishes in front of, May 28-29, 1862.—Occupation of, by Union forces, May 30, 1862.—Pursuit of Confederate forces from, to Guntown, May 30-June 10, 1862.—Skirmish near, Aug. 28, 1862.—Attack on Union camp near, Oct. 5, 1862.—Battle of, Oct. 3-4, 1862.—Skirmish near, June 11, 1863.—Skirmish near, Aug. 16, 1863.—Skirmish at, Nov. 2, 1863.—Skirmish at, Nov. 12, 1863.—Skirmish near, Dec. 23, 1863.—Evacuation of, by Union forces, Jan. 25, 1864.—Skirmish at, Jan. 19, 1865.
CORINTH ROAD, Reconnoissance on, April 8, 1862.—Reconnoissance on, April 13, 1862.—Skirmishes on, April 24-25, 1862.
COURTNEY'S PLANTATION, Skirmish at, April 11, 1863.
CRAVEN'S PLANTATION, Skirmish at, Aug. 14, 1863.
CRYSTAL SPRINGS, Raid on New Orleans and Jackson Railroad near, May 11, 1863.

MISSISSIPPI.

DANVILLE, Scouts from, July 19, 1863.—Skirmishes at, Nov. 14-15, 1863.
DAVIES, CAMP, Skirmish at, Nov. 22, 1863.
DAVIS'S MILLS, Skirmish at, Dec. 21, 1862.—Skirmish at, June 12, 1864.
DEER CREEK, Skirmish at, Feb. 23, 1863.—Expedition through (See Steele's Bayou Expedition, March 14-27, 1863).—Expedition to, April 2-14, 1863.—Expedition to, June —, 1863. —Expeditions from Vicksburg to, Sept. 21-26, 1864.
DRUMGOULD'S BLUFF, Demonstrations against, April 29-May 1, 1863.
DUCK RIVER, Skirmish at mouth of, Aug. 31, 1862.
EARLY GROVE, Scout from La Grange, Tenn., to, April 5-7, 1863.—Scout from La Grange, Tenn., to, April 10-11, 1863.
EASTPORT, Expedition from Cairo, Ill., to, Feb. 15-22, 1862.—Expedition from Pittsburg Landing, Tenn., to, April 1, 1862. Reconnoissance from Savannah, Tenn., to, April 3, 1862.—Expedition to, April 15-May 2, 1863.—Action at, Oct. 10, 1864.
EDWARDS' DEPOT, Battle near, May 16, 1863.
EDWARDS' FERRY, Skirmish at, Feb. 4, 1864.
EDWARDS' STATION, Skirmish near, May 15, 1863.—Skirmish near, May 31, 1863.—Skirmish near, June 6, 1863.—Skirmish at, June 10, 1863.—Skirmish at, July 1, 1863.
EGYPT, Engagement at, Dec. 28, 1864.
EGYPT STATION, Skirmish at, Feb. 19, 1864.
EIGHT-MILE POST, Natchez and Liberty Road, Skirmish near, Sept. 6, 1864.
ELLIS'S BRIDGE, Skirmish at, Feb. 21, 1864.
ELLISTOWN, Skirmish at, July 16, 1864.
ELLISVILLE, Skirmish near, June 25, 1865.
FARMINGTON, Reconnoissance to, and skirmish at, May 3, 1862.—Engagement at, May 9, 1862.—Skirmish near, May 10, 1862.—Skirmish near, May 12, 1862.—Skirmish near, May 19, 1862.—Skirmish near, May 22, 1862.
FARMINGTON HEIGHTS, Skirmish at, May 4, 1862.
FARRAR'S PLANTATION, Expeditions from Natchez to, Sept. 19-22, 1864.
FAYETTE, Skirmish at, Nov. 22, 1863.—Skirmish at, Dec. 22, 1863.—Expedition from Vicksburg to, Sept. 29-Oct. 3, 1864.
FISH LAKE BRIDGE, Skirmish at, Feb. 23, 1863.
FORKED DEER CREEK, Skirmish at, Oct. 3, 1863.
FORTY HILLS, Skirmish at, May 3, 1863.
FOURTEEN-MILE CREEK, Skirmish at, May 12, 1863.—Skirmish at, May 13, 1863.
FRANKLIN, Engagement at, Jan. 2, 1865.
FRANKLIN CREEK, Skirmish at, Dec. 21-22, 1864.
FREE BRIDGE, Yocknapatalfa River, Skirmish at, Dec. 3, 1862.

MISSISSIPPI.

FRIARS' POINT, Skirmish near, Sept. 28, 1862.—Expedition from Helena, Ark., to, Dec. 1-5, 1864.—Scout from and skirmish, Feb. 10, 1865.—Expedition from Helena, Ark., to, Feb. 19-22, 1865.
FULTON ROAD, Skirmish on, Sept. 20, 1862.
GARLANDVILLE, Skirmish at, April 24, 1863.
GLENDALE, Skirmish at, May 8, 1862.—Skirmish near, Sept. 7, 1863.
GRAND GULF, Affair at, May 26, 1862.—Engagement at, June 9, 1862.—Skirmish near, June 24, 1862.—Passage of the batteries at, by the U. S. S. Hartford and Monongahela, March 19, 1863.—Engagement at, March 31, 1863.—Bombardment and passage of batteries at, April 29, 1863.—Naval action at, Feb. 14, 1863.—Naval action near, Feb. 24, 1863.—Naval engagement at, April 22, 1863.—Capture of, by Union naval forces, May 3, 1863.—Skirmish at, Jan. 18, 1864.—Expedition from Vicksburg to, Feb. 15-March 6, 1864.—Expedition from Memphis, Tenn., to, July 4-24, 1864.—Expedition from Vicksburg to and vicinity, March 12-14, 1865.
GRANT'S FERRY, Pearl River, Skirmish at, July 16, 1863.
GRANT'S PASS (See Powell, Fort).
GREENVILLE, Skirmish at, Aug. 23, 1862.—Expedition to, Feb. 14-26, 1863.—Expedition to, April 2-14, 1863.—Skirmish at, May 12, 1863.—Skirmish near, May 18, 1863.—Expedition from Snyder's Bluff to, June 25-July 1, 1863.—Skirmish at, May 20, 1864.—Skirmish at, May 27, 1864.
GREENWOOD, Engagement near, March 11, 1863.—Engagement near, March 13, 1863.—Engagement near, March 16, 1863.—Engagement near, April 2, 1863.—Engagement near, April 4, 1863.—Attack on Union gunboats near, May 27, 1863.
GRENADA, Expedition from Helena, Ark., to the vicinity of, Nov. 27-Dec. 6, 1862.—Expeditions from Big Black River, Miss., and La Grange, Tenn., to, Aug. 10-23, 1863.
GRIFFIN'S LANDING, Expedition from Goodrich's Landing, La., to, Oct. 24-Nov. 10, 1863.
GUNTOWN, Pursuit of Confederate forces from Corinth to, May 30-June 10, 1862.—Reconnoissance toward, June 9, 1862.—Expedition to, July 10-11, 1862.—Engagement near, June 10, 1864.
HALL'S FERRY, Skirmish at, May 13, 1863.
HAMILTON'S PLANTATION, Skirmish at, June 24, 1862.
HANKINSON'S FERRY, Big Black River, Skirmish at, May 3, 1863.—Skirmish at, May 4, 1863.—Skirmish at, July 1, 1863.
HARBERT'S PLANTATION, Expedition from Helena, Ark., to, Jan. 11-13, 1865.
HARRISBURG, Engagement at, July 14-15, 1864.
HATCHIE BOTTOM, Affair at, July 20, 1862.

MISSISSIPPI.

HATCHIE RIVER, Skirmish on, July 5, 1862.—Reconnoissance from Rienzi to, Sept. 30, 1862.
HAYNES'S BLUFF, Demonstrations against, April 29-May 1, 1863.—Capture of, May 18, 1863.—Skirmish at, May 23, 1863.
HELENA ROAD, Skirmish on, June 21, 1863.
HERNANDO, Expedition to, June 21, 1862.—Expedition to, Sept. 8-13, 1862.—Skirmishes near, March 15-16, 1863.—Action at, April 18, 1863.—Expedition from Memphis, Tenn., to, May 23-24, 1863.—Expedition from Memphis, Tenn., toward, May 26, 1863.—Scout from Memphis, Tenn., toward, May 27, 1863.—Scout from Memphis, Tenn., toward, May 28, 1863.—Action near, June 19, 1863.—Expedition from Memphis, Tenn., to, Aug. 16-20, 1863.—Expedition from Memphis, Tenn., to, Oct. 10-11, 1863.—Scout from Memphis, Tenn., to, Nov. 19, 1863.—Scout from Memphis, Tenn., toward, Jan. 3, 1864.—Skirmish at, Oct. 15, 1864.
HILLSBOROUGH, Skirmish at, Feb. 6, 1864.—Skirmish at, Feb. 10, 1864.
HILL'S PLANTATION, Action at, June 22, 1863.
HOLLY SPRINGS, Expedition to, June 15-18, 1862.—Skirmish near, July 1, 1862.—Expedition from, to Bolivar and Jackson, Tenn., July 25-Aug. 1, 1862.—Scout toward, Sept. 5-6, 1862.—Skirmish at, Nov. 13, 1862.—Skirmishes at, Nov. 28-29, 1862.—Capture of, Dec. 20, 1862.—Evacuation of, by Union forces, Jan. 9-10, 1863.—Skirmishes near, June 16-17, 1863.—Skirmish at, Sept. 7, 1863.—Skirmish at, Nov. 5, 1863. —Skirmish at, Feb. 12, 1864.—Skirmish at, April 17, 1864.—Skirmish at, May 24, 1864.—Affair near, Aug. 28, 1864.
HOMOCHITTO RIVER, Expedition from Natchez to, Oct. 5-8, 1864.
HORN LAKE CREEK, Skirmish at, Aug. 16, 1862.
HOULKA SWAMP, Skirmish in, Feb. 17, 1864.
HOUSTON, Skirmish near, Feb. 17, 1864.—Skirmish near, Feb. 19, 1864.
HUDSONVILLE, Skirmish at, Nov. 8, 1862.—Skirmish at, Dec. 1, 1862.—Scout from La Grange, Tenn., to, March 2-3, 1863. —Scout from La Grange, Tenn., to April 10-11, 1863.— Skirmish at, June 21, 1863.—Affair near, Feb. 25, 1864.
HURRICANE CREEK, Skirmish at, Aug. 9, 1864.—Skirmishes at, Aug. 13-14, 1864.—Skirmish at, Aug. 19, 1864.
INDEPENDENCE, Skirmish at, Dec. 7, 1863.
INDIAN BAYOU, Affair at, June 8, 1864.
INGRAHAM'S HEIGHTS, Skirmish at, May 3, 1863.
INGRAHAM'S PLANTATION, Skirmish at, Oct. 10, 1863.
INGRAM'S MILL, Skirmish at, Oct. 12, 1863.
ISSAQUENA COUNTY, Skirmish in, March 22, 1864.—Skirmish in, July 10, 1864.—Skirmish in, Aug. 17, 1864.—Operations in, Oct. 24-31, 1864.

MISSISSIPPI.

IUKA, Reconnoissance to, May 22-23, 1862.—Skirmish near, Sept. 13, 1862.—Reconnoissance from Burnsville toward, Sept. 16, 1862, and skirmish.—Engagement at, Sept. 19, 1862. —Skirmish near, Sept. 20, 1862.—Skirmish near, Sept. 27, 1862.—Action at, July 7, 1863.—Skirmish near, July 14, 1863. —Reconnoissance from Eastport to, Jan. 9, 1865.—Expedition from Eastport to, Feb. 17-18, 1865.
IVEY'S HILL (or Farm), Skirmish at, Feb. 22, 1864.
JACINTO, Skirmish at, Aug. 13, 1863.—Skirmish near, Sept. 7, 1863.
JACKSON, Engagement at, May 14, 1863.—Investment of, July 10-17, 1863.—Skirmish at, Feb. 5, 1864.—Engagement near, July 7, 1864.
JACKSON CAMPAIGN, July 5-25, 1863.
JACKSON COUNTY, Scouts in, Jan. 15-17, 1864.
JONES COUNTY, Operations in, March 14, 1864.
JONES' CROSS ROADS, Skirmish at, May 3, 1863.
JONES' FERRY, Big Black River, Skirmish at, June 28, 1863.— Skirmish at, July 6, 1863.
JONES' PLANTATION, Skirmish at, June 22, 1863.
JUMPERTOWN, Skirmish at, Nov. 5, 1862.
KELLY'S MILL, Skirmish near, July 8, 1864.
KING'S CREEK, Action at, May 5, 1863.
KOSSUTH, Skirmish at, Aug. 27, 1862.
LAMAR, Reconnoissance from La Grange, Tenn., toward, Nov. 6, 1862.—Expedition from La Grange, Tenn., to, Feb. 13-14, 1863.—Skirmish at, Aug. 14, 1864.
LANGLEY'S PLANTATION, Issaquena County, Skirmish at, March 22, 1864.
LAUDERDALE SPRINGS, Skirmish at, Feb. 16, 1864.
LEXINGTON, Skirmish at, Jan. 2, 1865.
LIBERTY AND NATCHEZ ROAD (See Natchez and Liberty Road).
LIVERPOOL, Skirmish at, March 3, 1864.
LIVERPOOL HEIGHTS, Yazoo River, Action at, Feb. 3, 1864. —Skirmish opposite, Feb. 4, 1864.
LIVERPOOL LANDING, Skirmish at, May 23, 1863.
LIVINGSTON, Skirmish near, Oct. 17, 1863.—Skirmish at, March 27, 1864.
LIVINGSTON ROAD, Skirmish on, Oct. 18, 1863.
LOCKHART'S MILLS, Scout from La Grange, Tenn., to, April 10-11, 1863.—Skirmish at, Oct. 6, 1863.
LUCE'S PLANTATION, Skirmish at, May 13, 1864.
LUMPKIN'S MILL, Skirmish at, Nov. 29, 1862.
MACON FORD, Big Black River, Skirmish at, June 9, 1863.
MADISONVILLE, Affair at, Feb. 27, 1864.
MAGNOLIA CHURCH, Battle of, May 1, 1863.
MAGNOLIA HILLS, Battle of, May 1, 1863.
MARIETTA, Expedition from Rienzi to, Aug. 19-21, 1862, and skirmishes.—Skirmish near, Aug. 31, 1862.

MISSISSIPPI.

MARION STATION, Skirmishes at, Feb. 15-17, 1864.
MATTHEW'S FERRY, Coldwater River, Skirmish at, June 20, 1863.
MECHANICSBURG, Skirmish at, May 24, 1863.—Expedition from Haynes' Bluff to, May 26-June 4, 1863.—Skirmish at, May 29, 1863.—Expedition from Haynes' Bluff to, June 2-8, 1863.—Skirmish at, June 4, 1863.—Skirmishes at and near, April 19-23, 1864.—Skirmish near, Jan. 3, 1865.
MERIDIAN, Skirmishes near, Feb. 13-14, 1864.—Occupation of, by Union forces, Feb. 14-20, 1864.—Skirmish near, Feb. 19, 1864.
MERIDIAN EXPEDITION, Feb. 3-March 6, 1864, and co-operating expeditions from Memphis, Tenn., and up the Yazoo River.
MESSINGER'S FERRY, Big Black River, Skirmish at, June 26, 1863.—Skirmish at, June 29, 1863.—Skirmish at, June 30, 1863.—Skirmishes at, July 3, 4, and 6, 1863.
MESSINGER'S FORD, Skirmish at, July 6, 1863.
MIDWAY HILL, Battle of, May 16, 1863. (Champion's Hill.)
MISSISSIPPI SOUND, Naval action in, Oct. 19, 1861.
MISSISSIPPI SPRINGS, Skirmish at, May 13, 1863.
MITCHELL'S CROSS ROADS, Skirmish near, Dec. 1, 1862.
MOLINO, Skirmish near, Nov. 28, 1863.
MOORE'S BLUFF, Skirmish at, Sept. 29, 1864.
MOORE'S FORD, Skirmish at, Sept. 29, 1863.
MORTON, Skirmish at, Feb. 7, 1864.—Skirmish near, Feb. 8, 1864.—Skirmish at, Feb. 10, 1864.
MOUNT PLEASANT, Expedition from La Grange, Tenn., to, Feb. 13-14, 1863.—Scout from La Grange, Tenn., to, April 5-7, 1863.—Scout from La Grange, Tenn., to, April 10-11, 1863.—Skirmish at, Aug. 5, 1863.—Skirmish at, Aug. 27, 1863.—Skirmish at, Dec. 28, 1863.—Skirmish at, Jan. 25, 1864.—Skirmish near, May 22, 1864.
MUD CREEK, Skirmish at, June 20, 1863.
MUDDY BAYOU, Expedition through (See Steele's Bayou Expedition, March 14-27, 1863).
NATCHEZ, Occupation of, by Union naval forces, May 13, 1862.—Occupation of, by Union troops, July 13, 1863.—Expedition from, July 26-30, 1863.—Skirmish near, Nov. 11, 1863.—Operations about, Dec. 1-10, 1863.—Naval action near, Dec. 11, 1863.—Operations near, Jan. 24, 1864.—Skirmish near, April 25, 1864.
NATCHEZ AND LIBERTY ROAD, Skirmish near, Sept. 6, 1864.
NEW ALBANY, Skirmish at, April 18-19, 1863.—Expedition from Pocahontas, Tenn., to, June 12-14, 1863.—Skirmish at, June 19, 1863.—Skirmish at, Oct. 5, 1863.—Skirmish near, Feb. 23, 1864.
NEWTON STATION, Capture of, April 24, 1863.
NORTH FORK, Bayou Pierre, Skirmish on, May 3, 1863.

MISSISSIPPI.

OAKLAND, Skirmish at, Dec. 3, 1862.
OAK RIDGE, Skirmish at, Jan. 16, 1864.
OKOLONA, Skirmish at, Dec. 9, 1863.—Affair near, Feb. 18, 1864.—Skirmish near, Feb. 21, 1864.—Engagement near, Feb. 22, 1864.—Skirmish at, June 23, 1864.—Skirmish at, Dec. 27, 1864.
OLD LAMAR, Skirmish at, Nov. 6, 1862.—Skirmish at, Nov. 8, 1862.
OLD RIVER, Boat expedition into and skirmishes, Feb. 12-13, 1864.—Naval expedition into, Dec. 16, 1864.
OLD TOWN CREEK, Action at, July 15, 1864.
OLIVE BRANCH, Skirmish at, Sept. 6, 1862.
OSBORN'S CREEK, Skirmish at, June 4, 1862.
OXFORD, Skirmishes about, Dec. 1-3, 1862.—Affair near, Dec. 4, 1862.—Expedition from La Grange, Tenn., to, Aug. 1-30, 1864.
PALO ALTO, Skirmish at, April 21, 1863.
PANOLA, Expedition from La Grange, Tenn., to, May 11-15, 1863.—Expedition from La Grange, Tenn., to, June 16-24, 1863.—Skirmish near, Aug. 17, 1863.—Skirmish at, Aug. 20, 1863.
PASCAGOULA, Skirmish at, April 9, 1863.
PASS CHRISTIAN, Expedition from Ship Island to, April 3-4, 1862.—Expedition from Ship Island to, June 22, 1862.—Naval engagement in, March 25, 1862.
PAYNE'S PLANTATION, Skirmish at, Aug. 18, 1863.
PEARL RIVER, Reconnoissance toward, July 11, 1863.—Reconnoissance to, July 15, 1863.—Skirmish on, July 16, 1863.—Skirmish on, Feb. 28, 1864.—Expedition from Vicksburg to, July 2-10, 1864, and skirmishes.
PEMBERTON, FORT, Engagement at, March 11, 1863.—Engagement at, March 13, 1863.—Engagement at, March 16, 1863.—Engagement at, April 2, 1863.—Engagement at, April 4, 1863.
PERRY'S FERRY, Skirmish at, April 19, 1863.
PEYTON'S MILL, Skirmish at, Sept. 19, 1862.
PIERRE, BAYOU, Skirmish on South Fork of, May 2, 1863.—Skirmish on North Fork of, May 3, 1863.
PLENTYTUDE, Skirmish at, July 10, 1864.
PONDS, THE, Skirmish at, Jan. 4, 1865.
PONTOTOC, Skirmish at, April 19, 1863.—Expedition from Pocahontas, Tenn., toward, June 17-22, 1863.—Skirmish near, Feb. 17, 1864.—Skirmishes at and near, July 11-12, 1864.
PORT GIBSON, Battle of, May 1, 1863.—Skirmish near, Oct. 10, 1863.—Skirmish at, Dec. 26, 1863.—Skirmish at, July 14, 1864.—Skirmish at, Sept. 30, 1864.—Expedition from Rodney to, May 3-6, 1865, with skirmishes.

MISSISSIPPI.

POWELL, FORT, Shell Island, Naval attacks on, Feb. 21 and March 1, 1864.—Evacuation of, by Confederate forces, Aug. 8, 1864.
PRAIRIE STATION, Skirmish at, Feb. 21, 1864.
PRENTISS, Skirmish at, Sept. 19, 1862.
PROPHET BRIDGE, Yocknapatalfa River, Skirmish at, Dec. 3, 1862.
QUEEN'S HILL, Action at, July 7, 1863.—Skirmish at, Feb. 4, 1864.
QUINN AND JACKSON'S MILL, Skirmish at, June 16, 1863.—Skirmish at, Oct. 12, 1863.—Skirmish at, Nov. 1, 1863.—Skirmish at, Nov. 3, 1863.
RAIFORD'S PLANTATION, Affair at, Feb. 11, 1864.
RAMER'S CROSSING, Mobile and Ohio Railroad, Skirmish near, Oct. 2, 1862.
RAYMOND, Engagement at, May 12, 1863.—Skirmish near, May 13, 1863.—Capture of, May 24, 1863.
RED BONE, Skirmish at, April 21, 1864.
RIENZI, Affair near, June 2, 1862.—Skirmish near, Aug. 26, 1862.—Skirmish at, Sept. 9, 1862.—Skirmish at, Sept. 18, 1862.—Skirmish at, Aug. 8, 1863.
RIPLEY, Expedition from Rienzi to, July 27-29, 1862.—Skirmish near, Oct. 7, 1862.—Expedition from Grand Junction, Tenn., to, Nov. 19-20, 1862.—Skirmish at, Dec. 23, 1862.—Skirmish at, Dec. 25, 1862.—Scout near, Jan. 25, 1863.—Scout from La Grange, Tenn., toward, Jan. 28-30, 1863.—Scout from Pocahontas, Tenn., to, June 8-9, 1863.—Expedition from Pocahontas, Tenn., to, June 12-14, 1863, and skirmishes.—Skirmish at, July 7, 1863.—Skirmish at, Aug. 3, 1863.—Skirmish at, Dec. 1, 1863.—Affair at, Dec. 4, 1863.—Scout from La Grange, Tenn., to, Jan. 23, 1864.—Expedition from Memphis, Tenn., to, April 30-May 9, 1864.—Skirmish at, June 7, 1864.—Action at, June 11, 1864.—Skirmish near, July 7, 1864.
ROBINSON'S MILLS, Skirmish at, Oct. 17, 1863.
ROCKY CREEK, Skirmish at, June 25, 1863.
ROCKY FORD, Scout from Big Spring Creek to, Jan. 7, 1863.—Skirmish near, June 20, 1863.
RODNEY, Skirmish at, Dec. 17, 1863.—Skirmish at, Dec. 24, 1863.—Skirmish at, March 4, 1864.—Expedition from Vicksburg to, Sept. 29-Oct. 3, 1864.—Naval action near, June 25, 1862. (Cole's Creek.)—Naval affair at, Sept. 12, 1863.
RODNEY BEND, Naval action at, Dec. 11, 1863.
ROEBUCK LAKE, Expedition from Skipwith's Landing to, Nov. 18-22, 1863.
ROLLING FORK, Expedition to (See Steele's Bayou Expedition, March 14-27, 1863).—Skirmishes near, Sept. 22-23, 1864.
RUCKERSVILLE, Skirmish at, Oct. 1, 1862.—Skirmish near, Oct. 7, 1862.
SAINT CATHERINE'S CREEK, Skirmish at, July 31, 1863.

MISSISSIPPI.

SALEM, Scout from La Grange, Tenn., to, March 2-3, 1863.—Action at, Oct. 8, 1863.—Skirmish at, June 11, 1864.
SATARTIA, Expedition from Haynes's Bluff to, June 2-8, 1863.—Skirmish near, Oct. 17, 1863.—Skirmish at, Feb. 7, 1864.
SENATOBIA, Expedition from La Grange, Tenn., to, May 21-26, 1863.—Skirmish near, June 20, 1863.—Skirmishes at and near, Feb. 8-9, 1864.
SHARON, Skirmish at, Feb. 27, 1864.
SHARP'S MILL, Reconnoissance on the Alabama Road and toward, May 10, 1862.
SHELDON, CAMP, Affair near, Feb. 8, 1863.—Affair near, Feb. 10, 1863.
SHIP ISLAND, Seizure of fort on, by State troops, Jan. 20, 1861.—Affair at, July 9, 1861.—Affair at, Sept. 17, 1861.—Occupation of, by Union forces, Dec. 3, 1861.
SMITH'S BRIDGE, Skirmish at, June 11, 1863.—Skirmish at, Oct. 19, 1863.
SNYDER'S BLUFF, Attack on outpost at, March 30, 1864.
SNYDER'S MILL, Yazoo River, Affair at, Dec. 27, 1862.—Engagement at, April 30-May 1, 1863.—Capture of ordnance and ordnance stores at, May 17, 1863.
SOUTH FORK, Bayou Pierc, Skirmish on, May 2, 1863.
SPRINGDALE BRIDGE, Yocknapatalfa River, Skirmish at, Dec. 3, 1862.
STEELE'S BAYOU, Skirmish at, Oct. 25, 1864.
STEELE'S BAYOU EXPEDITION (to Rolling Fork, by Muddy, Steele's, and Black Bayou and Deer Creek), March 14-27, 1863.
TALLAHATCHIE BRIDGE, Skirmish at, June 18, 1862.
TALLAHATCHIE RIVER, Skirmish at, Nov. 28, 1862.—Expedition from Helena, Ark., to, Dec. 24, 1862.—Skirmish on Feb. 22, 1864.—Skirmishes at, Aug. 7-10, 1864.
TALLULAH COURT HOUSE, Expedition from Skipwith's Landing to, Nov. 10-13, 1863.
THOMPSON'S HILL, Battle of, May 1, 1863.
TIPPAH RIVER, Skirmish at, Feb. 24, 1864.
TISHOMINGO CREEK, Engagement at, June 10, 1864.
TOTTEN'S PLANTATION, Coahoma County, Skirmish near, Aug. 2, 1862.
TREADWELL'S PLANTATION, Skirmish at, Oct. 16, 1863.—Skirmish at, Oct. 20, 1863.
TUPELO, Expedition to, May 2-8, 1863.—Action near, May 5, 1863.—Expedition from La Grange, Tenn., to, July 5-21, 1864.
TUSCUMBIA BRIDGE, Burning of, May 30, 1862.
TUSCUMBIA CREEK, Skirmishes at, May 30-31, 1862.
UNION, Skirmishes at, Feb. 21-22, 1864.
UNION CHURCH, Skirmish at, April 28, 1863.
UTICA, Skirmishes at and near, May. 9-10, 1863.—Skirmish at, July 13, 1864.
VERONA, Engagement at, Dec. 25, 1864.

MISSISSIPPI.

VICKSBURG, Surrender of demanded and refused, May 18, 1862.—Operations against and about, May 18-July 27, 1862.—Expedition to, June 20-July 24, 1862.—Bombardment of, June 28, 1862.—Operations against, Dec. 20, 1862-Jan. 3, 1863.—Operations against and about, Jan. 20-July 4, 1863.—Expedition from, to Yazoo City, July 12-21, 1863.—Expedition from, to Monroe, La., Aug. 20-Sept. 2, 1863.—Expedition from, to Sunnyside Landing, Ark., Jan. 10-16, 1864.—Expedition from, to Waterproof, La., Jan. 29-Feb. 23, 1864, and skirmishes.—Expedition from, to Grand Gulf, Feb. 15-March 6, 1864.—Expedition from, to Yazoo City, May 4-21, 1864.—Skirmish near, June 4, 1864.—Expedition from, to Pearl River, July 2-10, 1864, and skirmishes.—Expedition from, to Grand Gulf, July 10-17, 1864.—Expedition from, to Deer Creek, Sept. 21-26, 1864.—Expedition from, to Rodney and Fayette, Sept. 29-Oct. 3, 1864.—Expedition from, to Gaines's Landing and Bayou Macon, La., Nov. 6-8, 1864.—Expedition from, to Grand Gulf and vicinity, March 12-14, 1865.
VICKSBURG BATTERIES, Naval actions with, March 25 and April 11, 1863.
VINCENT'S CROSS ROADS, Skirmish at, Oct. 26, 1863.
WALL HILL, Affair at, Feb. 12, 1864.
WALNUT HILLS, Skirmish at, May 14, 1863.
WARRENTON, Passage of the batteries at, Feb. 2-3, 1863.—Attack on the batteries at, by the U. S. S. Hartford and Monongahela, March 23, 1863.—Passage of the batteries at, by transports, April 22, 1863.—Naval actions at, Feb. 5 and 14, 1863, and March 27, 1863.—Destruction of water batteries at, May 10, 1863.
WASHINGTON COUNTY, Operations in, Oct. 24-31, 1864.
WATERFORD, Skirmishes at, Nov. 29-30, 1862.
WATER VALLEY, Skirmish at, Dec. 4, 1862.—Skirmish near, Dec. 18, 1862.
WEST POINT, Skirmish near, Feb. 20, 1864.—Skirmish at, Feb. 21, 1864.
WHITE OAK BAYOU, Skirmish at, July 24, 1862.
WILLOW SPRINGS, Skirmish at, May 3, 1863.
WOLF'S CREEK, Skirmish at, June 4, 1862.
WOODVILLE, Operations about, Aug. 3-6, 1864.—Expedition from Natchez to, Oct. 4-12, 1864.
WORSHAM'S CREEK, Skirmish at, Nov. 6, 1862.
WYATT, Action at, Oct. 13, 1863.—Expedition from Memphis, Tenn., to, Feb. 6-18, 1864.
YAZOO BATTERIES, Naval engagement with, Dec. 27-29, 1862.
YAZOO CITY, Capture of, July —, 1863.—Naval operations at, May 21 and July 18, 1863.—Naval actions at, April 21-22, 1864.—Expedition from Vicksburg to, July 12-21, 1863.—Expedition from Messinger's Ford to, Sept. 27-Oct. 1,

MISSISSIPPI—MISSISSIPPI• RIVER—MISSOURI.

1863.—Skirmish at, Oct. 31, 1863.—Occupation of, by Union forces, Feb. 9-March 6, 1864.—Skirmish near, Feb. 28, 1864.—Attack on, March 5, 1864.—Abandoned by Union forces, March 6, 1864.—Expedition from Vicksburg to, May 4-21, 1864.—Expedition from Vicksburg to, Nov. 23-Dec. 4, 1864.

YAZOO PASS, Skirmish at, Feb. 16, 1863.—Skirmish near, Feb. 19, 1863.

YAZOO PASS EXPEDITION (by Moon Lake, Yazoo Pass, and the Coldwater and Tallahatchie), Feb. 24-April 8, 1863.

YAZOO RIVER, Expedition from Helena, Ark., up, Aug. 16-27, 1862.—Expedition up, Dec. 12, 1862.—Expedition up, May 24-31, 1863.—Naval operations in, Dec. 23-29, 1862; May 20-23, 1863; Feb. 2-15, 1864.—Expedition up, April 19-23, 1864, and skirmishes at and near Mechanicsburg.—Skirmish at, May 29, 1864.—Expedition from Vicksburg up, Dec. 5-8, 1864.

YELLOW CREEK, Expedition from Savannah, Tenn., to, March 14-17, 1862.

YOCKNAPATALFA RIVER, Skirmish on, Dec. 1, 1862.—Skirmishes on, Dec. 3, 1862.

MISSISSIPPI RIVER.

BUCK ISLAND, Expedition from Helena, Ark., to, July 13-16, 1864.

ELLIS'S CLIFF, Affair near, June 21, 1862.—Naval actions at, June 24, 1862, and Feb. 16, 1863.

GAINES'S LANDING, Affair at, June 6, 1864.

HEAD OF THE PASSES, Naval affair near, Oct. 12, 1862.

ISLAND No. 70, Steamer Sir William Wallace fired on at, by guerrillas, Jan. 20, 1864.

PROPHET'S ISLAND, Naval action at, Dec. 14, 1862.

RED RIVER, Naval action near mouth of, Nov. 21, 1863.

SMITH'S PLANTATION, Confederate operations near, May 24-June 4, 1864.

SOUTHWEST PASS, Naval affair at, Sept. 22, 1863.

MISSOURI.

ALBANY, Skirmish at, Oct. 26, 1864.
ALLEN, Skirmish at, July 23, 1864.
ALTON, Scout from Pilot Knob to, Oct. 29-Nov. 5, 1863.
ARCADIA, Skirmish at, Sept. 27, 1864.
ARCADIA VALLEY, Skirmish in, Sept. 26, 1864.
ARNOLDSVILLE, Skirmish near, June 1, 1864.
ARROW ROCK, Skirmish at, July 29, 1862.—Skirmish at, Oct. 12, 1862.—Attack on, July 20, 1864.—Skirmish at, Aug. 7, 1864.

MISSOURI.

ARROW ROCK ROAD, Skirmish on, Sept. 23, 1864.
ASH HILLS, Scout from Cape Girardeau to, Aug. 9-18, 1863.
ASHLEY, Skirmish at, Aug. 28, 1862.
ATHENS, Skirmish at, Aug. 5, 1861.
AUXVASSE CREEK, Callaway County, Skirmish at, Oct. 16, 1862.
BALL'S MILL, Skirmish at, Aug. 28, 1861.
BALL TOWN, Affair on Clear Creek near, Aug. 8, 1863.
BARRY, Skirmish near, Aug. 14, 1862.
BARRY COUNTY, Skirmishes in, Oct. 8, 18, 29, 1864.
BARTON COUNTY, Expedition from Greenfield into, Nov. 24-26, 1862.—Scout in, Feb. 19-22, 1863.
BATES COUNTY, Scouts in, May 3-11 and Sept. 27-28, 1863.—Operations in, Oct. 3-7, 1863.
BEAR CREEK, Johnson County, Skirmish on, Feb. 5, 1863.
BEAR SKIN LAKE, Skirmish at, Sept. 7, 1863.
BEAVER CREEK, Skirmish on, Nov. 24, 1862.
BEE CREEK, Affair on, May 2, 1864.
BELMONT, Skirmish near, Sept. 26, 1861.—Engagement at, Nov. 7, 1861.
BENNETT'S BAYOU, Scout on and skirmishes, Aug. 23, 1863.
BENNIGHT'S MILL, Skirmish at, Sept. 1, 1861.
BENTON, Expedition to, Aug. 7-10, 1861.—Expeditions to, Jan. 15-17, 1862.
BERTRAND, Skirmish near, Dec. 11, 1861.
BIG BLUE, Action at the, Oct. 22, 1864.—Engagement at the, Oct. 23, 1864.
BIG CREEK, Skirmish on, March 9, 1862.—Skirmish at, Sept. 9, 1862.—Scout from Salem to, April 18-21, 1863.—Skirmish at, May 15, 1863.—Skirmish on, Aug. 22, 1863.—Scout from Cold Water Grove to, Sept. 4-7, 1863, and skirmishes.—Skirmish on, July 28, 1864.—Scout to Crisp's Mill on, Aug. 25-30, 1864.
BIG CREEK BLUFFS, Skirmish at, July 11, 1862.
BIG GRAVOIS, Skirmish near mouth of, April 22, 1865.
BIG GROVE, Scout from Warrensburg to, Feb. 1-5, 1865.
BIG HURRICANE CREEK, Action at, Oct. 19, 1861.
BIG NORTH FORK CREEK, Affair on, June 16, 1864.
BIG PINEY, Scout from Waynesville to the, July 6-8, 1862.—Skirmish on the, Nov. 25, 1863.—Scouts from, July 5-6, 1864.—Skirmish on the, Nov. 1, 1864.—Skirmish on the, Dec. 2, 1864.—Skirmish near (See Waynesville, Operations about, etc., Jan. 16-22, 1865).
BIG RIVER, Skirmish at, Oct. 7, 1864.
BIG RIVER BRIDGE, Destruction of, Oct. 15, 1861.
BIG SPRINGS, Expedition to, Sept. 7, 1861.
BIRD'S POINT, Skirmish near, Oct. 14, 1861.
BLACK FORK HILLS, Affair at, July 4, 1863.
BLACK RIVER, Skirmish at, Sept. 12, 1861.
BLACK RUN, Skirmish at, July 8, 1862.

MISSOURI.

BLACKWATER CREEK (or River), Skirmish at, Dec. 18, 1861.—Skirmish on, March 29, 1862.—Skirmish near, April 16, 1862.—Expedition toward, July 6-9, 1862.—Skirmish on, July 23, 1862.—Scout from Sedalia to, June 3-5, 1864.—Skirmish on, July 27, 1864.—Expedition from Sedalia to Scott's Ford on, Sept. 2-4, 1864.—Skirmish on, May 20, 1865.

BLACKWELL'S STATION, Skirmishes at and near, Oct. 15, 1861.

BLOOMFIELD, Expeditions to, Jan. 15-17, 1862.—Skirmish near, May 10, 1862.—Skirmish at, July 29, 1862.—Affair near, Aug. 24, 1862.—Skirmish near, Aug. 29, 1862.—Action at, Sept. 11, 1862.—Affair at, Jan. 27, 1863.—Capture of, by Union forces, March 1, 1863.—Skirmish near, March 2, 1863.—Affair at, April 20, 1863.—Skirmish at, May 12, 1863.—Mutiny at, Oct. 22, 1863.—Attack on, and pursuit of Confederates to Brown's Ferry, Ark., Nov. 29-30, 1863.—Affair near, April 1, 1864.—Scout from, May 6, 1864.—Expedition from Patterson to, May 16-25, 1864.—Skirmish near, July 14, 1864.—Expeditions from, into Dunklin County, March 3-7, 1865.

BLUE MILLS, Action at, July 24, 1861.

BLUE MILLS LANDING, Action at, Sept. 17, 1861.

BLUE RIVER, Affair on, May 21, 1864.

BLUE SPRINGS, Expedition to, Jan. 29-Feb. 3, 1862.—Skirmish at, March 22, 1863.

BOB'S CREEK, Skirmish at, March 7, 1862.

BOLE'S FARM, Skirmish at, July 23, 1862.

BOLIVAR, Affair at, Feb. 8, 1862.

BOLLINGER COUNTY, Skirmish in, Jan. 14, 1864.—Scout from Cape Girardeau into, March 9-15, 1865.

BOLLINGER'S MILLS, Skirmishes at, July 28, 1862.

BOONE COUNTY, Skirmish in, Sept. —, 1862.—Operations in, Nov. 1-10, 1862.—Scouts in, Sept. 6-12, 1864.—Operations in, Sept. 15-19, 1864.

BOONEVILLE, Engagement at, June 17, 1861.—Action at, Sept. 13, 1861.—Skirmishes at, Oct. 11-12, 1863.—Skirmish at, Oct. 9, 1864.—Skirmishes near, Oct. 11-12, 1864.—Skirmish near, May 3, 1865.

BOWERS' MILL, Skirmish at, Oct. 4, 1863.

BRAGG'S FARM, Skirmish near, Sept. 13, 1862.

BRECKINRIDGE, Affair near, June 9, 1864.

BRIER FORK, Action at, July 5, 1861.

BROWN'S SPRINGS, Skirmish at, July 27, 1862.

BRUNSWICK, Skirmish at, Aug. 17, 1861.—Affair near, Sept. 6, 1864.—Skirmish at, Oct. 11, 1864.—Expedition from Brookfield to, Nov. 16-23, 1864.

BUFFALO CREEK, McDonald County, Skirmish on, Aug. 7, 1864.

BUFFALO CREEK, Ripley County, Scout from Patterson to, July 8-12, 1864.

MISSOURI.

BULL CREEK, Christian County, Skirmish at, March 28, 1865.
BUSH CREEK, Skirmish at, May 26, 1863.
BUSHY CREEK, Scouts from Salem to, Nov. 24-28, 1863.
BUTLER, Skirmish at, Nov. 20, 1861.—Skirmish near, May 15, 1862.
BYRAM'S FORD, Action at, Oct. 22, 1864.
CALEDONIA, Skirmish at, Sept. 12, 1864.—Skirmish at, Sept. 28, 1864.
CALHOUN, Raid on, June 12, 1864.
CALIFORNIA, Skirmish at, Oct. 9, 1864.
CALIFORNIA HOUSE, Skirmish at, Aug. 29, 1862.—Skirmish at, Oct. 18, 1862.—Affair near, Feb. 12, 1864.
CALLAWAY COUNTY, Scouts in, Sept. 4, 1862.—Scout in, Nov. 6-7, 1864.
CAMBRIDGE, Scout to, June 5-7, 1862.—Skirmish near, Sept. 26, 1862.
CAMDEN POINT, Action at, July 13, 1864.—Skirmish near, July 22, 1864.
CAPE GIRARDEAU, Surrender of, demanded by Confederate forces, April 25, 1863.—Action at, April 26, 1863.—Scout from, to Ash Hill and Poplar Bluff, Aug. 9-18, 1863.—Scout from, to Doniphan, Mo., and Pocahontas, Ark., Oct. 26-Nov. 12, 1863.—Skirmish near, Feb. 5, 1864.—Skirmish near, Dec. 14, 1864.
CARROLL COUNTY, Operations in, July 27-Aug. 4, 1862.—Skirmishes in, April —, 1863.—Operations in, Aug. 12-16, 1864.—Scout and skirmishes in, May 26-27, 1865.
CARROLLTON, Skirmish at, Aug. 1, 1862.—Surrender of, by Union forces, Oct. 17, 1864.
CARTHAGE, Engagement near, July 5, 1861.—Expedition to, March 19-20, 1862.—Skirmish at, Nov. 27, 1862.—Skirmish at, Jan. 13, 1863.—Skirmish near, May 16, 1863.—Skirmish near, May 26, 1863.—Skirmishes at, June 27-28, 1863.—Attack on train between Carthage, Mo., and Fort Scott, Kans., Sept. 6, 1863.—Skirmish at, Oct. 2, 1863.—Scout from Greenfield to, Aug. 6-9, 1863.—Skirmish at, Oct. 18, 1863.—Scouts near, May 18-23, 1864.—Skirmish near, July 21, 1864.—Skirmish at, Sept. 22, 1864.
CARUTHERSVILLE, Expedition from New Madrid to, July 5-10, 1864, with skirmishes.—Skirmish near, Dec. 30, 1864.
CASS COUNTY, Operations in, July 9-11, 1862.—Expedition from Fort Leavenworth, Kans., through, Sept. 8-23, 1862.—Scout in, May 3-11, 1863.—Expedition from Lexington into, Aug. 28-Sept. 7, 1863.—Scout in, Aug. 25-29, 1864.
CASSVILLE, Skirmish near, June 11, 1862.—Skirmish at, Sept. 21, 1862.—Operations about, Nov. 17-18, 1862.—Scout from, through Northwestern Arkansas, into Newton and Jasper Counties, May 21-30, 1863.—Skirmish at, July 4, 1863.—Affair near, July 27, 1863.—Skirmish at, Sept. 26, 1863.—Scout from, Dec. 24-29, 1863.

MISSOURI.

CASTOR RIVER, Skirmish at, April 29, 1863.—Affair near, Aug. 1, 1863.
CEDAR COUNTY, Skirmish in, Oct. 17, 1863.
CENTRALIA, Affair at, Sept. 7, 1864.—Affair at, Sept. 27, 1864.—
—Skirmish near, Sept. 28, 1864.
CENTRE CREEK, Scout from Newtonia to, May 13-18, 1863, and skirmishes.—Skirmish at, May 15, 1863.—Skirmish at, Feb. 20, 1865.
CENTREVILLE, Reconnoissance from Ironton to, Aug. 2, 1861.—Attack on, Dec. 23, 1863.—Skirmish near, Nov. 12, 1864.
CHAPEL HILL, Expedition toward, July 6-9, 1862.—Expedition from Independence to, Oct. 24-26, 1862.—Expedition from Warrensburg to, July 29-Aug. 2, 1864.
CHARITON BRIDGE, Skirmish at, Aug. 3, 1862.
CHARITON COUNTY, Affair in, April 11, 1864.—Scout in, July 27-30, 1864.—Skirmish in, May 27, 1865.
CHARITON ROAD, Skirmish on, near Keytesville, July 30, 1864.
CHARLESTON, Skirmishes at, Aug. 19-20, 1861.—Expedition from Bird's Point to, Oct. 2, 1861.—Skirmish at, Dec. 13, 1861.—Skirmish at, Jan. 8, 1862.—Affair near, Feb. 15, 1864.—Skirmishes near, April 19-20, 1864.—Skirmish at, Nov. 5, 1864.
CHARLOT, Battle of, Oct. 25, 1864.
CHERRY GROVE, Schuyler County, Skirmish at, June 26, 1862.—Skirmish at, July 1, 1862.
CLARK COUNTY, Operations in, Oct. 11, 1862.
CLARK'S MILL, Chariton County, Skirmish at, July 30, 1862.
CLARK'S MILL, Douglas County, Action at, Nov. 7, 1862.
CLARKTON, Skirmish at, Oct. 23, 1862.—Expedition from New Madrid to, Dec. 17-21, 1862.—Expedition from Cape Girardeau to, Oct. 27-Nov. 15, 1863.
CLAY COUNTY, Skirmish in, July 4, 1864.
CLEAR CREEK, Skirmish on, near Taberville, Aug. 2, 1862.—Skirmish on, Aug. 19, 1862.—Affair on, near Ball Town, Aug. 8, 1863.
CLEAR FORK, Skirmish on, near Warrensburg, Sept. —, 1862.—Skirmish at, Aug. 26, 1863.—Skirmish on, near Warrensburg, July 16, 1864.
CLEAR LAKE, Expedition from Fort Scott, Kans., to, Aug. 6-10, 1863.
CLINTON, Skirmish near, March 30, 1862.—Attack on, Oct. 25, 1864.
CLINTONVILLE, Skirmishes near, Oct. 12-13, 1861.
COAL CAMP CREEK, Scout from Warrensburg to mouth of, May 23-26, 1865.
COLD WATER GROVE, Scout from, to Pleasant Hill and Big Creek, Sept. 4-7, 1863, and skirmishes.

MISSOURI.

COLE CAMP, Skirmish at, Oct. 5, 1862.—Skirmish at, June 8, 1863.—Skirmish near, Oct. 9, 1863.
COLE COUNTY, Skirmish in, Oct. 6, 1864.
COLUMBIA, Expedition toward, Sept. 2, 1861.—Skirmish near, Oct. 2, 1862.—Skirmish near, Jan. 21, 1863.—Skirmish near, June 17, 1864.—Skirmish at, Aug. 16, 1864.—Skirmish at, Sept. 16, 1864.—Skirmish near, Feb. 12, 1865.
COLUMBUS, Skirmish at, Jan. 9, 1862.—Skirmish near, Aug. 23, 1862.—Skirmish at, July 12, 1864.—Scout from Warrensburg to, March 19-23, 1865, with a skirmish near Greenton.
COMMERCE, Expedition to, Aug. 7-10, 1861.—Descent upon, and attack on the steamer City of Alton, Dec. 29, 1861.
COMPTON'S FERRY, Grand River, Skirmish at, Aug. 11, 1862.
COON CREEK, Skirmish on, near Lamar, Aug. 24, 1862.
COOPER COUNTY, Scout in, May 8-10, 1865.
COWSKIN BOTTOM, Newton County, Affair at, Jan. 23, 1864.
CRANE CREEK, Skirmish at, Feb. 14, 1862.
CRAVENSVILLE, Skirmish at, Aug. 5, 1862.
CRISP'S MILL, on Big Creek, Scout to, Aug. 25-30, 1864, with skirmish near Rose Hill.
CROOKED CREEK, Skirmish on, near Dallas, Aug. 24, 1862.
CROSS TIMBERS, Skirmish at, July 28, 1862.—Skirmish at, Oct. 15, 1863.
CROW'S STATION, near Licking, Skirmish at, May 26, 1862.
CUBA, Skirmish near, May 13, 1864.—Affair at, Sept. 29, 1864.
CURRENT HILLS, Expedition through the, Dec. 5-9, 1861.
CURRENT RIVER, Scout from Salem to, Aug. 24-28, 1862.—Scout from Salem to, April 18-21, 1863.
CYPRESS SWAMP, Skirmish in, near Cape Girardeau, Dec. 14, 1864.
DADE COUNTY, Skirmish in, July 24, 1863.
DALLAS, Skirmish at, Sept. 2, 1861.—Expeditions to, Jan. 15-17, 1862.—Reconnoissance from Cape Girardeau to, April 2-4, 1862.—Skirmish on Crooked Creek near, Aug. 24, 1862.
DALLAS COUNTY, Scout in, July 19-23, 1862.
DANVILLE, Expedition to, Dec. 25, 1861.—Attack on, Oct. 14, 1864.
DAVIDSON, FORT, Pilot Knob, Attack on, Sept. 27, 1864.
DAVIS'S CREEK, Scout from Warrensburg to, Feb. 1-5, 1865.
DAYTON, Skirmish at, Dec. 23, 1861.—Expedition from Morristown to, Jan. 1-3, 1862, and skirmish en route.—Destruction of, by Union forces, Jan. 3, 1862.—Skirmish at, Aug. 10, 1863.—Skirmish at, April 27, 1864.
DEEP WATER, Skirmish at, June 11, 1862.
DEEPWATER TOWNSHIP, Affair in, March 27, 1864.
DEER CREEK, Skirmish on, Oct. 16, 1863.
DIAMOND GROVE, Skirmish at, April 14, 1862.—Skirmish at, Aug. 21, 1864.
DIAMOND GROVE PRAIRIE, Skirmish at, Aug. 1, 1864.

MISSOURI.

DONIPHAN, Expedition from Greenville to, Nov. 13-15, 1861.—Occupation of, by Union forces, Feb. —, 1862.—Skirmish at, April 1, 1862.—Scout toward, March 19-23, 1863.—Skirmish near, June 1, 1863.—Scout from Cape Girardeau to, and Pocahontas, Ark., Oct. 26-Nov. 12, 1863.—Affair at, Sept. 19, 1864.
DOUGLAS COUNTY, Scout through, March 4-11, 1862.—Scout from Forsyth through, June 5-12, 1864.
DOVER, Skirmish near, Sept. 10, 1864.—Skirmish at, Oct. 20, 1864.—Scout from Warrensburg to, Feb. 1-5, 1865.
DRIPPING SPRINGS, Skirmish at, Aug. 15, 1864.
DRY FORK CREEK, Action at, July 5, 1861.—Scouts from Salem to, Nov. 24-28, 1863.
DRY WOOD, Action at, Sept. 2, 1861.—Skirmish at, Nov. 9, 1862.—Skirmish near, July 7, 1863.—Skirmish near, May 16, 1864.
DUG FORD, near Jonesborough, Skirmish at, Oct. 12, 1863.
DUG SPRINGS, Skirmish at, July 25, 1861.—Skirmish at, Aug. 2, 1861.
DUNKLIN COUNTY, Operations in, May 16-20, 1862, and capture of the steamer Daniel E. Miller.—Scout in, Aug. 20-27, 1862.—Expeditions from Bloomfield into, March 3-7, 1865.
DUNKSBURG, Affairs near, June 27-28, 1864.
DUTCH HOLLOW, Action at, Oct. 13, 1861.
EDINA, Skirmish at, Aug. 1, 1861.
ELEVEN POINTS, Skirmish at, June 1, 1862.
ELEVEN POINTS RIVER, Skirmish near, Oct. 25, 1862.
ELK CHUTE, Skirmish at, Aug. 4, 1864.
ELK FORK RIVER, Scout on, April —, 1862.
EMINENCE, Skirmish at, June 17, 1862.
ENTERPRISE, Skirmish near, Sept. 15, 1863.—Skirmish near, Aug. 7, 1864.
ETNA, Skirmish at, July 22, 1861.
EUREKA, Boone County, Expedition to, Sept. 23-24, 1862.
FARLEY, Expedition from Fort Leavenworth, Kans., to, June 16-17, 1864.
FARMINGTON, Skirmish at, July 4, 1861.—Raid on, Nov. 25 1863.—Skirmishes at, Sept. 24-25, 1864.—Pursuit of bushwhackers near, April 3, 1865.
FAYETTE, Skirmish near, July 1, 1864.—Skirmish near, Aug. 3, 1864.—Attack on, Sept. 24, 1864.—Skirmish at, Nov. 18, 1864.
FAYETTE ROAD, Skirmish on, near Huntsville, July 16, 1864.
FISH LAKE, Skirmish at, Aug. 19-20, 1861.
FLAT CREEK, Skirmish near, Feb. 15, 1862.
FLORENCE, Skirmish at, July 10, 1863.
FLORIDA, Skirmish on Salt River near, May 31, 1862.—Skirmish at, July 22, 1862.

MISSOURI.

FORSYTH, Skirmish at, July 22, 1861.—Skirmish on White River near, Aug. 4. 1862.—Scout from Ozark to, Aug. 7-9, 1862, and skirmishes.—Expedition from Ozark to, Aug. 14-17, 1862.
FOUR MILE, Skirmish at, Aug. 23, 1862.
FOX CREEK, Skirmish at, March 7, 1862.
FRANKFORT, Scout to, June 5-7, 1862.
FRANKLIN, Skirmish at, Oct. 1, 1864.—Affair at Moselle Bridge near, Dec. 7, 1864.
FREDERICKSBURG, Skirmish near, July 14, 1864.—Action near, July 17, 1864. (Ray County.)—Skirmish at, Aug. 12, 1864.
FREDERICKTOWN, Expedition to, Aug. 16, 1861.—Operations about, Oct. 12-25, 1861.—Skirmish at, April 22, 1863.
FRENCH POINT, Scout from Newtonia to, May 13-18, 1863, and skirmishes.
FULTON, Skirmish at, July 17, 1861.—Expedition to, Oct. 28, 1861.—Skirmish at Moore's Mill near, July 24, 1862.—Action at Moore's Mill near, July 28, 1862.—Scout from, July 25-26, 1864.—Operations in the vicinity of, Nov. 21-30, 1864.
GADFLY, Scout through, April 8, 1862.
GAMBLE, CAMP, Expedition from, in search of guerrillas, Aug. 12-18, 1862.
GARDEN HOLLOW, Skirmish at, near Pineville, Aug. 9, 1863.
GAYOSO, Skirmish at, Aug. 4, 1862.—Skirmish near, Sept. 8, 1864.
GLADEN VALLEY, Scouts from Salem to, Nov. 24-28, 1863.
GLASGOW, Skirmish near, Oct. 14, 1864.—Action at, Oct. 15, 1864.—Skirmish near, Oct. 26, 1864.—Skirmish near, Jan. 10, 1865.
GOLDEN GROVE, Scout from Greenfield to, Aug. 6-9, 1863.
GOUGE'S MILL, Skirmish near, March 26, 1862.
GRANBY, Scout through, April 8, 1862.—Skirmish at, Sept. 24, 1862.—Affair at, Oct. 4, 1862.—Raid by guerrillas on, March 3, 1863.
GRAND RIVER, Skirmish at, Nov. 30, 1861.—Skirmish at, Aug. 1, 1862.
GREENFIELD, Scout from, Sept. 15-18, 1863.—Skirmish at, Oct. 5, 1863.
GREENTON, Expedition from Independence to, Oct. 24-26, 1862.—Affair near, March 30, 1864.—Affair at, Nov. 1, 1864.—Scout from Warrensburg to, Feb. 1-5, 1865.—Skirmish near, March —, 1865.
GREENTON VALLEY, Affair in, near Hopewell, Oct. 21, 1863.—Scout from Warrensburg to the, Nov. 29-Dec. 3, 1864.
GREENVILLE, Skirmish at, July 20, 1862.
GRUNDY COUNTY, Affair at Lindley in, July 15, 1864.
GUM SLOUGH, Expedition from Bloomfield to, March 9-15, 1863, and skirmishes.

MISSOURI.

GUNTER'S MILLS, Scout on the Independence Road to, Aug. 1-3, 1864.
HALCOMB ISLAND, Skirmish at, Feb. 2, 1864.
HALLSVILLE, Skirmish near, Dec. 27, 1861.
HAMBRIGHT'S STATION, Skirmish at, June 18, 1862.
HAMBURG, Expedition to, Aug. 7-10, 1861.—Affair at, Aug. 11, 1861.
HARRISON, Skirmishes at, Sept. 29-Oct. 1, 1864.
HARRISONVILLE, Action at, July 18, 1861.—Skirmishes at, July 25-27, 1861.—Skirmish near, Nov. 3, 1862.—Skirmish near, Oct. 24, 1863.
HARTVILLE, Affair near, Nov. —, 1862.—Garrison of, surrendered to the Confederate forces, Jan. 9, 1863.—Engagement at, Jan. 11, 1863.—Skirmish at, May 23, 1863.—Skirmish at, Aug. 11, 1864.
HAZEL BOTTOM, Skirmish at, Oct. 14, 1862.
HENRY COUNTY, Operations in, March 18-30, 1862.—Expedition from Lexington into, Aug. 28-Sept. 7, 1863.
HENRYTOWN, Action near, Oct. 13, 1861.
HERMANN, Skirmish at, Oct. 3, 1864.
HICKORY GROVE, Expedition from Fort Leavenworth, Kans., to, Aug. 17-27, 1862.—Skirmish at, Sept. 19, 1862.
HIGH GROVE, Skirmish near, July 28, 1863.
HOG ISLAND, Bates County, Affair at, May 18, 1863.
HOLDEN, Operations near, Aug. 2-8, 1864.—Skirmish near, Aug. 12, 1864.
HONEY CREEK, Affair on, Oct. 19, 1863.—Skirmishes on, May 30-31, 1864.
HOPEWELL, Expedition from Independence to, Oct. 24-26, 1862.—Scout from Lexington to vicinity of, Aug. 6-9, 1863.—Skirmishes near, Aug. 25-26, 1863.—Affair in Greenton Valley near, Oct. 21, 1863.
HORNERSVILLE, Expedition from Bloomfield to, March 9-15, 1863, and skirmishes.—Skirmish at, Sept. 20, 1863.—Skirmish near, Sept. 8, 1864.
HORSE CREEK, Skirmish at, May 7, 1862.—Skirmish on, Sept. 17, 1863.
HOUSTON, Scout from Rolla toward, Dec. 18, 1861.—Affair at, Sept. 12, 1863. (Texas County.)—Scouts from, Nov. 23-29, 1863.—Scouts from, Dec. 9-19, 1863.—Scouts from, Nov. 17-27, 1863.—Affair near, Nov. 22, 1863.—Scout from, into Arkansas, Feb. 5-17, 1864, and skirmishes.
HOWARD COUNTY, Skirmish in, Aug. 28, 1862.—Operations in, Aug. 13-22, 1864, and skirmishes.—Scouts in, Sept. 6-12, 1864.—Operations in, Sept. 15-19, 1864.
HOWELL COUNTY, Expedition from Springfield to, Nov. 23-Dec. 18, 1863.
HUMANSVILLE, Action at, March 26, 1862.—Skirmish near, Aug. 12, 1862.—Affair at, Oct. 6, 1863.—Skirmishes at and near, Oct. 16, 1863.

MISSOURI.

HUNNEWELL, Affair at, Aug. 17, 1861.—Skirmish at, Jan. 3, 1862.—Affair at, April 18, 1864.
HUNTER'S FARM, Skirmish at, near Belmont, Sept. 26, 1861.
HUNTSVILLE, Skirmish at, Nov. 9, 1862.—Attack on, July 15, 1864.—Skirmish on Fayette Road near, July 16, 1864.—Skirmish at, July 24, 1864.—Skirmish near, Aug. 7, 1864.—Affair at, Sept. 25, 1864.
HUTTON VALLEY, Skirmish in, Sept. 6, 1863.—Scouts from Waynesville to, March 5-12, 1865.
IBERIA, Expedition toward, Sept. 2, 1861.—Skirmish near, Aug. 29, 1862.
INDEPENDENCE, Skirmish at, Nov. 26, 1861.—Skirmish at, Feb. 22, 1862.—Skirmish near, May 17, 1862.—Action at, and surrender of, by Union forces, Aug. 11, 1862.—Expedition from Fort Leavenworth, Kans., to, Aug. 12-14, 1862.—Skirmish near, Feb. 8, 1863.—Skirmish at Blue Springs near, March 22, 1863.—Confederate attack on steamer Sam. Gaty at, March 28, 1863.—Skirmish at, April 23, 1863.—Skirmish near, Aug. 25, 1863.—Skirmish near, Feb. 19, 1864.—Skirmish at, April 23, 1864.—Skirmishes near, Aug. 1, 1864.—Scout from, into La Fayette County, Aug. 7-8, 1864.—Action at, Oct. 22, 1864.
INDEPENDENCE ROAD, Scout on, to Gunter's Mills, Aug. 1-3, 1864.
INDIAN CREEK VALLEY, Scout through, April 8, 1862.
INMAN HOLLOW, Skirmish at, July 7, 1862.
IRONTON, Operations about, Oct. 12-25, 1861.—Skirmishes at, Sept. 26-27, 1864.
ISLAND, THE, Vernon Co., Skirmish at, March 30, 1863.
ISLAND MOUND, Skirmish at, Oct. 29, 1862.
JACK'S FORK, Skirmish near, Aug. 14, 1863.—Scout from Houston to, Nov. 4-9, 1863.
JACKSON, Skirmish at, June 24, 1861.—Expeditions to, Aug. 28-Sept. 5, 1861.—Reconnoissance from Cape Girardeau to, April 2-4, 1862.—Skirmish at, April 9, 1862.—Skirmish near, April 26, 1863.—Skirmish at, April 27, 1863.—Skirmish at, Sept. 24, 1864.
JACKSON, CAMP, near Saint Louis, Capture of, by Union forces, May 10, 1861.
JACKSON COUNTY, Expedition from Fort Leavenworth, Kans., through, Sept. 8-23, 1862.—Operations in, Nov. 1-5, 1862.—Affair in, April 2, 1863.—Skirmish in, Sept. 15, 1863.—Affairs in, Nov. 26-30, 1862.—Scouts in, Jan. 15-17, 1864.—Scouts in, March 20-30, 1864.—Skirmish in, July 6, 1864.—Operations in, Aug. 25-30, 1864.—Scouts in, Sept. 2-10, 1864.
JAMES CREEK, Affair near, April 27, 1865.
JASPER COUNTY, Expeditions from Greenfield into, Nov. 24-26, 1862.—Scout in, Feb. 19-22, 1863.—Operations in, March 5-13, 1863.—Scout from Creek Agency, Ind. Ter., to,

MISSOURI.

May 6-19, 1863.—Scout from Cassville through Northwestern Arkansas into, May 21-30, 1863.
JEFFERSON CITY, Skirmish at, Oct. 7, 1864.—Skirmish near, Oct. 8, 1864.
JEFFERSON COUNTY, Expeditions through, Sept. 1-3, 1861.
JOHNSON COUNTY, Operations in, Jan. 5-12, 1862.—Operations in, March 18-30, 1862.—Operations in, June 28-29, 1862.—Expedition from Fort Leavenworth, Kans., through, Sept. 8-23, 1862.—Expedition from Lexington into, Aug. 28-Sept. 7, 1863.—Skirmishes in, April 28-30, 1864.—Operations and skirmishes in, July 20-31, 1864.—Operations in, Aug. 11-19, 1864.—Operations in, Sept. 1-9, 1864.—Operations in, May —, 1865.
JOHNSTOWN, Skirmish at, Nov. 24, 1861.—Skirmish at, Oct. 16, 1863.
JOLLIFICATION, Skirmish at, Oct. 3, 1862.
JONESBOROUGH, Skirmishes at, Aug. 21-22, 1861.
KANSAS CITY, Seizure of U. S. ordnance stores at, May 4, 1861.—Operations of guerrillas on Santa Fe Road near, May 21, 1863.—Scout from, June 18-20, 1864.
KEETSVILLE, Barry County, Skirmish at, Feb. 25, 1862.—Operations about, Nov. 17-18, 1862.
KENNETT, Expedition from Bloomfield to, March 9-15, 1863, and skirmishes.
KEYTESVILLE, Skirmish on Chariton Road near, July 30, 1864.—Surrender of, by Union forces, Sept. 20, 1864.—Expedition from Brookfield to, Nov. 16-23, 1864.
KING'S HOUSE, Skirmish at, near Waynesville, Oct. 26, 1863.
KINGSVILLE, Skirmish near, June 12, 1864.—Scout from, May 19-22, 1865.
KIRKSVILLE, Operations around, Aug. 16-21, 1861.—Action at, Aug. 6, 1862.
KLAPSFORD, Skirmish at, Aug. 19, 1861.
KNOBNOSTER, Skirmish at, Jan. 22, 1862.
LACLEDE, Descent upon, June 18-19, 1864.
LACLEDE COUNTY, Scout through, March 4-11, 1862.
LA FAYETTE COUNTY, Operations in, Jan. 5-12, 1862.—Skirmish in, March 10, 1862.—Operations in, June 4-10, 1862.—Expedition from Fort Leavenworth, Kans., through, Sept. 8-23, 1862.—Affairs in, Nov. 26-30, 1862.—Expedition from Lexington into, Aug. 28-Sept. 7, 1863.—Scout in, Sept. 22-25, 1863, with skirmishes.—Scouts in, March 20-30, 1864, with skirmishes.—Operations in, July 20-31, 1864, with skirmishes.—Scout from Independence into, Aug. 7-8, 1864.—Operations in, Aug. 13-30, 1864.—Scout in, Sept. 20-25, 1864.—Skirmish in, Jan. 30, 1865.—Scouts in, Feb. 3-8, 1865.—Scout in, May 8-10, 1865.
LAKE SPRINGS, Skirmish near, Oct. 1, 1864.

MISSOURI.

LAMAR, Skirmish on Coon Creek near, Aug. 24, 1862.—Action at, Nov. 5, 1862.—Skirmish at, May 20, 1864.—Destruction of, by Confederate forces, May 28, 1864.
LA MINE BRIDGE, Affair at, Oct. 10, 1863.
LANCASTER, Skirmish at, Nov. 24, 1861.—Skirmish at, Sept. 7, 1862.
LANE'S PRAIRIE, Maries County, Affair on, May 26, 1864.
LAWRENCE, FORT, Beaver Station, Skirmish at, Jan. 3, 1863.
LEASBURG, Skirmishes at, Sept. 29-Oct. 1, 1864.
LEBANON, Occupation of, by Union forces, Jan. 22, 1862.—Skirmish near, Nov. 1, 1864.—Scouts from Waynesville to, March 5-12, 1865.
LEESVILLE, Skirmish near, March 19, 1862.
LEWIS COUNTY, Operations in, Oct. 11, 1862.
LEXINGTON, Skirmish near, Sept. 12, 1861.—Siege of, Sept. 13-20, 1861.—Surrender of, by Union forces, Sept. 20, 1861.—Descent upon, by Union forces, Oct. 16, 1861.—Expedition to, Dec. 23, 1861.—Skirmish at, Oct. 17, 1862.—Operations about, May 4, 1863.—Skirmish at, July 30, 1863.—Skirmish near, Nov. 4, 1863.—Scout from, Dec. 19-20, 1863.—Skirmish at, Feb. 22, 1864.—Scout from, March 19-22, 1864.—Skirmish near, June 14, 1864.—Skirmish near, Sept. 18, 1864.—Skirmish near, Oct. 17, 1864.—Action at, Oct. 19, 1864.—Skirmish near, Jan. 11, 1865.—Scout from, March 20-22, 1865.—Skirmish at Star House near, May 4, 1865.
LIBERTY, Skirmish at, Oct. 6, 1862.—Skirmish near, July 23, 1864.—Seizure of U. S. Arsenal at, April 20, 1861.
LICKING, Texas County, Expedition from Rolla to, Nov. 5-9, 1864.—Operations about, March 7-25, 1865.—Scouts from, April 1-30, 1865.
LINDLEY, Grundy County, Affair at, July 15, 1864.
LINN CREEK, Affair at, Oct. 14, 1861.—Skirmish near, Oct. 16, 1861.—Skirmish at, Aug. 10, 1862.—Affair near, Jan. 6, 1863.—Skirmish near, April 22, 1865.—Skirmish at, April 25, 1865.
LITTLE BLACK RIVER, Skirmish at Ponder's Mill on, Sept. 20, 1864.
LITTLE BLUE RIVER, Action at, Nov. 11, 1861.—Scout to, May 15-17, 1862.—Skirmish on, June 2, 1862. (Jackson County.)—Skirmish at Taylor's Farm on the, Aug. 1, 1863.—Skirmish near the, July 6, 1864. (Jackson County.)—Scouts on the, in Jackson County, Sept. 2-10, 1864.—Action at the, Oct. 21, 1864.—Affair near the, March 11, 1865.
LITTLE COMPTON, Grand River, Skirmish at, Aug. 11, 1862.
LITTLE NIANGUA, Scout to, April —, 1862.
LITTLE PINEY, Skirmish on, May 14, 1865.
LITTLE RIVER, Expedition from Cairo, Ill., to, June 22-23, 1861.—Expedition to, March 23, 1862.—Skirmish on, in New Madrid County, Dec. 18, 1864.
LITTLE RIVER BRIDGE, Skirmish at, Aug. 31, 1862.

MISSOURI.

LITTLE SANTA FE, Action at, Nov. 6, 1861.—Skirmish at, Nov. 20, 1861.—Skirmish at, March 22, 1862.
LITTLE SNI, Skirmish on the, April 1, 1862.
LIVINGSTON COUNTY, Operations in, July 27-Aug. 4, 1862.
LONE JACK, Action at, Aug. 16, 1862.—Skirmish near, Sept. 1, 1864.—Affair near, March 12, 1865.
LONGWOOD, Skirmish at, Sept. 13, 1864.—Skirmish near, Sept. 22, 1864.—Skirmish on the Blackwater near, May 20, 1865.
LOOKOUT STATION, Attack on railroad train near, Aug. 20, 1861.
LOST CREEK, Skirmish at, April 15, 1862.
LOTSPEICH FARM, Skirmish at, near Wadesburg, July 9, 1862.
LUCAS BEND, Engagements at, Sept. 8-10, 1861.—Reconnoissance from Cairo, Ill., to, Oct. 7, 1861.
McCOURTNEY'S MILLS, on Big Piney, Skirmish near, Jan. —, 1865.
McCULLA'S STORE, Skirmish at, July 26, 1861.—Skirmish at, Aug. 3, 1861.
McKAY'S FARM, Affair at, March 21, 1862.
McKENZIE CREEK, Skirmish at, near Pattersonville, April 15, 1865.
MACON, Skirmish at, Feb. 12, 1864.—Skirmish at, Feb. 12, 1865.
MAN'S CREEK, Shannon County, Skirmish near, Oct. 14, 1863.
MARAIS-DES-CYGNES, Scout on the, April —, 1862.
MARIES COUNTY, Scout in, July 30-Aug. 1, 1864.
MARMITON RIVER, Engagement at, Oct. 25, 1864.
MARSHALL, Skirmish near, March 15, 1862.—Skirmish near, March 16, 1862.—Skirmish at, July 28, 1863.—Skirmish near, July 30, 1863.—Expedition from Sedalia to, Oct. 7-17, 1863.—Action at, Oct. 13, 1863.
MARSHALL AND SEDALIA ROAD, Affair near, June 26, 1864.
MARSHFIELD, Skirmish at, Feb. 9, 1862.—Skirmish near, Oct. 20, 1862.
MARTINSBURG, Skirmish at, July 18, 1861.
MEDICINE CREEK, Skirmish at, April 8, 1862.
MEDOC, Skirmish at, Aug. 23, 1861.
MELVILLE, Raid on, June 14, 1864.
MEMPHIS, Skirmish near, July 18, 1862.
MERRILL'S CROSSING, Skirmish at, near Jonesborough, O t. 12, 1863.
MEXICO, Skirmish at, July 15, 1861.
MIAMI, Operations about, May 25-28, 1862.—Scout to, June 4-5, 1862.—Scout from Warrensburg to, Jan. 12-17, 1865.—Skirmish near, April 24, 1865.
MIDDLE CREEK BRIDGE, Skirmish at, April 24, 1863.
MILFORD, Skirmish at, Dec. 18, 1861.
MILL CREEK, Skirmishes on, May 30-31, 1864.
MILL CREEK BRIDGE, Skirmish at, April 24, 1863.

MISSOURI.

MILLER'S STATION, Affair at, Oct. 3, 1864.
MINERAL POINT, Skirmish at, Sept. 27, 1864.
MINGO SWAMP, Scouts and skirmishes in and about, Feb. 2-13, 1863.
MISSISSIPPI COUNTY, Operations in, Nov. 5-6, 1864.—Skirmish in, Feb. 13, 1865.
MONAGAN SPRINGS, Skirmish at, March 25, 1862.—Skirmi h on the Osage near, April 25, 1862.—Skirmish at, near Osceola, May 27, 1862.
MONDAx HOLLOW, Action at, Oct. 13, 1861.
MONITEAU COUNTY, Expedition into, March 25-28, 1862.—Sco ts in, Sept. 11-18, 1864.
MONROE COUNTY, Skirmish in, Sept. 16, 1862.—Skirm'sh in, Oct. 4, 1862.—Scout in, Oct. 31, 1862.—Operations in, Sept. 11-16, 1864.
MONROE STATION, Skirmishes at and near, July 9-11, 1861.
MONTEVALLO, Vernon County, Scout from Humansville to, April 9-16, 1862.—Skirmish at, April 14, 1862.—Skirmish at, Aug. 5, 1862.—Skirmish near, Aug. 7, 1862.—Affair at, June 12, 1864.—Skirmish near, Oct. 19, 1864.
MONTICELLO BRIDGE, Skirmish at, Sept. 6, 1861.
MOORE'S MILL, Skirmish at, near Fulton, July 24, 1862.—Action at, near Fulton, July 28, 1862.
MOREAU CREEK, Skirmish at, Oct. 7, 1864.
MORGAN COUNTY, Scouts in, Sept. 11-18, 1864.
MORRISTOWN, Skirmish at, Sept. 17, 1861.
MORSE'S MILLS, Skirmish at, Aug. 29, 1861.
MOSELLE BRIDGE, Affair at, near Franklin, Dec. 7, 1864.
MOUNTAIN GROVE, Skirmish at, March 9, 1862.
MOUNTAIN STORE, Skirmishes near, July 25-26, 1862.—Skirmish at, May 26, 1863.
MOUNT VERNON, Expedition to, Feb. 18-19, 1862.—Skirmish at, Sept. 19, 1862.—Scout from, June 19-25, 1864.—Skirmish near, Sept. 2, 1864.
MOUNT ZION CHURCH, Action at, Dec. 28, 1861.
MUSCLE FORK, Chariton River, Skirmish at, Aug. 13, 1862.
NEOSHO, Capture of Union troops at, July 5, 1861.—Scout through, April 8, 1862.—Skirmish at, April 26, 1862.—Skirmish near, May 31, 1862.—Skirmish at, Aug. 21, 1862.—Skirmish at, Sept. 1, 1862.—Skirmish at, Sept. 3, 1862.—Skirmish at, Sept. 5, 1862.—Skirmish at, Dec. 15, 1862.—Skirmish at, March 2, 1863.—Scout near, April 19-20, 1863.—Action at, Oct. 4, 1863.—Scout from, Nov. —, 1863.—Skirmishes at and near, Nov. 4-6, 1863.—Scouts near, May 18-23, 1864.—Skirmish near, June 3, 1864.—Skirmish at, Nov. 10, 1864.
NEWARK, Skirmish near, July 7, 1862.
NEW FRANKFORT, Raid on, June 7, 1864.
NEW FRANKLIN, Skirmish near, Oct. 7, 1862.—Skirmish at, Oct. 13, 1862.

MISSOURI.

NEW MADRID, Occupation of, by Confederate forces, July 28, 1861.—Skirmish near, March 2, 1862.—Siege of, March 3-14, 1862.—Capture of, by Union forces, March 14, 1862.—Evacuation of, by the Union forces, Dec. 28, 1862.—Reoccupation of, by the Union forces, Jan. 2, 1863.—Skirmish at, Aug. 7, 1863.—Scout from Island No. 10, Tenn., to, March 18, 1864.—Expedition from, April 5-9, 1864, and skirmishes in the swamps of Little River, near Osceola, and on Pemiscot Bayou, Ark.—Skirmish near, Dec. 3, 1864.
NEW MADRID COUNTY, Skirmish on Little River in, Dec. 18, 1864.
NEW MARKET, Raid on, June 1, 1864.
NEWTON COUNTY, Operations in, March 5-13, 1863.—Scout from Cassville, through Northwestern Arkansas into, May 21-30, 1863.
NEWTONIA, Scout through, April 8, 1862.—Skirmish near, Aug. 8, 1862.—Skirmish at, Sept. 13, 1862.—Engagement at, Sept. 30, 1862.—Skirmish at, Oct. 4, 1862.—Skirmish at, Oct. 7, 1862.—Skirmish at, Sept. 27, 1863.—Engagement at, Oct. 28, 1864.
NORFOLK, Reconnoissance toward, Sept. 10, 1861, and engagement.—Skirmish near, Sept. 27, 1861.
NORRIS CREEK, Skirmish on, Aug. 8, 1864.
NORTH BLACKWATER RIVER, Scout from Warrensburg to, June 5-9, 1864.
OAK HILLS, Battle of, Aug. 10, 1861.
OAKLIN CHURCH, Scout from Warrensburg to, Feb. 1-5, 1865.
OLD RANDOLPH, Skirmish at, Sept. 14, 1861.
OLIVER'S PRAIRIE, Scout from Newtonia to, July 28-30, 1863.
OREGON, Skirmish at, Oct. 4, 1863.
OREGON COUNTY, Operations in, June 1-5, 1862.—Expeditions from Pilot Knob to, Sept. 29-Oct. 26, 1863.—Scouts in, Nov. 4-19, 1863.—Expedition from Springfield to, Nov. 23-Dec. 18, 1863.
OSAGE, Skirmish at, Nov. 26, 1864.
OSAGE RIVER, Skirmish on, near Monagan Springs, April 25, 1862.—Scout on, and in the vicinity of, June 8-19, 1864.—Skirmishes on, Oct. 5-6, 1864.
OSCEOLA, Skirmish at, and destruction of, by Union forces, Sept. 22, 1861.—Skirmish at Monagan Springs near, May 27, 1862.
OWENSVILLE, Skirmish at, March 31, 1863.
OZARK, Skirmish at, Aug. 1, 1862.—Capture of, by the Confederate forces, Jan. 7, 1863.
OZARK COUNTY, Scout from Forsyth through, June 5-12, 1864.—Operations in, Feb. 6-8, 1865.—Scout in, Feb. 16-20, 1865.

MISSOURI.

OZARK MOUNTAINS, Expedition from Rolla to, Nov. 30-Dec. 6, 1862, and skirmishes.
PALMYRA, Affair at, Aug. 17, 1861.—Execution of rebel citizens at, Oct. 18, 1862.
PANTHER CREEK, Skirmish on, Aug. 8, 1862.
PAPINSVILLE, Skirmish at, Sept. 5, 1861.—Skirmish near, June 23, 1863.
PARIS, Surrender of, by Union forces, Oct. 15, 1864.
PARKERSVILLE, Skirmishes at, July 17-19, 1861.—Skirmish at, Dec. 6, 1862.
PARKVILLE, Attack on, July 7, 1864.
PATTERSON, Skirmish at, April 20, 1863.—Affair at, May —, 1863.—Scout to, Aug. —, 1863.—Scout from, May 6-11, 1864. —Affair at, Sept. 22, 1864.—Expedition from Capt Girardeau to, Nov. 16-25, 1864.—Skirmish at McKenzie's Creek near, April 15, 1865.
PEA RIDGE PRAIRIE, Reconnoissance to and skirmish, Feb. 23-24, 1862.
PEMISCOT COUNTY, Scout in, Oct. 10-12, 1864.—Scout in, Nov. 13-16, 1864, and skirmish.
PERCHE HILLS, Scout from Glasgow to the, March 7-15, 1865.—Skirmish in the, May 5, 1865.
PETTIS COUNTY, Scout in, July 28-31, 1862.
PHELPS COUNTY, Scout in, July 30-Aug. 1, 1864.
PIGEON CREEK, Scouts from Salem to, Nov. 24-28, 1863.
PIKE CREEK, Skirmish near, Oct. 25, 1862.
PILOT KNOB, Expedition from Patterson to, May 16-25, 1864. Attack on Fort Davidson at, Sept. 27, 1864.
PINEVILLE, Skirmish at, June 23, 1862.—Skirmish at, Nov. 19, 1862.—Skirmish at Garden Hollow near, Aug. 9, 1863.— Skirmish at, Aug. 13, 1863.
PINEY RIVER, Affair near headwaters of, Feb. 18, 1864.
PINK HILL, Skirmish at, March 31, 1862.—Scout to, June 10, 1862.—Skirmish at, June 11, 1862.—Operations about, June 23-July 1, 1862.
PISGAH, Skirmish near, Sept. 10, 1864.
PLATTE CITY, Affair at, July 10, 1864.
PLATTE COUNTY, Skirmish in, July 3, 1864.—Scout in, Aug. 25-30, 1864.
PLATTSBURG, Attack on, July 21, 1864.
PLEASANT HILL, Skirmish at, July 8, 1862.—Skirmishes at Sear's House and Big Creek Bluffs near, July 11, 1862.— Skirmish at Big Creek near, May 15, 1863.—Scout from Cold Water Grove to, Sept. 4-7, 1863, and skirmishes.—Skirmish at, May 28, 1864.—Scouts from, June 14-16, 1864.—Skirmish near, Aug. 26, 1864.—Affair near, May 3, 1865.
POINT PLEASANT, Engagement at, March 7, 1862.—Engagement at, March 18, 1862.
POLK COUNTY, Scout in, July 19-23, 1862.—Skirmish in, Aug. 28, 1864.—Skirmish in, Sept. 28, 1864.

MISSOURI.

POMME DE TERRE, Skirmish on, Oct. 13, 1861.
PONDER'S MILL, Little Black River, Skirmish at, Sept. 20, 1864.
POPLAR BLUFF, Occupation of, by Union forces, Feb. —, 1862.—Scout from Cape Girardeau to, Aug. 9-18, 1863.—Affair near, Feb. 27, 1864.—Expedition from Bloomfield to, Jan. 4-16, 1865.
PORTLAND, Affair at, Oct. 16, 1862.
POST OAK CREEK, Skirmish on, March 22, 1862.—Action on, at the mouth of the Brier, March 26, 1862.
POTOSI, Expedition from St. Louis to, May 15, 1861.—Skirmish at, Aug. 10, 1861.
PRAIRIE CHAPEL, Skirmish at, Sept. 4, 1862.
PRESTON, Affair on Big North Fork Creek near, June 16, 1864.
PRICE'S EXPEDITION, Aug. 29-Dec. 2, 1864.
PRICE'S LANDING, Expedition to, Aug. 7-10, 1861.—Attack on the steamer Platte Valley at, Nov. 18, 1861.
PULLIAM'S, Skirmish at, Dec. 25, 1863.
PUTNAM, Skirmish at, Sept. 1, 1862.
QUINCEY, Scout to Shiloh Camp, on Hoyle's Run near, April 9-16, 1862, and skirmishes.—Affair at, Sept. 4, 1863.—Expedition to, Oct. 29-Nov. 8, 1864.
RALLS COUNTY, Operations in, Sept. 11-16, 1864.
RANDOLPH COUNTY, Operations in, July 23-24, 1864.—Operations in, Sept. 15-19, 1864.
RAY COUNTY, Operations in, July 27-Aug. 4, 1862.—Action in, near Fredericksburg, July 17, 1864.—Operations in, Aug. 12-16, 1864.—Scout and skirmishes in, May 26-27, 1865.
RAYTOWN, Skirmish near, June 23, 1862.
READSVILLE, Skirmish near, May 8, 1865.
REEVES'S MILL, Skirmish at, Nov. 19, 1864.
RENICK'S FARM, Scout from Sedalia to, June 10-15, 1864.
REYNOLDS COUNTY, Scouts in, Nov. 4-19, 1863.
RICHFIELD, Clay County, Skirmish near, May 19, 1863.
RICHMOND, Skirmish near, July 8, 1864.
RICHWOOD'S, Skirmish near, Oct. 4, 1864.
RIDDLE'S POINT, Action at, March 17, 1862.
RIDGELEY, Skirmish at, June 11, 1864.—Capture of, by guerrillas, Oct. 16, 1864.
RIPLEY COUNTY, Scout in, from Patterson to Buffalo Creek, July 8-12, 1864.
ROANOKE, Skirmish near, Sept. 6, 1862.—Skirmish near, Sept. 10, 1864.
ROAN'S TAN-YARD, Silver Creek, Action at, Jan. 8, 1862.
ROCHEPORT, Skirmish near, June 1, 1863.—Skirmish near, June 18, 1863.—Skirmish near, Aug. 20, 1864.—Skirmish near, Aug. 28, 1864.—Skirmishes near, Sept. 3, 1864.—Skirmishes near, Sept. 23, 1864.—Skirmish near, May 24, 1865.
ROCKY BLUFF, Platte County, Skirmish at, Aug. 7, 1862.

MISSOURI.

ROLLA, Operations about, March 8-9, 1862.—Union expedition from, Nov. 1-9, 1861.—Scouts from, Feb. 1-March 1, 1864.—Skirmish at, Aug. 1, 1864.—Skirmish at, Nov. 1, 1864. —Scouts from Waynesville to, March 5-12, 1865.—Affair near, March 24, 1865.
ROSE HILL, Expedition from Morristown to, Jan. 1-3, 1862.—Skirmish near, Aug. —, 1864.
ROUND PONDS, Affair at, near Castor River, Aug. 1, 1863.
RUSSELLVILLE, Skirmish at, Oct. 9, 1864.
RUTLEDGE, Skirmish at, Aug. 4, 1864.
SAINT CLAIR COUNTY, Operations in, March 18-30, 1862.
SAINT FRANCIS RIVER, Expedition from Cape Girardeau and Dallas, Mo., to Cherokee Bay, Ark., and the Saint Francis River, Dec. 20, 1864-Jan. 4, 1865, and skirmishes.
SAINT FRANCISVILLE, Reconnoissance to, and skirmish near, Feb. 23-25, 1862.
SAINT FRANCOIS COUNTY, Scout in, and skirmishes, Oct. 9, 1864.
SAINT GENEVIEVE, Expedition to, Aug. 15-16, 1861.
SAINT JAMES, Affair near, June 10, 1864.
SAINT LOUIS, Riot in, May 11, 1861.—Expedition from, to receive the surrender of Gen. M. Jeff Thompson, C. S. Army, April 29-June 11, 1865.
SALEM, Action at, Dec. 3, 1861.—Skirmish at, July 6, 1862.—Skirmish at, Aug. 9, 1862.—Scout from, and skirmish, July 3, 1863.—Attack on, and skirmish near, Sept. 13, 1863.—Scout from, Dec. 26-28, 1863.
SALINE COUNTY, Scout through, Dec. 3-12, 1861.—Operations in, March 7-10, 1862.—Operations in, June 4-10, 1862.—Operations in, July 29-Aug. 2, 1862.—Scout in, Aug. 6-9, 1864.—Operations in, Aug. 13-22, 1864, and skirmishes.—Scout in, May 8-10, 1865.
SALISBURY, Expedition from Brookfield to, Nov. 16-23, 1864.
SALT RIVER, Skirmish on, near Florida, May 31, 1862.
SANTA FE, Skirmishes near, July 24-25, 1862.
SANTA FE ROAD, Skirmish near, April 14, 1862.—Expedition on, May 3, 1863.—Operations of guerillas on, near Kansas City, May 21, 1863.
SARCOXIE PRAIRIE, Skirmish on, Feb. 10, 1863.
SCHUYLER COUNTY, Operations in, Oct. 11, 1862.
SCOTLAND COUNTY, Skirmishes in, Sept. —, 1862.—Operations in, Oct. 11, 1862.
SCOTT'S FORD, Skirmish at, Oct. 14, 1863.—Expedition from Sedalia to, Sept. 2-4, 1864.
SEARS'S FORD, Chariton River, Skirmish at, Aug. 9, 1862.
SEARS'S HOUSE, Skirmish at, July 11, 1862.
SEDALIA, Skirmish near, June 5, 1862.—Skirmish at, April 9, 1863—Scout from, Aug. 25-28, 1863.—Affair at, Oct. 15, 1864.
SEDALIA AND MARSHALL ROAD (See Marshall and Sedalia Road, June 26, 1864).

MISSOURI.

SHANGHAI, Skirmish at, Dec. 1, 1861.—Skirmish near, May 27, 1864.
SHANNON COUNTY, Scout through, April 18, 1863.—Scouts in, Nov. 4-19, 1863.—Scout in, July 18-21, 1864.—Scout in, Jan. 2-7, 1865.
SHELBINA, Action at, Sept. 4, 1861.—Attack on, July 26, 1864.
SHELL'S MILL, Skirmish at, Oct. 16, 1862.
SHERWOOD, Skirmish near, March 9, 1863.—Scout from Fort Scott, Kans., to, May 5-9, 1863, and skirmishes.—Skirmish near, May 18, 1863.—Destruction of, by Union forces, May 19, 1863.—Skirmish near, Aug. 14, 1863.
SHILOH, Skirmish near, April 11, 1862.
SHILOH, CAMP, on Hoyle's Run, near Quincey, Scout to, April 9-16, 1862, and skirmishes.
SHIRLEY'S FORD, Spring River, Skirmish at, Sept. 20, 1862.
SHOAL CREEK, Scout to, Nov. —, 1863.—Skirmish on, in Jasper County, Nov. 18, 1863.
SHUT-IN GAP, Skirmish in, Sept. 26, 1864.
SIBLEY, Operations about, June 23-July 1, 1862.—Skirmish at, Oct. 6, 1862.—Skirmish at, and destruction of, by Union forces, June 23, 1863.
SIKESTON, Skirmish at, March 1, 1862.—Affair at, June 7, 1864.—Skirmish near, Sept. 22, 1864.—Skirmish near, Nov. 6, 1864.
SIM'S COVE, Skirmish at, on Cedar Creek, Oct. 5, 1862.
SINKINK CREEK, Scout on, Aug. 4-11, 1862.—Scout from Salem to, April 18-21, 1863.
SMITHVILLE, Burning of, Oct. 17, 1864.
SNIBAR HILLS, Scout from Warrensburg to the, Jan. 18-22, 1865.
SNI HILLS, Scout in the, Feb. 6-10, 1864.—Skirmish in the, April 29, 1864.
SPRINGFIELD, Battle of, Aug. 10, 1861.—Action at, Oct. 25, 1861.—Skirmish at, Feb. 12, 1862.—Engagement at, Jan. 8, 1863.—Expedition from, into Arkansas and Indian Territory, Sept. 7-19, 1863.—Expedition from, to Huntsville; Carrollton, and Berryville, Ark., Nov. 10-18, 1863.—Expedition from, to Howell, Wright, and Oregon Counties, Nov. 23-Dec. 18, 1863.—Skirmish near, Dec. 16, 1863.
SPRING HILL, Skirmish near, Oct. 27, 1861.—Expedition to, May 24, 1862.
SPRING RIVER, Skirmish at, Sept. 1, 1862.
SPRING VALLEY, Skirmish at, April 23, 1865.
STAR HOUSE, Skirmish at, near Lexington, May 4, 1865.
STATE LINE, Action at, Oct. 22, 1864.
STEELVILLE, Affair at, Aug. 31, 1864.
STEPHENSON'S MILL, Operations about, March 22-23, 1865.
STOCKTON, Cedar County, Skirmish near, Aug. 12, 1862.—Skirmish at, July 11, 1863.—Skirmish at, Oct. 5, 1863.
STOCKTON, Macon County, Skirmish near, Aug. 8, 1862.

MISSOURI.

STODDARD COUNTY, Scout in, Aug. 20-27, 1862.—Scout from Cape Girardeau into, March 9-15, 1865.
STONE COUNTY, Skirmish in, May 9, 1863.
STROTHER FORK OF BLACK RIVER, Iron County, Skirmish on, Sept. 13, 1862.
STUMPTOWN, Skirmish at, Aug. 2, 1863.
STURGEON, Skirmish near, Feb. 27, 1865.
SUGAR CREEK HILLS, Operations in the, Dec. 23-31, 1862.
SWITZLER'S MILL, Skirmish at, Aug. 10, 1862.—Skirmish near, July 12, 1863. (Chariton County.)—Affair at, Feb. 24, 1865.—Skirmish at, May 27, 1865. (Chariton County.)
SYRACUSE, Skirmish near, Oct. 5, 1863.—Skirmish at, Oct. 10, 1863.
TABERVILLE, Skirmish at, July 20, 1862.—Skirmish on Clear Creek near, Aug. 2, 1862.—Skirmish at, Aug. 11, 1862.
TABO CREEK, Scout from Warrensburg to, Feb. 1-5, 1865.
TAOS, Scout to, July 19, 1864.
TAYLOR'S FARM, on the Little Blue, Skirmish at, Aug. 1, 1863.
TEXAS COUNTY, Scout through, Nov. 13-18, 1861.—Scout in, Sept. 14-21, 1864.—Skirmishes in, Jan. 9-11, 1865.
TEXAS PRAIRIE, Skirmish at, Aug. 29, 1863.—Operations on, Sept. 14-21, 1864.—Skirmishes in, Jan. 9-11, 1865. Grover to, Jan. 12-15, 1865.—Scout from Warrensburg to, Feb. 1-5, 1865.
THE ISLAND, Vernon County, Skirmish at, March 30, 1863.
THOMASVILLE, Skirmish at, Sept. 18, 1864.—Scout from Rolla toward, April 21-27, 1865.
TIPTON, Affair at, Oct. 10, 1863.—Attack on, Sept. 1, 1864.
TURKEY CREEK, Jasper County, Skirmish on, Nov. 18, 1863.
TURNBACK CREEK, Skirmish at, April 26, 1862.
TUSCUMBIA, Affair at, Dec. 8, 1864.
TYLER'S MILLS, Big River, Skirmish at, Oct. 7, 1864.
UNDERWOOD'S FARM, near Bird's Point, Skirmish at, Oct. 14, 1861.
UNION, Skirmish at, Oct. 1, 1864.
UNION CHURCH, Skirmish at, July 30, 1864.
UNION MILLS, Skirmish at, Dec. 9, 1861.—Skirmish near, July 22, 1864.
UNIONTOWN, Skirmish at, Oct. 18, 1862.
UPSHAW'S FARM, Barry County, Skirmish at, Oct. 29, 1864.
VALLEY MINES, Skirmish at, May 22, 1865.
VAN BUREN, Skirmish at, Aug. 12, 1862.—Skirmish near, Oct. 22, 1862.
VERA CRUZ, Skirmish at, Nov. 3, 1864.
VERNON COUNTY, Operations in, Oct. 3-7, 1863.
VERSAILLES, Affair at, July 13, 1864.
WADESBURG, Skirmish at, Dec. 24, 1861.—Skirmish at Lotspeich Farm near, July 9, 1862.
WAGON KNOB, Scout from Warrensburg to, Feb. 1-5, 1865.

MISSOURI

WALKERSVILLE, Skirmish near, April 2, 1862.
WALNUT CREEK, Skirmish at, Aug. 9, 1862.
WARDER'S CHURCH, Skirmish at, July 10, 1864.
WARRENSBURG, Skirmish at, Oct. 18, 1861.—Affair near, Nov. 18, 1861.—Skirmish near, April 8, 1862.—Skirmish near, June 17, 1862.—Skirmish near, Sept. —, 1862.—Operations about, Feb. 22-24, 1864.—Scout from, May 23-25, 1864.—Skirmish at, May 28, 1864.—Scout from, to the North Blackwater River, June 5-9, 1864.—Skirmish on the Clear Fork near, July 16, 1864.—Expedition from, to Chapel Hill, July 29-Aug. 2, 1864.—Affair on Warrensburg Road near, Sept. 9, 1864.—Scout from, to the Greenton Valley, Nov. 29-Dec. 3, 1864.—Scout from, to Miami, Jan. 12-17, 1865.—Scout from, to the Snibar Hills, Jan. 18-22, 1865.—Scouts from, to Wagon Knob, Big Grove, Greenton, Texas Prairie, Tabo Creek, Dover, Oaklin Church, and Davis' Creek, Feb. 1-5, 1865.—Scout from, to Columbus, March 19-23, 1865, with skirmish near Greenton.—Scout from, to mouth of Coal Camp Creek, May 23-26, 1865.
WARRENSBURG ROAD, Affair on, near Warrensburg, Sept. 9, 1864.
WARRENTON, Skirmish near, Oct. 29, 1864.
WARSAW, Destruction of U. S. stores at, Nov. 21, 1861.—Skirmish near, April 8, 1862.—Skirmish at, April 17, 1862.—Skirmish at, April 28, 1862.—Skirmish near, Oct. 7, 1863.—Affair near, Oct. 29, 1863.—Scout from Lebanon to, May 18-20, 1865.
WASHINGTON, Occupation of, by Confederate forces, Oct. 2, 1864.
WASHINGTON COUNTY, Attack on Webster in, July 19, 1864.
WAVERLY, Operations about, May 25-28, 1862.—Scout to, June 8-9, 1862.—Affair at, June 1, 1863.
WAYMAN'S MILL, on Spring Creek, Skirmish near, Aug. 23, 1862.
WAYNE COUNTY, Scout in, Aug. 20-27, 1862.—Skirmish in, April 26, 1864.—Scout from Cape Girardeau into, March 9-15, 1865.
WAYNESVILLE, Skirmish near, May 31, 1862.—Expeditions from, Aug. 29-Sept. —, 1862.—Scouts from, June 20-23, 1863.—Skirmish near, Aug. 25, 1863.—Skirmish at King's House near, Oct. 26, 1863.—Scout in the vicinity of, Nov. 25, 1863.—Skirmish at, Sept. 30, 1864.—Skirmish on the Big Piney near, Nov. 1, 1864.—Operations in the vicinity of, Dec. 1-3, 1864.—Operations about, Jan. 16-22, 1865, including skirmish near McCourtney's Mills, on Big Piney.—Scouts from, to Hutton Valley, Rolla, and Lebanon, March 5-12, 1865.—Scout from, March 29-April 2, 1865.—Skirmish near, May 23, 1865.

MISSOURI—MONTANA—NEBRASKA.

WEBSTER, Washington County, Attack on, July 19, 1864.—Affair at, Aug. 23, 1864.
WELLINGTON, Affair near, June 17, 1863.—Skirmish near, Aug. 14, 1863.—Operations in the vicinity of, July 9-13, 1864.
WENTZVILLE, Skirmishes at, July 15-17, 1861.
WESTERN MISSOURI, Operations in, July 6-30, 1864.
WESTON, Scout from Fort Leavenworth, Kans., to, June 13-16, 1864.
WEST PLAINS, Skirmish at, Feb. 19, 1862.
WESTPORT, Skirmish near, June 17, 1863.—Engagement at, Oct. 23, 1864.
WET GLAZE, Action at, Oct. 13, 1861.
WHALEY'S MILL, Skirmish near, Sept. 13, 1862.
WHITE HARE, Skirmish near, June 15, 1864.
WHITE OAK RIDGE, Skirmish at, Aug. 18, 1862.
WHITE RIVER, Skirmish on, near Forsyth, Aug. 4, 1862.—Scout from Linden to, April 1-5, 1863.—Skirmish on, April 17, 1863.
WHITEWATER, Reconnoissance from Cape Girardeau to, April 2-4, 1862.
WHITE WATER BRIDGE, Skirmish near, April 27, 1863.
WILSON'S CREEK, Battle of, Aug. 10, 1861.
WOOD CREEK, Skirmish at, Jan. 11, 1863.
WOODSON, Skirmish near, Nov. 26, 1863.
WRIGHT COUNTY, Scout through, Nov. 13-18, 1861.—Scout through, March 4-11, 1862.—Expedition from Springfield to, Nov. 23-Dec. 18, 1863, Skirmish in, July 22, 1864.
YELLOW CREEK, Skirmish on, Aug. 13, 1862.
YOCUM CREEK, Skirmish at, Nov. 15, 1862.

MONTANA.

POWDER RIVER, Skirmish at, Sept. 1, 1865.—Skirmish at, Sept. 2, 1865.—Skirmish at, Sept. 4, 1865.—Engagement at, Sept. 5, 1865.—Skirmish at, Sept. 7, 1865.—Engagement at, Sept. 8, 1865.

NEBRASKA.

COTTONWOOD, Scout from, May 12-14, 1865.
COTTONWOOD, FORT, Skirmish near, Sept. 20, 1864.
DAKOTA CITY, Scout from, April 12-16, 1865.
KEARNEY, FORT, Skirmish with Indians near, May 18, 1865.—Scout from, May 19-26, 1865.
LITTLE BLUE RIVER, Scout from Fort Kearney to, May 19 to June 12, 1865.
MIDDLE BOW RIVER, Scout from Dakota City to, April 22-27, 1865.
MIDWAY STATION, Scout from Plum Creek to, May 8-20, 1865.

NEBRASKA—NEVADA—NEW MEXICO.

MUD SPRINGS, Action at, Feb. 4-6, 1865.
MULLAHLA'S STATION, Attack on wagon train near, May 5, 1865.
NIOBRARA, Skirmish with Indians at, Dec. 4, 1863.
NIOBRARA RIVER, Expedition to, June 12-July 5, 1865.
OVERLAND STAGE ROAD, Operations against Indians on, May 26-June 14, 1865.
PAWNEE AGENCY, Attack on, June 23, 1863.
PLUM CREEK, Skirmish near, Dec. 8, 1864.—Scout from, May 26-27, 1865.
RUSH CREEK, Action on the North Platte River near, Feb. 8-9, 1865.
SAINT MARY'S STATION, Skirmish with Indians at. May 27, 1865.
SMITH'S STATION, Skirmish at, May 12, 1864.
SWEETWATER RIVER, Operations against Indians on, May 26-June 9, 1865.
SWEETWATER STATION, Attack on, by Indians, April 3, 1863.—Skirmish at, May 26, 1865.—Skirmish with Indians at, May 28, 1865.—Skirmish with Indians at, June 1, 1865.

NEVADA.

AUSTIN, Skirmish near, May 29, 1865.
CANNON STATION, Affair at, June 23, 1863.
CARSON LAKE, Expedition from Fort Churchill to, May 3-June 15, 1865.
FAIRBANK'S STATION, Expedition from Dun Glen to, June 13-26, 1865.
HUMBOLDT RIVER, Affair on, Oct. 11, 1862.—Affair on, Oct. 15, 1862.—Expedition from Fort Churchill to, June 8-Aug. 9, 1864.—Expeditions from Fort Churchill to, May 3-June 15, 1865.
MUD LAKE, Skirmish at, March 14, 1865.
PYRAMID LAKE, Expedition from Fort Churchill to, March 12-19, 1865.
SIERRA NEVADA MOUNTAINS, Expedition from Fort Ruby to, Nov. 22-27, 1862.
TRUCKEE RIVER, Expedition from Fort Churchill to, May 3-June 15, 1865.
WALKER'S LAKE, Expedition from Fort Churchill to, March 12-19, 1865.—Affair near, March 16, 1965.

NEW MEXICO.

ADOBE FORT, on the Canadian River, Engagement with Indians at, Nov. 25, 1864.
AGUA FRIA, Operations about, March 31-April 1, 1865.

NEW MEXICO.

ALBUQUERQUE, Evacuation of, by Union forces, March 2-4, 1862.—Skirmish at, April 8, 1862.
APACHE CANON, Skirmish at, March 26, 1862.—Skirmish at, July 15, 1862.
APACHE PASS, Skirmish at, April 25, 1863.
BONITA, RIO, Skirmish on the, March 27, 1863.
BRECKINRIDGE, FORT, Abandoned by Union forces, July 10, 1861.
BUCHANAN, FORT, Abandoned by Union forces, July 23, 1861.
CAJOUDE ARIVAYPO, Skirmish at, May 7, 1863.
CANADA ALAMOSA, Skirmish at, Sept. 25, 1861.
CANADIAN RIVER, Expedition from Fort Union to, Oct. 9-Nov. 25, 1862.—Engagement with Indians at Adobe Fort on, Nov. 25, 1864.
CIMARRON RIVER, Scout on the, Sept. 18-Oct. 5, 1864.
COMANCHE PASS, Skirmish at, March 3, 1862.
CONCHAS SPRINGS, Skirmish with Indians at, July 29, 1863.
COOK'S CANON, Skirmish with Indians at, July 10, 1863.—Skirmish with Indians at, July 24, 1863.
CRAIG, FORT, Skirmish near, Aug. 23, 1861.—Affair near, May 23, 1862.—Skirmish with Indians near, July 4, 1863.
CUBERO, Capture of, by Confederate forces, March 3, 1862.
CUMMINGS, FORT, Scout from, April 28-May 13, 1865.
DOUBTFUL CANON, Skirmish in, May 4, 1864.
FILLMORE, FORT, Abandoned by Union forces, July 26, 1861.
GILA RIVER, Skirmish on, Nov. —, 1863.
GLORIETA, Engagement at, March 28, 1862.
JACOB'S WELL, Scout from Fort Wingate to, Sept. 15-Oct. 5, 1863.
JORNADA DEL MUERTO, Skirmish on the, June 16, 1863.
McLANE, FORT, Abandoned by Union forces, July 3, 1861.
MESILLA, Skirmish at, July 25, 1861.
MIMBRES, CAMP, Scout from, Feb. 24-29, 1864.
NAVAJO INDIANS, Operations against, July 7-Dec. 16, 1863. —Expedition against, Jan. 6-21, 1864.
NICHOLS, CAMP, Scout from, June 13-17, 1865.
OJO DE ANAYA, Scout from, May 1-9, 1865.
OJO REDONDO, Scout from Fort Wingate to, Sept. 15-Oct. 5, 1863.
OSCURA MOUNTAINS, Scout from Fort Sumner to, June 15-22, 1865.
PARAJE, Affair at, May 21, 1862.
PECOS RIVER, Skirmish on, near Fort Sumner, Jan. 5, 1864.
PERALTA, Skirmish at, April 15, 1862.
PIGEON'S RANCH, Engagement at, March 28, 1862.
PINOS ALTOS MINES, Skirmish at, Jan. 29, 1863.
PUEBLO COLORADO, Skirmish with Indians at, Aug. 18, 1863.

NEW MEXICO—NEW YORK.

RED RIVER, Skirmish on, Dec. 1, 1864.
RIO BONITA, Skirmish on, March 27, 1863.
RIO DE LAS ANIMAS, Skirmish with Indians on, July 19, 1863.
RIO HONDO, Skirmish with Indians on, July 18, 1863.
ROBLEDO, CAMP, Operations against Indians from, Sept. 30-Oct. 7, 1861.
SACRAMENTO MOUNTAINS, Skirmish at, Aug. 26, 1864.—Scout in the, Oct. 13-21, 1864.
SAN ANDRES MOUNTAINS, Affair in, Jan. 26, 1864.—Affair in, Aug. 12, 1864.
SAN AUGUSTINE SPRINGS, Surrender of Union forces at, July 27, 1861.
SANTA FE, Abandoned by Union forces, March 4, 1862.
SANTA FE ROAD, Action on, June 14, 1865.
SIERRA BONITO, Skirmish at the foot of the, April 7, 1864.—Skirmish at the foot of the, April 15, 1864.
SIERRA DEL DATIL, Scouts from Fort Wingate to, Jan. 2-10 and 11-21, 1865.
SOCORRO, Affair at, April 25, 1862.
SOUTHWESTERN NEW MEXICO, Expedition to, July 23-Oct. 10, 1864.
SPENCER'S RANCH, near Presidio del Norte, Skirmishes at, April 7 and 15, 1864.
STANTON, FORT, Abandoned by Union forces, Aug. 2, 1861.—Operations against Indians about, Aug. 25-Sept. 8, 1861.—Scout from, April 12-25, 1865.
SUMNER, FORT, Scouts from, Aug. 3-Nov. 4, 1864.—Scout from, March 15-21, 1865.—Scout from, May 10-19, 1865.
THORN, FORT, Skirmish near, Sept. 26, 1861.
UNION, FORT, Expedition from, to the Canadian River and Utah Creek, Oct. 9-Nov. 25, 1862.—Scout from, Aug. 4-Sept. 15, 1864.
UTAH CREEK, Expedition from Fort Union to, Oct. 9-Nov. 25, 1862.
VALVERDE, Engagement at, Feb. 21, 1862.
WINGATE, FORT, Expedition from, against Indians, Nov. 23-Dec. 10, 1864.—Scouts from, to Sierra del Datil, Jan. 2-10 and 11-21, 1865.

NEW YORK.

NEW YORK CITY, Draft riots in, July 13-16, 1863.
TROY, Draft riots in, July 13-16, 1863.

NORTH CAROLINA.

NORTH CAROLINA.

Seceded May 20, 1861.

ALBEMARLE, C. S. S., Engagement with, May 5, 1864.
ALBEMARLE SOUND, Operations in, May 4-6, 1864.
ANDERSON, FORT, Attack on, March 14, 1863.—Action at, Feb. 18, 1865.—Capture of, by Union forces, Feb. 19, 1865.
ASHVILLE, Expedition to, April 3-11, 1865.
AVERASBOROUGH, Battle of, March 16, 1865.—Skirmish at, March 17, 1865.
BATCHELDER'S CREEK, Skirmish at, April 29, 1862.—Skirmish at, Feb. 10, 1863.—Expedition from, Feb. 12-13, 1863.—Skirmish at, May 23, 1863.—Skirmish at, Feb. 1-3, 1864.
BEACON ISLAND, Expedition to, Sept. 16, 1861.
BEAR INLET, Destruction of Confederate salt works on, Dec. 25, 1863.—Expdition to, March 25-26, 1864.
BEAUFORT, Occupation of, March 25, 1862.—Expedition from, to Port Royal, S. C., Jan. 29, 1863.
BEAVER CREEK, Skirmish at, April 17, 1864.
BEECH GROVE, Action at, Feb. 2, 1864.
BENNETT'S HOUSE, near Durham Station, Surrender of Gen. Joseph E. Johnston's army to Gen. William T. Sherman, April 26, 1865.
BENTON'S CROSS ROADS, Skirmish near, March 18, 1865.
BENTONVILLE, Action at, March 18, 1865.—Battle of, March 19-21, 1865.
BEST'S STATION, Skirmish at, April 13, 1865.
BEULAH, Skirmish near, April 11, 1865.
BIG SWIFT CREEK, Skirmish at, April 19, 1863.
BLACK JACK CHURCH, Skirmish near, March 26, 1864.
BLACK RIVER, Reconnoissance from Fayetteville, on the Goldsborough Road, to, March 14, 1865.—Skirmish on, near Smith's Mills, March 15, 1865.
BLOUNT'S CREEK, Action at, April 9, 1863.—Affair near, April 5, 1864.
BOGUE INLET, Expedition to, March 25-26, 1864.
BOGUE SOUND BLOCK HOUSE, Skirmish at, Feb. 2, 1864.
BOONE, Skirmish at, March 28, 1865.—Skirmish at, April 1, 1865.
BOONEVILLE, Skirmish at, April 10, 1865.—Action near, March 27, 1865.
BUSHY SWAMP, Skirmish at, March 18, 1865.
BUTCHER'S BRIDGE, Skirmish at, Dec. 12, 1864.
CAMDEN COUNTY, Expedition from Kempsville, Va., to, Aug. 5-12, 1863.
CAMDEN COURT HOUSE, Skirmish near, Oct. 17, 1863.—Expedition from Norfolk, Va., to, Dec. 5-24, 1863.

NORTH CAROLINA.

CAPE FEAR RIVER, Engagement on, Oct. 11, 1862.—Actions at, Dec. 15, 1864, and April 15, 1865.—Reconnoissance to entrances of the, Nov. 13-14, 1863.—Boat expedition into, March 4-12, 1865.—Naval reconnoissance in, March 7-9, 1865.
CAPE LOOKOUT LIGHT, Destruction of, April 2, 1864.
CASWELL, FORT, Seizure of, by citizens of Smithville and Wilmington, Jan. 10, 1861.—Seizure of, by State troops, April 16, 1861.—Engagement at, Feb. 23, 1863.—Naval affair near, June 2, 1864.—Blown up, by Confederate forces, Jan. 16-17, 1865.
CATAWBA RIVER, Action at, near Morganton, April 17, 1865. —Skirmishes on, March 1-2 and April 19, 1865.
CEDAR POINT, Expedition from Newport Barracks to, March 7-10, 1863.—Reconnoissance from Newport Barracks to, July 13-16, 1863.—Skirmish at, Dec. 1, 1863.
CHAPPEL HILL, Skirmish near, April 15, 1865.
CHEROKEE COUNTY, Skirmish in, Oct. 27, 1863.
CHICAMACOMICO, Affair at, Oct. 4, 1861.
CHICOA CREEK, Expedition from Washington to, Dec. 17, 1863.
CHINCOPIN CREEK, Skirmish at, Dec. 16, 1863.
CHINCOTEAGUE INLET, Naval affair in, Oct. 5, 1861.— Naval expedition from, to Swann's Big Creek, Oct. 27, 1861.
CHOWAN RIVER, Reconnoissance down, June 5-7, 1863.— Expedition up, Nov. 4-9, 1863.—Naval expedition from Plymouth up, March 1-5, 1864.—Expedition up, July 28-30, 1864.
CLINTON, Skirmish at, May 19, 1862.
COBB'S POINT, Naval engagement with batteries at, Feb. 9, 1862.
CORE CREEK, Skirmish at, Nov. 18, 1862.—Skirmish at, March 7, 1863.—Skirmish at, April 17-18, 1863, and April 20 and May 22, 1863.—Scout from Rocky Run to, June 17-18, 1863.
COX'S BRIDGE, Neuse River, Skirmishes at and near, March 19-20, 1865.—Skirmish at, March 23, 1865.
CROATON, Surrender of Union outpost at, May 5, 1864.
CURRITUCK CANAL, Naval expedition to, Feb. 13, 1862.
CURRITUCK COUNTY, Expedition from Kempsville, Va., to, Aug. 5-12, 1863.
CURRITUCK SOUND, Expedition into, Feb. 19-20, 1862.
DALLAS, Skirmish near, April 19, 1865.
DANBURY, Skirmish near, April 9, 1865.
DEEP CREEK, Action at, Feb. 2, 1864.—Skirmish on, Feb. 5, 1864.
DEEP GULLY, Skirmish at, March 31, 1862.—Skirmish near, May 2, 1862.—Skirmish at, March 13-14, 1863.—Skirmish near, March 30, 1863.
DIXIE, FORT (See Neuse River, March 13-14, 1862).
DOVER, Skirmish near, March 7, 1863.—Scout from Rocky Run to, June 17-18, 1863.

NORTH CAROLINA.

DOVER ROAD, Reconnoissances on, Jan. 27-28, 1863.—Skirmish on, April 28, 1863.
DUDLEY STATION, Raid on, Dec. 17, 1862.
DURHAM STATION (See Bennett's House, April 26, 1865).
EAGLE ISLAND, Skirmish at, Feb. 21, 1865.
EDENTON, Reconnoissance from Norfolk, Va., to, May 27-31, 1862.—Naval expedition to, Feb. 11-12, 1862.—Boat expedition to, June 8, 1864.—Skirmish near, Feb. 7, 1863, and Feb. 10, 1863.—Expedition from Portsmouth, Va., to, Aug. 11-19, 1863, and skirmishes.—Action at, Oct. 9, 1864.—Expedition from New Berne to, Oct. 10-17, 1863.
ELBOW CROSS ROADS, Skirmish near, March 26, 1865.
ELIZABETH CITY, Action at, Feb. 10, 1862.—Expedition to, April 7-8, 1862.—Naval expeditions to, May 12-17, 1862, and Sept. 10-11, 1864.—Skirmish at, Dec. 27, 1862.—Expedition from New Berne to, Oct. 10-17, 1863.
ELLIS, FORT (See Neuse River, March 13-14, 1862).
EVANS'S MILLS, Occupation of, April 5, 1862.—Action near, Feb. 2, 1864.
EVERETTSVILLE, Affair at, Dec. 17, 1862.—Skirmish near, Feb. 20, 1865.
FAIRFIELD, Skirmish near, March 3, 1863.—Affair at, Feb. 16, 1864.
FALLING CREEK, Skirmish at, March 17, 1865.—Skirmish near, March 20, 1865.
FAYETTEVILLE, Skirmish at, March 11, 1865.—Skirmish near, March 13, 1865.—Seizure of U. S. Arsenal at, by State troops, April 22, 1861.
FISHER, FORT, Expedition to, and operations against, Dec. 7-27, 1864.—Expedition to, and capture of, and its dependencies, Jan. 3-17, 1865.—Skirmish near, Jan. 13, 1865.—Naval bombardment of, Jan. 13, 1865.—Combined naval and military operations against, Jan. 13-15, 1865.—Assault on, and capture of, Jan. 15, 1865.—Explosion of magazine at, Jan. 16, 1865.—Skirmish at, Feb. 8, 1865.
FORD'S MILL, near New Berne, Affair at, Oct. 30, 1863.
FOSTER'S BRIDGE, Skirmish at, Dec. 10, 1864.
FOSTER'S MILLS, Expedition from Plymouth to, July 26-29, 1863.
FOY'S PLANTATION, Skirmish at, April 7, 1862.
FREE BRIDGE, near Trenton, Skirmish at, July 6, 1863.—Skirmish at, Dec. 16, 1863.
GALES'S CREEK, Skirmish at, Feb. 2, 1864.
GARDNER'S BRIDGE, Expedition from Plymouth to, July 5-7, 1863.
GATES COUNTY, Reconnoissance through, June 5-7, 1863.—Naval expedition to, May 6-8, 1862.
GATESVILLE, Expedition from Roanoke Island toward, May 7-8, 1862.
GILLETT'S FARM, Pebbly Run, Skirmish at, April 13, 1862.

NORTH CAROLINA.

GOLDSBOROUGH, Expedition from New Berne to, Dec. 11-20, 1862.—Skirmish at Neuse River Bridge near, March 19, 1865.—Occupation of, by Union forces, March 21, 1865.—Skirmish near, April 2, 1865.—Skirmishes at, March 23, 24, 25, 27, 29, April 8, 9 and 10, 1865.
GOLDSBOROUGH AND WILMINGTON RAILROAD, Affairs on, Dec. 16-17, 1862.
GOLDSBOROUGH BRIDGE, Engagement at, Dec. 17, 1862.
GOLDSBOROUGH ROAD, Reconnoissance from Fayetteville, on the, to Black River, March 14, 1865, and skirmish.
GOSHEN SWAMP, Affair at, Dec. 16, 1862.
GRANT'S CREEK, Skirmish at, near Salisbury, April 12, 1865.
GREENVILLE, Occupation of, July 19, 1863.—Skirmish near, Nov. 25, 1863.—Action at, Dec. 20, 1863.—Skirmish near, Dec. 30, 1863.
GREENVILLE ROAD, Action on, May 31, 1862.
GULLEY'S, Skirmish at, March 31, 1865.
GUM SWAMP, Skirmish at, May 22, 1863.—Scout from Camp Palmer to, Oct. 11-13, 1864.
HALF MOON BATTERY, Skirmish at, Jan. 19, 1865.
HALL'S BRIDGE, Action near, July 26, 1863.
HAMILTON, Capture of, by Union forces, July 9, 1862.—Naval expedition to, Nov. 2-9, 1862.
HANNAH'S CREEK, Skirmish at, March 22, 1865.
HARRELLSVILLE, Skirmish at, Jan. 20, 1864.
HATTERAS INLET, Capture of Confederate batteries at, Aug. 28-29, 1861.—Naval action in, Oct. 5, 1861.—Naval action in, Nov. 14, 1861.
HENDERSONVILLE, Action near, April 23, 1865.
HERTFORD, Skirmish at, Dec. 10, 1863.—Naval expedition to, Jan. 30, 1863.—Expedition from Portsmouth, Va., to, Dec. 6-10, 1864.
HILL'S POINT, Pamlico River, Engagement at, April 2, 1863.—Affair at, April 16, 1863.—Affair at, March 31, 1863.—Actions at, April 5-7, 1863.
HOOKERTON, Skirmish at, March 31, 1865.
HOUGHTON'S MILL, Pollocksville Road, Skirmish near, April 27, 1862, and skirmish at, May 15, 1862.
HOWARD'S GAP, Blue Ridge Mountains, Skirmish at, April 22, 1865.
INDIANTOWN, Expedition from Great Bridge, Va., to, Sept. 15-19, 1863.—Skirmish at, Sept. 20, 1863.—Scout from Great Bridge to, Oct. 13, 1863.—Skirmish at, Dec. 18, 1863.
JACKSON, Expedition from Portsmouth, Va., to, July 25-Aug. 3, 1863.
JACKSON'S MILLS, Action at, June 22, 1864.—Skirmish at, March 7, 1865.
JACKSONVILLE, Skirmish near, Jan. 20, 1863.—Occupation of, by Union naval forces, Nov. —, 1862.—Expedition from Newport Barracks to, Dec. 27-29, 1863.

NORTH CAROLINA.

JAMESVILLE, Naval reconnoissance to, Jan. 29, 1863.—Naval action at, Dec. 10, 1864.
JOHNSTON, FORT, Seizure of, by citizens of Smithville, Jan. 9, 1861.—Seizure of, by State troops, April 16, 1861.
KENANSVILLE, Skirmish at, July 5, 1863.
KINNEKEET, Naval action at, Oct. 15, 1861.
KINSTON, Engagement at, Dec. 14, 1862.—Skirmish near, Jan. 25, 1863.—Demonstration on, March 6-8, 1863.—Expedition from New Berne toward, April 16-21, 1863.—Expedition from New Berne toward, April 27-May 1, 1863.—Demonstrations on, May 20-23, 1863.—Scout from New Berne to, Dec. 5, 1863.—Expedition from Batchelder's Creek to the vicinity of, June 20-23, 1864.—Skirmish at, June 28, 1864.—Battle of, March 8-10, 1865.—Occupation of, by Union forces, March 14, 1865.
KINSTON ROAD, Skirmishes on the, Dec. 11-12, 1862.
LAUREL VALLEY, Expedition from Greenville, Tenn., to, April 6-11, 1862.
LITTLE COHERA CREEK, Skirmish at, March 16, 1865.
LITTLE CREEK, Skirmish at, Nov. 2, 1862.
LITTLE RIVER, Naval expeditions into, Jan. 4-6, 1863; Jan. 7, 1864; Feb. 4-6, 1865.
LOCKWOOD'S FOLLY INLET, Affair at, Jan. 4, 1864.—Affair at, Jan. 11, 1864.
LOGGERHEAD INLET, Capture of U. S. S. Fanny in, Oct. 1, 1861.
MACON, FORT, Seizure of, by State troops, April 15, 1861.—Siege of, March 23-April 26, 1862.—Capture of, by Union forces, April 26, 1862.
MAGNOLIA STATION, Skirmish near, April 1, 1865.
MANNING'S NECK, Expedition from New Berne to, July 28-31, 1864.
MARTINSVILLE, Action at, April 8, 1865.
MASONBOROUGH INLET, Destruction of salt-works at, April 21, 1864.—Affairs at, April 27-29, 1864.—Naval actions in, Jan. 16-17, 1863.—Naval operations near, Feb. 1-10, 1864.
MATTAMUSKEET, LAKE, Expedition from New Berne to, March 7-14, 1863.
MILL CREEK, Skirmish at, near Pollocksville, July 26, 1862.—Skirmish at, March 22, 1865.
MINGO CREEK, Skirmish at, March 18, 1865.
MOCCASIN CREEK, Skirmish near, March 24, 1865.
MOCCASIN SWAMP, Skirmish at, April 10, 1865.
MOCKSVILLE, Skirmish at, April 11, 1865.
MOREHEAD CITY, Occupation of, March 22, 1862.
MORGANTON, Action on the Catawba River near, April 16-17, 1865.
MORRISVILLE, Skirmish at, April 13, 1865.—Skirmish near, April 14, 1865.

NORTH CAROLINA.

MOSELEY HALL, Skirmish near, March 29, 1865.—Skirmish at, March 20, 1865.—Skirmish near, April 2, 1865.
MOUNT OLIVE STATION, Affair at, Dec. 16, 1862.
MURFREE'S DEPOT, Expedition from Suffolk, Va., to, March 10-11, 1865.
MURPHY, Expedition from Motley's Ford, Tenn., to, and vicinity, Feb. 17-22, 1864.—Skirmish near, Aug. 2, 1864.
MYRTLE SOUND, Reconnoissance to, Jan. 19, 1865.
NAHUNTA STATION, Skirmish near, April 10, 1865.
NEUSE RIVER, Naval operations on, Dec. 12-15, 1862.—Actions with batteries on, March 13-14, 1862. (Fort Dixie, Fort Ellis.)—Naval operations on, Dec. 12-20, 1862.—Affair on, Feb. 2, 1864.—Skirmishes at and near Cox's Bridge on, March 19-20, 1865.—Skirmish at Cox's Bridge on, March 23, 1865.—Destruction of U. S. transports on, April 5-7, 1865.—Skirmishes near, April 10 and May 10, 1865.
NEUSE RIVER BRIDGE, Skirmish at, near Goldsborough, March 19, 1865.
NEUSE RIVER ROAD, Expedition on, from Batchelder's Creek, July 28, 1862.—Reconnoissances on, Jan. 27-28, 1863.
NEW BERNE, Battle of, March 14, 1862.—Skirmish near, May 22, 1862.—Expedition from, Nov. 1-12, 1862.—Reconnoissance from, to Pollocksville, Trenton, Young's Cross Roads, and Onslow, Jan. 17-21, 1863.—Skirmish near, Feb. 27, 1863.—Expedition from, to Trenton, Pollocksville, Young's Cross Roads, and Swansborough, March 6-10, 1863.—Expedition against, March 8-16, 1863.—Action near, March 14, 1863.—Affair at Ford's Mill near, Oct. 30, 1863.—Expedition against, Jan. 28-Feb. 10, 1864.—Skirmish at, Feb. 29, 1864.—Operations about, May 4-6, 1864.
NEW INLET, Naval actions near, Aug. 23 and Oct. 21, 1863.--Naval engagement in, May 6, 1864.
NEWPORT, Skirmish near, April 7, 1862.
NEWPORT BARRACKS, Skirmish at, Feb. 2 and 3, 1864.—Skirmish near, Feb. 6, 1864.
NEW RIVER INLET, Naval operations in, and occupation of Jacksonville, by Union naval forces, Nov. 23-24, 1862.
NEW TOPSAIL INLET, Naval reconnoissance in, and engagement with batteries, Aug. 22, 1863.
NICHOL'S MILLS, Reconnoissance from Plymouth to, June 28, 1863.
NIXONTON, Skirmish at, April 6, 1863.
NORTHEAST FERRY, Skirmish at, Feb. 22, 1865.
OLDFIELD BANK LANDING, Naval action at, Dec. 14, 1862.
OLD FORD MILL, Skirmish at, Oct. 30, 1863.
ONSLOW, Reconnoissance to, Jan. 20, 1863.
ORTON POND, Action at, Feb. 18, 1865.
PASQUOTANK, Skirmish near, Aug. 18, 1863.
PEBBLY RUN, Skirmishes at, April 13 and 27, 1862.
PELETIER'S MILLS, Skirmish at, May 5, 1863.

NORTH CAROLINA.

PHILLIPS'S CROSS ROADS, Skirmish at, March 4, 1865.
PIKEVILLE, Affair near, April 11, 1865.
PLYMOUTH, Skirmish near, Aug. 30, 1862.—Action at, Sept. 2, 1862.—Naval affair near, Oct. 31, 1862.—Attack on, Dec. 10, 1862.—Expedition from New Berne to, Feb. 1-10, 1863.—Demonstration on, March 10-13, 1863.—Skirmish at, Nov. 26, 1863.—Skirmish near, April 1, 1864.—Operations against, April 17-20, 1864.—Capture of, by Confederate forces, April 20, 1864.—Destruction of Confederate ram Albemarle at, Oct. 27, 1864.—Naval action with batteries near, Oct. 29-31, 1864.—Skirmishes at, Dec. 10-11, 1864.
POLLOCKSVILLE, Skirmishes at, May 15-16, 1862.—Expeditions from New Berne to, July 24-28, 1862.—Action near, April 21, 1862.—Skirmish near, July 26, 1862.—Reconnoissance from New Berne to, Jan. 17-21, 1863.—Expedition from New Berne to, March 6-8, 1863.
POLLOCKSVILLE AND TRENTON CROSS ROADS (See Trenton and Pollocksville Cross Roads).
POTECASI CREEK, Skirmish at, July 26, 1863.
PUNGO LANDING, Affairs at, Oct. 16-17, 1863.
QUAKER BRIDGE, Action at, July 6, 1863.
QUALLATOWN, Expedition from Maryville, Tenn., to, Jan. 31-Feb. 7, 1864.
RAINBOW BLUFF, Expedition to, Dec. 9-12, 1864.
RALEIGH, Action near, April 12, 1865.—Occupation of, by Union forces, April 13, 1865.—Surrender of Johnston's Confederate army near, April 26, 1865.
RALEIGH ROAD, Reconnoissance from Fayetteville on the, to Silver Run Creek, March 14, 1865.
RAWLES'S MILLS, Skirmish at, Nov. 2, 1862.
RED HOUSE TOWER, Engagement at, Feb. 1, 1864.
REEVES'S POINT, Defensive works at, abandoned by Confederate forces, Jan. 16-17, 1865.
ROANOKE ISLAND, Battle of, Feb. 8, 1862.
ROANOKE RIVER, Engagements on, May 5 and Oct. 24, 1864.
ROCKINGHAM, Skirmish at, March 7-15, 1865.
ROCKY HOOK CREEK, Skirmish at, March 24, 1863.
ROCKY MOUNT, Expedition from New Berne to, July 18-24, 1863.
ROCKY RUN, Scout from, to Dover and Core Creek, June 17-18, 1863.—Skirmish near, Nov. 4, 1863.
RODMAN'S POINT, Pamlico River, Skirmish at, March 30, 1863.—Engagement at, April 1, 1863.—Engagement at, April 4-5, 1863.—Affair at, April 16, 1863.
ROUSE'S STATION, Action at, April 28, 1863.
SALISBURY, Skirmish at Grant's Creek near, April 12, 1865.—Engagement at, April 12, 1865.—Occupation of, by Union forces, April 12, 1865.
SANDY RIDGE, Skirmish at, Feb. 13, 1863.—Skirmishes at, April 17, 18, 27 and 28, 1863.—Skirmish at, April 20, 1863.

NORTH CAROLINA.

SANDY SWAMP, Skirmish at, Dec. 18, 1863.
SAUNDERS'S FARM, Affair near, April 14, 1865.
SCUPPERNONG RIVER, Naval expedition into, to Columbia, July 12-13, 1864.—Naval action at mouth of, Sept. 29, 1864.
SCUPPERTON, Skirmish at, July 22, 1863.
SHALLOW FORD, Skirmish at, April 11, 1865.
SHILOH, Operations at and about, Sept. 17-20, 1862.
SILVER RUN CREEK, Reconnoissance from Fayetteville to, March 14, 1865.
SMITHFIELD, Skirmish near, April 11, 1865.
SMITH'S CREEK, Skirmish at, Feb. 22, 1865.
SMITH'S MILLS, Black River, Skirmish near, March 15, 1865.
SMITHVILLE, Defensive works at, abandoned by Confederate forces, Jan. 16-17, 1865.—Boat expedition to, Feb. 29-March 1, 1864.—Skirmish near, Feb. 17, 1865.—Occupation of, by Union naval forces, Jan. 18, 1865.
SNEAD'S FERRY, Scout from Piney Green to, June 22-23, 1864.
SNOW HILL, Skirmish near, March 28, 1865.—Skirmish at, April 1, 1865.—Skirmishes at, March 23 and 27, 1865.
SOUTH MILLS, Camden County, Engagement at, April 19, 1862.—Scout from Suffolk, Va., to, June 8, 1863.—Skirmish at, Sept. 12, 1863.—Expedition from Norfolk, Va., to, Dec. 5-24, 1863.
SOUTH RIVER, Skirmish at, March 15, 1865.
SOUTHWEST CREEK, Skirmishes at, Dec. 13-14, 1862.—Skirmish at, June 22, 1864.—Scout from Core Creek to, Dec. 10-15, 1864.—Skirmish at, March 7, 1865.
SPARTA, Skirmish at, July 20, 1863.
STATESVILLE, Skirmishes near, April 10, 11, 13, 14 and 20, 1865.
STREET'S FERRY, Skirmish at, July 21, 1863.
STRONG, FORT, Skirmish at, Feb. 21, 1865.
SUGAR LOAF, Action near, Feb. 11, 1865.
SWAIN'S BIG CREEK, Naval expedition to, Oct. 27, 1861.
SWAN QUARTER, Expedition from New Berne to, March 1-6, 1863.
SWANSBOROUGH, Reconnoissance from Newport to, Aug. 14-15, 1862.—Expedition from Newport Barracks to, Dec. 27-29, 1863.—Reconnoissance toward, Feb. 9, 1864.—Expedition to, March 25-26, 1864.—Expedition from Newport Barracks to, April 29-30, 1864.—Scout from Piney Green to, June 22-23, 1864.—Expedition to, March 9, 1865.
SWEED'S MILL, Skirmish near, March 14, 1865.
SWIFT CREEK, Action at, April 12, 1865.—Skirmishes at, Oct. 30, 1862; July 18, 1863; Oct. 7, 1864; April 13, 17 and 19, 1865.
SWIFT CREEK VILLAGE, Expeditions from New Berne to, April 13-21, 1863.—Expedition from New Berne to, July 17-20, 1863, and skirmishes.

NORTH CAROLINA.

TARBOROUGH, Expedition from New Berne to, July 18-24, 1863.
TAYLOR'S HOLE CREEK, Battle of, March 16, 1865.
THOMPSON, FORT (See Neuse River, March 13-14, 1862).
THOMPSON'S BRIDGE, Skirmish at, Dec. 17, 1862.
TOWN CREEK, Skirmish at, Feb. 19-20, 1865.
TRANTER'S CREEK, Skirmish at, May 30, 1862.—Skirmish at, June 2, 1862.—Action at, June 5, 1862.—Reconnoissance from Washington to, June 24, 1862.
TRENTON, Expeditions from New Berne to, July 24-28, 1862.—Skirmish at, Dec. 12, 1862.—Reconnoissance from New Berne to, Jan. 18, 1863.—Expedition from New Berne to, March 6-7, 1863.—Skirmish at Free Bridge near, July 6, 1863.—Scout from Rocky Run toward, Dec. 21-24, 1863.
TRENTON BRIDGE, Skirmishes near, May 15-16, 1862.
TRENTON AND POLLOCKSVILLE CROSS ROADS, Skirmishes at, April 27 and May 22, 1862.
TRENT RIVER, Skirmish on south side of, May 5, 1864.
TRENT ROAD, Skirmish on, April 19, 1862.—Skirmish on, Dec. 11, 1862.—Reconnoissance on, Jan. 27-28, 1863.—Skirmish on, May 4, 1864.—Skirmish on, March 11, 1865.
VANCE, CAMP, Capture of, by Union forces, June 28, 1864.
WACCOMO NECK, Affair at, Feb. 7, 1864.
WALE'S HEAD, Currituck Beach, Destruction of salt-works at, Feb. 2, 1863.
WARM SPRINGS, Skirmishes at, Oct. 20, 23, 26 and Nov. 26, 1863.
WARSAW, Skirmish at, July 5, 1863.
WASHINGTON, Expedition to, March 20-21, 1862.—Destruction of light-ship near, by Union naval forces, Dec. 30, 1861.—Occupation of, by Union naval forces, March 21, 1862.—Skirmish near, June 1, 1862.—Action near, June 5, 1862.—Attack on, Sept. 6, 1862.—Skirmish at, Oct. 30, 1862.—Skirmish near, Feb. 13, 1863.—Skirmish near, March 30, 1863.—Siege of, March 30-April 15, 1863.—Action at, March 31, 1863.—Expedition from New Berne to, April 17-19, 1863.—Skirmish at, Aug. 14, 1863.—Skirmish at, Nov. 1, 1863.—Expedition from, to Chicoa Creek, Dec. 17, 1863.—Evacuation of, by Union forces, April 26-30, 1864.
WELDON, Operations near, Nov. 9, 1863.—Expedition from Deep Bottom, Va., to near, March 28-April 11, 1865, and skirmishes.
WESTERN BAR, Naval operations at, Jan. 18-19, 1865.
WESTERN NORTH CAROLINA, Stoneman's Raid in, March 21-April 25, 1865.
WHITE HALL, Engagement at, Dec. 16, 1862.
WHITE HALL RIDGE, Affair at, Dec. 15, 1862.
WHITE OAK CREEK, Skirmish at, Jan. 19, 1863.
WHITE OAK RIVER, Reconnoissance from Newport Barracks to, July 13-16, 1863.

NORTH CAROLINA—OHIO.

WILKESBOROUGH, Skirmish at, March 28-29, 1865.
WILLIAMSTON, Expedition from Plymouth to, July 5-7, 1863.—Skirmish near, Nov. 2, 1862.—Naval expedition to, June 13-15, 1863.
WILMINGTON, Occupation of, by Union forces, Feb. 22, 1865.
WILMINGTON HARBOR, Boat expedition into, June 23, 1864.
WILMINGTON RIVER, Naval reconnoissance in, Feb. 1, 1863.
WILMINGTON AND WELDON RAILROAD, Raid on, July 3-7, 1863.—Expedition from Beaufort against, June 20-23, 1864.
WINDSOR, Skirmish at, Jan. 30, 1864.
WINFIELD, Skirmish at, March 23, 1863.
WINTON, Expedition to, Feb. 18-21, 1862.—Expedition from New Berne to, July 25-31, 1863.
WISE'S CROSS ROADS, Skirmish at, April 28, 1863, and skirmish near, Dec. 12, 1862.
WISE'S FORKS, Battle of, March 8-10, 1865.
YEOPIN RIVER, Boat expedition into, Feb. 2, 1863.
YOUNG'S CROSS ROADS, Skirmishes near, May 15-16, 1862.—Reconnoissance from Newport to, July 26-29, 1862.—Reconnoissance from New Berne to, Jan. 19, 1863.—Expedition from New Berne to, March 7, 1863.—Expedition from Newport Barracks to, Dec. 27-29, 1863.

OHIO.

ATHENS, Skirmish at, July 24, 1863.
BERLIN, Skirmish at, July 17, 1863.
BUFFINGTON ISLAND, Ohio River, Engagement near, July 19, 1863.
CHESIRE, Skirmish at Coal Hill near, July 20, 1863.
COAL HILL, Skirmish at, near Chesire, July 20, 1863.
DENNISON, CAMP, Skirmish at, July 14, 1863.
EAGLEPORT, Skirmish at, July 22, 1863.
HAMDEN, Skirmish near, July 17, 1863.
HOCKINGPORT, Skirmish near, July 20, 1863.
HOLMES COUNTY, Affairs in, June 16-20, 1863.
MORGAN'S RAID into Ohio, July 13-26, 1863.
NEW LISBON, Remnant of Morgan's command surrendered near, July 26, 1863.
JENKINS' RAID into Ohio, Sept. 4, 1862.
POMEROY, Skirmish at, July 18, 1863.
ROCKVILLE, Skirmish at, July 23, 1863.
SALINEVILLE, Skirmish at, July 26, 1863.
SPRINGFIELD, Skirmish near, July 25, 1863.
STEUBENVILLE, Skirmish near, July 25, 1863.
WASHINGTON, Skirmish at, July 24, 1863.

OREGON.

BUTTER CREEK, Scouts to, Feb. 5-17, 1861.
CANYON CITY, Expedition from Camp Lincoln near, to Harney Valley, March 24-April 16, 1864, and skirmishes.
CANYON CITY ROAD, Operations on, Jan. 1-Nov. 30, 1865.
COLUMBIA RIVER, Skirmish on, Feb. 8, 1861.—Skirmish on, Feb. 10, 1861.
COOS BAY, Expedition from Siletz River Block House to, April 21-May 12, 1864.
HARNEY LAKE VALLEY, Expedition from Camp Lincoln, near Canyon City, to, March 24-April 16, 1864.
JOHN DAY'S ROAD, Attack on wagon train on, near Fort Klamath, June 24, 1864.
KLAMATH, FORT (See John Day's Road, June 24, 1864).
LINCOLN, CAMP (See Canyon City, March 24-April 16, 1864).
MALHEUR RIVER, Expedition from Camp Lyon, Idaho, to the, July 2-13, 1865.
PORTLAND, Emigrant Road expedition from Omaha, Neb., to, June 16-Oct. 30, 1862.
UMATILLA RIVER, Scouts to, Feb. 5-17, 1861.
WILLOW CREEK, Scouts to, Feb. 5-17, 1861.

PENNSYLVANIA.

CALEDONIA IRON-WORKS, Skirmish at, July 5, 1863.
CARLISLE, Evacuation of, by Union forces, and occupation of, by Confederate forces, June 27, 1863.—Skirmish at, July 1, 1863.
CHAMBERSBURG, Capture of, by Confederate forces, Oct. 10, 1862.—Evacuation of, by Confederate forces, Oct. 11, 1862.—Evacuation of, by Confederate forces, June 18, 1863.—Reoccupation of, by Confederate forces, June 23, 1863.—Skirmish near, July 2, 1863.—Burning of, by Confederate forces, July 30, 1864.
COLUMBIA, Skirmish near, June 28, 1863.
CUNNINGHAM'S CROSS ROADS, Skirmish at, July 5, 1863.
FAIRFIELD, Skirmish at, June 30, 1863.—Action at, July 3, 1863.—Skirmish near, July 5, 1863.—Skirmish at, July 7, 1863.
FAIRFIELD GAP, Skirmish at, July 4, 1863.
FOUNTAIN DALE, Skirmish at, June 28, 1863.
GETTYSBURG, Skirmish near, Oct. 11, 1862.—Skirmish at, June 26, 1863.—Battle of, July 1-3, 1863.
GREENCASTLE, Skirmishes at, June 20, 22, July 1 and 5, 1863.
GREEN OAK, Skirmish near, July 5, 1863.
HANOVER, Confederate operations in, June 27, 1863.—Action at, June 30, 1863.

PENNSYLVANIA—SOUTH CAROLINA.

HARRISBURG, Skirmish at Sporting Hill near, June 30, 1863.
HUNTERSTOWN, Skirmish at, July 2, 1863.
LITTLESTOWN, Skirmish at, June 30, 1863.
McCONNELLSBURG, Skirmishes near, June 24-25, 1863.—Skirmishes at, June 29, 1863; July 30, 1864.
MECHANICSBURG, Occupation of, by Confederate forces, June 28, 1863.
MERCERSBURG, Skirmish near, July 5, 1863.—Skirmish at, July 29, 1864.
MONTEREY GAP, Action at, July 4, 1863.
MONTEREY PASS, Skirmish near, July 6, 1863.
OYSTER POINT, Skirmish near, June 28-29, 1863.
SHIPPENSBURG, Occupation of, by Confederate forces, June 24, 1863.
STEVENS' FURNACE, Skirmish at, July 5, 1863.
STONE FARM, near Carlisle, Skirmish at, June 27, 1863.
SPORTING HILL, near Harrisburg, Skirmish at, June 30, 1863.
TETTERSBURG, Skirmish at, July 7, 1863.
WAYNESBOROUGH, Attack on Confederate trains at, July 6, 1863.
WRIGHTSVILLE, Skirmish at, June 28, 1863.
YORK, Occupation of, by Union forces, June 30, 1863.

SOUTH CAROLINA.

Ordinance of secession adopted by Convention, Dec. 20, 1860.

AIKEN, Action at, Feb. 11, 1865.
ANDERSONVILLE, Naval action with batteries near, Feb. 13-14, 1865.
ANGLEY'S POST OFFICE, Skirmish at, Feb. 4, 1865.
ASHEPOO RIVER, Skirmish on, May 16, 1864.
ASHLEY RIVER, Naval expedition into, March 5-9, 1865.
BACK RIVER, Boat expeditions into, July 30 and Aug. 2-4, 1864.
BARKER'S MILL, Whippy Swamp, Skirmish at, Feb. 2, 1865.
BARNWELL, Skirmish near, Feb. 6, 1865.
BARNWELL'S ISLAND, Skirmish on, Feb. 10, 1862.—Expedition to, July 30, 1863.
BATES' FERRY, Congaree River, Skirmish at, Feb. 15, 1865.
BATTERY ISLAND, Affair near, May 21, 1862.—Affair on, Sept. 7, 1863.—Demonstration on, April 15, 1864.
BATTERY PRINGLE, Naval action with, Jan. 28, 1865.
BEAUFORT, Expedition to, Dec. 6-7, 1861.—Occupation of, by Union naval forces, Nov. 9, 1861.
BEAUREGARD, BATTERY, Occupation of, by Union naval forces, Feb. 18, 1865.
BEAUREGARD, FORT, Capture of, by U. S. naval forces, Nov. 7, 1861.
BEECH CREEK, Skirmish at, near Statesburg, April 19, 1865.

SOUTH CAROLINA.

BIG BLACK CREEK, Affair near, March 3, 1865.
BINNAKER'S BRIDGE, South Edisto River, Skirmish at, Feb. 9, 1865.
BLACK RIVER, Engagement on, Aug. 13, 1862.
BLACKVILLE, Skirmish at, Feb. 7, 1865.
BLAKENY'S, Skirmish near, March 3, 1865.
BLUE'S BRIDGE, Skirmish at, March 8, 1865.
BLUFFTON, Operations near, March 20-24, 1862, including affairs at Buckingham and Hunting Island.—Expedition from Fort Pulaski, Ga., to, June 4, 1863.
BOYD'S LANDING, Skirmish near, Nov. 29, 1864.
BOYKIN'S MILLS, Skirmish at, April 18, 1865.
BRADDOCK'S POINT, Expedition from Hilton Head to, Nov. 10-11, 1861.
BRADFORD SPRINGS, Skirmish at, April 18, 1865.
BROAD RIVER, Naval operations in, Nov. 28-Dec. 10, 1864.
BROXTON'S BRIDGE, Salkahatchie River, Skirmish at, Feb. 2, 1865.
BUCKINGHAM, Affair at, March 20, 1862.
BUFORD'S BRIDGE, Skirmish at, Feb. 4, 1865.
BUGBEE BRIDGE, Skirmishes near, Feb. 9-11, 1864.
BULL ISLAND, Affair on, Jan. 31, 1863.
BULL RIVER, Reconnoissance on, Feb. 23-26, 1862.
BULL'S BAY, Naval operations in, Feb. 13-14, 1862; April 4-9, 1862; March 9-11, 1864; and Feb. 12-19, 1865.
BURDEN'S CAUSEWAY, John's Island, Action at, July 9, 1864.
CAMDEN, Skirmishes near, Feb. 22-23, 1865.—Skirmish at, Feb. 24, 1865.—Occupation of, by Union forces, Feb. 25, 1865.—Expedition from Georgetown to, April 5-25, 1865.
CANNON'S BRIDGE, South Edisto River, Reconnoissance to, Feb. 7, 1865.—Skirmish at, Feb. 8, 1865.
CASTLE PINCKNEY, Reconnoissance of, by steamers, Dec. 20, 1860.—Seizure of, by State troops, Dec. 27, 1860.
CASTON'S PLANTATION, Engagement at, Oct. 22, 1862.
CHAPMAN'S FORT, Ashepoo River, Destruction of U. S. transport Boston at, May 26, 1864.
CHARLESTON, Attack on blockading squadron off, Jan. 31, 1863.—Bombardment of, Aug. 21-Dec. 31, 1863.—Evacuation of, by Confederate forces, Feb. 17, 1865.—Occupation of, by Union forces, Feb. 18, 1865.—Seizure of U. S. Arsenal at, by State troops, Dec. 30, 1860.
CHARLESTON HARBOR, Operations in, Dec. 20, 1860-April 14, 1861.—Star of the West fired on in, Jan. 9, 1861.—Schooner Rhoda M. Shannon fired on in, April 3, 1861.—C. S. S. Savannah captured off, June 3, 1861.—Sinking of stone fleet at entrance of, Dec. 20, 1861.—Abduction of the armed steamer Planter from, May 13, 1862.—Sinking of stone fleet at entrance of, Jan. 20, 1862.—Engagement in, April 7, 1863.—Engagement in, Sept. 7-8, 1863.—Attempt to

SOUTH CAROLINA.

blow up U. S. S. New Ironsides off, Oct. 5, 1863.—Operations in and vicinity, Jan. 1-Nov. 13, 1864.—Destruction of U. S. monitor Patapsco in, Jan. 15, 1865.—Removal of obstructions in, Feb. 19-March 18, 1865.
CHARLESTON AND SAVANNAH RAILROAD, Expedition against, Oct. 22-23, 1862.—Naval expedition against, May 25-28, 1864.—Demonstrations against, Dec. 6-9, 1864.
CHERAW, Skirmish near, Feb. 28, 1865.—Skirmish at Juniper Creek near, March 3, 1865.—Skirmish at Thompson's Creek near, March 3, 1865.—Occupation of, by Union forces, March 3, 1865.—Expedition from near, to Florence, March 4-6, 1865, and skirmishes.—Skirmish near, March 5, 1865.
CHESTERFIELD, Skirmishes at and near, and occupation of, by Union forces, March 2, 1865.
CHEVES, BATTERY, James Island, Explosion at, Sept. 15, 1863.
CHICKISSEE RIVER, Naval reconnoissance in, March 31, 1864.
CHISOLM'S ISLAND, Skirmish on, Dec. 17, 1861.
CLOUD'S HOUSE, Skirmish at, Feb. 27, 1865.
COLE'S ISLAND, Bombardment of, May 20, 1862.
COLUMBIA, Skirmishes about, Feb. 16-17, 1865.
COMBAHEE FERRY, Skirmish at, Feb. 5, 1865.
COMBAHEE RIVER, Union raid on, June 2, 1863.—Skirmish at, Jan. 28, 1865.—Naval reconnoissance in, Feb. 8-9, 1865.
CONGAREE CREEK, Skirmish at, Feb. 15, 1865.
CONGAREE RIVER, Skirmish at Bates's Ferry, on, Feb. 15, 1865.
COOPER RIVER, Naval expedition into, Feb. 25-28, 1865.
COOSAWHATCHIE, Skirmish at, Oct. 22, 1862.
COOSAW RIVER, Naval engagement in, Jan. 1, 1863.
COWPEN'S FORD, Little Salkehatchie River, Skirmish at, Feb. 6, 1865.
CUMMINGS'S POINT BATTERIES, Naval engagement with, Nov. 16, 1863.
CUNNINGHAM'S BLUFF, Skirmish near, Nov. 24, 1863.
DAUFUSKIE ISLAND, Expedition to, Jan. 29, 1863.—Reconnoissance to, May 11, 1864.
DENKIN'S MILL, Skirmish at, April 19, 1865.
DILLINGHAM'S CROSS ROADS, Skirmish at, Feb. 3, 1865.
DINGLE'S MILLS, near Sumterville, Skirmish at, April 9, 1865.
DIXON'S ISLAND, Affair near, May 25, 1862.—Affair on, June 21, 1863.
DUCK BRANCH, Skirmishes at, Feb. 2-3, 1865.
DUNCANVILLE, Skirmish at, Feb. 5, 1865.
EDISTO ISLAND, Expedition to, Jan. 22-25, 1862.—Occupation of, by Union forces, Feb. 11, 1862.—Affair on, March 29, 1862.—Occupation of, by Union forces, April 5, 1862.—Skirmish on, April 19, 1862.—Skirmish on, June 18, 1863.

SOUTH CAROLINA.

EDISTO RAILROAD BRIDGE, Skirmish at, Feb. 7, 1865.
EDISTO RIVER, Skirmish at Walker's (or Valley Bridge), on, Feb. 8, 1865.—Naval demonstration in, Feb. 15-16, 1865.
ENNIS'S CROSS ROADS, Skirmish at, Jan. 27, 1865.
FENWICK'S ISLAND, Expeditions to, Dec. 10 and 12, 1861, and July 9, 1862.
FISHBURN'S PLANTATION, Action at, Feb. 6, 1865.
FLORENCE, Expedition from near Cheraw to, March 4-6, 1865, and skirmishes.
FOLLY ISLAND, Skirmish on, April 10, 1863.
FRAMPTON'S PLANTATION, Engagement at, Oct. 22, 1862.
GEORGETOWN, Naval expedition to, May 22, 1862.—Occupation of, by Union naval forces, Feb. 23, 1865.
GRAHAM'S POINT, Naval action at, Feb. 16, 1865.
GRAHAMVILLE, Engagement at Honey Hill near, Nov. 30, 1864.
GREGG, BATTERY, Morris Island, Boat expeditions against, Sept. 4-6, 1863.—Evacuation of, by the Confederates, and occupation of, by the Union forces, Sept. 6-7, 1863.
GRIMBALL'S LANDING, James Island, Engagement near, July 16, 1863.
GRIMBALL'S PLANTATION, Naval expedition to, April 29, 1862.—Naval attacks on, July 11 and 16, 1862.
GUNTER'S BRIDGE, North Edisto River, Skirmish at, Feb. 14, 1865.
HARDEEVILLE, Skirmish near, Jan. 3, 1865.
HICKORY HILL, Skirmish at, Feb. 1, 1865.
HILTON HEAD, Reconnoissance on, Nov. 8, 1861.
HOLMAN'S BRIDGE, South Edisto River, Skirmish at, Feb. 19, 1865.
HONEY HILL, ENGAGEMENT at, Nov. 30, 1864.
HORNSBOROUGH, Skirmish near, March 3, 1865.
HUNTING ISLAND, Affair at, March —, 1862.
HUTCHINSON'S ISLAND, Reconnoissance on, June 12, 1862.
JAMES ISLAND, Affair near, May 25, 1862.—Skirmish on, June 3, 1862.—Skirmish on, June 8, 1862.—Skirmish on, June 10, 1862.—Operations against, June 11-July 2, 1862.—Evacuation of, by Union forces, June 28-July 7, 1862.—Affair on, May 31, 1863.—Naval action at, July 9, 1863.—Expedition to, Feb. 6-14, 1864.—Demonstrations on, April 8, 1864.—Affair on, May 13, 1864.—Demonstration on, May 21-23, 1864.—Skirmish on, July 2, 1864.—Skirmish on, July 16, 1864.—Skirmish at, Feb. 10, 1865.—Naval demonstration on, Feb. 14, 1865.
JOHN'S ISLAND, Expedition to, May 22, 1862.—Skirmish on, June 7, 1862.—Affairs on, June 8-9, 1862.—Naval actions at, July 11 and Dec. 25, 1863.—Demonstrations on, Nov. 15, 1863.—Affairs on, Dec. 28, 1863.—Expedition to, Feb. 6-14, 1864.—Skirmish on, July 3, 1864.—Skirmish on, July 7, 1864.

SOUTH CAROLINA.

JOHNSON, FORT, Seizure of, by State troops, Jan. 2, 1861.—Assault on, July 3, 1864.—Attack on, July 10, 1864.
JOHNSON'S STATION, Skirmish at, Feb. 10, 1865.—Action at, Feb. 11, 1865.
JUNIPER CREEK, near Cheraw, Skirmish at, March 3, 1865.
KILKENNY RIVER, Skirmish on, Sept. 10, 1862.
KING'S CREEK, Skirmish at, July 3, 1864.
KIRK'S BLUFF, Affair at, Oct. 18, 1862.
LANE'S BRIDGE, Little Salkehatchie River, Action near, Feb. 6, 1865.
LAWTONVILLE, Skirmish near, Jan. 30, 1865.—Skirmish at, Feb. 2, 1865.
LEE, BATTERY, Occupation of, by Union naval forces, Feb. 18, 1865.
LEGARE'S POINT, James Island, Bombardment of, July 20, 1863.
LEGAREVILLE, Burning of, by Confederate forces, Aug. 20, 1864.
LEXINGTON, Skirmish near, Feb. 15, 1865.
LITTLE FOLLY ISLAND, Operations on, June 11-13, 1863.
LITTLE SALKEHATCHIE RIVER, Action near Lane's Bridge on, Feb. 6, 1865.—Skirmish at Cowpen's Ford on, Feb. 6, 1865.
LOPER'S CROSS ROADS, Skirmish at Duck Branch near, Feb. 2, 1865.
LOVE'S BRIDGE, Skirmish at, March 8, 1865.
LOWNDES'S MILL, Combahee River, Capture of Union telegraph party near, Sept. 13-14, 1863.
LYNCH'S CREEK, Skirmish at, Feb. 26, 1865.
McCLELLANSVILLE, Affair at, March 25, 1864.
MAGNOLIA BEACH, Boat expedition to and skirmish, Dec. 5, 1863.
MARSHALL BATTERY, Naval action with, Nov. 7, 1864.
MATTIS'S PLANTATION, Affair at, March 13, 1862.
MAY RIVER, Reconnoissance on, March 19-24, 1862.—Reconnoissance on, Sept. 30-Oct. 3, 1862.
MONROE'S CROSS ROADS, Engagement at, March 10, 1865.
MORRIS ISLAND, Occupation of, by State troops, Dec. 30, 1860.—Operations on, July 10-Sept. 7, 1863.
MOULTRIE, FORT, Evacuation of, by Union forces, Dec. 26, 1860.—Seizure of, by State troops, Dec. 27, 1860.—Naval engagement with, Sept. 21, 1863.—Naval action near, Feb. 2, 1864.—Naval action with, Nov. 5, 1864.—Naval attack on, Feb. 17, 1865.—Occupation of, by Union forces, Feb. 18, 1865.
MOUNT ELON, Skirmish near, Feb. 27, 1865.
MURRAY'S INLET, Affair at, April 27, 1863.—Affair at, May 4, 1863.
MURRELL'S INLET, Affair at, Oct. 19, 1863.—Affair at, Dec. 5, 1863.—Boat expeditions into, April 27 and May 3, 1863.—

SOUTH CAROLINA.

Naval engagement in, Jan. 1, 1864.—Naval expedition into, April 21-23, 1864.
NORTH EDISTO RIVER, Naval reconnoissance into, Dec. 16-29, 1861.—Skirmishes at, Feb. 12-14, 1865.
ORANGEBURG, Skirmishes about, Feb. 11-12, 1865.
PALMETTO POINT, Boat expedition to, Feb. 23, 1865.
PINCKNEY ISLAND, Affair on, Aug. 21, 1862.
PINEBERRY BATTERY, Engagement at, April 29, 1862.
PINE ISLAND, Skirmish at, May 10, 1864.
POCOTALIGO, Skirmish at, May 29, 1862.—Demonstrations against, July 9-10, 1862.—Skirmish and engagements near, Oct. 22, 1862.—Advance of Union forces from Beaufort to, Jan. 14, 1865, and skirmishes.—Skirmish near, Jan. 26, 1865.
POCOTALIGO ROAD, Skirmish near, Dec. 20, 1864.
POPE'S ISLAND, Skirmish on, May 19, 1863.
PORT ROYAL, Naval expedition to, Oct. 29-Nov. 6, 1861.
PORT ROYAL FERRY, Expedition to, Dec. 6-7, 1861.—Engagement at, Jan. 1, 1862.—Affair at, June 6, 1862.—Affair at, July 4, 1862.
PRINGLE, BATTERY, Attack on, July 4-9, 1864.
RED BANK CREEK, Skirmish at, Feb. 15, 1865.
RHODA M. SHANNON, Schooner, fired on in Charleston Harbor, April 3, 1861.
RICEBOROUGH RIVER, Naval reconnoissance of, April 26-27, 1862.
RIVER'S BRIDGE, Salkehatchie River, Skirmish at, Feb. 2, 1865.—Action at, Feb. 3, 1865.
ROBERTSVILLE, Skirmish at, Jan. 29, 1865.
ROCKVILLE, Evacuation of, by Confederate forces, Dec. 17, 1861.—Boat expedition to, Feb. 28, 1862.
ROCKY MOUNT, Skirmish near, Feb. 28, 1865.
ROSELAND PLANTATION, Boat expedition to, Dec. 15, 1864.
SAINT HELENA ISLAND, Affair on, Oct. 24, 1862.
SAINT HELENA BAY, Naval expedition to, Nov. 4-9, 1861.
SAINT HELENA SOUND, Naval expedition into, Nov. 25-27, 1861.
SALKEHATCHIE RIVER, Reconnoissance from Pocotaligo to, Jan. 20, 1865, and skirmish.—Reconnoissance from Pocotaligo to, Jan. 25, 1865.—Skirmishes at River's and Broxton's Bridges on, Feb. 2, 1865.—Action at River's Bridge on, Feb. 3, 1865.
SANTEE RIVER, Expedition from Charleston to, April 5-15, 1865.—Boat expedition up, March 23-24, 1864.
SAVANNAH CREEK, Skirmish at, Feb. 15, 1865.
SCHOONER CHANNEL, Reconnoissance on, Feb. 23-26, 1862.
SEABROOK ISLAND, Reconnoissance on, April 14, 1862.
SEABROOK'S PLANTATION, Boat expedition to, April 18, 1862.

SOUTH CAROLINA.

SECESSIONVILLE, James Island, Engagement at, June 16, 1862.—Skirmish near, July 2, 1864.
SHANNON, RHODA M. (See Rhoda M. Shannon, April 3, 1861).
SIMMON'S BLUFF, Engagement at, June 21, 1862.
SIMPKINS, BATTERY, Assault on, July 3, 1864.—Attack on, July 10, 1864.—Attack on, Feb. 11, 1865.
SKULL CREEK, Affair at, Sept. 24, 1862.—Torpedo operations in, May 18-21, 1863.
SLANN'S BLUFF, Naval action at, April 29, 1862.
SOUTH EDISTO RIVER, Reconnoissance to Cannon's Bridge on, Feb. 7, 1865.—Naval reconnoissance in, Dec. 16-19 and 27, 1861, and Jan. 10-12, 1862.—Skirmish at Cannon's Bridge on, Feb. 8, 1865.—Skirmish at Binnaker's Bridge on, Feb. 9, 1865.—Skirmish at Holman's Bridge on, Feb. 9, 1865.
SPRING ISLAND, Affair at, March 31, 1864.
STATESBURG, Skirmish near, April 15, 1865.—Skirmish at Beech Creek near, April 19, 1865.
STAR OF THE WEST fired on in Charleston Harbor, Jan. 9, 1861.
STONO INLET, Naval action with batteries in, Dec. 26, 1861.—Naval actions in, Feb. 10-11, 1865.
STONO RIVER, Occupation of, by Union naval forces, May 20, 1862.—Naval action in, near Wappoo Cut, May 29, 1862.—Naval action in, Jan. 30, 1863.—Attack on U. S. S. Marblehead in, Dec. 25, 1863.
STROUD'S MILL, Skirmish near, Feb. 26, 1865.
SULLIVAN'S ISLAND BATTERIES, Naval engagement with, Nov. 16, 1863, and naval attack on, Feb. 17, 1865.
SUMTER, FORT, Bombardment of, April 12-14, 1861.—Evacuation of, by Union forces, April 14, 1861.—Attack on, April 7, 1863.—Bombardment of, Aug. 17-Dec. 31, 1863.—Boat expedition to, and assault on, Sept. 8, 1863.
SUMTERVILLE, Skirmish at Dingle's Mills near, April 9, 1865.
THOMPSON'S CREEK, Skirmish at, near Chesterfield, March 2, 1865.—Skirmish at, near Cheraw, March 3, 1865.
TOGADOO CREEK, Naval action with batteries in, Feb. 9-10, 1865.
TWO-LEAGUE CROSS ROADS, near Lexington, Skirmish at, Feb. 15, 1865.
VALLEY BRIDGE, Edisto River, Skirmish at, Feb. 8, 1865.
VINCENT'S CREEK, Affair at mouth of, Aug. 4, 1863.
WACCAMAW NECK, Affair on, Jan. 7, 1864.
WACKINANA RIVER, Naval expedition up, to Conwaysborough, March 23-27, 1865.
WADLEMAW RIVER, Naval action in, Feb. 5, 1865.
WADLEMAW SOUND, Naval expedition up, to Simmon's Bluff, June 21, 1862.

SOUTH CAROLINA—TENNESSEE.

WAGNER, BATTERY, First assault on, July 11, 1863.—Sortie from, July 14-15, 1863.—Siege of, July 18-Sept. 7, 1863.—Evacuation of, by Confederate forces, and occupation of, by Union forces, Sept. 6-7, 1863.
WALKER, FORT, Capture of, by Union naval forces, Nov. 7, 1861.
WALKER'S BRIDGE, Edisto River, Skirmish at, Feb. 8, 1865.
WAPPOO CUT, Naval action near, May 29, 1862.
WATEREE RIVER, Skirmish near, Feb. 22, 1865.
WEST'S CROSS ROADS, Skirmish at, Feb. 25, 1865.
WHALE BRANCH, Naval reconnoissance of, Dec. 4, 1864.
WHIPPY SWAMP, Skirmish at Barker's Mill on, Feb. 2, 1865.
WHIPPY SWAMP CREEK, Skirmish at, Feb. 1, 1865.
WHITE, FORT, Pedee River, Occupation of, by Union naval forces, Feb. 23, 1865.
WHITE HOUSE, near Hilton Head, Affair at, June 13, 1862.
WHITE POINT, Engagement at, April 29, 1862.—Skirmish near, July 3, 1864.—Naval action at, Jan. 30, 1865.
WHITE POND, Skirmish near, Feb. 8, 1865.
WILLISTON, Skirmish at, Feb. 8, 1865.
WILLSTOWN, Engagement at, April 29, 1862.
WILLSTOWN BLUFF, Pon Pon River, Engagement at, July 10, 1863.
WILSON'S STORE, Skirmish at, March 1, 1865.
WINYAW BAY, Naval operations in, May 21-25, 1862, and April 20-21, 1864.
WITHER'S SWASH, Naval expedition to, April 22, 1864.
WOLF'S PLANTATION, Skirmish at, Feb. 14, 1865.
WOODVILLE ISLAND, Naval action at, April 27, 1862.
WRIGHT RIVER, Reconnoissance to, Feb. 6, 1862.

TENNESSEE.

Seceded May 6, 1861.

ADAMSVILLE, Skirmish on Purdy Road near, March 31, 1862.
AGNEW'S FERRY, Reconnoissance to, March 25, 1862.
ALEXANDRIA, Expedition from Murfreesborough to, Feb. 3-5, 1863.
ALTAMONT, Skirmish at, Aug. 30, 1862.
ANDERSON, Reconnoissance from Cowan to, July 11-14, 1863.
ANDERSON'S CROSS ROADS, Skirmish at, Oct. 2, 1863.
ANTHONY'S HILL, Action at, Dec. 25, 1864.
ANTIOCH, Capture of construction train near, Jan. 25, 1863.
ANTIOCH CHURCH, Expedition from Bolivar to, May 26-29, 1863, and skirmishes.
ANTIOCH STATION, Affair at, April 10, 1863.
ARMSTRONG'S FERRY, Skirmish at, Jan. 22, 1864.
ASHLAND, Affair at, Jan. 12, 1863.

TENNESSEE.

ATHENS, Skirmish at, Sept. 10, 1863.—Skirmish at, Sept. 25, 1863.—Skirmish at, Sept. 27, 1863.—Pursuit of Confederates from, into North Carolina, Aug. 1-3, 1864.—Action at, Jan. 28, 1865.—Attack upon the garrison at, Feb. 16, 1865.—Operations about, March 2-4, 1865.

ATKIN'S MILL, Skirmish at, April 26, 1862.

AUBURN, Expedition from Murfreesborough to, Feb. 3-5, 1863.—Skirmishes near, Feb. 15, 1863.—Reconnoissance from near Murfreesborough to, April 2-6, 1863.—Reconnoissance from Murfreesborough to, Jan. 21-22, 1863.—Reconnoissance from Murfreesborough to, Jan. 25, 1863.

BAINBRIDGE, Skirmish at, Oct. 30, 1864.

BAIRD'S MILL, Reconnoissance from Stewart's Ferry to, Nov. 29-Dec. 1, 1862, and skirmishes.

BATTLE CREEK, Skirmish at, June 21, 1862.—Skirmish at, July 5, 1862.—Attack on Fort McCook at, Aug. 27, 1862.

BEACH CREEK BRIDGE, Mobile and Ohio Railroad, Destruction of, March 13, 1862.

BEAN'S STATION, Skirmishes at, and near, Dec. 9-13, 1863.—Engagement at, Dec. 14, 1863.—Skirmish at, Dec. 15, 1863.—Skirmish at, Dec. 18, 1863.—Scout to, Dec. 29-30, 1863.—Skirmish at, June 14, 1864.—Skirmish at Thorn Hill near, Oct. 10, 1864.

BEAR CREEK, Skirmish near, March 3, 1863.—Skirmish at, Oct. 3, 1863.

BEARDSTOWN, Skirmish at, Sept. 27, 1864.

BEAVER CREEK SWAMP, Scout in, April 2-6, 1863.

BEECH GROVE, Skirmish at, June 26, 1863.

BEERSHEBA, Skirmish at Hill's Gap near, Oct. 3, 1863.

BEERSHEBA SPRINGS, Skirmish at, March 19, 1864.

BELL'S LANDING, Naval actions at, Dec. 3, 4, 6, and 14, 1864.

BELL'S MILLS, Action at, Dec. 4, 1864.—Action at, Dec. 6, 1864.

BELMONT, Action near, March 29, 1863.

BEND OF CHUCKY ROAD, Skirmish on, Jan. 16, 1864.

BENT CREEK, Skirmish at, March 14, 1864.

BERRY COUNTY, Skirmish in, April 29, 1864.

BETHPAGE BRIDGE, Elk River, Skirmishes at and near, July 1-2, 1863.

BIG CREEK, Skirmish at, near Rogersville, Dec. 12, 1864.

BIG CREEK GAP, Skirmish at, March 14, 1862.—Action at, June 15, 1862.—Skirmishes at, June 11-13, 1862.—Operations at, Sept. 10, 1862.

BIG EDDY, Naval engagement at, April 29, 1865.

BIG HATCHIE, Engagement at, Oct. 5, 1862.

BIG HILL, Skirmish near, Oct. 5, 1862.

BIG SPRING BRANCH, Skirmish at, June 24, 1863.

BIG SPRINGS, Skirmish at, near Tazewell, Jan. 19, 1864.

BLAIN'S CROSS ROADS, Skirmishes at, and near, Dec. 16-19, 1863.

TENNESSEE.

BLOOD'S (See Insane Asylum, Jan. 3, 1863).
BLOOMINGTON, on Hatchie River, Skirmish near, Feb. 27, 1863.
BLOUNT COUNTY, Skirmish in, July 20, 1864.
BLOUNTSVILLE, Capture of Confederates at, Dec. 30, 1862.—Engagement at, Sept. 22, 1863.—Skirmish at, Oct. 14, 1863.
BLOUNTSVILLE ROAD, Capture of Confederates on, Dec. 29, 1862.
BLUE SPRINGS, Skirmish at, Oct. 5, 1863.—Action at, Oct. 10, 1863.—Skirmish at, Aug. 23, 1864.
BLYTHE'S FERRY, Tennessee River, Skirmish at, Nov. 13, 1863.
BOBO'S CROSS ROADS, Skirmish near, July 1, 1863.
BOILING FORK, Skirmish at, near Winchester, July 3, 1863.
BOILING SPRINGS, Skirmishes at, April 19-20, 1864.
BOLIVAR, Expedition from Holly Springs, Miss., to, July 25-Aug. 1, 1862.—Skirmish near, Aug. 30, 1862.—Skirmish at, Dec. 24, 1862.—Scout near, Jan. 25, 1863.—Guerrilla attack on railway train near, March 21, 1863.—Skirmish at, July 10, 1863.—Affair at, Feb. 6, 1864.—Skirmish near, March 29, 1864.—Skirmish at, May 2, 1864.
BRADYVILLE, Skirmish at, Feb. 16, 1863.—Skirmish at, March 1, 1863.—Reconnoissance from Murfreesborough to, March 26, 1863.—Skirmish near, June 24, 1863.
BRADYVILLE PIKE, Skirmish on, near Murfreesborough, Jan. 23, 1863.—Skirmish on, May 17, 1863.
BRAWLEY FORKS, Skirmish at, March 25, 1865.
BRECKINRIDGE'S ADVANCE into East Tennessee, Nov. 4-17, 1864.
BRENTWOOD, Skirmishes at, Sept. 19-20, 1862.—Skirmish near, Dec. 9, 1862.—Reconnoissance to, Feb. 2, 1863.—Action at, March 25, 1863.
BRISTOL, Skirmish at, Sept. 19, 1863.—Skirmish at, Oct. 15, 1863.—Affair at, Dec. 14, 1864.
BRITTON'S LANE, near Denmark, Skirmish at, Sept. 1, 1862.
BROWN'S FERRY, Skirmish at, Oct. 27, 1863.
BROWNSVILLE, Guerrilla raid on, July 19, 1862.—Reconnoissance from, toward mouth of the Hatchie River, Aug. 10-11, 1862.
BUCK LODGE, Skirmish at Butler's Mill near, June 30, 1863.
BUELL'S FORD, Skirmish at, Sept. 28, 1863.
BULL'S GAP, Skirmish at, March 15, 1864.—Reconnoissance from Powder Springs Gap toward, April 2-4, 1864.—Skirmish near, Oct. 16, 1864.—Action at, Nov. 11-13, 1864.
BURNT BRIDGE, near Humboldt, Skirmish at, Sept. 5, 1862.
BUSHY KNOB, Skirmish at, Nov. 23, 1863.
BUTLER'S MILL, near Buck Lodge, Skirmish at, June 30, 1863.

TENNESSEE.

CAINSVILLE, Reconnoissance from Murfreesborough to, Jan. 21-22, 1863.—Skirmish near, Feb. 15, 1863.—Reconnoissance from near Murfreesborough to, April 2-6, 1863.
CALFKILLER CREEK, Skirmish at, near Sparta, Aug. 17, 1863.—Skirmish on, Feb. 22, 1864.—Skirmish on, March 11, 1864.
CALHOUN, Skirmish at, Sept. 18, 1863.—Skirmishes at, Sept. 25-26, 1863.—Action at, Dec. 28, 1863.
CAMPBELL'S STATION, Engagement at, Nov. 16, 1863.
CAMPBELLSVILLE, Action at, Nov. 24, 1864.
CANEY FORK, Affair near, May 9, 1863.
CARROLL STATION, Affair at, Dec. 19, 1862.
CARTER CREEK PIKE, Skirmish on, April 2, 1863.—Skirmish on, April 27, 1863.
CARTER CREEK ROAD, Reconnoissance from Franklin on, Feb. 21, 1863.
CARTER CREEK STATION, Surrender of block-houses at, Oct. 1, 1864.
CARTER'S DEPOT, Capture of, by Union forces, Dec. 30, 1862.—Skirmishes at, Sept. 20-22, 1863.
CARTER'S STATION, Skirmishes at, Sept. 30-Oct. 1, 1864.
CARTHAGE, Skirmish at, Jan. 23, 1863.—Capture of Union forage train near, March 8, 1863.—Expedition from Murfreesborough to, April 1-8, 1863.—Expedition from Gallatin to, Oct. 10-14, 1863.
CARTHAGE ROAD, Skirmishes on, near Hartsville and Rome, Nov. 28, 1862.
CELINA, Skirmish at, March 19, 1865.—Skirmish at, March 22, 1865.
CENTREVILLE, Expedition to, July —, 1863.—Skirmish at, Oct. 29, 1863.—Skirmish at, Nov. 2, 1863.—Skirmish at, Sept. 29, 1864.
CHAMBERS'S CREEK, Skirmish at, near Hamburg, Jan. 13, 1863.
CHAPEL HILL, Expedition from Concord Church to, March 3-6, 1863.—Skirmish at, March 5, 1863.—Skirmish near, April 13, 1863.
CHAPEL HILL PIKE, Reconnoissance on, April 29, 1863.
CHARLESTON, Skirmish at, Sept. 25, 1863.—Skirmish at, Nov. 26, 1863.—Affair at, Nov. 30, 1863.—Skirmish at, Dec. 28, 1863.—Skirmishes at, Aug. 18-19, 1864.
CHARLOTTE, Capture of conscripts near, March 13-14, 1863.
CHATTANOOGA, Occupation of, by Confederate forces, March 8, 1862.—Attack on, June 7-8, 1862.—Bombardment of, Aug. 21, 1863.—Reconnoissance from Shellmound toward, Aug. 30-31, 1863.—Reconnoissance toward, Sept. 7, 1863.—Evacuation of, by Confederate forces, Sept. 8, 1863.—Occupation of, by Union forces, Sept. 9, 1863.—Skirmish at Missionary Ridge near, Sept. 22, 1863.—Skirmish at Shallow Ford Gap near, Sept. 22, 1863.—Skirmishes in front of, Sept. 23-26,

TENNESSEE.

1863.—Skirmish near, Oct. 2, 1863.—Skirmish near, Oct. 8, 1863.—Battles about, Nov. 23-25, 1863.—Explosion of ordnance building at, June 9, 1865.
CHEEK'S CROSS ROADS, Skirmish at, Dec. 12, 1863.—Skirmish at, March 13, 1864.
CHERRY VALLEY, Reconnoissance from near Murfreesborough to, April 2-6, 1863.
CHEWALLA, Skirmish near, Oct. 5, 1862.
CHICKAMAUGA STATION, Skirmish at, Nov. 26, 1863.
CHRISTIANA, Skirmish near, March 6, 1863.—Skirmish at, June 24, 1863.—Affair at, Oct. 6, 1863.
CHUCKY ROAD, Skirmish on Bend of, Jan. 16, 1864.
CLARKSBURG, Skirmish at, Dec. 30, 1862.
CLARK'S CREEK CHURCH, Skirmish at, Sept. 13, 1863.
CLARK'S FERRY, Scout from near Dandridge to, Jan. 10-11, 1864.
CLARKSVILLE, Occupation of, by Union forces, Feb. 19, 1862.—Surrender of, by Union forces, Aug. 18, 1862.—Expedition from Fort Donelson to, Sept. 5-10, 1862.—Reconnoissance from Edgefield Junction toward, Nov. 15-20, 1862.—Skirmish at, Nov. 25, 1862.—Expedition to, Nov. 28-30, 1862.—Scout from, May 20-22, 1863.—Skirmish at, Oct. 28, 1863.
CLEVELAND, Skirmish at, Sept. 18, 1863.—Skirmish at, Oct. 9, 1863.—Skirmish at, Nov. 27, 1863.—Skirmish at, Dec. 22, 1863.—Skirmish at, Dec. 29, 1863.—Skirmish at, April 2, 1864.—Skirmish at Mink Springs near, April 13, 1864.
CLIFTON, Skirmish near, Jan. 1, 1863.—Skirmish near, Jan. 3, 1863.—Skirmish at, Jan. 10, 1863.—Expedition from Lexington to, Feb. 17-21, 1863.—Skirmishes at, July 22-23, 1864.—Skirmish at, July 30, 1864.—Skirmish at, Aug. 31, 1864.
CLINCH MOUNTAIN, Skirmish at, Oct. 27, 1863.—Skirmish at, Dec. 6, 1863.—Skirmish at, Oct. 18, 1864.—Expedition from Strawberry Plains to, Jan. 28-31, 1865.
CLINCH MOUNTAIN GAP, Skirmish at, Dec. 14, 1863.
CLINCH RIVER, Skirmish at, Dec. 21, 1863.—Skirmish at, Oct. 1, 1864.
CLINCH VALLEY, Skirmish in, near Sneedville, Oct. 21, 1864.
CLINTON FERRY, Skirmish at, July 25, 1862.
COLLEGE GROVE, Skirmish near, March 19, 1863.—Affair near, April 26, 1863.
COLLIERVILLE, Scout to, Oct. 21, 1862.—Skirmish near, Jan. 28, 1863.—Expedition from, March 8-12, 1863.—Skirmish at, May 20, 1863.—Action at, Oct. 11, 1863.—Action at, Nov. 3, 1863.—Skirmish at, Dec. 27, 1863.—Skirmish near, Jan. 13, 1864.—Scout from, Jan. 14, 1864.—Skirmish near, June 13, 1864.—Skirmish at, June 23, 1864.—Skirmish near, July 2, 1864.—Skirmish near, July 24, 1864.—Skirmish near, Nov. 15, 1864.
COLUMBIA, Skirmish near, July 17, 1862.—Skirmish at, Sept.

TENNESSEE.

9, 1862.—Skirmish at, Sept. 10, 1862.—Expedition from Murfreesborough toward, March 4-14, 1863.—Expedition to, July —, 1863.—Skirmish near, Oct. 2, 1864.—Skirmishes in front of, Nov. 24-27, 1864.—Skirmish at, Dec. 20, 1864.—Skirmish at Warfield's near, Dec. 23, 1864.

COLUMBIA FORD, Action at, Nov. 29, 1864.

COLUMBIA PIKE, Skirmish on, April 1, 1863.

COLUMBIA ROAD, Reconnoissance from Franklin on the, Feb. 21, 1863.

COLWELL'S FORD, Skirmish at, Nov. 19, 1863.

COMO, Skirmish at, Sept. 19, 1863.

CONYERSVILLE, Expeditions from Paducah, Ky., and Union City, Tenn., to, Sept. 10, 1863.

CORNERSVILLE PIKE, Affair at Lee's House on, Jan. 28, 1864.

CORN'S FARM, Franklin County, Affair at, Feb. 6, 1865.

COTTON PORT FORD, Tennessee River, Skirmish at, Sept. 30, 1863.

COVINGTON, Expedition from Columbus, Ky., to, Sept. 28-Oct. 1, 1862.—Skirmish near, March 9-10, 1863.

COWAN, Affair near the railroad tunnel near, Oct. 9, 1863.

COX'S HILL (See Insane Asylum, Jan. 3, 1863).

CRAB GAP, Skirmish at, Dec. 5, 1863.

CRIPPLE CREEK, Woodbury Pike, Skirmish near, May 25, 1864.

CROSSVILLE, Affair at Cumberland Mountain, on road to, Dec. 9, 1863.

CRUMP'S LANDING, Expedition toward Purdy and operations about, March 9-14, 1862.

CUBA, Expedition from Memphis to, Aug. 10-11, 1863.

CUMBERLAND GAP, Skirmish near, Feb. 14, 1862.—Reconnoissance to and skirmish at, March 21-23, 1862.—Campaign, March 28-June 18, 1862.—Skirmish near, April 29, 1862.—Operations about, July 7-11, 1862.—Operations at, Aug. 2-6, 1862.—Occupation of, by Union forces, June 18, 1862.—Operations about, Aug. 16-22, 1862.—Operations about, Aug. 16-Sept. 17, 1862.—Skirmish at, Aug. 26, 1862.—Skirmish near, Aug. 27, 1862.—Expedition from, to Pine Mountain, Sept. 6-10, 1862, and skirmishes.—Evacuation of, by Union forces, Sept. 17, 1862.—Operations about, Sept. 7-10, 1863.—Skirmish at, Sept. 23, 1863.—Skirmish near, Nov. 12, 1863.—Scout from, Jan. 23-27, 1865.

CUMBERLAND IRON WORKS, Skirmish at, Aug. 26, 1862.—Skirmish at, Feb. 3, 1863.

CUMBERLAND MOUNTAINS, Affair at, Dec. 9, 1863.—Expedition from Gallatin to, Jan. 28-Feb. 8, 1864.

CUMBERLAND RIVER, Skirmish on, near Gallatin, Nov. 8, 1862.—Reconnoissance from Nashville to, Jan. 13-19, 1863.—Scout from Columbia, Ky., to south side of, Nov. 26, 1863.—Skirmishes on, Nov. —, 1863.

TENNESSEE.

CURTIS'S CREEK, Skirmish at, Dec. 19, 1864.
CYPRESS CREEK BRIDGE, Destruction of, May 30, 1862.
CYPRESS SWAMP, Skirmish at, April 3, 1864.—Skirmish at, April 10, 1864.
DANDRIDGE, Scouts from, Dec. 22-23, 1863, and skirmish.—Operations about, Dec. 24-28, 1863.—Skirmish at, Jan. 1, 1864.—Skirmish at, Jan. 14, 1864.—Operations about, Jan. 16-17, 1864.—Operations about, Jan. 26-28, 1864.—Skirmish at, May 19, 1864.
DANDRIDGE'S MILL, Skirmish near, Dec. 13, 1863.
DAVIDSON'S FERRY, Tennessee River, Attack on gunboats at, Nov. 2-3, 1864.
DAVIS'S BRIDGE, Skirmish at, Oct. 1, 1862.—Skirmish at, Sept. 25, 1862.—Engagement at, Oct. 5, 1862.
DAVIS'S MILL, Skirmish at, March 14, 1863.—Skirmish at, April 5, 1863.
DAVIS'S MILL ROAD, Skirmish on, near La Grange, March 24, 1863.
DECATUR COUNTY, Skirmish in, June 21, 1864.
DECHERD, Skirmish at, June 29, 1863.—Expedition from, to Nashville, Ala., Aug. 5-9, 1863.
DENMARK, Affair at Hatchie Bottom near, July 29, 1862.—Skirmish at Britton's Lane near, Sept. 1, 1862.—Skirmish near, Aug. 3, 1863.
DEVIL'S GAP, Action at, Dec. 25, 1864.
DIXON SPRINGS, Skirmish at, June 20, 1863.
DOBBIN'S FERRY, near La Vergne, Skirmish at, Dec. 9, 1862.
DONELSON, FORT, Siege of, Feb. 12-16, 1862.—Capture of, by Union forces, Feb. 16, 1862.—Skirmish near, Aug. 23, 1862.—Skirmish at, Aug. 25, 1862.—Operations about, Sept. 18-23, 1862, and skirmish.—Skirmish near, Jan. 2, 1863.—Attack on, Feb. 3, 1863.—Skirmish near, July 29, 1863.—Affair near, Sept. 18, 1863.—Skirmish near, Oct. 11, 1864.
DOUBLE BRIDGE, Skirmish at, Nov. 18, 1862.
DOVER, Naval attack on, Feb. 3, 1863.
DRAKE'S CREEK, Skirmish at, Aug. 20, 1862.
DRESDEN, Expedition from Trenton to, May 2-9, 1862.
DUCK RIVER, Scout from Lexington to mouth of, March 31-April 3, 1863.—Skirmish on, April 22, 1864.—Skirmishes at crossings of, Nov. 28, 1864.—Skirmish at, Dec. 22, 1864.
DUCK RIVER ISLAND, Engagement at, April 26, 1863.
DUKEDOM, Skirmish at, Feb. 28, 1864.
DUNLAP, Skirmish near, Oct. 2, 1863.
DURHAMVILLE, Expedition from Columbus, Ky., to, Sept. 28-Oct. 1, 1862.
DUVALL'S FORD, Skirmish at, Sept. 30, 1864.
DYERSBURG, Skirmish at Wood Springs near, Aug. 7, 1862.—Skirmish near, Aug. 18, 1862.—Skirmish at, Jan. 30, 1863.

TENNESSEE.

EAGLEVILLE, Skirmish near, March 2, 1863.—Skirmishes near, March 31-April 1, 1863.—Skirmish near, April 16, 1863.—Expedition from Triune to, May 3, 1863.—Skirmish at, Dec. 7, 1863.
EAGLEVILLE PIKE, Scout on, June 10, 1863.
EASTPORT, Skirmish at, Nov. 1, 1863.
EAST TENNESSEE AND GEORGIA RAILROAD, Raid on, Nov. 24-27, 1863.
EDDYVILLE, Naval action at, Aug. 26, 1861.
EDGEFIELD, Expedition from, to Harpeth Shoals, Clarksville, etc., Nov. 26-Dec. 1, 1862.
EDGEFIELD JUNCTION, Skirmishes near, Aug. 20, 1862.
ELK RIVER, Skirmish on, near Bethel, May 9, 1862.—Skirmish on, May 20, 1862.—Skirmish at, Oct. 9, 1863.
ENGLAND COVE, Scout from Kingston to, July 7-9, 1864.—Scout from Kingston to, July 12-18, 1864.
ESTENAULA, Skirmish at, Dec. 24, 1863.
ESTILL SPRINGS, Skirmish at, July 2, 1863.
EVANS'S ISLAND, Expedition from Irish Bottom to, Jan. 25, 1865.
FAIN'S ISLAND, Skirmish at, Jan. 28, 1864.
FAIRFIELD, Skirmish at, June 27, 1863.
FAIR GARDEN, Engagement near, Jan. 27, 1864.
FARLEY'S MILL, Holston River, Skirmish at, Dec. 13, 1863.
FARMINGTON, Skirmish at, Oct. 7, 1863.
FAYETTEVILLE, Skirmish at, May 14, 1862.—Reconnoissance from, to Athens, Ala., Aug. 7-8, 1863.—Skirmishes at, Oct. 13-14, 1863.—Scout from Winchester to, Oct. 29-Nov. 2, 1863.—Affair near, Dec. 6, 1863.
FENTRESS COUNTY, Skirmish in, Feb. 13, 1864.
FLAT CREEK, Skirmish at, Jan. 26, 1864.—Expedition from Knoxville to, Feb. 1, 1864.—Skirmish at, Feb. 20, 1864.—Skirmish at, Nov. 17, 1864.
FLAT CREEK VALLEY, Skirmish in, March 15, 1864.
FORKED DEER RIVER, Scout on, April 26-29, 1862.—Skirmish at Railroad Crossing of, Dec. 20, 1862.—Skirmish on, July 13, 1863.—Skirmish on, July 15, 1863.
FOSTERVILLE, Skirmish at, June 25, 1863.—Skirmish at, June 27, 1863.—Skirmish at Garrison's Creek near, Oct. 6, 1863.
FOUCHE SPRINGS, Skirmish at, Nov. 23, 1864.
FRANKLIN, Reconnoissance toward, Dec. 9, 1862.—Skirmish at, Dec. 12, 1862.—Skirmishes at, Dec. 26-27, 1862.—Expedition from Murfreesboro to, Jan. 31-Feb. 13, 1863.—Reconnoisance from, on the Lewisburg, Columbia and Carter Creek Roads, Feb. 21, 1863.—Skirmish near, March 4, 1863.—Skirmish near, March 31, 1863.—Skirmish at, April 9, 1863.—Engagement at, April 10, 1863.—Engagement at, June 4, 1863.—Battle of, Nov. 30, 1864.—Action at, Dec. 17, 1864.—Scouts about, Jan. 16-Feb. 20, 1865.
FRANKLIN COUNTY, Affair at Corn's Farm, in, Feb. 6, 1865.

TENNESSEE.

FRANKLIN PIKE, Skirmish on, near Nashville, Dec. 14, 1862.
FRIAR'S ISLAND, Skirmish at, Sept. 9, 1863.
FRIENDSHIP CHURCH, Skirmish at, Sept. 29, 1863.
GALLATIN, Operations about, March 15-18, 1862.—Capture of, by Confederate forces, Aug. 12, 1862.—Skirmish near, Aug. 13, 1862.—Action on the Hartsville Road near, Aug. 21, 1862.—Skirmish at, Nov. 7, 1862.—Skirmish on the Cumberland River near, Nov. 8, 1862.—Affair at South Tunnel near, Oct. 10, 1864.
GALLATIN PIKE, Skirmish on, near Nashville, Oct. 20, 1862.
GALLATIN ROAD, Affair on, Sept. 6, 1862.
GALLOWAY SWITCH, Scout to, Oct. 23, 1862.
GARRISON'S CREEK, Skirmish at, near Fosterville, Oct. 6, 1863.
GATLINSBURG, Skirmish at, Dec. 10, 1863.
GERMANTOWN, Affair near, Jan. 27, 1863.—Scout from, July 8, 1863.—Scout from, July 16-20, 1863.—Skirmish at, March 28, 1865.—Skirmish near, April 18, 1865.
GOODLETSVILLE, Skirmish at, Sept. 30, 1862.
GRAND JUNCTION, Expedition from Bolivar to, Sept. 20-22, 1862, and skirmish.—Occupation of, by Union forces, Nov. 4, 1862.—Guerrilla attack on railway train near, March 21, 1863.—Skirmish at, July 30, 1863.
GRANGER'S MILL, Skirmish at, Dec. 14, 1863.
GRANNY WHITE'S PIKE, Skirmish on, near Nashville, March 9, 1862.
GREENVILLE, Skirmish at, Oct. 2, 1863.—Skirmish near, April 15, 1864.—Skirmish at, May 30, 1864.—Scout from Strawberry Plains to, Aug. 1-5, 1864.—Skirmish at, Sept. 4, 1864.—Skirmish at, Oct. 12, 1864.—Expedition to, Feb. 20-24, 1865.
GREEN HILL, Skirmish near, April 6, 1863.—Skirmish near, June 14, 1863.
GRISSON'S BRIDGE, Skirmish at, Dec. 27, 1863.
GUY'S GAP, Skirmish at, June 25, 1863.—Skirmish at, June 27, 1863.
HAMBURG, Skirmish at Chambers Creek near, Jan. 13, 1863.
HAMBURG LANDING, Skirmishes at, May 29-30, 1863.
HARDIN COUNTY, Skirmish in, Feb. 9, 1864.
HARPETH RIVER, Reconnoissance from Nashville to, Jan. 13-19, 1863.—Skirmish on, March 8, 1863.
HARPETH SHOALS, Expedition from Edgefield to, Nov. 26-27, 1862.—Affair at, Jan. 13, 1863.
HARRISON, Scout from Chattanooga to, Jan. 21, 1864.
HARRISON'S LANDING, Skirmishes at, Aug. 26-27, 1863.
HARTSVILLE, Skirmish on the Carthage Road near, Nov. 28, 1862.—Action at, Dec. 7, 1862.—Skirmish at, April 18, 1863.—Skirmish at, April 22, 1863.—Skirmish near, Oct. 10, 1863.
HARTSVILLE ROAD, Action on, near Gallatin, Aug. 21, 1862.

TENNESSEE.

HATCHIE BOTTOM, Affair at, near Denmark, July 29, 1862.
HATCHIE BRIDGE, Engagement at, Oct. 5, 1862.
HATCHIE RIVER, Reconnoissance towara mouth of, Aug. 10-11, 1862.—Skirmish near Bloomington on the, Feb. 27, 1863.—Expedition from Jackson to, April 1-16, 1863, and skirmishes.—Scout from Memphis to, June 16, 1863.
HAY'S FERRY, near Dandridge, Action at, Dec. 24, 1863.
HENDERSON, Expedition from Corinth, Miss., to, Sept. 11-16, 1863.
HENDERSON'S MILL, Skirmish at, Oct. 11, 1863.
HENDERSON'S STATION, Mobile and Ohio Railroad, Capture of, by Confederate forces, Nov. 25, 1862.
HENRY, FORT, Reconnoissance from Paducah, Ky., to, Jan. 15-25, 1862.—Gunboat reconnoissance to, Feb. 4, 1862.—Capture of, by Union forces, Feb. 6, 1862.—Operations about, Sept. 18-23, 1862.
HENRYVILLE, Skirmish at, Nov. 23, 1864.
HERMITAGE FORD, Skirmish at, Oct. 20, 1862.
HERNANDO ROAD, Scout on, Feb. 7, 1865.
HICKMAN COUNTY, Scout in, May 2-12, 1864.
HICKORY, Scout to, Oct. 23, 1862.
HILLSBOROUGH, Skirmish near, June 29, 1863.
HILL'S GAP, near Beersheba, Skirmish at, Oct. 3, 1863.
HOLLY TREE GAP, Skirmish on Franklin Pike near, Dec. 4, 1862.—Action at, Dec. 17, 1864.
HOLSTON RIVER, Destruction of railroad bridge over, Dec. 30, 1862.—Skirmish at Leiper's Ferry on, Oct. 30, 1863.
HOOVER'S GAP, Skirmishes at, June 24-26, 1863.
HORN LAKE CREEK, Skirmish on, May 18, 1863.
HUFF'S FERRY, Skirmish at, Nov. 14, 1863.
HUMBOLDT, Skirmish near, July 28, 1862.—Skirmish at Burnt Bridge near, Sept. 5, 1862.—Affair near, Oct. 9, 1862.—Capture of, by Confederate forces, Dec. 20, 1862.
HUNTINGDON, Skirmish near, Dec. 27, 1862.—Skirmishes at, Dec. 29-30, 1862.—Skirmish at, Dec. 27, 1863.
HUNTSVILLE, Scott County, Skirmish at, Aug. 13, 1862.
INDIAN CREEK, Skirmish at, Jan. 28, 1864.
INDIAN HILL, Skirmish at, Nov. 23, 1863.
INSANE ASYLUM (or Cox's Hill, Blood's), Skirmish at the, Jan. 3, 1863.
ISLAND FORD, Skirmish at, Jan. 28, 1864.
JACKSBOROUGH, Skirmish at, March 14, 1862.
JACK'S CREEK, Skirmish at, Dec. 24, 1863.
JACKSON, Capture of, by Union forces, June 7, 1862.—Expedition from Holly Springs, Miss., to, July 25-Aug. 1, 1862.—Engagement near, Dec. 19, 1862.—Expedition across Tennessee River from, June — to 7, 1863.—Skirmish at, July 13, 1863.—Skirmish near, July 15, 1863.—Expedition from Fort Pillow to, Sept. 19-25, 1863.
JACKSON, CAMP, Skirmish at, March 24, 1862.

142

TENNESSEE.

JACKSONBOROUGH, Skirmish at, Aug. 28, 1863.
JACKSON COUNTY, Skirmish in, March 8, 1865.
JASPER, Skirmish at Rankins' Ferry near, June 21, 1862.—Skirmish on the Valley Road near, Oct. 2, 1863.
JEFFERSON, Skirmish at, Dec. 30, 1862.
JEFFERSON PIKE, Skirmish on, at Stewart's Creek Bridge, Dec. 27, 1862.
JOHNSONVILLE, Skirmish near, Sept. 25, 1864.—Action at, Nov. 4-5, 1864.
JONESBOROUGH, Action at, Sept. 21, 1863.—Skirmish at, Sept. 28, 1863.—Skirmish at, Sept. 29, 1864.
JONES' HILL, Skirmish at, Oct. 26, 1863.
JORDAN'S STORE, Skirmish at, May 30, 1863.
KELLY'S FORD, Skirmish at, Jan. 27, 1864.—Skirmish at, Jan. 28, 1864.
KIMBROUGH'S CROSS ROADS, Skirmish at, Jan. 16, 1864.
KIMBROUGH'S MILL, Mill Creek, Skirmish near, Dec. 6, 1862.
KINDERHOOK, Affair near, Aug. 11, 1862.
KING'S HILL, Action at, Dec. 25, 1864.
KINGSPORT, Skirmish at, Sept. 18, 1863.—Skirmish at, Oct. 6, 1864.—Action at, Dec. 13, 1864.
KINGSTON, Skirmishes at, and about, Nov. 16-23, 1863.—Action at, Nov. 24, 1863.—Skirmish near, Dec. 4, 1863.—Skirmish at. Oct. 7, 1864.
KNOB CREEK, near Ripley, Skirmish at, Jan. 8, 1863.
KNOB GAP, Skirmish at, Dec. 26, 1862.
KNOXVILLE, Skirmishes near, June 19-20, 1863.—Occupation of, by Union forces, Sept. 2, 1863.—Skirmish near, Nov. 16, 1863.—Siege of, Nov. 17-Dec. 4, 1863.—Assault on Confederate lines, about, Nov. 23, 1863.—Assault on Union lines about, Nov. 23, 1863.—Capture of Union pickets at Love's Hill near, Jan. 24, 1864.—Skirmish near, Jan. 26, 1864.—Skirmish near, Jan. 27, 1864.—Scout near, Feb. 13, 1864.—Skirmish on Sevierville Road near, Feb. 20, 1864.
LA FAYETTE, Macon County, Expedition to, Oct. —, 1862.—Scout to, March 10-16, 1863, and skirmish.—Skirmish at, May 11, 1863.—Skirmish at, Nov. 5, 1863.—Skirmish at, Dec. 4, 1863.—Skirmish at, Dec. 27, 1863.—Skirmish at, June 9, 1864.—Attack on train near, June 23, 1864.—Skirmish at, June 29, 1864.—Skirmish at, Aug. 8, 1864.
LA FAYETTE DEPOT, Skirmish at, March 15, 1863.
LA FAYETTE LANDING, Affair near, Oct. 3, 1862.
LA FAYETTE STATION, Affair near, June 25, 1862.
LA GRANGE, Expedition from Bolivar to, Sept. 20-22, 1862, and skirmish.—Occupation of, by Union forces, Nov. 4, 1862.—Reconnoissance from, Nov. 8-9, 1862.—Expedition from, March 8-12, 1863.—Skirmish on Davis's Mill Road near, March 24, 1863.—Scout from, May 17, 1863.—Scouts

TENNESSEE.

from, May 19, 1863.—Skirmish at, Dec. 13, 1863.—Skirmish at, Jan. 2, 1864.—Skirmish at, Jan. 25, 1864.—Skirmish near, Feb. 2, 1864.—Skirmish near, July 3, 1864.
LAUREL CREEK GAP, Skirmish at, Oct. 1, 1864.
LA VERGNE, Skirmish near, Oct. 7, 1862.—Reconnoissance toward, Nov. 19, 1862.—Reconnoissance to, Nov. 26-27, 1862, and skirmish.—Skirmish at Dobbin's Ferry near, Dec. 9, 1862.—Skirmish at, Dec. 11, 1862.—Skirmishes at, Dec. 26-27, 1862.—Operations near, Dec. 29-31, 1862.—Skirmish at, Dec. 30, 1862.—Skirmish at, Jan. 1, 1863.—Skirmish near, April 10, 1863.—Reconnoissance from, May 12, 1863.—Skirmish at, Dec. 29, 1863.
LAWRENCEBURG, Skirmish at, April 4, 1862.—Skirmish at, Nov. 3, 1863.—Action at, Nov. 22, 1864.
LAWRENCE'S MILL, Skirmish at, Jan. 5, 1864.
LEBANON, Action at, May 5, 1862.—Skirmish at, Nov. 9, 1862.—Expedition from Murfreesborough to, April 1-8, 1863.—Reconnoissance from Murfreesborough toward, May 12-16, 1863.—Expedition to and skirmish near, June 15-17, 1863.
LEBANON ROAD, Skirmish on, near Nashville, Oct. 13, 1862.
LEESBURG, Skirmish at, Sept. 29, 1863.—Skirmish at, Sept. 28, 1864.
LEE'S HOUSE, on Cornersville Pike, Affair at, Jan. 28, 1864.
LEIPER'S FERRY, Skirmish at, Oct. 28, 1863.—Skirmish at, Oct. 30, 1863. (Holston River.)
LENOIR STATION, Affair at, June 19, 1863.—Skirmish at, Nov. 15, 1863.
LEWISBURG PIKE, Skirmish on, April 4, 1863.
LEWISBURG ROAD, Reconnoissance from Franklin on, Feb. 21, 1863.
LEXINGTON, Skirmish at, Dec. 18, 1862.—Skirmish near, June 29, 1863.—Scout to, Jan. 11, 1864.
LIBERTY, Reconnoissance from Murfreesborough to, Jan. 21-22, 1863.—Expedition from Murfreesborough to, Feb. 3-5, 1863.—Expedition from Murfreesborough to, Feb. 17-20, 1863.—Skirmish at, March 19, 1863.—Expedition from Murfreesborough to, April 1-8, 1863.—Reconnoissance from Murfreesborough toward, May 12-16, 1863.—Skirmish at, June 4, 1863.
LIBERTY GAP, Skirmishes at, June 24-27, 1863.
LICK CREEK, Skirmish at, April 24, 1862.
LIMESTONE STATION, Action at, Sept. 8, 1863.
LINCOLN COUNTY, Skirmish in, June 14, 1864.—Scout in, July 12-15, 1864.
LINDEN, Skirmish at, May 12, 1863.
LITTLE HARPETH RIVER, Action on, March 25, 1863.
LITTLE POND, near McMinnville, Skirmish at, Aug. 30, 1862.
LITTLE RIVER, Skirmish at, Nov. 14, 1863.
LITTLE ROCK LANDING, Engagement at, April 26, 1863.

TENNESSEE.

LITTLE TENNESSEE RIVER, Skirmish at Motley's Ford on, Nov. 4, 1863.—Expedition from Maryville up, Jan. 11-12, 1864.
LIVINGSTON, Skirmish near, Dec. 15, 1863.—Skirmish at, March 18, 1865.
LIZZARD, Skirmish at, Dec. 29, 1862.—Reconnoissance from Murfreesborough to, May 1, 1863.
LOBELVILLE, Skirmish at, Sept. 27, 1864.
LOCKRIDGE'S MILL, Skirmish at, May 5, 1862.
LOG MOUNTAIN, Skirmish at, Dec. 3, 1863.
LONG FORD, Skirmish at, Dec. 10, 1863.
LONG'S MILLS, near Mulberry Gap, Skirmish at, July 28, 1864.
LOOKOUT MOUNTAIN, Skirmish at, Sept. 23, 1863.—Battle of, Nov. 24, 1863.
LOOKOUT VALLEY, Skirmish in, Sept. 7, 1863.
LOUDON, Skirmish near, Oct. 14, 1863.—Skirmish near, Nov. 15, 1863.—Skirmishes at and near, Dec. 4-5, 1863.
LOUDON COUNTY, Skirmish in, Nov. 5, 1863.
LOUDON, FORT. (See Sanders, Fort, Nov. 29, 1863.)
LOUISVILLE, Affair at, March 27, 1864.
LOUISVILLE AND NASHVILLE RAILROAD, Raid on, Aug. 19-21, 1862.—Raid on, April 7-11, 1863.
LOVE'S HILL, near Knoxville, Capture of Union pickets at, Jan. 24, 1864.
LOWER POST FERRY, Affair near, July 27, 1862.
LOWRY'S FERRY, Skirmish at, Jan. 11, 1863.
LYNCHBURG, Skirmish near, Sept. 29, 1864.
LYNNVILLE, Skirmish at, Nov. 24, 1864.—Skirmish at, Dec. 24, 1864.
LYTLE'S CREEK, on Manchester Pike, Skirmish at, Jan. 5, 1863.
McCOOK, FORT, Battle Creek, Attack on, Aug. 27, 1862.
McLEMORESVILLE, Expedition from Paduach, Ky., to, Sept. 20-30, 1863.
McMINNVILLE, Reconnoissance from Murfreesborough to, March 25-28, 1862.—Expedition from Murfreesborough to, April 20-30, 1863.—Skirmishes near, Oct. 3-4, 1863.—Skirmish at, Dec. 21, 1863.—Skirmish near, Feb. 5, 1865.
McNUTT'S BRIDGE, Skirmish at, Jan. 27, 1864.
MACON, Expeditions from La Grange to, March 28-April 3, 1863.
MAGNOLIA, Skirmish at, March 31, 1865.
MANCHESTER, Reconnoissance from Murfreesborough to, March 25-28, 1862.—Occupation of, by Union forces, June 27, 1863.—Skirmish at, March 17, 1864.
MANCHESTER PIKE, Skirmish on, Jan. 4, 1863.—Skirmish on, Feb. 22, 1863.—Reconnoissance from Murfreesborough on, April 29-May 2, 1863.—Reconnoissance from Murfreesborough to, May 27-28, 1863.
MANSCOE CREEK, Skirmish at, Aug. 20, 1862.

TENNESSEE.

MARSHALL KNOB, Skirmish at, June 4, 1863.
MARYVILLE, Skirmish at, Nov. 14, 1863.—Skirmish near, Feb. 8, 1864.—Skirmish near, Feb. 18, 1864.
MAURY COUNTY, Scout in, May 2-12, 1864.
MAYNARDVILLE, Skirmish near, Dec. 1, 1863.
MEDON, Skirmish near, Aug. 13, 1862.—Skirmishes near, Aug. 31, 1862.
MEDON STATION, Skirmish at, Aug. 30, 1862.—Skirmish at, Oct. 10, 1862.
MEMPHIS, Naval engagement off, June 6, 1862.—Occupation of, by Union forces, June 6, 1862.—Skirmish near, Sept. 2, 1862.—Expedition from, against guerrillas, Feb. 17, 1863.—Skirmish on Nonconnah Creek near, April 4, 1863.—Operations on the Mississippi River near, and attack on transports, June 17-18, 1863.—Scouts from, July 3, 1863.—Skirmish near, July 18, 1863.—Scouts from, July 20-21, 1863.—Scout from, Dec. 10, 1863.—Expedition from, into Mississippi, June 1-13, 1864.—Attack on, Aug. 21, 1864.—Skirmish near, Sept. 12, 1864.—Skirmish near, Oct. 4, 1864.—Skirmish near, Oct. 20, 1864.—Skirmish near, Oct. 25, 1864.—Scout near, Nov. 10, 1864.—Skirmish on Germantown Road near, Dec. 14, 1864.—Expedition from, to destroy the Mobile and Ohio Railroad, Dec. 21, 1864-Jan. 5, 1865.—Skirmish near, Feb. 9, 1865.—Loss of the steamer Sultana in the Mississippi River near, April 27, 1865.
MEMPHIS AND CHARLESTON RAILROAD, Operations against, March 14-15, 1862.—Reconnoissances to the, May 3, 1862.—Reconnoissance toward the, and skirmish, May 15, 1862.—Operations on the, Oct. 20-29, 1863.—Operations on the, Nov. 3-5, 1863.—Operations against the, Nov. 28-Dec. 10, 1863.
MERIWETHER'S FERRY, Obion River, Skirmish at, Aug. 16, 1862.—Skirmish at, near Union City, Nov. 19, 1863.
METAMORA, Engagement at, Oct. 5, 1862.
MIDDLEBURG, Skirmish at, Dec. 24, 1862.
MIDDLE TENNESSEE, or Tullahoma Campaign, June 23-July 7, 1863.
MIDDLETON, Skirmish near, Oct. 4, 1862.—Skirmish at, Jan. 31, 1863.—Skirmish at, March 6, 1863.—Expedition from Murfreesborough to, May 21-22, 1863, and action.—Skirmish at, June 24, 1863.—Skirmish at, Jan. 14, 1864.
MIDDLETON PIKE, Scout on, June 10, 1863.
MIFFLIN, Skirmish at, Feb. 18, 1864.
MILL CREEK, Skirmish at, Nov. 27, 1862.—Affair at, Jan. —, 1863.—Skirmish near, Jan. 25, 1863.
MILTON, Action at Vaught's Hill near, March 20, 1863.
MINK SPRINGS, near Cleveland, Skirmish at, April 13, 1864.
MISSIONARY RIDGE, Skirmish at, near Chattanooga, Sept. 22, 1863.—Skirmishes at the foot of, Nov. 24, 1863.—Battle of, Nov. 25, 1863.

TENNESSEE.

MOCCASIN GAP, Passage of, Dec. 29, 1862.
MONTEREY, Skirmish near, April 3, 1862.—Skirmish near, April 17, 1862.—Skirmishes near, April 28-29, 1862.—Skirmish at, Jan. 4, 1863.
MONTEZUMA, Skirmish at, Sept. 16, 1863.
MONTGOMERY, Affair at Wartburg near, June 17, 1863.
MORGAN COUNTY, Skirmish in, Feb. 2, 1862.—Expedition into, March 28, 1862.
MORRIS' FORD, Elk River, Skirmish at, July 2, 1863.
MORRISTOWN, Skirmish at, Dec. 10, 1863.—Skirmish near, Dec. 14, 1863.—Scout to Nola Chucky Bend near, March 12, 1864.—Raid from, into North Carolina, June 13-July 15, 1864.—Skirmish at, Aug. 2, 1864.—Action at, Oct. 28, 1864.
MOSCOW, Affair near, Feb. 9, 1863.—Affair near, Feb. 18, 1863.—Scout to, March 10-16, 1863, and skirmish.—Expeditions from La Grange to, March 28-April 3, 1863.—Skirmish at Locke's Mill near, Sept. 27, 1863.—Skirmish at, Nov. 5, 1863.—Skirmish near, Dec. 27, 1863.—Skirmish near, June 15, 1864.—Expedition from Memphis to, Nov. 9-13, 1864.
MOSSY CREEK, Operations near, Dec. 24-28, 1863.—Skirmish at, Dec. 29, 1863.—Skirmish near, Jan. 10, 1864.—Skirmish near, Jan. 12, 1864.—Skirmish at, Oct. 15, 1864.—Skirmish at, Oct. 27, 1864.
MOSSY CREEK STATION, Skirmish at, Dec. 24, 1863.
MOTLEY'S FORD, Little Tennessee River, Skirmish at, Nov. 4, 1863.
MOUNTAIN GAP, near Smith's Cross Roads, Skirmish at, Oct. 1, 1863.
MOUNT CARMEL, Skirmish at, Nov. 29, 1864.
MOUNT PLEASANT, Skirmish near, July 17, 1862.—Skirmish near, Aug. 14, 1862.—Action at, Nov. 23, 1864.—Skirmish at, April 3, 1865.—Skirmish at, April 14, 1865.
MUDDY CREEK, Skirmish at, Jan. 26, 1864.
MULBERRY GAP, Skirmish at, Nov. 19, 1863.—Skirmish at Long's Mills near, July 28, 1864.
MULBERRY VILLAGE, Skirmish at, Dec. 23, 1863.
MURFREESBOROUGH, Action at, and surrender of, by Union forces, July 13, 1862.—Skirmish near, Aug. 27, 1862.—Skirmish near, Sept. 7, 1862.—Skirmishes near, Dec. 29-30, 1862.—Battle of, or Stone's River, Dec. 31, 1862-Jan. 3, 1863.—Skirmish at, Jan. 4, 1863.—Occupation of, by Union forces, Jan. 5, 1863.—Reconnoissance from, to Nolensville and Versailles, Jan. 13-15, 1863.—Capture of Union forage train near, Jan. 21, 1863.—Capture of Union forage train near, Jan. 21, 1863.—Skirmish near, Feb. 4, 1863.—Skirmish near, Feb. 7, 1863.—Reconnoissances from, March 6-7, 1863.—Skirmish near, March 10, 1863.—Skirmish near, March 22, 1863.—Skirmish near, June 3, 1863.—Operations on Shelbyville Pike near, June 4, 1863.—Skirmish at Stone's River Railroad Bridge near, Oct. 5, 1865.—Skirmish near,

TENNESSEE.

March 4, 1864.—Demonstrations against, Dec. 5-7, 1864.—Attack on railroad train near, Dec. 13, 1864.—Capture of railroad train near, Dec. 15, 1864.
MURFREESBOROUGH, or Stone's River Campaign, Dec. 26, 1862-Jan. 5, 1863.
MURFREESBOROUGH PIKE, Skirmish on, at Stewart's Creek Bridge, Dec. 27, 1862.
NARROWS, near Shellmound, Skirmishes at the, Aug. 27-28, 1863.
NASHVILLE, Evacuation of, by Confederate forces, Feb. 23, 1862.—Occupation of, by Union forces, Feb. 25, 1862.—Scout to, Feb. 26, 1862.—Operations near, March 8, 1862.—Operations around, July 8-24, 1862.—Skirmish near, Sept. 2, 1862.—Operations around, Oct. 1-Dec. 4, 1862.—Skirmish near, Oct. 1, 1862.—Skirmish at Fort Riley near, Oct. 5, 1862.—Skirmish on Lebanon Road near, Oct. 13, 1862.—Skirmish on Gallatin Pike near, Oct. 20, 1862.—Action at, Nov. 5, 1862.—Skirmish near, Nov. 13, 1862.—Affair on Hardin Pike near, Dec. 3, 1862.—Skirmish near, Dec. 11, 1862.—Skirmish on Franklin Pike near, Dec. 14, 1862.—Violation of flag of truce near, Dec. 15-16, 1862.—Skirmishes near, Dec. 23-24, 1862.—Skirmish near, Jan. 28, 1863.—Affair near, May 4, 1863.—Skirmish near, May 24, 1864.—Operations about, Dec. 1-14, 1864.—Battle of, Dec. 15-16, 1864.—Scout from, on the Nolensville Pike, Feb. 15-16, 1865.
NASHVILLE AND CHATTANOOGA RAILROAD, Raid on, April 7-11, 1863.—Raid on, near Tullahoma, March 16, 1864.—Operations against stockades and block-houses on, Dec. 2-4, 1864.
NASHVILLE AND NORTHWESTERN RAILROAD, Raid on, Aug. 15, 1864.—Raid on, Oct. 18, 1864.—Raid on, Oct. 21, 1864.
NEELY'S BEND, Cumberland River, Skirmish at, Oct. 5, 1862.—Skirmish at, Oct. 15, 1862.
NEW CASTLE, Skirmish near, Dec. 26, 1863.
NEW MADRID BEND, Skirmish at, Oct. 22, 1863.—Scouts to, Nov. 30-Dec. 3, 1863.
NEWPORT, Skirmish at, Jan. 23, 1864.
NEW PROVIDENCE, Skirmish at, Sept. 6, 1862.
NOLA CHUCKY BEND, near Morristown, Scout to, March 12, 1864.
NOLENSVILLE, Skirmish near, Dec. 1, 1862.—Skirmish at, Dec. 26, 1862.—Skirmish at, Dec. 30, 1862.—Reconnoissance from Murfreesborough to, Jan. 13-15, 1863.—Skirmish near, Feb. 15, 1863.
NOLENSVILLE PIKE, Scout from Nashville on the, Feb. 15-16, 1865.
NONCONAH CREEK, Skirmish on, Aug. 3, 1862.—Skirmish on, near Memphis, April 4, 1863.—Skirmish at, Oct. 29, 1864.

TENNESSEE.

OBEY'S RIVER, Skirmish on, March 28, 1864.—Expedition from Burkesville, Ky., to, April 18-20, 1864.
OBION PLANK ROAD CROSSING, Affair at, May —, 1863.
OBION RIVER, Skirmish near, April 9. 1863.—Skirmish on the, June 17, 1863.
OOLTEWAH, Scout from Chattanooga to, Jan. 21, 1864.—Scout from, to Burke's and Ellidge's Mills, Ga., Feb. 18-19, 1864.
ORCHARD KNOB, Skirmish at, Nov. 23, 1863.
OVERALL'S CREEK, Skirmish at, Dec. 31, 1862.
OWENS' CROSS ROADS, Action at, Dec. 1, 1864.
PALMYRA, Skirmish at, Nov. 13, 1863.
PANTHER SPRINGS, Skirmish near, March 5, 1864.—Skirmish at, Oct. 27, 1864.
PARIS, Skirmish near, March 11, 1862.—Expedition to, March 31-April 2, 1862.—Expedition from Trenton to, May 2-9, 1862.—Skirmish at, Sept. 13, 1863.
PARKER'S CROSS ROADS, Engagement at, Dec. 31, 1862.
PARK'S GAP, Skirmish at, Sept. 4, 1864.
PEA RIDGE, Skirmish at, April 15, 1862.—Skirmish at, April 27, 1862.
PEA VINE VALLEY, Skirmish in, Nov. 26, 1863.
PECK'S HOUSE, near New Market, Skirmish at, Dec. 24, 1863.
PELHAM, Skirmish at, July 2, 1863.
PERKINS' MILL, on Elk Fork, Skirmish at, Dec. 28, 1862.
PERRYVILLE, Expedition from Columbus, Ky., to, March 12-20, 1863.
PETERSBURG, Skirmish near, March 2, 1863.
PHILADELPHIA, Skirmish at, Sept. 27, 1863.—Skirmish near, Oct. 15, 1863.—Action at, Oct. 20, 1863.—Skirmishes at, Oct. 25-26, 1863.—Skirmish at, Dec. 2, 1863.—Skirmish near, March 1, 1865.
PIGEON HILLS, Skirmish at, Nov. 26, 1863.
PILLOW, FORT, Expedition down the Mississippi to, May 19-23, 1862.—Naval engagement near, April 13. 1862.—Naval operations against, April 14-June 5, 1862.—Evacuation of, by Confederate forces, June 4, 1862.—Occupation of, by Union forces, June 5, 1862.—Scout in the vicinity of, Feb. 6, 1863.—Expedition from, Feb. 27, 1863.—Scout from, Aug. 3, 1863.—Scout from, Nov. 21-22, 1863.—Capture of, by Confederate forces, April 12, 1864.
PILLOWVILLE, Skirmish at, Nov. 15, 1863.
PILOT KNOB, Skirmish at, Aug. 20, 1862.
PINE BLUFF, Skirmish at, Aug. 20, 1864.
PINE MOUNTAIN, Skirmish at, Aug. 17, 1862.—Expedition from Cumberland Gap to, Sept. 6-10, 1862, and skirmishes.
PINE MOUNTAIN GAP, Skirmish at, Sept. 7, 1862.
PINE WOOD, Expedition from Nashville to, Feb. 20-24, 1865.
PINEY FACTORY, Skirmish at, Nov. 3, 1863.
PITTSBURG, Engagement at, March 1, 1862.

TENNESSEE.

PITTSBURG LANDING, Occupation of, by Union forces, March 14-15, 1862.—Skirmish near, April 4, 1862.—Battle of, April 6-7, 1862.
PITT'S CROSS ROADS, Sequatchie Valley, Skirmish at, Oct. 2, 1863.
PLEASANT HILL LANDING, Skirmish at, April 12, 1864.
PLUM POINT, near Fort Pillow, Naval engagement at, May 10, 1862.
POCAHONTAS, Skirmish at, Sept. 26, 1862.
PORTERSVILLE, Scout to, Oct. 23-24, 1862.
POWDER SPRING GAP, Skirmish at, June 21, 1863.—Reconnoisance from Blain's Cross Roads to, Dec. 23, 1863.—Reconnoissance from, toward Rogersville and Bull's Gap, April 2-4, 1864.
POWELL RIVER, Affair at, June 30, 1862.—Skirmish at, Dec. 13, 1863.
POWELL'S BRIDGE, Skirmish at, Feb. 22, 1864.
POWELL VALLEY, Skirmish at, June 22, 1863.
PRIM'S BLACKSMITH SHOP, Edmondson Pike, Skirmish at, Dec. 25, 1862.
PULASKI, Skirmish near, May 1, 1862.—Skirmish at, May 4, 1862.—Skirmish at, May 11, 1862.—Skirmish on Richland Creek near, Aug. 27, 1862.—Skirmish at, July 15, 1863.—Scout from Columbia toward, Oct. 27, 1863, and skirmish.—Scouts from, and skirmishes, Dec. 1, 1863.—Affair near, Dec. 15, 1863.—Skirmish at, May 13, 1864.—Skirmish at Richland Creek near, Sept. 26, 1864.—Skirmish at, Sept. 27, 1864.—Scout from, to Florence, Ala., July 20-25, 1864.
PURDY, Expedition toward, March 9-14, 1862.—Expedition to, April 28-29, 1862.
PURDY ROAD, Skirmish on, near Adamsville, March 31, 1862.
PUTNAM COUNTY, Scout in, Feb. 1-7, 1864.
RAILROAD TUNNEL near Cowan, Affair near the, Oct. 9, 1863.
RALEIGH, Expedition from Memphis to, July 19-23, 1863.—Skirmish near, April 3, 1864.—Skirmish near, April 9, 1864.
RALLY HILL, Skirmish near, Nov. 29, 1864.
RANDOLPH, Burning of, by Union forces, Sept. 25, 1862.
RANDOLPH, FORT, Expedition from Columbus, Ky., to, Oct. 2, 1862.—Attack on steamer Belle St. Louis at, Oct. 27, 1864.
RANKINS'S FERRY, near Jasper, Skirmish at, June 21, 1862.
READYVILLE, Skirmish at, June 7, 1862.—Skirmish near, Oct. 5, 1863.—Skirmish at, Oct. 6, 1863.—Skirmish at, Sept. 6, 1864.
RED MOUND, Engagement at, Dec. 31, 1862.
REYNOLDSBURG, Skirmish at, March 21, 1864.
REYNOLDS'S STATION, Nashville and Decatur Railroad, Skirmish near, Aug. 27, 1862.
RHEATOWN, Skirmish at, Sept. 12, 1863.—Skirmish at, Oct. 11, 1863.—Skirmish at, April 16, 1864.—Skirmish near, Sept. 28, 1864.

TENNESSEE.

RICHLAND CREEK, Skirmish on, near Pulaski, Aug. 27, 1862.—Skirmish near, Oct. 23, 1862.—Skirmish at, near Pulaski, Sept. 26, 1864.—Skirmish at, Dec. 24, 1864.—Skirmish at, Dec. 25, 1864.
RICHLAND STATION, Skirmish at, March 19, 1863.
RIGGIN'S HILL, near Clarksville, Skirmish at, Sept. 7, 1862.
RILEY, FORT, near Nashville, Skirmish at, Oct. 5, 1862.
RILEY'S LANDING, Expedition from Island No. 10 to, Feb. 17, 1864.
RIPLEY, Skirmish at Knob Gap, near, Jan. 8, 1863.
RISING SUN, Skirmish at, June 30, 1862.
ROCK CREEK FORD, Elk River, Skirmish at, July 2, 1863.
ROCKFORD, Skirmish at, Nov. 14, 1863.
ROCK ISLAND FERRY, Reconnoissance to, Aug. 4-5, 1863.
ROCK SPRING, Skirmish at, Dec. 30, 1862.
ROGER'S GAP, Skirmish at, June 10, 1862.—Skirmish at, Aug. 31, 1862.—Operations about, Sept. 10, 1862.—Skirmish at, June 20, 1863.
ROGERSVILLE, Action near, Nov. 6, 1863.—Reconnoissance from Powder Springs Gap toward, April 2-4, 1864.—Skirmish at, Aug. 21, 1864.—Skirmish at, Oct. 8, 1864.—Skirmish at Big Creek near, Dec. 12, 1864.
ROME, Skirmish on the Carthage Road near, Nov. 28, 1862.
ROUND MOUNTAIN, near Woodbury, Skirmish at, Aug. 27, 1862.
ROVER, Skirmish at, Jan. 31, 1863.—Skirmish at, Feb. 13, 1863.—Skirmish near, Feb. 19, 1863.—Skirmish at, March 4, 1863.—Skirmish at, March 13, 1863.—Skirmish at, March 15, 1863.—Skirmish at, May 5, 1863.—Skirmish at, June 23, 1863.—Skirmish at, June 28, 1863.
RURAL HILL, Reconnoissance to, Dec. 10, 1862.
RUSSELLVILLE, Affair at, Dec. 10, 1863.—Skirmishes at, Dec. 12-13, 1863.—Skirmish at, Oct. 28, 1864.—Skirmish at, Nov. 11, 1864.—Action near, Nov. 14, 1864.
RUTHERFORD CREEK, Skirmishes at, March 10-11, 1863.—Skirmish at, Dec. 19, 1864.
RUTHERFORD'S STATION, Action at, Dec. 21, 1862.
RUTLEDGE, Skirmish at, Dec. 7, 1863.—Skirmish at, Dec. 16, 1863.—Skirmish at, Dec. 18, 1863.
SALEM, Skirmish at, March 21, 1863.—Skirmish at, May 20, 1863.
SALEM PIKE, Scouts on, June 12, 1863.
SANDERS, FORT, Knoxville, Assault on, Nov. 29, 1863.
SAULSBURY, Skirmish at, Aug. 11, 1862.—Reconnoissance in the vicinity of, Feb. 2-5, 1863.—Scout from La Grange to, March 2-3, 1863.—Scout from La Grange to, March 21-22, 1863.—Scout from Grand Junction to, April 5-6, 1863.—Scout from La Grange to, April 11, 1863.—Expedition from La Grange to, April 15, 1863.—Descent on, Dec. 2, 1863.
SCHULTZ'S MILL, Cosby Creek, Skirmish at, Jan. 14, 1864.

TENNESSEE.

SCOTT COUNTY, Expedition into, March 28, 1862.
SEQUATCHIE VALLEY, Scout in, July —, 1863.—Scout in, Sept. 21-23, 1863.—Skirmish in, Feb. 27, 1864.
SEVIERVILLE, Affair at, Jan. 13, 1864.—Skirmish at, Jan. 26, 1864.—Reconnoissance from Maryville toward, Feb. 1-2, 1864.—Skirmish at, Feb. 18, 1864.
SEVIERVILLE ROAD, Skirmish on, near Knoxville, Feb. 20, 1864.
SHALLOW FORK GAP, near Chattanooga, Skirmish at, Sept. 22, 1863.
SHELBY DEPOT, Scout to, Oct. 22, 1862.
SHELBYVILLE, Reconnoissance from Murfreesborough to, March 25-28, 1862.—Skirmish at, June 27, 1863.—Skirmish at Sim's Farm near, Oct. 7, 1863.—Skirmish at, Nov. 28, 1864.
SHELBYVILLE PIKE, Skirmish on, Jan. 5, 1863.—Skirmish on, Jan. 21, 1863.—Skirmish on, Feb. 20, 1863.—Skirmish on, April 23, 1863.—Operations on, near Murfreesborough, June 4, 1863.—Skirmish on, June 6, 1863.
SHELBYVILLE ROAD, Skirmish on, April 24, 1862.
SHELLMOUND, Action at, Aug. 21, 1863.—Skirmishes at the Narrows near, Aug. 27-28, 1863.
SHILOH, Battle of, April 6-7, 1862.
SHOAL CREEK, Skirmish on, near Wayland Springs, Dec. 12, 1863.
SHORT MOUNTAIN CROSS ROADS, Skirmish at, Aug. 29, 1862.
SILVER SPRINGS, Skirmish at, Nov. 9, 1862.
SIM'S FARM, near Shelbyville, Skirmish at, Oct. 7, 1863.
SMITH'S CROSS ROADS, Skirmish at Mountain Gap near, Oct. 1, 1863.
SMITH'S FORD, Skirmish at, April 3, 1863.
SMITHVILLE, Scout to, June 4-5, 1863.
SNEEDVILLE, Skirmish in Clinch Valley near, Oct. 21, 1864.
SNOW HILL, Reconnoissance from near Murfreesborough to, April 2-6, 1863.—Skirmish at, April 3, 1863.—Skirmish at, June 4, 1863.
SOMERVILLE, Reconnoissance from La Grange toward, Nov. 5, 1862.—Skirmish near, Nov. 26, 1862.—Action at, Jan. 3, 1863.—Skirmish at, March 28, 1863.—Expedition from Bolivar to, May 26-29, 1863, and skirmishes.—Skirmish at, Dec. 26, 1863.
SOUTH TUNNEL, near Gallatin, Affair at, Oct. 10, 1864.
SPARTA, Skirmish at, June 28, 1862.—Skirmish at, Aug. 5, 1862.—Expedition from, into Kentucky, Nov. 17-29, 1862.—Skirmish at, Aug. 9, 1863.—Skirmish at Calfkiller Creek near, Aug. 17, 1863.—Skirmish at, Nov. 20, 1863.—Skirmishes at and near, Nov. 24-26, 1863.—Skirmish near, Nov. 27, 1863.—Operations about, Jan. 4-14, 1864.—Operations about, March 11-28, 1864.
SPRING CREEK, Affair at, Dec. 19, 1862.

TENNESSEE.

SPRINGFIELD, Operations about, Nov. 26-30, 1862.
SPRING HILL, Expedition toward, March 4-5, 1863.—Engagement at, March 5, 1863.—Skirmish at, March 13, 1864.—Engagement at, Nov. 29, 1864.—Skirmish at, Dec. 18, 1864.
SPURGEON'S MILL, Skirmish at, Oct. 19, 1863.
STATESVILLE, Reconnoissance from near Murfreesborough to, April 2-6, 1863.
STEWARTSBOROUGH, Skirmish at, April 12, 1863.
STEWART'S CREEK, Skirmish at, Jan. 1, 1863.
STEWART'S CREEK BRIDGE, Skirmish on the Jefferson Pike at, Dec. 27, 1862.—Skirmish on the Murfreesborough Pike at, Dec. 27, 1862.
STEWART'S FERRY (or Ford), Stone's River, Capture of Union outpost near, Dec. 4, 1862.
STOCK CREEK, Skirmish at, Nov. 15, 1863.
STONE'S MILL, Skirmish at, Dec. 19, 1863.
STONE'S RIVER, Capture of Union courier station on, Nov. 12, 1862.—Battle of (or Murfreesborough), Dec. 31, 1862-Jan. 3, 1863.—Skirmish on, July 17, 1863.
STONE'S RIVER CAMPAIGN, Dec. 26, 1862-Jan. 5, 1863.
STONE'S RIVER RAILROAD BRIDGE, near Murfreesborough, Skirmish at, Oct. 5, 1863.
STRAWBERRY PLAINS, Skirmish at, June 20, 1863.—Skirmish at, Jan. 21, 1864.—Skirmish at, Feb. 20, 1864.—Skirmishes at, Nov. 16-17, 1864.
SUGAR CREEK, Skirmish at, Oct. 9, 1863.—Action at, Dec. 26, 1864.
SULPHUR SPRINGS, Skirmish at, Oct. 21, 1863.—Skirmish at, Feb. 26, 1864.
SUMMERTOWN, Skirmish at, Sept. 23, 1863.
SWALLOW BLUFFS, Skirmish at, Sept. 30, 1863.
SWANN'S ISLAND, Skirmish at, Jan. 28, 1864.
SWEEDEN'S COVE, near Jasper, Skirmish at, June 4, 1862.
SWEET WATER, Skirmishes near, Sept. 6, 1863.—Skirmishes at, Oct. 10-11, 1863.—Skirmish at, Oct. 23, 1863.—Skirmishes at and near, Oct. 26-27, 1863.—Attack upon garrison at, Feb. 16, 1865.
SYCAMORE CREEK, Expedition to, Nov. 30, 1862.
TALBOTT'S STATION, Skirmish at, Dec. 27, 1863.—Skirmish at, Dec. 29, 1863.
TAZEWELL, Affair near, July 22, 1862.—Skirmish at, July 26, 1862.—Skirmish near, Aug. 6, 1862.—Skirmish at, Sept. 5, 1863.—Skirmish at Big Springs near, Jan. 19, 1864.—Skirmish at, Jan. 24, 1864.—Scout from Cumberland Gap to, Aug. 3-6, 1864.—Skirmish at, March 5, 1865.
TELFORD'S STATION, Action at, Sept. 8, 1863.
TENNESSEE RIVER, Naval expedition up, Nov. 18-26, 1861.—Operations of Mississippi Marine Brigade on, April 5-May 29, 1863.—Naval operations on, Dec. 14, 1864-Jan. 4, 1865.

TENNESSEE.

TENNESSEE STATE LINE, Expedition from Bowling Green, Ky., to, May 2-6, 1863.—Expedition from Glasgow, Ky., to, June 8-10, 1863.
THOMPSON'S STATION, Engagement at, March 5, 1863.—Skirmish at, March 9, 1863.—Skirmishes near, March 23, 1863.—Skirmish near, May 2, 1863.—Affair at, Nov. 29, 1864.—Skirmish at, Nov. 30, 1864.
THORN HILL, near Bean's Station, Skirmish at, Oct. 10, 1864.
TIPTONVILLE, Expedition from Island No. 10 to, Nov. 21, 1863.
TOONE'S STATION, Affair near, July 27, 1862.—Skirmish near, Aug. 31, 1862.—Expedition from La Grange to, Sept. 11-16, 1863.
TRACY CITY, Expedition from, to the Tennessee River, Aug. 22-24, 1863.—Skirmish at, Jan. 20, 1864.—Skirmish at, Aug. 4, 1864.
TRENTON, Capture of, by Confederate forces, Dec. 20, 1862.—Expedition from Jackson to, March 16-18, 1863.—Skirmish at, April 19, 1863.—Affair near, June 15, 1863.—Operations in the vicinity of, July 19-29, 1863.—Expedition from Union City to, Jan. 22-27, 1864.
TRIUNE, Skirmish at, Dec. 27, 1862.—Skirmish near, March 8, 1863.—Skirmish near, March 21, 1863.—Skirmish at, June 8, 1863.—Skirmish near, June 9, 1863.—Action at, June 11, 1863.—Skirmish at, June 19, 1863.—Skirmishes at, Aug. 3-4, 1864.—Affair near, Feb. 10, 1865.
TULLAHOMA, Reconnoissance from Murfreesborough to, March 25-28, 1862.—Skirmishes near, June 29-30, 1863.—Occupation of, by Union forces, July 1, 1863.—Raid on the Nashville and Chattanooga Railroad near, March 16, 1864.
TULLAHOMA (or Middle Tennessee) CAMPAIGN, June 23-July 7, 1863.
TYREE SPRINGS, Skirmish at, Nov. 7, 1862.
UNION, Capture of, by Union forces, Dec. 30, 1862.
UNION CITY, Descent upon, March 30-31, 1862.—Capture of, by Confederate forces, Dec. 21, 1862.—Capture of Union outpost at, July 10, 1863.—Expedition from, to Conyersville, Sept. 1-10, 1863.—Skirmish at Meriwether's Ferry near, Nov. 19, 1863.—Expedition from, to Trenton, Jan. 22-27, 1864.—Skirmish near, March 12, 1864.—Capture of, by Confederate forces, March 24, 1864.
UNION STATION, Skirmishes at, Nov. 1, 1864.
UNIONTOWN, Skirmish at, June 23, 1863.
UNIONVILLE, Skirmish at, Jan. 31, 1863.—Skirmish at, March 4, 1863.
UNIVERSITY DEPOT, Skirmish at, July 4, 1863.
VALLEY ROAD, Skirmish on, near Jasper, Oct. 2, 1863.
VAN BUREN, Skirmish near, Sept. 21, 1862.
VAUGHT'S HILL, near Milton, Action at, March 20, 1863.

TENNESSEE.

VERSAILLES, Reconnoissance from Murfreesborough to, Jan. 13-15, 1863.—Reconnoissance from Salem to, March 9-14, 1863.
WALDEN'S RIDGE, Affair at, July 5, 1862.
WALKER'S FORD, Clinch River, Action at, Dec. 2, 1863.—Skirmish at, Dec. 5, 1863.
WALLACE'S CROSS ROADS, Skirmish at, July 15, 1862.
WARFIELD'S, near Columbia, Skirmish at, Dec. 23, 1864.
WARRENSBURG, Expedition to, Feb. 20-24, 1865.
WARTBURG, near Montgomery, Affair at, June 17, 1863.
WARTRACE, Skirmish at, April 11, 1862.—Skirmish at, Sept. 6, 1863.—Skirmish at, Oct. 6, 1863.
WASHINGTON, Capture of, by Confederate forces, Feb. 26, 1864.
WATAUGA BRIDGE, Destruction of, Dec. 30, 1862.
WATAUGA RIVER, Expedition from Bull's Gap to, April 25-27, 1864.—Skirmish at, Sept. 29, 1864.
WATERHOUSE'S MILL, Skirmishes at, April 19-20, 1864.
WAUHATCHIE, Engagement at, Oct. 28-29, 1863.
WAVERLY, Expedition from Fort Donelson to, Oct. 22-25, 1862, and skirmishes.—Expedition from Fort Henry to, Jan. 16, 1863.—Skirmish near, Oct. 23, 1862.—Skirmish near, Oct. 28, 1862.
WAYLAND'S SPRINGS, Skirmish on Shoal Creek near, Dec. 12, 1863.
WEEM'S SPRINGS, Skirmish at, Aug. 19, 1863.
WELLS'S HILL, Skirmish at, Sept. 28, 1864.
WESLEY CAMP, Expedition from Bolivar to, May 26-29, 1863, and skirmishes.
WEST HARPETH RIVER, Action at, Dec. 17, 1864.
WHITE COUNTY, Skirmish in, Jan. 16, 1864.—Scout in, Feb. 1-7, 1864.
WHITE OAK CREEK, Skirmish at, April 1, 1865.
WHITE OAK SPRINGS, Skirmish near, Oct. 24, 1862.
WHITE RANGE, Skirmish at, Nov. 7, 1862.
WHITESIDE'S, Scout from, to Stevens's and Frick's Gaps, Ga., Feb. 25-26, 1864.—Scout from, to Sulphur Springs, Ga., Sept. 2-5, 1864.
WHITE'S STATION, Skirmish at, June 20, 1864.—Skirmish at, July 26, 1864.—Skirmish at, Dec. 4, 1864.—Skirmish near, Dec. 25, 1864.
WILKINSON'S (or Wilkerson's) CROSS ROADS, Skirmish at, Dec. 29, 1862.—Skirmish near, Dec. 31, 1862.
WILLIAMSPORT, Skirmish near, Aug. 11, 1862.
WILSON CREEK PIKE, Skirmish on, Dec. 11, 1862.—Skirmish on, Dec. 21, 1862.—Skirmish on, Dec. 25, 1862.
WILSON'S GAP, Skirmish at, June 10, 1862.—Skirmish at, June 18, 1862.
WILSONVILLE, Capture of forage trains near, Jan. 22, 1864.

TENNESSEE—TEXAS.

WINCHESTER, Skirmish at, May 24, 1862.—Skirmish at, June 4, 1862.—Skirmish at, June 10, 1862.—Skirmish at, June 16, 1862.—Skirmish at Boiling Fork near, July 3, 1863.—Skirmish near, Sept. 26, 1863.—Scout from, to Fayetteville, Oct. 29-Nov. 2, 1863.—Skirmish at, Nov. 22, 1863.—Affair at, May 10, 1864.—Guerrilla depredations at, May 29, 1864.

WINTER'S GAP, Skirmish at, Aug. 31, 1863.

WOLF CREEK BRIDGE, near Memphis, Skirmish at, Sept. 23, 1862.

WOLF RIVER, Skirmish near, July 13, 1862.

WOLF RIVER BRIDGE, near Moscow, Action at, Dec. 3-4, 1863.

WOODBURY, Skirmish at Round Mountain near, Aug. 27, 1862.—Skirmish near, Jan. 19, 1863.—Skirmish at, Jan. 24, 1863.—Skirmish near, March 1, 1863.—Expedition from Murfreesborough to, March 3-8, 1863.—Expedition from Readyville to, April 2, 1863.—Skirmish at, April 4, 1863.—Skirmish at, May 24, 1863.—Skirmish near, March 25, 1863.—Skirmish at, Sept. 10, 1864.

WOODBURY PIKE, Skirmish on, March 27, 1863.—Skirmish near Cripple Creek on, May 25, 1864.

WOODSON'S GAP, Capture of Union refugees near, April 17, 1862.

WOOD SPRINGS, near Dyersburg, Skirmish at, Aug. 7, 1862.

WOODVILLE, Skirmish at, Oct. 21, 1862.

YANKEETOWN, Skirmish near, Nov. 25, 1863.—Skirmish at, Nov. 30, 1863.

YELLOW CREEK, Skirmish on, May 22, 1863.—Skirmish at, July 5, 1863.

YORKVILLE, Skirmish near, Jan. 28, 1863.

ZOLLICOFFER, Action at, Sept. 20-21, 1863.—Skirmish at, Sept. 24, 1863.—Skirmish at, Oct. 19, 1863.

TEXAS.

Seceded Feb. 1, 1861.

ARANSAS BAY, Engagement in, Feb. 22, 1862.—Capture of Union launches in, April 22, 1862.—Operations in, July 7-17, 1862.

ARANSAS PASS, Operations at, Feb. 11-13, 1862.—Capture of Confederate battery at, Nov. 17, 1863.

BEAUMONT, Destruction of railroad depot near, Oct. 2, 1862.

BELKNAP, FORT, Operations against Indians near, Oct. 13-20, 1864.

BLISS, FORT, Abandoned by Union forces, March 31, 1861.—Skirmish with Indians near, Aug. —, 1861.

BOCA CHICA PASS, Skirmish at the, Oct. 14, 1864.

BRAZOS ISLAND, Occupation of, by Union forces, Nov. 2, 1863.

TEXAS.

BRAZOS SANTIAGO, Seizure of U. S. property at, Feb. 21, 1861.—Expedition to, Oct. 27-Nov. 3, 1863.—Operations in the vicinity of, Aug. 4-15, 1864.—Skirmish at Palmetto Ranch near, Sept. 6, 1864.—Expedition from, May 11-14, 1865.
BROWN, FORT, Abandoned by U. S. troops, March 20, 1861.
BROWNSVILLE, Occupation of, by Union forces, Nov. 6, 1863.—Reoccupation of, by Confederate forces, July 30, 1864.
CALCASIEU BAY, Naval action in, May 6, 1864.
CALCASIEU RIVER, Naval expedition into, Sept. 26-30, 1862.
CANEY BAYOU, Bombardment of Confederate works at mouth of, Jan. 8-9, 1864.—Affair at mouth of, Feb. 7, 1864.
CEDAR BAYOU, Skirmish at, Nov. 23, 1863.
CEDAR LAKE, Boat expedition into, Nov. 27-28, 1862.
CHADBOURNE, FORT, Surrender of, by U. S. forces, Feb. 28, 1861.
CLARK, FORT, Affair on the Nueces River near, Aug. 10, 1862.
COLORADO, CAMP, Abandoned by U. S. forces, Feb. 26, 1861.
CONCHO RIVER, Action at Dove Creek on, Jan. 8, 1865.
COOPER, CAMP, Abandoned by U. S. forces, Feb. 21, 1861.
CORPUS CHRISTI, Bombardment of, Aug. 16-18, 1862.—Capture of, by Union naval forces, Oct. 5, 1862.—Affair at, March 17, 1864.—Affair at, March 22, 1864.
CORPUS CHRISTI BAY, Naval action in, Aug. 12, 1862.
CORPUS CHRISTI PASS, Naval operations near, Dec. 6, 1862.
DAVIS, FORT, Abandoned by U. S. forces, April 13, 1861.
DOVE CREEK, Concho River, Action at, Jan. 8, 1865.
DUNCAN, FORT, Abandoned by U. S. forces, March 20, 1861.
EAGLE PASS, Affair at, June 19, 1864.
ELM CREEK, Skirmish on, Oct. 13, 1864.
ESPERENZA, FORT, Matagorda Island, Expedition against, Nov. 22-30, 1863.
FLOUR BLUFFS, Operations at, Sept. 13-14, 1862. (Near Corpus Christi.)
GALVESTON, Blockade of, and operations about, May 14-25, 1862.—Bombardment of, Aug. 3, 1862.—Naval demonstration on, May 15, 1862.—Capture of, by Union naval forces, Oct. 5, 1862.—Surrender of, to Union naval forces, May 2, 1865.—Occupation of, by Union forces, Dec. 24, 1862.—Capture of, by Confederate forces, Jan. 1, 1863.—Naval engagement off, Jan. 11, 1863.—Mutiny at, Aug. 10-13, 1863.
GALVESTON BAY, Boat expedition in, and destruction of blockade-runners, July 7-8, 1864.
HUDSON, CAMP, Abandoned by U. S. forces, March 17, 1861.
INDIANOLA, Surrender of U. S. troops at, April 25, 1861.—Affair near, Feb. 22, 1864.
INGE, FORT, Abandoned by U. S. troops, March 19, 1861.—Operations against Indians from, Oct. 11-16, 1861.

TEXAS.

LAGUNA MADRE (See Flour Bluffs, Sept. 13-14, 1862).
LAMAR, Descent upon, Feb. 11, 1864.
LANCASTER, FORT, Abandoned by U. S. forces, March 19, 1861.
LAREDO, Attack on, March 19, 1864.
LAVACCA, Bombardment of, Oct. 31-Nov. 1, 1862.
LOS PATRICIOS, Skirmish at, March 13, 1864.
McINTOSH, FORT, Abandoned by U. S. troops, March 12, 1861.
MATAGORDA, Affair near, Nov. 20, 1862.
MATAGORDA BAY, Expedition up, April 12-13, 1864.—Naval operations in, March 28-April 6, 1864.
MATAGORDA PENINSULA, Skirmish on, Dec. 29, 1863.—Reconnoissance on, Jan. 21-25, 1864.
NORTHWESTERN TEXAS, ARIZONA, AND NEW MEXICO, Expedition from Southern California through, April 13-Sept. 20, 1862.
NEUCES RIVER, Affair on, near Fort Clark, Aug. 10, 1862.
PADRE ISLAND, Affair at, Dec. 7, 1862.
PALMETTO RANCH, Skirmish at, near Brazos Santiago, Sept. 6, 1864.—Skirmish at, May 12-13, 1865.
PASS CABELLO, Naval action at, Dec. 29-30, 1863.
PASS CAVALLO, Evacuation of, by Union forces, June 15, 1864.
PEOSI RIVER, Skirmish with Indians on, Nov. 1, 1861.
POINT ISABEL, Affair at, May 30, 1863.—Skirmish at, Aug. 9, 1864.
QUITMAN, FORT, Abandoned by U. S. troops, April 5, 1861.
RANCHO LAS RINAS, Skirmish at, June 25, 1864.
RIO GRANDE CITY, Expedition to, Nov. 23-Dec. 2, 1863.
RIO GRANDE, Expedition from New Orleans, La., to the mouth of the, March 2-30, 1863.
RIO GRANDE, Expedition and operations on the coast of Texas, Oct. 27-Dec. 2, 1863.
RIO GRANDE RIVER, Operations in Texas and on the, May 29, 1865-Nov. 14, 1866.
SABINE CITY, Surrender of, to Union naval forces, Oct. 9, 1862.
SABINE PASS, Engagement at, Sept. 24-25, 1862.—Affair at, Oct. 29, 1862.—Attack on blockading squadron at, Jan. 21, 1863.—Boat expedition into, and skirmish, April 18, 1863.—Occupation of, by Union naval forces, May 25, 1865.—Expedition, Sept. 4-11, 1863.—Attack on, Sept. 8, 1863.
SAINT JOSEPH'S ISLAND, Affair at, May 3, 1863.
SALURIA, Capture of U. S. troops at, April 25, 1861.
SAN ANTONIA, Seizure of U. S. Arsenal and Barracks at, Feb. 16, 1861.—Capture of U. S. troops at and near, April 23, 1861.
SAN LUCAS SPRINGS, Capture of U. S. troops at, May 9, 1861.
SAN LUIS PASS, Affair at, April 5-6, 1862.

TEXAS—UTAH—VERMONT—VIRGINIA.

STOCKTON, FORT, Abandoned by U. S. troops, April —, 1861.
TAYLOR'S BAYOU, Naval action in, Oct. 15, 1862.—Affair at, Sept. 27, 1862.
VELASCO, Attack on U. S. vessels at, July 4, 1862.—Affair at, Aug. 11, 1862.—Affair at, March 21, 1864.
VERDE, CAMP, Abandoned by U. S. troops, March 7, 1861.
WHITE'S RANCH, Skirmish at, May 13, 1865.

UTAH.

BEAR RIVER, Engagement on, Jan. 29, 1863.
CACHE VALLEY, Expedition from Camp Douglas to the, Nov. 20-27, 1862.
CEDAR FORT, Skirmish at, April 1, 1863.
CEDAR MOUNTAINS, Expedition from Camp Douglas to the, March 26-April 3, 1863.
DOUGLAS, CAMP, Expedition from Fort Ruby, Nev. T., to, Sept. 30-Oct. 29, 1862.
GOVERNMENT SPRINGS, Skirmish near, June 20, 1863.
GREAT SALT LAKE, Attack on emigrant train near, Aug. 8-9, 1861.
PLEASANT GROVE, Skirmish at, April 12, 1863.
SPANISH FORK, Expedition from Camp Douglas to the, April 2-6, 1863.
SPANISH FORK CANON, Expedition from Camp Douglas to, April 11-20, 1863.—Action at, April 4, 1863.—Action at, April 15, 1863.

VERMONT.

SAINT ALBANS, Raid on, Oct. 19, 1864.

VIRGINIA.

Seceded April 17, 1861.

ABINGDON, Skirmish near, Dec. 15, 1864.
ABRAHAM'S CREEK, Skirmish at, Sept. 13, 1864.
ACCOMAC COUNTY, Expedition through, Nov. 14-22, 1861.
ACCOTINK, Scout to, Aug. 18, 1861.—Affairs at, Oct. 17, 1863, and July 15, 1864.—Affair near, Jan. 12, 1864.
AENON CHURCH, Combat at, May 28, 1864.
ALBEMARLE COUNTY, Union raid into, Feb. 28-March 1, 1864.
ALDIE, Reconnoissance toward, Sept. 16, 1862.—Reconnoissances from Fairfax Court House to, Oct. 8-9, 1862, and Feb. 15-16, 1865.—Skirmish at, Oct. 31, 1862.—Skirmishes near, March 2, June 18, 22, July 31, 1863, and Feb. 5, 1864.—Scout from Snicker's Ferry to, May 27-29, 1863.—Expedition from Brightwood, D. C., to, June 11-13, 1863.—Action at, June 17, 1863.—Scout from Centreville to, Aug. 15-19, 1863.—Scout to, March 28-29, 1864.—Action near, July 6, 1864.

VIRGINIA.

ALEXANDRIA, Abandoned by State troops, May 5, 1861.—Occupation of, by Union troops, May 24, 1861.—Reconnoissances from, July 14, 1861.
ALLEN'S FARM, Engagement at, June 29, 1862.
ALSOP'S FARM, Combat at, May 8, 1864.
AMELIA COURT HOUSE, Skirmishes at, April 4-5, 1865.
AMELIA SPRINGS, Engagement at, April 5, 1865.—Skirmish near, April 6, 1865.
AMHERST COURT HOUSE, Skirmish near, June 12, 1864.
AMISSVILLE, Action near, Nov. 10, 1862.—Skirmish near, Aug. 4, 1863.
ANGLE, THE (or the Salient), Combat at, May 12, 1864.
ANNANDALE, Skirmishes at, Dec. 2, 1861, and Aug. 24, 1864.—Capture of Union wagon train near, Aug. 11, 1863.—Affairs near, Oct. 18 and 22, 1863, and March 16, 1864.
ANTIOCH CHURCH, Skirmish at, May 23, 1863.
APPOMATTOX CAMPAIGN, March 29-April 9, 1865.
APPOMATTOX COURT HOUSE, Engagement at and Surrender of Lee's Army, April 9, 1865.
APPOMATTOX STATION, Engagement at, April 8, 1865.
AQUIA CREEK, Attack on batteries at, May 31-June 1, 1861.—Evacuation of, Sept. 6, 1862.
ARLINGTON HEIGHTS, Occupation of, by Union forces, May 24, 1861.
ARLINGTON MILLS, Skirmish at, June 1, 1861.
ARMSTRONG'S FARM, Combat at, May 30, 1864.
ARMSTRONG'S MILL (See Hatcher's Run, Feb. 5-7, 1865).
ARRINGTON'S DEPOT, Raid on, June 11, 1864.
ARROW, Steamer, Capture of, at Currituck Canal, May 15, 1863.
ARROWFIELD CHURCH, Engagement at, May 9, 1864.
ARUNDEL'S FARM, Skirmish at, April 10, 1865.
ASHBY'S GAP, Skirmishes at, Sept. 20, 22, Nov. 3, 1862; July 19, 20, 1864; Feb. 19, 1865.—Reconnoissance to, July 11-14, 1863.
ASHLAND, Destruction of Confederate supplies at, May 28, 1862.—Skirmishes near, June 25, 1862; March 1-5, 1865.—Skirmishes at, May 3, 1863; March 1, 1864.—Combats at, May 11, June 1, 1864.
ASHLAND CHURCH, Skirmish at, May 4, 1863.
ATLEE'S, Skirmish near, March 1, 1864.
ATLEE'S STATION, Virginia Central Railroad, Skirmish at, June 26, 1862.
AUBURN, Skirmish near, Oct. 1, 1863.—Action at, Oct. 13, 1863.
AUGUSTA COUNTY, Operations in, Nov. 5-14, 1862.
AYLETT'S, Skirmish at, May 5, 1863.—Expedition from Yorktown to, June 4-5, 1863.
BACK BAY, Destruction of Confederate salt-works on, Sept. 30, 1863.
BACK RIVER, Operations on, July 24, 1861.
BACK RIVER ROAD, Affair on, July 19, 1861.

160

VIRGINIA.

BACK ROAD, Skirmish on, Oct. 7, 1864.
BAILEY'S CORNERS (or Cross Roads), Skirmishes near, Aug. 28-30, 1861.
BAILEY'S CREEK, Combat at, Aug. 16, 1864.
BAILEY'S CROSS ROADS, Skirmishes near, Aug. 27-28, 1861.
BALLAHOCK, Skirmishes at, Feb. 29-March 1, 1864.
BALL'S BLUFF (or Battle of Leesburg, Harrison's Island, or Conrad's Ferry), Engagement at, Oct. 21, 1861.
BALL'S BRIDGE, Skirmish at, March 4, 1865.
BALL'S CROSS ROADS, Skirmishes at, Aug. 27-28, 1861.
BALTIMORE CROSS ROADS, Skirmishes at, May 13, 1862; July 1-2, 1863.
BALTIMORE STORE, Skirmish at, July 2, 1863.—Skirmishes near, Feb. 6-8, 1864.
BANKS'S FORD, Battle near, May 4, 1863.
BARBEE'S CROSS ROADS, Action at, Nov. 5, 1862.—Skirmishes at, July 25, Sept. 1, 1863.—Scout to, Aug. 24, 1863.
BARBER'S CREEK, Skirmish on, Dec. 19, 1863.
BARBER'S CROSS ROADS, Skirmish at, May 23, 1863.
BARHAMSVILLE, Engagement at, May 7, 1862.
BARNETT'S FORD, Skirmishes at, Aug. 1, 1862; Feb. 6-7, 1864.
BASSETT'S LANDING, Naval expedition from White House to, May 17, 1862.
BATH COUNTY, Operations in, Nov. 5-14, 1862.—Scout through, April 15-23, 1865.
BATTLE MOUNTAIN, Skirmish at, July 24, 1863.
BEALTON STATION, Affair at, March 28, 1862.—Skirmishes at, March 17, Oct. 24, 1863.—Skirmishes near, Oct. 22, 27, 1863.—Operations about, March 3-8, 1865.
BEAR QUARTER ROAD, Skirmishes on, Feb. 29-March 1, 1864.
BEAVER DAM CHURCH, Skirmish at, Dec. 1, 1862.
BEAVER DAM CREEK, Battle of, June 26, 1862.
BEAVER DAM STATION, Expedition from Fredericksburg to, July 19-20, 1862.—Skirmish at, Feb. 29, 1864.—Combats at, May 9-10, 1864.—Skirmish near, March 13, 1865.
BEAVER POND CREEK, (See Tabernacle Church, April 4, 1865.)
BELL GROVE (See Cedar Creek, Oct. 19, 1864).
BENN'S CHURCH (See Isle of Wight County, Expedition into, etc., Jan. 29-Feb. 1, 1864.)
BERMUDA HUNDRED FRONT, Operations on, May 17-June 2, 1864.—Action on, June 16, 1864.—Skirmish on, June 17, 1864.
BERRY'S FERRY, Accident at, April 15, 1862.—Skirmish at, May 16, 1863.—Skirmish near, July 20, 1863.
BERRY'S FORD, Engagement at, July 19, 1864.
BERRY'S FORD GAP, Skirmish at, Nov. 1, 1862.
BERRYVILLE, Skirmishes at, May 24, Dec. 2, 1862; June 13,

VIRGINIA.

14, Oct. 17, 1863; Aug. 19-20, Sept. 4, 1864.—Skirmishes near, June 6, 1863; July 22, Aug. 21, Sept. 14, 1864.—Skirmish on road to, Oct. 18, 1863.—Affair at, Aug. 13, 1864.—Engagement at, Sept. 3, 1864.—Affair near, Sept. 13, 1864.
BERRYVILLE AND WINCHESTER PIKE, Skirmish on, Aug. 19, 1864.
BETHEL CHURCH (See Big Bethel, June 10, 1861).
BETHESDA CHURCH, Combat at, May 31, 1864.—Battles of, June 1-3, 1864.
BETHSAIDA CHURCH, Skirmish at, Oct. 10, 1863.
BEVERLY FORD (or Cunningham's Ford, Rappahannock River), Skirmish at, Aug. 21, 1862—Action at, Aug. 23, 1862.—Operations at, April 14-15, 1863.—Engagement at, June 9, 1863.—Skirmish at, Aug. 15, 1863.
BIG BETHEL (or Bethel Church), Engagement at, June 10, 1861.—Reconnoissance from Camp Hamilton to, Jan. 3, 1862.
BIRCH ISLAND BRIDGES, Blackwater River, Skirmish at, May 6, 1864.
BLACKBURN'S FORD, Bull Run, Action at, July 18, 1861.—Skirmish at, Oct. 15, 1863.
BLACK CREEK (or Tunstall's Station), Combat at, June 21, 1864.
BLACKSBURG, Skirmish at, May 11, 1864.
BLACKWATER BRIDGE, Skirmish at, Nov. 14, 1862.
BLACKWATER RIVER, Skirmishes on, Oct. 3, 29, Dec. 2, 1862; Oct. 16, 1864.—Reconnoissance from Suffolk to, Dec. 8-12, 1862.—Expeditions from Suffolk to, Jan. 8-10, June 12-18, 1863.—Reconnoissance to, Sept. 14-17, 1863.—Reconnoissance from Portsmouth to, April 13-15, 1864.—Skirmish on, May 6, 1864.
BLICK'S STATION, Combats at, Aug. 18-21, 1864.
BLOODY ANGLE (See Angle, The, May 12, 1864).
BLUE RIDGE MOUNTAINS, Reconnoissance from Vienna toward, Nov. 18-23, 1863.
BOHLER'S ROCKS, Rappahannock River, Naval action at, April 19, 1864.
BOTTOM'S BRIDGE, Chickahominy River, Operations about, May 20-23, June 25-29, 1862.—Expeditions from White House to, July 1-7, 1863.—Expedition from Williamsburg to, Aug. 26-29, 1863.—Skirmishes at, Feb. 6-8, 1864.—Scout to, Jan. 30, 1865.
BOWLING GREEN ROAD, Skirmish on, May 11, 1862.
BOYDTON PLANK ROAD, Engagement at, Oct. 27-28, 1864.
BOYDTON ROAD Skirmish at, March 29, 1865. (See Hatcher's Run, March 31, 1865.)
BRACKETT'S, Action at, June 30, 1862.
BRADY, FORT, James River, Action at, Jan. 23-24, 1865.
BRANDER'S (or Brandon) BRIDGE, Skirmish at, May 9, 1864.

VIRGINIA.

BRANDY STATION, Skirmishes at, Aug. 20, 1862; Aug. 4, 9, Sept. 8, 13, Oct. 11, 12, Nov. 8, 1863.—Skirmish near, April 29, 1863.—Engagement at, June 9, 1863.—Action at, Aug. 1, 1863.
BRANDYWINE HILL, Potomac River, Naval action at, Dec. 4, 1862.
BRENTSVILLE, Scout to, Dec. 21-23, 1862.—Skirmishes at, Jan. 9, Oct. 14, Nov. 26, 29, 1863.—Affair near, Feb. 14, 1864.—Scout from Bristoe Station to, March 8, 1864.—Scout from Fairfax Court House to, Feb. 6-7, 1865.
BRIDGEWATER, Skirmish at, Oct. 2, 1864.
BRISTOE CAMPAIGN, Oct. 9-22, 1863.
BRISTOE STATION, Skirmishes at, Aug. 26, 1862; Aug. 18, Sept. 24, Oct. 18, 1863; Feb. 1, March 16, 1864.—Expedition from Centreville to, Sept. 25-28, 1862.—Skirmishes near, Oct. 24, 1862; Sept. 12, 1863.—Engagement at, Oct. 14, 1863.—Affair at, April 15, 1864.
BROAD RUN, Skirmish at, Aug. 27, 1862.—Skirmish near mouth of, April 1, 1863.
BROADWATER FERRY, Operations about, Dec. 11-19, 1864.
BROCK ROAD, Combats at, May 5-7, 1864.
BROCK'S GAP, Skirmish near, Oct. 6, 1864.
BROOK CHURCH (or Richmond Fortifications), Combat at, May 12, 1864.
BROOK TURNPIKE, Skirmishes on, March 1, 1864.
BROWNSBURG, Skirmish at, June 10, 1864.
BROWN'S FERRY, Skirmishes at, May 12-13, 1864.
BROWN'S GAP, Skirmish at, Sept. 26, 1864.
BROWNTOWN, Reconnoissance from Front Royal to, May 21, 1862.
BRUCETOWN, Skirmish near, Sept. 7, 1864.
BUCHANAN, Skirmish near, June 13, 1864.
BUCKLAND BRIDGE, Broad Run, Skirmish at, Aug. 27, 1862.
BUCKLAND MILLS, Expedition from Centreville to, Sept. 29, 1862.—Action at, Oct. 19, 1863.
BUCK'S FORD, Operations about, May 12-14, 1863.
BUCKTON, Skirmish at, July 3, 1864.
BUCKTON STATION, Skirmish at, May 23, 1862.
BUFORD'S GAP, Skirmish at, June 20, 1864.
BULL PASTURE MOUNTAIN, Engagement near, May 8, 1862.
BULL RUN (or Manassas), Battles of, July 21, 1861; Aug. 30, 1862. (See Blackburn's Ford, Oct. 15, 1863.)
BULL RUN BRIDGE, Skirmish at, Aug. 26, 1862.—Action at, Aug. 27, 1862.
BULL RUN CAMPAIGN, July 16-22, 1861.
BULL RUN MOUNTAINS, Scout to, Aug. 14, 1863.
BURKE'S STATION, Skirmish at, Dec. 4, 1861.—Scout to vicinity of, Jan. 17, 1862.—Affair at, Aug. 7, 1863.—Skirmish near, April 10, 1865.

VIRGINIA.

BURNSIDE'S SECOND CAMPAIGN (See Mud March, Jan. 20-24, 1863).
BURNT CHIMNEYS, Engagement at, April 16, 1862.
BURNT ORDINARY, Reconnoissance to, Dec. 17, 1862.—Skirmish at, Jan. 19, 1863.
BURTON'S FORD, Skirmish at, March 1, 1864.
BYRD'S PLANTATION, Expedition from Yorktown to, April 1, 1863.
CABIN POINT, Skirmish at, Aug. 5, 1864.
CALLAGHAN'S STATION, Affair at, May 4, 1864.
CAPE HENRY, Capture of steamer Maple Leaf off, June 10, 1863.
CARMEL CHURCH, Skirmish near, July 23, 1862.
CARRSVILLE, Skirmishes near, Oct. 15, 1862; May 15-16, 1863.—Affair near, Nov. 17, 1862.
CARTER'S CREEK, Naval reconnoissance to, April 29, 1864.
CARTER'S RUN, Skirmish at, Sept. 6, 1863.
CASTLEMAN'S FERRY, Skirmish at, Nov. 2, 1862.—Skirmish near, Nov. 3, 1862.
CATAWBA MOUNTAINS, Skirmish at, June 21, 1864.
CATLETT'S STATION, Raid on, Aug. 22, 1862.—Skirmishes near, Sept. 26, Oct. 19, 1862; Oct. 30, 1863.—Scout to, Dec. 21-23, 1862.—Reconnoissances to, Jan. 8-10, 1863.—Affairs near, Oct. 6, Dec. 14, 1863; April 16, 1864.—Skirmishes at, Oct. 14, 19, Nov. 1, 27, 1863.—Scout about, Nov. 3, 1863.
CEDAR CREEK, Skirmishes at, Aug. 12, 15, 1864.—Actions at, Oct. 13, Nov. 12, 1864.—Battle of, Oct. 19, 1864.
CEDAR CREEK VALLEY, Reconnoissance from Winchester up, April 12-13, 1863.
CEDAR MOUNTAIN, Battle of, Aug. 9, 1862.
CEDAR RUN, Reconnoissance to, March 14-16, 1862.—Battle of, Aug. 9, 1862.—Skirmish at, Aug. 10, 1862.
CEDAR RUN CHURCH, Affair at, Oct. 17, 1864.
CEDARVILLE, Skirmish at, June 12, 1863.—Engagement at, Aug. 16, 1864.—Skirmish near, Sept. 20, 1864.
CENTREVILLE, Skirmish at, Aug. 28, 1862.—Operations about, Aug. 31, 1862; March 3-8, 1865.—Expedition from, to Bristoe Station and Warrenton Junction, Sept. 25-28, 1862.—Expedition from, to Warrenton and Buckland Mills, Sept. 29, 1862.—Reconnoissance from, Oct. 13, 1862.—Skirmishes near, Sept. 22, Oct. 14, 1863; June 23-24, 1864.
CHAFFIN'S FARM, Battle of, Sept. 29-30, 1864.—Naval action with batteries at, May 7, 1864.
CHANCELLORSVILLE, Skirmishes at and near, April 30, 1863; May 4, 1864.—Battle of, May 1-3, 1863.
CHANCELLORSVILLE CAMPAIGN, April 27-May 6, 1863.
CHANTILLY, Operations about, Aug. 31, 1862.—Battle of, Sept. 1, 1862.—Reconnoissance from, to Snicker's Ferry and Berryville, Nov. 28-30, 1862, and skirmishes.—Skirmishes

VIRGINIA.

near, Dec. 29, 1862; March 23, 1863.—Skirmishes at, Feb. 10, 25-26, 1863.—Expedition from Brightwood, D. C., to, June 11-13, 1863.—Affair near, Oct. 17, 1863.
CHAPPELL HOUSE, Combats at and near, Sept. 29-Oct. 2, 1864.
CHARLES CITY COUNTY, Scout from Bermuda Hundred into, Nov. 1-5, 1864.
CHARLES CITY COURT HOUSE, Reconnoissance from Harrison's Landing beyond, July 11, 1862.—Expedition from Williamsburg to, Dec. 12-14, 1863, and skirmish.
CHARLES CITY CROSS ROADS, Battle of, June 30, 1862.
CHARLES CITY ROAD, Skirmish on, June 19, 1862.—Reconnoissance from Harrison's Landing on, July 3, 1862.—Combats at, Aug. 13-20, 1864.
CHARLOTTESVILLE, Skirmish near, Feb. 29, 1864.—Occupation of, March 3, 1865.—Expedition from Richmond to, May 6-14, 1865.
CHERRY GROVE, Capture of Confederate outpost at, March 30, 1864.
CHERRY GROVE LANDING, Skirmish near, April 11, 1864.
CHESNESSEX CREEK, Expedition to and vicinity, Oct. 9-13, 1863.
CHESTER GAP, Skirmishes at, Nov. 16, 1862; July 21-22, 1863.—Skirmish near, July 23, 1863.
CHESTER STATION, Engagement at, May 6-7, 1864.—Action at, May 10, 1864.
CHICKAHOMINY, THE, Battle of, June 27, 1862.
CHICKAHOMINY RIVER, Reconnoissance on east bank of, June 7, 1862.
CHIMNEYS, Assault on Confederate works at, Sept. 10, 1864.
CHOWAN RIVER, Operations about, Dec. 11-19, 1864.
CHUCKATUCK, Affair at, April 23, 1863.—Skirmish at, May 3, 1863.
CHUCKATUCK CREEK, Boat expedition up, March 29-30, 1864.
CHULA DEPOT, Skirmish near, May 14, 1864.
CIRCLEVILLE, Skirmishes near, Feb. 21-22, 1864.
CIRCUS POINT, Rappahannock River, Naval expedition to, April 18-22, 1864.
CITY POINT, James River, Skirmishes at, May 19, 1862; May 18, 1864.—Explosion at, Aug. 9, 1864.
CLARK'S MOUNTAIN, Skirmish on, Aug. 18, 1862.
CLIFTON, FORT, Engagement at, May 9, 1864.—Joint engagements with, June 9 and 16, 1864.
CLOVER HILL, Surrender of Lee's Army at, April 9, 1865.
CLOYD'S MOUNTAIN (or Farm), Engagement at, May 9, 1864.
COAN RIVER, Expedition from Belle Plain to, March 3-8, 1863.—Naval expedition to, Dec. 15, 1864.
COCKLETOWN, Skirmish near, April 4, 1862.

VIRGINIA.

COCKPIT POINT, Naval actions at, Jan. 3 and March 9, 1862.
COGGINS' POINT, Affair at, Sept. 16, 1864.
COLD HARBOR, Battle of, June 27, 1862.—Operations at and about, May 31-June 12, 1864.
COLUMBIA, Occupation of, March 9, 1865.
COLUMBIA BRIDGE, Skirmish at, May 5, 1862.—Reconnoissance from Luray to, July 22, 1862.
COLUMBIA FURNACE, Skirmishes at, April 7, 16, 1862.—Skirmish near, Oct. 7, 1864.
CORBIN'S BRIDGE, Combat at, May 8, 1864.
CORBIN'S CROSS ROADS, Action at, Nov. 10, 1862.—Skirmish at, Sept. 1, 1863.
COVE MOUNTAIN, Engagement at, May 10, 1864.
COVINGTON, Reconnoissance to, and destruction of saltpetre-works on Jackson's River, Aug. 5-31, 1863.—Skirmishes near, Nov. 9, Dec. 19, 1863.—Affair at, June 2, 1864.
COX'S FARM, Destruction of Confederate signal station at, July 11, 1864.—Naval affair near, Aug. 3, 1864.
COYLE'S TAVERN, Skirmish at, Aug. 24, 1863.
CRAIG'S MEETING HOUUSE (See Wilderness, May 5-7, 1864).
CRANEY'S ISLAND, Naval reconnoissance to, June 5, 1861.—Occupation of, by Union naval forces, May 10, 1862.
CRATER, THE, Assault on, July 30, 1864.
CREW'S FARM, Battle of, July 1, 1862.
CRICKET HILL, Skirmish at, March —, 1864.
CROOKED RUN, Skirmish at, Sept. 18, 1863.
CROOK'S RUN, Skirmish at, April 29, 1863.
CROSS KEYS, Battle of, June 8, 1862.
CROSS ROADS, Skirmishes near, Aug. 28-30, 1861.
CROW'S HOUSE, Action at, March 31, 1865.
CRUMP'S CREEK, Combat at, May 28, 1864.
CRUMP'S CROSS ROADS, Skirmish at, July 2, 1863.
CUB RUN, Skirmish at, Jan. 5, 1863.
CULPEPER, Skirmish at, Sept. 10, 1864.
CULPEPER COURT HOUSE, Reconnoissance to, May 4-5, July 12-17, 1862.—Skirmish at, Sept. 13, 1863.—Skirmishes near, Oct. 1, 11, Dec. 23, 1863.—Affair near, Dec. 18, 1863.
CULPEPER FORD, Skirmishes at, Feb. 6-7, 1864.
CUMBERLAND HEIGHTS, Naval operations at, June 6, 1864.
CUMBERLAND POINT, Naval action near, June 21, 1864.
CUNNINGHAM'S FORD, Skirmish at, Aug. 21, 1862.—Action at, Aug. 23, 1862.
CURRIOMAN BAY, Expedition from Belle Plain to, Feb. 12-14, 1863.
CURRITOMAN CREEK, Naval affair in, Nov. 6, 1861.
CURRITUCK BRIDGE, Skirmish at, Sept. 9, 1864.
CURRITUCK CANAL, Capture of the steamers Emily and Arrow in, May 15, 1863.
DABNEY'S FERRY, Combat at, May 27, 1864.

VIRGINIA.

DABNEY'S MILL, Battle of, Feb. 5-7, 1865.
DAM No. 1, Engagement at, April 16, 1862.
DANVILLE, Expedition from Burkeville and Petersburg to, April 23-29, 1865.
DANVILLE RAILROAD, Expedition against, June 22-July 2, 1864.
DARBYTOWN, Engagement at, July 27, 1864.
DARBYTOWN ROAD, Engagements on, Oct. 7, 13, 27, 28, 1864.
DARLING, FORT, James River, Engagements at, May 15, 1862; May 12-16, 1864.
DAVENPORT, Combat at, May 9, 1864.
DAVENPORT CHURCH, Skirmish near, Dec. 4, 1864.
DAVENPORT FORD, Combats at, May 9-10, 1864.
DAVIS HOUSE, Skirmish near, Aug. 31, 1864.
DEEP BOTTOM, Action at, June 30-July 1, 1864.—Engagement at, July 27, 1864.—Skirmish at, Aug. 1, 1864.—Demonstrations at, Aug. 13-20, 1864.—Expedition from, to near Weldon, N. C., March 28-April 11, 1865.
DEEP CREEK, Skirmishes at, Feb. 29-March 1, 1864.—Combats at and near, Aug. 13-20, 1864.
DEEP RUN (or Franklin's Crossing), Operations at, April 29-May 2, 1863.—Skirmishes at, June 5-13, 1863.
DESERTED HOUSE, Engagement at, Jan. 30, 1863.
DIAMOND HILL, Skirmish at, June 17, 1864.
DIASCUND BRIDGE, Reconnoissance to, Dec. 17, 1862.—Skirmishes at, June 11. 20, 1863.
DINWIDDIE COURT HOUSE, Reconnoissance toward, and skirmish, Sept. 15, 1864.—Engagement at. March 31, 1865.
DINWIDDIE ROAD, Action on, Aug. 23, 1864.
DISPATCH STATION, Skirmish at, June 28, 1862.
DISPUTANTA STATION, Skirmish near, Jan. 9, 1865.
DOOLAN'S FARM, Capture of Union foraging party at, Nov. 16, 1861.
DOVER, Skirmish near, June 22, 1863.
DRANESVILLE, Expedition to, and skirmish, Nov. 26-27, 1861.—Expedition to Gunnell's Farm near, Dec. 6, 1861.—Engagement at, Dec. 20, 1861.—Reconnoissance to, Aug. 31, 1862.—Skirmishes at, Feb. 6 and 13, 1863.—Skirmishes near, Feb. 21-22, 1864: March 18, 1865.
DREWRY'S BLUFF, Engagement at, May 12-16, 1864.—Naval engagement at. May 15, 1862.
DRY RUN. Skirmish at, Oct. 23, 1864.
DUGUIDSVILLE, Skirmish at. March 8, 1865.
DUMFRIES, Reconnoissance to, March 20-21, 1862.—Affair in, Oct. 11, 1861. (Quantico Creek.)—Capture of Union pickets near, Dec. 2. 1862.—Skirmish at, Dec. 12, 1862.—Raid on, Dec. 27-29, 1862.—Affairs near, March 15 and 29, 1863.—Skirmish near, May 17, 1863.

VIRGINIA.

DUTCH GAP, Actions at, Aug. 13 and 15, 1864.—Confederate demonstrations near, and naval engagement, June 21, 1864.

EASTERN SHORE, Expedition through, Nov. 14-22, 1861.—Operations on, Aug. 20, 1862-June 3, 1863.—Affairs on, Nov. 14-15, 1863.—Raid on, March 5, 1864.

EAST RIVER, Joint expedition into, Dec. 12-14, 1862.

EASTVILLE, Capture of schooners near, Sept. 18-23, 1863.

EDENBURG, Advance of Union forces from Strasburg to, April 1-2, 1862.—Skirmish at, Nov. 16, 1863.—Skirmishes near, Sept. 23 and Nov. 7, 1864.—Expedition from Camp Russell to, Feb. 13-17, 1865.—Scouts from Winchester to, March 17-19 and 20-21, 1865.

EDENTON ROAD, Skirmishes on, April 12, 15, 24, 1863.

EDWARDS'S FERRY, Skirmishes near, Oct. 4 and 21, 1861.—Action near, Oct. 22, 1861.

ELK RUN, Skirmishes at, Jan. 9, 1862; April 13, 1863.

ELLIS' FORD, Expedition from Potomac Creek to, Dec. 30-31, 1862.—Skirmish at, Dec. 3, 1863.—Affairs near, Jan. 12, April 17, 1864.—Affairs at, Jan. 17 and 22, 1864.

ELLISON'S MILL, Skirmish at, May 23, 1862.—Battle of, June 26, 1862.

ELTHAM'S LANDING, Engagement at, May 7, 1862.

ELY'S FORD, Skirmish at, May 2, 1863.—Skirmish near, Dec. 1, 1863.—Affairs near, Jan. 13 and 17, 1864.—Affair at, Feb. 28, 1864.

EMILY, STEAMER, Capture of, in Currituck Canal, May 15, 1863.

FAIRFAX COURT HOUSE, Skirmishes at, June 1, July 17, 1861; Jan. 9, 1863.—Skirmishes near, Nov. 18, 27, 1861; Sept. 2, 1862; Jan. 26, 27, June 4, 27, Aug. 24, 1863.—Scout toward, Dec. 24-25, 1861.—Skirmishes at and near, Dec. 27-28, 1862.—Affair at, March 9, 1863.—Scout from Snicker's Ferry to, May 27-29, 1863.—Confederate operations about, July 28-Aug. 3, 1863.—Expedition to, Aug. 4, 1863.—Capture and recapture of sutlers' wagons near, Aug. 6, 1863.

FAIRFAX STATION, Raid on, Dec. 27-29, 1862.—Skirmishes at, Aug. 8, Nov. 26, 1864.

FAIR OAKS, Skirmishes near, May 30, June 8, 18, 1862.—Battle of, May 31-June 1, 1862.—Skirmish at, June 27, 1862.—Engagement at, Oct. 27-28, 1864.

FAIR OAKS STATION, Skirmish near, June 21, 1862.—Engagement near, June 29, 1862.

FALLS CHURCH, Skirmishes near, Sept. 2-4, 1862; June 23-24, 1864.—Skirmishes at, Sept. 3, 4, 1862; Aug. 16, 1863.—Scout from, July 18-21, 1864.

FALMOUTH, Skirmishes near, April 17-19, 1862; Nov. 6, 1863.—Skirmishes at, Nov. 17, 1862; Nov. 4, 1863.—Scout from Centreville to, Feb. 27-28, 1863.

FANT'S FORD, Skirmish at, Aug. 23, 1862.

FARMVILLE, Engagement at, April 6-7, 1865.

168

VIRGINIA.

FARMWELL STATION, Scout from Vienna to, Feb. 25-26, 1864.
FAUQUIER COUNTY, Operations in, Oct. 26-Nov. 10, 1862.—Scouts in, Jan. 24-26, 1863.—Expedition from Winchester into, Nov. 28-Dec. 3, 1864.
FAUQUIER WHITE SULPHUR SPRINGS, Actions and skirmishes at and near, Aug. 23-26, 1862.
FAWN, Steamer, Capture of, Sept. 9, 1864.
FAYETTEVILLE, Skirmish near, June 3, 1863.—Skirmish at, Oct. 23, 1863.
FEARNSVILLE, Expedition from Bermuda Hundred to, Feb. 11-15, 1865.
FISHER, FORT, Action at, March 25, 1865.
FISHER'S HILL, Skirmishes at, April 22, Sept. 21, 1863; Sept. 21, Oct. 20, 1864.—Battle of, Sept. 22, 1864.—Skirmishes near, Oct. 6, 1864; March 21, 1865.
FITZHUGH'S CROSSING, Operations at, April 29-May 2, 1863.
FIVE FORKS, Skirmish near, March 30, 1865.—Battle of, April 1, 1865.
FLAT CREEK, Skirmish at, April 6, 1865.
FLAT CREEK BRIDGE, Skirmish at, May 14, 1864.
FLEET'S POINT, Shelling of, by Union naval forces, Oct. 25, 1864.
FLEETWOOD, Engagement at, June 9, 1863.—Skirmish at, Oct. 12, 1863.
FLEMMING'S (Shannon's) CROSS ROADS, Skirmish at, May 4, 1863.
FLINT HILL, Expeditions to, Feb. 7 and 22, 1862.—Affairs at, Sept. 2, 1862; Jan. 6 and 18, 1864.—Skirmish near, March 7, 1865.
FOREST HILL (Timberville), Skirmish at, Sept. 24, 1864.
FORGE BRIDGE (See Jones's Bridge), June 29-30, 1862.—Reconnoissance toward, Aug. 17, 1862.
FORT FURNACE, Powell's Big Fort Valley, Skirmish near, July 1, 1862.
FOSTER'S PLANTATION, Skirmish at, May 18, 1864.
FOUUR MILE CREEK, Actions at, Aug. 6, 1863; June 29-July 1, July 16, 21, 26, 28, Aug. 13-18, 1864.—Combat at, Oct. 7, 1864.
FOX'S FORD, Skirmish at, Oct. 13, 1863.
FRANKLIN, Skirmishes at, Aug. 31, Oct. 31, Nov. 18, 1862.—Skirmishes near, Oct. 3, Dec. 2, 1862; March 17, 1863.
FRANKLIN'S CROSSING, Operations at, April 29-May 2, 1863.—Skirmishes at, June 5-13, 1863.
FRAZIER'S FARM (See Glendale, June 30, 1862).
FREDERICK COUNTY, Scout in, Dec. 7-11, 1863.
FREDERICKSBURG, Skirmishes near, April 17-19, 1862.—Confederate expedition from Hanover Court House to vicinity of, Aug. 4-8, 1862.—Skirmish at, Nov. 9, 1862.—Surrender of, demanded, Nov. 21, 1862.—Battles of, Dec. 11-15,

VIRGINIA.

1862; May 3-4, 1863.—Operations near, April 29-May 2, 1863.—Naval expedition to, May 12-19, 1864.—Expedition from Fort Monroe to, March 5-8, 1865.
FREDERICK'S HALL STATION, Expeditions from Fredericksburg to, Aug. 5-8, 1862.
FREEMAN'S FORD, Rappahannock River, Skirmish at, Aug. 21, 1862.—Action at, Aug. 22, 1862.
FREEPORT, Naval engagement at, March 7, 1864.
FREESTONE POINT, Engagement at, Sept. 25, 1861.—Naval action at, Dec. 9, 1861.
FRENCH'S FIELD, Engagement at, June 25, 1862.
FRONT ROYAL, Actions at, May 23, 30, 1862.—Skirmish near, May 31, 1862.—Expedition from Bealton to, Jan. 1-4, 1864.—Skirmishes at, Feb. 20, Sept. 21, 23, Nov. 22, 1864.—Engagement at, Aug. 16, 1864.—Scout from near Winchester to, March 16, 1865.
FRONT ROYAL FORD, Operations about, May 12-14, 1863.
FRYING PAN, Reconnoissance to, Aug. 31, 1862.—Skirmish near, Dec. 29, 1862.—Skirmish at, June 4, 1863.
FRYING PAN CHURCH, Skirmish at, Oct. 17, 1863.
FURNACES, THE, Combats at, May 6, 1864.
FUSSELL'S MILL, Combats at, Aug. 16-18, 1864.
GAINES' CROSS ROADS, Rappahannock County, Skirmishes at, May 14, 15, Nov. 10, 1862; Oct. 12, 1863.—Skirmish near, July 23, 1863.
GAINES' MILL, Skirmish at, May 19, 1862.—Battle of, June 27, 1862.
GAINESVILLE, Reconnoissance to, March 20, 1862.—Skirmishes at, Aug. 26, 1862; Oct. 14, 15, 19, 1863.—Engagement near, Aug. 28, 1862.—Expedition from, June 7-8, 1863.—Skirmish near, June 21, 1863.
GAP MOUNTAIN, Skirmishes at, May 12-13, 1864.
GARLICK'S LANDING, Attack on, June 13, 1862.
GARNETT'S FARM, Actions at, June 27-28, 1862.
GARRETT'S FARM, near Port Royal, Capture of Booth and Harold at, April 26, 1865.
GERMANNA FORD, Skirmishes at, April 29, Oct. 10, 1863.—Skirmish near, Nov. 18, 1863.
GERMANTOWN, Skirmishes at, Aug. 31, 1862; Jan. 22, 1864.—Affairs near, Feb. 26, 1863; Dec. 24, 1863.—Affairs at, Nov. 16, Dec. 13, 1863.
GIBSON'S MILLS, Indian Creek, Skirmish at, Feb. 22, 1864.
GILBERT'S FORD, Opequon Creek, Skirmish at, Sept. 13, 1864.
GILL'S BLUFF, James River, Affair at, June 20, 1862.
GILMER, FORT, Combats at, Sept. 29-30, 1864.
GLADE SPRINGS, Skirmish near, Dec. 15, 1864.
GLADESVILLE, Skirmishes at, July 7, 1863; Oct. 2, 1864.
GLEN ALLEN STATION, Combat at, May 11, 1864.

VIRGINIA.

GLENDALE (Nelson's Farm, Charles City Cross Roads, New Market Road, Frazier's Farm, or Willis's Church), Battle of, June 30, 1862.
GLOBE TAVERN, Combats at, Aug. 18-21, 1864.
GLOUCESTER COUNTY, Reconnoissance through, July 7-9, 1862.—Scouts in, July 22-30, 1862; March 28, 1864.—Reconnoissance to, Dec. 12, 1862.—Skirmish in, Feb. 28, 1864.
GLOUCESTER COURT HOUSE, Expedition from Gloucester Point to, April 7, 1863.—Expedition to, July 25, 1863.—Affair near, Jan. 29, 1864.
GLOUCESTER PENINSULA, Operations on, Aug. 20, 1862-June 4, 1863.
GLOUCESTER POINT, Exchange of shots between U. S. S. Yankee and batteries at, May 9, 1861.—Skirmish at, Nov. 16, 1862.—Operations against, April 9-14, 1863.
GOLDING'S FARM, Actions at, June 27-28, 1862.
GOOCHLAND COURT HOUSE, Skirmish at, March 11, 1865.
GOOSE CREEK, Scout to, July 25-27, 1863.—Skirmish at, March 23, 1865.
GORDONSVILLE, Skirmish near, July 17, 1862.—Expedition from Winchester to near, Dec. 19-28, 1864.
GORESVILLE, Skirmish at, Nov. 28, 1864.
GRACIES' SALIENT, Explosion of Confederate mine at, Aug. 5, 1864.
GRASSY LICK, Engagement at, May 10, 1864.
GRAVEL HILL, Combats at, Aug. 13-20, 1864.
GRAVELLY FORD, Skirmish at, April 2, 1865.
GRAVELLY RUN, Skirmishes at, Oct. 27-28, 1864; Feb. 5-7, and March 29-30, 1865.
GREAT RUN, Action at, Aug. 23, 1862.
GREENWICH, Skirmishes near, May 30, 1863; March 9, 1864.—Scout from Bristoe Station to, March 11, 1864.—Affair near, April 11, 1864.
GRIFFINSBURG, Skirmish at, Oct. 11, 1863.
GROUND SQUIRREL BRIDGE (or Church), Combat at, May 11, 1864.
GROVE CHURCH, Reconniossance to, Dec. 1, 1862.—Skirmishes near, Jan. 9, May 8, Nov. 19, 1863.—Skirmishes at, Jan. 26, Oct. 14, 1863.—Operations at, Feb. 5-7, 1863.
GROVETON, Battle of, Aug. 29, 1862. (Manassas Plains.) Skirmishes at, Oct. 17-18, 1863.
GROVETON HEIGHTS, Battle of, Aug. 30, 1862.
GUARD HILL, Engagement at, Aug. 16, 1864.
GUINEY'S STATION, Combat at, May 21, 1864.
GUM SPRINGS, Scout from Vienna to, Oct. 12-13, 1863.
GUNNELL'S FARM, near Dranesville, Expedition to, Dec. 6, 1861.
HAMILTON, Skirmish near, March 21, 1865.
HAMPTON, Demonstration on, May 23, 1861.—Burning of, Aug. 7, 1861.

VIRGINIA.

HAMPTON ROADS, Naval Engagement in, March 8-9, 1862. (Destruction of the U. S. S. Congress and Cumberland by the C. S. S. Virginia, formerly the Merrimac.)—Confederate naval operations in, April 11, 1862.
HANOVER COURT HOUSE, Reconnoissance toward, May 24, 1862.—Operations about, May 27-29, 1862.—Engagement at, May 27, 1862.—Skirmish near June 26, 1862.—Skirmishes at, May 29-31, 1864; March 15, 1865.
HANOVER JUNCTION, Combat at, May 27, 1864.
HANOVER STATION, Skirmish at, May 3, 1863.
HANOVERTOWN, Combat at, May 27, 1864.
HANOVERTOWN FERRY, Reconnoissance to, May 22 1862.—Skirmish at, May 4, 1863
HARE'S HILL, Action at, June 24, 1864.
HARRIS FARM, Combat at, May 19, 1864.
HARRISON, FORT, Combats at, Sept. 29-30, 1864.
HARRISONBURG, Occupation of, by Union forces, April 22, 1862.—Skirmishes near, April 24, May 6, June 1, 6-7, 1862.—Action near, June 6, 1862.—Affair at, June 4, 1864.—Skirmish at, March 5, 1865.
HARRISON'S LANDING, Reconnoissance from, on Charles City Road, July 3, 1862.—Reconnoissance from, July 4, 1862.—Attack on Union camps and shipping near, July 31-Aug. 1, 1862.—Skirmish near, June 14, 1864.—Action near, Aug. 4, 1864.
HARTWOOD CHURCH, Affair near, Nov. 28, 1862.—Skirmishes at, Feb. 25, Aug. 15, 25, 28, Oct. 12, Nov. 5, 1863.
HASKELL, FORT, Skirmishes in front of, Nov. 5 and 24, 1864.
HATCHER'S RUN, Engagement at, Oct. 27-28, 1864.—Skirmishes at, Dec. 8, 1864; April 2, 1865.—Reconnoissance to, and skimishes, Dec. 9-10, 1864.—Battle of, Feb. 5-7, 1865.—Skirmish near, March 29, 1865.—Skirmishes on the line of, March 30, 1865.—Action at, March 31, 1865.
HAW'S SHOP, Skirmish at, June 13, 1862.—Combat at, May 28, 1864.—Action at, June 3, 1864.
HAXALL'S, Combat at, May 18, 1864.
HAYMARKET, Skirmishes at, Aug. 26, 28, 1862; June 21-25 Oct. 19, 1863.
HAZEL RIVER, Action at, Aug. 22, 1862.—Skirmishes at, Nov. 8, 1862; Oct. 7, 1863.—Scout on, Sept. 27-28, 1863.
HEATHSVILLE, Expedition from Pratt's Landing to, Feb. 12-14, 1863.
HERNDON STATION, Reconnoissance from Dranesville to, Oct. 20, 1861.—Reconnoissance to, Aug. 31, 1862.—Affair at, March 17, 1863.
HERRING CREEK, Skirmishes near, July 3-4, 1862.—Skirmish at, July 17, 1864.
HICKORY FORKS, Reconnoissance from Gloucester Point to the vicinity of, April 12, 1863.—Expedition from Yorktown beyond, April 27, 1863.

VIRGINIA.

HICKSFORD, Expedition to, and skirmishes, Dec. 7-12, 1864.
HIGH BRIDGE, Action near, April 6, 1865.—Engagement at, April 7, 1865.
HIGHLAND COUNTY, Operations in, Nov. 5-14, 1862.—Scout through, April 15-23, 1865.—Expedition through, June 1-13, 1865.
HILLSBOROUGH, Reconnoissance from Loudoun Heights to, Oct. 4-6, 1862.—Skirmishes near, July 15, 1864.
HILLSBOROUGH ROAD, Loudoun County, Affair on, and scout to Leesburg, Feb. 14-16, 1863.
HILL'S POINT, Skirmish near, May 3, 1863.
HILLSVILLE, Skirmish near, April 3, 1865.
HOGAN'S, Skirmish at, May 23, 1862.
HOLLY, FORT, Skirmish in front of, Dec. 10, 1864.
HOPEWELL GAP, Scouts from Vienna to, Dec. 28-31, 1863.—Scouts from Fairfax Court House to, Dec. 26-27, 1864.
HOWARD'S MILL, Skirmish at, April 4, 1862.
HOWLETT'S BLUFF, Actions at, June 21, 28, 1864.
HOWLETT'S HOUSE BATTERIES, James River, Naval actions with, May 19, 22, 24, June 21, 28, 1864; Jan. 24, 1865.
HUGER, BATTERY, Capture of, April 19, 1863.
HUNDLEY'S CORNER, Skirmishes at, June 26-27, 1862.
HUNGARY STATION, Skirmish at, May 4 and 11, 1863.
HUNTER'S MILL, Reconnoissance to, Oct. 20, 1861.—Expedition to, Feb. 7, 1862.—Affair near, Dec. 21, 1863; April 23, 1864.
HUPP'S HILL, Skirmish at, Oct. 14, 1864.
INDEPENDENT HILL, Prince William County, Skirmish at, March 4, 1863.
INDIAN CREEK, Skirmish on, Feb. 22, 1864.
ISLE OF WIGHT COUNTY, Expedition to, skirmishes near Benn's Church and at Smithfield, and destruction of the U. S. S. Smith Briggs, Jan. 29-Feb. 1, 1864.—Expedition from Norfolk to, and skirmishes near Cherry Grove Landing and at Smithfield, April 13-15, 1864.
JACKSON'S RIVER, Destruction of saltpetre-works on, and reconnoissance to Covington, Aug. 5-31, 1863.—Skirmishes on Dec. 19, 1863.
JACKSON'S RIVER DEPOT, Raid on the Virginia Central Railroad at, May 20, 1862.
JAMES CITY, Reconnoissance to, July 22, 1862.—Skirmishes near, Oct. 8, 9, and 10, 1863.
JAMES RIVER, Expedition from Bottom's Bridge to, May 25-26, 1862.—Reconnoissance to, to communicate with the Union fleet, June 3-7, 1862.—Operations against Union shipping on, July 5-7, 1862.—Reconnoissance on the south side of, Aug. 3, 1862.—Operations on the south side of, Aug. 20, 1862-June 3, 1863.—Army and naval reconnoissance on, Aug. 4-7, 1863.—Engagement on, Aug. 6, 1863.—Expedition up, Jan. 24-25, 1864.—Joint operations in, Jan. 31-Feb. 1, April

VIRGINIA.

13-15, 1864.—Operations on the south side of, May 4-June 2, 1864.—Naval engagement in, May 31, 1864.—Campaign from the Rapidan to, May 4-June 12, 1864.—Sheridan's expedition from Todd's Tavern to, May 9-24, 1864.—Demonstration on the north bank of, July 27-29, 1864, and engagement at Deep Bottom (or Darbytown, Strawberry Plains, and New Market Road).—Demonstrations on the north bank of, Aug. 13-20, 1864, at Deep Bottom (including combats at Fussell's Mills, Gravel, Hill Bailey's Creek, Deep Run (or Creek), White's Tavern, Charles City Road, New Market Road, etc.).—Action on, Jan. 23-24, 1865.—Sheridan's command crossed, March 26, 1865.

JAMES RIVER ROAD, Skirmish on, June 29, 1862.
JAMESTOWN, Naval reconnoissance to, April 12-13, 1863.
JARRATT'S STATION, Skirmish at, May 8, 1864.
JEFFERSON, Skirmishes at, Nov. 7, 8, 11, 14, 1862.
JEFFERSONTON, Skirmishes at, Oct. 12-13, 1863.—Skirmish near, Nov. 8, 1863.
JENNING'S FARM, Skirmish at, Dec. 1, 1863.
JERICHO FORD (or Bridge, or Mills), Combat at, May 25, 1864.
JERUSALEM PLANK ROAD, Engagement near, June 22, 1864.
JOHNSON'S FARM, Combat at, Oct. 7, 1864.—Skirmish at, Oct. 29, 1864.
JONES' BRIDGE, Operations about, June 29-30, 1862. (Forge Bridge.)—Reconnoissance toward, Aug. 17, 1862.—Combat at, May 17, 1864.—Combat at, June 23, 1864.
JONES' FARM, Combat at, May 28, 1864.
JONESVILLE, Skirmish at, Jan. 2, 1863. (Lee County.)—Skirmishes near, Nov. 29, Dec. 1, 1863; Jan. 28-29, Aug. 4, 1864.—Action at, Jan. 3, 1864.—Reconnoissance from Cumberland Gap, Tenn., toward, March 3-5, 1865.
JONESVILLE ROAD, Skirmishes on, Feb. 12, 1864.
JORDAN'S FORD, Skirmish at, June 27-29, 1862.
JOYNER'S FERRY, Blackwater River, Skirmish at, Dec. 22, 1862.
KELLY'S FORD, Rappahannock River, Skirmishes near, Aug. 20, 1862; Oct. 11, 1863.—Skirmishes at, Aug. 21, Dec. 20-22, 1862; March 29, July 31-Aug. 1, 1863.—Engagement at, March 17, 1863. (Kellysville.)—Operations at, April 14-15, 1863.—Action at, Nov. 7, 1863.
KELLY'S STORE, Engagement at, Jan. 30, 1863.
KELLYSVILLE, Reconnoissance from Stafford Court House to, Dec. 21-23, 1862.—Skirmish near, April 29, 1863.
KEMPSVILLE, Affair near, Sept. 15, 1863.
KERNSTOWN, Skirmish at, March 22, 1862.—Battle of, March 23, 1862.—Skirmishes near, July 23, Nov. 10, 11, 12, 1864.—Engagement at, July 24, 1864.
KETTLE RUN, Engagement at, Aug. 27, 1862.

VIRGINIA.

KING AND QUEEN COUNTY, Reconnoissance through, July 7-9, 1862.—Scout in, July 22-30, 1862.—Reconnoissance to, Dec. 12, 1862.—Expedition into, March 9-12, 1864.
KING AND QUEEN COURT HOUSE, Combats at, June 18 and 20, 1864.
KING GEORGE COURT HOUSE, Skirmish near, Aug. 24, 1863.
KING'S SCHOOL-HOUSE, Engagement at, June 25, 1862.
KING WILLIAM COUNTY, Scout in, July 22-30, 1862.
KINNEY'S FARM, Engagement at, May 27, 1862.
LACEY'S SPRINGS, Action at, Dec. 20-21, 1864.
LAMB'S CREEK CHURCH, Skirmish at, Sept. 1, 1863.
LAMB'S FERRY, Chickahominy River, Skirmish near, Aug. 25, 1863.
LAUREL HILL (Henrico County), Combats at, Sept. 29-30, 1864.—Spottsylvania County, Combat at, May 8, 1864.
LAWYER'S ROAD, Skirmish on, June 4, 1863.
LEAD MINES, Capture and destruction of the, Dec. 17, 1864.
LEE COUNTY, Skirmish in, Dec. 24, 1863.—Scout from Cumberland Gap, Tenn., into, Aug. 3-6, 1864.
LEED'S FERRY, Rappahannock River, Skirmish at, Dec. 2, 1862.
LEESBURG, Engagements near, Oct. 21-22, 1861.—Occupation of, by Union forces, March 8, 1862.—Skirmishes near, Sept. 2, 14, Dec. 12, 1862; Sept. 14, 1863.—Reconnoissance from Upton's Hill to, Sept. 16-19, 1862, and skirmishes.—Reconnoissance from Harper's Ferry to, Oct. 1-2, 1862.—Reconnoissance from Conrad's Ferry to, Oct. 8, 1862.—Skirmishes at, Dec. 13, 1862; Feb. 19, 1863.—Scouts to, Dec. 20, 1862; April 21-24, 1863.—(See Hillsborough Road, Feb. 14-16, 1863.)—Scout from Harper's Ferry to, March 15, 1863.—Scout from Snicker's Ferry to, May 27-29, 1863.—Expedition from Brightwood, D. C., to, June 11-13, 1863.—Expeditions to, Aug. 30-Sept. 2, 1863.—Scout from Vienna to, Dec. 25-27, 1863, and skirmish.—Affair at, April 19, 1864.
LEE'S HOUSE, on the Occoquan, Affair at, Jan. 28-29, 1862.
LEE'S MILL, Skirmishes near, April 5, 1862; July 27, Nov. 16, 1864.—Engagement at, April 16, 1862.—Reconnoissances to, April 22, 28, 29, 1862.—Skirmish at, July 30, 1864.—Scout to, Sept. 19, 1864.
LEESVILLE, Skirmish at, April 4, 1863.
LEWINSVILLE, Skirmish near, Sept. 10, 1861.—Reconnoissance from Chain Bridge to, and action at, Sept. 11, 1861.—Reconnoissance to, and skirmish at, Sept. 25, 1861.—Skirmishes at, Oct. 1 and 3, 1863.—Affairs at and near, Dec. 9, 1863.
LEWIS' CHAPEL, Affair at, Feb. 24, 1862.
LEWIS' FARM, Engagement at, March 29, 1865.
LEWIS' FORD, Skirmishes at, Aug. 28, 30, 1862.
LEXINGTON, Skirmish at, June 11, 1864.

VIRGINIA.

LIBERTY, Skirmishes at, Oct. 24, 1863; June 19, 1864.—Affair at, Nov. 21, 1863.—Skirmish near, June 16, 1864.
LIBERTY CHURCH, Reconnoissance to, April 16, 1862.
LIBERTY MILLS, Skirmish near, Sept. 23, 1863.—Skirmish at, Dec. 22, 1864.
LICKING RUN BRIDGE, Skirmish at, Nov. 30, 1863.
LIMESTONE RIDGE, Affair at, Sept. 17, 1864.
LINDEN, Skirmishes at, May 15 and 24, 1862.
LITTLE BOSTON, Skirmish near, Nov. 24, 1863.
LITTLE FORT VALLEY, Expedition from Camp Russell to, Feb. 13-17, 1865, and skirmishes.
LITTLE RIVER, Combat at, May 27, 1864.
LITTLE RIVER TURNPIKE, Skirmishes on, Oct. 15, 1861; March 23, 1863.—Affair on, June 28-29, 1863.
LITTLE WASHINGTON, Skirmishes at, Nov. 8, 1862; Aug. 5, 27, 1863.
LOCKE'S FORD, Opequon Creek, Affair at, Sept. 13, 1864.
LOCK GROVE, Skirmishes at, Nov. 27, 1863.
LOCUST GROVE (Robertson's Tavern), Engagement at, Nov. 27, 1863.
LONG BRIDGE ROAD, Reconnoissance on, July 9, 1862.
LOUDOUN COUNTY, Operations in, Feb. 25-May 6, Oct. 26-Nov. 10, Dec. 12-20, 1862.—Scout in, Sept. 12-17, 1862.—Scouts from Harper's Ferry into, Sept. 12-16, 1863; March 20-25, 1865.—Affair in, June 9, 1864.—Skirmish in, Aug. 21, 1864.—Expedition from Winchester into, Nov. 28-Dec. 3, 1864.—Expedition from Camp Averill into, Feb. 18-19, 1865.—Scout into, March 10-14, 1865.—Scout from Vienna into, April 8-10, 1865.
LOUDOUN HEIGHTS, Skirmishes at, May 27, 1862; Jan. 10, 1864.—Reconnoissance from, Oct. 4-6, 1862.
LOUDOUN VALLEY, Scout from Harper's Ferry into, Sept. 21-26, 1863.
LOUISA COURT HOUSE, Skirmish at, May 2, 1862.—Reconnoissance toward, Aug. 16-17, 1862.—Skirmish near, May 2, 1863.
LOVETTSVILLE, Skirmish at, Aug. 8, 1861.—Reconnoissance to, Sept. 3, 1862.—Reconnoissance from Loudoun Heights to, and skirmishes, Oct. 21, 1862.—Affair near, Jan. 18, 1865.
LOWRY, FORT, Rappahannock River, Naval action near, Feb. 24, 1863.—Naval action with, March 15, 1865.
LURAY, Occupation of, and skirmish near, April 22, 1862.—Reconnoissance from Front Royal to, June 29-30, 1862, and skirmish.—Occupation of, July 21, 1862.—Expedition from Bealton to, Dec. 21-23, 1863, and skirmishes.—Skirmish at, Sept. 24, 1864.
LURAY VALLEY, Skirmish in, Oct. 8, 1864.
LYNCHBURG, Scout from Lexington around, June 13-15, 1864.—Engagement at, June 17-18, 1864.

VIRGINIA.

LYNCHBURG CAMPAIGN, May 26-June 29, 1864.
LYNNHAVEN BAY, Naval action at, Oct. 10, 1861.
LYON, FORT, Explosion at, July 9, 1863.
McDOWELL, Skirmishes near, May 7 and 9, 1862.—Engagement near, May 8, 1862.
McGAHEYSVILLE, Skirmish at, April 27, 1862.
MACHODOC CREEK, Expedition from Belle Plain to, March 3-8, 1863.—Joint expedition from Point Lookout, Md., to, April 13-14, 1864.
McLEAN'S FORD, Bull Run, Operations at, July 18, 1861.—Skirmish at, Oct. 15, 1863.
MADISON COURT HOUSE, Reconnoissances to, July 12-17, 23, 1862; Jan. 31, April 28, 1864.—Action near, Aug. 8. 1862.—Skirmishes at, Sept. 21, 1863; Dec. 21, 1864.—Scout from Culpeper to, Jan. 30, 1864.
MAGRUDER'S FERRY, Skirmish at, Sept. 16, 1861.
MALLORY'S CROSS ROADS, Combats at, June 11-12, 1864.
MALVERN CLIFF, Engagement at, June 30, 1862.
MALVERN HILL, Battle of, July 1, 1862.—Skirmish near, July 2, 1862.—Reconnoissance to, July 23, 1862.—Reconnoissance to and reoccupation of, by Union forces, Aug. 2-8, 1862.—Skirmishes at and near, Aug. 5-6, 1862.—Skirmish at, June 15, 1864.—Actions at, July 14, 16, 1864.
MANASSAS, Battles of, July 21, 1861; Aug. 30, 1862.—Skirmish at, Oct. 15, 1863.
MANASSAS GAP, Reconnoissance to, Nov. 5-6, 1862, and skirmish.—Skirmishes at, July 21-22, 1863.—Action at, July 23, 1863.
MANASSAS JUNCTION, Skirmishes at, Aug. 26-28, Oct. 24, 1862; Oct. 15, 17, 1863; Nov. 11, 1864.
MANASSAS PLAINS, Battle of, Aug. 29, 1862.
MANASSAS STATION, Operations about, Aug. 25-27, 1862.—Capture of, Aug. 26, 1862.
MAPLE LEAF, U. S. Transport, Capture of, off Cape Henry, June 10, 1863.
MARION, Action at, Dec. 16, 1864.—Engagement near, Dec. 17-18, 1864.
MARKHAM'S STATION, Skirmishes at, Nov. 4 and 10, 1862.
MARSTELLER'S PLACE, Skirmish at, May 14, 1863.
MARYE'S HEIGHTS, Battle of, May 3, 1863.
MASSAPONAX CHURCH, Affairs at, Aug. 5-6, 1862.
MATADEQUIN CHURCH, Combat at, May 29-30, 1864.
MATHEWS COUNTY, Reconnoissance through, July 7-9, 1862.—Expedition into, Nov. 22-25, 1862.—Destruction of salt-works in, Nov. 22, 1862.—Reconnoissance to, Dec. 12, 1862.—Expedition from Gloucester Point into, May 19-22, 1863.—Expeditions from Yorktown into, Oct. 4-9, Nov. 16-19, 1863; March 17-21, 1864.

VIRGINIA.

MATHIAS POINT, Attack on, June 27, 1861.—Action at, Aug. 15, 1861.—Expedition to, Nov. 9, 1861.—Expedition from Richmond to, July —, 1863.
MATTAPONY CHURCH, Skirmish at, May 9, 1864.
MATTAPONY RIVER, Boat expedition into, May 22-23, 1863.—Naval operations in, June 4-6, 1863.
MATTOX CREEK, Expedition from Belle Plain to, Feb. 12-14, 1863.—Naval reconnoissance of, March 15-17, 1865.
MEADOW BRIDGE, Skirmish at, June 26, 1862.—Combat at, May 12, 1864.
MECHANICSVILLE, Skirmishes near, May 23, June 26, 1862.—Skirmish at, May 24, 1862.—Combat at, May 12, 1864.
MECHUMP'S CREEK, Combat at, May 31, 1864.
MERRIMAC, C. S. S. (See Hampton Roads, March 8-9, 1862.)—Destruction of, May 11, 1862.
MIDDLEBROOK, Skirmish at, June 10, 1864.
MIDDLEBURG, Operations about, March 27-28, Oct. 13, 1862.—Skirmishes at, Jan. 26-27, 1863.—Scouts from Fairfax Court House to, April 3-6, 1863; Feb. 15-16, 1865.—Skirmishes at and near, June 17-19, 1863.—Scouts to, Sept. 10-11, 1863; March 28-29, 1864.—Scouts from Vienna to, Dec. 18-20, 1863.—Scouts from Manassas Junction to, Jan. 22-23, 1864.
MIDDLESEX COUNTY, Reconnoissance to, Dec. 13, 1862.—Operations in, May 20-26, 1863.—Expedition from Yorktown into, March 17-21, 1864.
MIDDLETOWN, Skirmishes at, March 18, 1862; June 12, 1863; Sept. 20, 1864.—Actions at, May 24, 1862; Nov. 12, 1864.—Skirmishes near, July 15, 1862; April 24, 1864.
MILFORD, Skirmishes at, June 24, 1862; Sept. 22, Oct. 25-26, 1864.—Affair at, April 15, 1864.
MILLWOOD, Skirmish near, Feb. 6, 1863.
MILLWOOD ROAD, Skirmish on, April 8, 1863.
MINE, THE, Explosion of, at Petersburg, July 30, 1864.—Explosion of (Confederate), at Gracie's Salient, Aug. 5, 1864.
MINE RUN, Skirmishes on, Nov. 28 and 30, 1863.
MINE RUN CAMPAIGN, Nov. 26-Dec. 2, 1863.
MITCHELL'S FORD, Bull Run, Skirmishes at, July 18, 1861; Oct. 7 and 15, 1863.
MONITOR, U. S. S., Engagement between the, and the C. S. S. Merrimac, March 9, 1862.
MONROE, FORT, Expedition from, to open communication with the Army of the Potomac, June 28-July 4, 1862.—Expedition from, to Pagan Creek, Dec. 15, 1864.—Expedition from, to Fredericksburg, March 5-8, 1865.—Expedition from, into Westmoreland County, March 11-13, 1865.
MONTEREY, Skirmishes at, April 12, 21, May 12, 1862.
MORRISVILLE, Skirmish near, Jan. 26, 1863.
MORTON, FORT, Skirmishes in front of, Oct. 27 and Nov. 5, 1864.

VIRGINIA.

MORTON'S FORD, Skirmishes at, Oct. 10, 11, and Nov. 14, 15, 26, and Dec. 3-4, 1863.—Engagement at, Feb. 6-7, 1864.
MOSEBY'S OPERATIONS, Aug. 9-Oct. 14, 1864.
MOUNT AIRY, Skirmish near, Dec. 17, 1864.
MOUNT CARMEL, Skirmish at, June 1, 1862.
MOUNT CARMEL CHURCH, Reconnoissance to, Jan. 31, 1864.—Combat at, May 27, 1864.
MOUNT CRAWFORD, Skirmishes at, Oct. 2, 1864; March 1, 2, and 8, 1865.
MOUNT JACKSON, Skirmishes at, March 25, June 3, 1862; Nov. 16, 1863; Sept. 23, 24, 1864.—Occupation of, April 17, 1862.—Skirmishes near, June 6, 13, and 16, 1862; Oct. 3, 1864; March 7, 1865.—Action near, Nov. 22, 1864.
MOUNTVILLE, Skirmish near, Oct. 31, 1862.
MOUNT ZION CHURCH, Action at, July 6, 1864.
MRS. VIOLETT'S, Affair at, March 22, 1863.
MUDDY RUN, Skirmishes at, Aug. 5, Sept. 13, Nov. 8, 1863.
MUD MARCH, THE, Jan. 20-24, 1863.
MULBERRY LANDING, Potomac River, Affair at, Dec. 15, 1861.
MULBERRY POINT, James River, Reconnoissance to, May 7-8, 1862.
MULBERRY ROAD, Skirmish on, Feb. 12, 1864.
MUNSON'S HILL, Skirmish at, Aug. 31, 1861.—Affair at, Sept. 18, 1861.
MURFREE'S STATION, Reconnoissance from Barnard's Mills to, Oct. 15-17, 1864.
NAMOZINE CHURCH, Action at, April 3, 1865.
NANSEMOND RIVER, Naval engagement on, near Suffolk, April 14, 1863.—Joint operations in, April 13-15, 1864.
NEERSVILLE, Reconnoissance from Loudoun Heights to, Oct. 4-6, 1862.—Skirmish at, Sept. 30, 1863.
NELSON'S FARM, Battle of, June 30, 1862.
NEWARK, Combat at, June 12, 1864.
NEW BALTIMORE, Skirmish at, Oct. 13, 19, 1863.—Attack on wagon train near, Oct. 26, 1863.
NEW BRIDGE, Skirmishes near, May 23, June 5, 20, 1862.—Skirmishes at, May 24, June 5, 1862.
NEWBY'S CROSS ROADS, Skirmish at, Nov. 9, 1862; July 24, 1863.
NEW CASTLE, Skirmish at, June 23, 1864.
NEW CASTLE FERRY, Reconnoissance to, May 22, 1862.
NEW GLASGOW, Affair at, June 14, 1864.
NEW HOPE CHURCH, Action near, Nov. 27, 1863.—Skirmish at, Nov. 29, 1863.
NEW KENT COURT HOUSE, Skirmish at, May 9, 1862.—Operations about, June 23, 1862.—Skirmish near, June 30, 1862.—Expedition from Williamsburg toward, Nov. 9-10, 1863.
NEW LONDON, Skirmish at, June 16, 1864.

VIRGINIA.

NEW MARKET, Occupation of, April 17, 1862.—Operations in the vicinity of, April 19-24, 1862.—Skirmishes at, June 13, 1862; May 14, Sept. 24, 1864.—Reconnoissance to near, June 15, 1862.—Expedition from Charlestown, W. Va., to near, Nov. 15-18, 1863.—Skirmish near, May 13, 1864.—Engagement at, May 15, 1864.
NEW MARKET BRIDGE, Affair near, July 19, 1861.—Skirmish near, Oct. 21, 1861.
NEW MARKET HEIGHTS, Combat at, Sept. 29-30, 1864.
NEW MARKET ROAD, Reconnoissance on, June 8, 1862.—Battle of, June 30, 1862.—Engagements on, July 27, Oct. 7, 1864.—Combat on, Aug. 14-15, 1864.
NEWPORT, Skirmishes near, May 12-13, 1864.
NEWPORT NEWS, Occupation of, by Union forces, May 27-29, 1861.—Reconnoissance from Yorktown to, June 7, 1861.—Skirmishes near, July 5 and 12, 1861.—Attack on U. S. S. Minnesota at, April 8, 1864.
NEW RIVER BRIDGE, Skirmish at, May 10, 1864.
NEWTON, Actions at, May 24, 1862; Nov. 11-12, 1864.—Skirmishes at, Nov. 24, 1862; June 12, Aug. 2, 1863; May 29-30, July 14, 22, 1864.—Skirmishes near, Jan. 17, 1863; Oct. 26-28, 1864.—Action near, Aug. 11, 1864.
NINE MILE ORDINARY, Skirmish at, June 14, 1863.
NINE MILE ROAD, Skirmish on, June 18, 1862.
NINEVEH, Action at, Nov. 12, 1864.
NOKESVILLE, Affair near, April 13, 1864.
NOMONI, Potomac River, Boat expedition to, and engagement at, Jan. 5, 1864.
NOMINI BAY, Expedition from Belle Plain to, Feb. 12-14, 1863.
NORFLEET HOUSE, Engagements near, April 14, 15, 1863.
NORFOLK, Evacuation of, by Confederate forces, May 9, 1862.—Occupation of, by Union forces, May 10, 1862.—Affair at, March 25, 1863.—Expedition from, into North Carolina, July 27-Aug. 4, 1864.
NORFOLK AND PETERSBURG RAILROAD, Operations on, May 15-28, 1863.
NORFOLK NAVY YARD, Expedition to destroy the dry-dock at, April 20, 1861.
NORTHAMPTON COUNTY, Expedition through, Nov. 14-22, 1861.
NORTH ANNA RIVER, Combat at, May 9, 1864.—Operations on, May 22-June 1, 1864.
NORTHERN NECK, Operations in, May 20-26, 1863.—Raid on, Jan. 12-14, 1864.—Joint expedition to, June 11-21, 1864.
NORTHERN VIRGINIA, ARMY OF, Surrender of, April 9, 1865.
NORTHERN VIRGINIA CAMPAIGN, Aug. 16-Sept. 2, 1862.
NORTH RIVER, Skirmish at, Oct. 3, 1864.
NORTHWESTERN (B. & O.) R. R., Confederate raid on, April 21-May 21, 1863.

VIRGINIA.

NOTTOWAY COURT HOUSE, Skirmish near, June 23, 1864.
NY RIVER, Combat at, May 10, 1864.
OAK GROVE (Henrico County), Engagement at, June 25, 1862.—(Westmoreland County), Skirmish at, April 26, 1863.
OAK HILL, Skirmish at, Oct. 15, 1863.
OAK SHADE, Skirmish near, Sept. 2, 1863.
OCCOQUAN, Reconnoissance to, Feb. 3, 1862.—Skirmish near, Dec. 20, 1862.—Skirmishes at and near, Dec. 27-28, 1862.—Affair near, March 22, 1863.
OCCOQUAN RIVER, Reconnoissance toward, Oct. 18, 1861.—Reconnoissance to, Nov. 12, 1861.—Skirmish on, Dec. 19, 1862.
OLD CHURCH, Reconnoissance toward, May 18-19, 1862.—Skirmishes at, June —, 1862; June 10, 1864.—Skirmish near, March 2, 1864.—Combat at, May 30, 1864.
OLIVE BRANCH CHURCH, Skirmish near, Feb. 5, 1863.—Skirmish at, Feb. 7, 1863.
OPEQUON CREEK, Skirmishes at, June 13, 1863; Aug. 18, 20, Sept. 15, 1864.—Skirmish near, Aug. 19, 1864.—Affair at, Sept. 13, 1864.—Battle of, Sept. 19, 1864.
ORANGE AND ALEXANDRIA RAILROAD, Operations on, March 28-31, Nov. 10-12, 1862.
ORANGE COURT HOUSE, Reconnoissance to, July 12-17, 1862.—Skirmishes at, July 15, Aug. 2, 1862; Sept. 21, 1863.—Reconnoissance from Fredericksburg toward, July 24-26, 1862.—Operations about, July 29, 1862.—Reconnoissance toward, and skirmish, Aug. 13, 1862.
ORCHARD, THE, Engagement at, June 25, 1862.
ORLEANS, Scout to, March 19, 1864.
OTTER CREEK, Skirmish on, June 16, 1864.
OX FORD, Combat at, May 24, 1864.
OX HILL, Battle of, Sept. 1, 1862.
PAGAN CREEK, Expedition from Fort Monroe to, Dec. 15, 1864.—Joint expedition up, Feb. 5-6, 1865.
PAINE'S CROSS ROADS, Skirmish at, April 5, 1865.
PAMUNKEY PENINSULA, Operations on, Aug. 20, 1862-June 3, 1863.
PAMUNKEY RIVER, Expedition up, May 17, 1862.—Naval expedition up, Jan. 7-8, 1863.—Affair on, April 16, 1863.—Joint operations in, March 9-13, 1864.—Operations on, May 22-June 1, 1864.
PARIS, Operations about, Oct. 13, 1862.
PARKER'S FORD, Engagement at, July 17-18, 1864.
PARKER'S STORE, Action at, Nov. 29, 1863.—Combat at, May 5, 1864.
PARKINS, MILL, Skirmish at, Nov. 24, 1864.
PAYNE'S FARM, Engagement at, Nov. 27, 1863.
PEACH GROVE, Skirmish near, March 12, 1865.
PEACH ORCHARD, Engagement at, June 29, 1862. (Or Allen's Farm, near Fair Oaks Station.)

VIRGINIA.

PEEBLES' FARM, Combats at, Sept. 29, Oct. 2, 1864.
PEGRAM'S FARM, Combats at, Sept. 29, Oct. 2, 1864.
PENINSLA, THE, Operations on, Aug. 20, 1862-June 3, 1863.—Scout on, June 18, 1863.
PENINSULAR CAMPAIGN, March 17-Sept. 2, 1862.
PETERSBURG, Engagement at, June 9, 1864.—Assaults on, June 15-18, 1864.—Siege of, June 19, 1864-April 2, 1865.—Expedition from Winchester to the front of, Feb. 27-March 28, 1865.—Assault on, and capture of, April 2, 1865.—Occupation of, April 3, 1865.
PETERSBURG AND WELDON RAILROAD, Union raid against, May 5-11, 1864.
PHILOMONT, Skirmishes at, Nov. 1, 9, 19, 1862.
PIANKATANK RIVER, Expedition to, March 9-22, 1864.—Naval engagement in, April 29, 1862.—Expedition up, Aug. 10-11, 1863.—Naval action in, March 7, 1864.
PIEDMONT, Skirmish at, April 17, 1862.—Skirmishes near, Feb. 17-18, June 5, Oct. 9, 1864.—Engagement at, June 5, 1864.
PIEDMONT STATION, Skirmish at, May 16, 1863.
PIG POINT, Attack on batteries at, June 5, 1861.
PINEY BRANCH CHURCH, Combats at, May 8 and 15, 1864.
PINEY RIVER, Skirmish at, June 12, 1864.
POHICK CHURCH, Skirmish at, Aug. 18, 1861.—Expedition to, Oct. 3, 1861.—Reconnoissances to, Nov. 12 and Dec. 18, 1861.—Skirmish near, March 5, 1862.
POHICK RUN, Skirmish near, Jan. 9, 1862.
POINDEXTER'S FARM, Battle of, July 1, 1862.
POINT OF ROCKS, Appomattox River, Engagement at, June 26, 1862.
POLE CAT CREEK, Combat at, May 27, 1864.
POLLOCK'S MILL CREEK, Operations at, April 29-May 2, 1863.
PONY MOUNTAIN, Skirmish at, Sept. 13, 1863.
POPE'S CREEK, Expedition from Point Lookout, Md., to, June 11-21, 1864.
POPLAR SPRING CHURCH, Scout to, Sept. 13, 15, 1864.—Battle of, Sept. 29-Oct. 2, 1864.
PO RIVER, Combat at, May 10, 1864.
PORT CONWAY, Expedition from Belle Plain to, April 20-23, 1863.—Skirmish near, Sept. 1, 1863.—Destruction of gunboats Satellite and Reliance at, Sept. 2, 1863.
PORTOPANK CREEK, York River, Naval action near, May 5, 1864.
PORT REPUBLIC, Engagements at, June 8-9, 1862.—Affair at, June 4, 1864.—Skirmishes at, Sept. 26-28, 1864.
PORT ROYAL, Expedition from Fredericksburg to, Aug. 15-16, 1862.—Expeditions from Belle Plain to, April 20-23, 1863.—Naval reconnoissance to, Oct. 26-27, 1864.—Capture of **Booth and Harold at Garrett's Farm near, April 26, 1865.**

VIRGINIA.

PORTSMOUTH, Occupation of, by Union forces, May 10, 1862.—Demonstrations on, March 4-5, 1864.
PORT WALTHAL JUNCTION, Engagement at, May 6-7, 1864.—Skirmish at, May 16, 1864.
POTOMAC CREEK, Engagement with batteries at mouth of, Aug. 23, 1861.—Expedition from, to Richards's and Ellis's Fords, Dec. 30-31, 1862.
POWELL'S BIG FORT VALLEY, Reconnoissance up, July 2, 1862.
POWHATAN, Skirmish near, Jan. 25, 1865.
POWHATAN, FORT, Skirmish at, May 21, 1864.
PRATT'S LANDING, Potomac River, Naval action at, Dec. 11, 1862.
PRINCE EDWARD COURT HOUSE, Skirmish at, April 7, 1865.
PRINCE GEORGE COURT HOUSE, Skirmish near, Nov. 24, 1864.
PRINCESS ANNE COURT HOUSE, Operations about, Sept. 21-25, 1863.
PRINCE WILLIAM COUNTY, Scout in, Feb. 18-19, 1865.
PRITCHARD'S MILL, Skirmish at, Sept. 15, 1861.
PROCTOR'S CREEK, Engagement at, May 12-16, 1864.
PROCTOR'S HOUSE, Scout to, Sept. 19, 1864.
PROVIDENCE CHURCH, Skirmishes at, Nov. 12 and Dec. 28, 1862.—Skirmishes near, Jan. 9 and May 17, 1863.
PROVIDENCE CHURCH ROAD, Skirmish on, April 12, 1863.—Reconnoissance on, May 3, 1863.
PURCELLVILLE, Capture of Confederate wagon-train near, July 16, 1864.
QUAKER ROAD, Skirmishes at, March 28-29, 31, 1865.
QUARLES' MILLS, Combat at May 23, 1864.
RACCOON FORD, Reconnoissance from Culpeper to, July 28, 1862.—Skirmishes at, Aug. 20, 1862; April 30, Sept. 15, 17, 19, 22, Oct. 10, Dec. 5, 1863.—Skirmishes at and near, Nov. 26-27, 1863.—Skirmish near, Nov. 30, 1863.
RAPIDAN RIVER, Advance of the Union forces from the Rappahannock to, Sept. 13-17, 1863.—Reconnoissance across, Sept. 21-23, 1863.—Demonstration on, Feb. 6-7, 1864.—Campaign from the, to the James River, May 4-June 12, 1864.
RAPIDAN STATION, Skirmishes at, May 1, July 13, 1862: May 1, Sept. 15, 16, 1863.—Skirmish near, Aug. 18, 1862.—Scout toward, July 26, 1864.
RAPPAHANNOCK BRIDGE, Operations at, Feb. 5-7, April 14-15, 1863.—Skirmish at, Oct. 22, 1863.
RAPPAHANNOCK COUNTY, Operations in, Oct. 26-Nov. 10, 1862.
RAPPAHANNOCK FORDS, Reconnoissance of, Feb. 2, 1863.
RAPPAHANNOCK RIVER, Affairs on, June 24, 1861; May 13, 1862.—Reconnoissances to, April 2, 7, 15, 16, 18, 1862.—

VIRGINIA.

Expedition up, April 12-19, 1862.—Operations on, Aug. 18-25, 1862.—Engagement on, Dec. 4, 1862.—Capture of U. S. Gunboats Satellite and Reliance near mouth of, Aug. 23, 1863.—Expedition up, in search of the U. S. S. Satellite and Reliance, Aug. 30-Sept. 3, 1863.—Advance of the Union forces from, to the Rapidan, Sept. 13-17, 1863.—Advance of the Union forces to the line of the, Nov. 7-8, 1863.—Expedition from Point Lookout, Md., to, May 11-14, 1864.—Naval expedition up, to Fredericksburg, May 12-19, 1864.—Reconnoissance up, to Port Royal, Oct. 26-27, 1864.

RAPPAHANNOCK STATION, Affair at, March 29, 1862.—Skirmishes at, Aug. 20, Nov. 7-8, 1862; Feb. 2, 1863.—Engagements at, Aug. 23, 1862; Nov. 7, 1863.—Skirmishes near, Nov. 9, 1862; Oct. 12, 23, 27, 1863.—Reconnoissance to, Jan. 8-10, 1863.

REAMS' STATION, Skirmish at, June 22, 1864.—Engagement at, June 29, 1864.—Actions near, Aug. 23, 24, 1864.—Battle of, Aug. 25, 1864.

RECTORTOWN, Skirmish at, Jan. 1, 1864.—Skirmish near, Oct. 10, 1864.

REED'S BLUFF (See Watkins's Bluff, June 20, 1862).

REED'S FERRY, Nansemond River, Skirmish near, May 3, 1863.

RELIANCE, U. S. Gunboat, Capture of, near mouth of Rappahannock River, Aug. 23, 1863.—Expedition against and destruction of, at Port Conway, Sept. 1-3, 1863.

RICE'S STATION, Engagement at, April 6, 1865.

RICHARDS' FORD, Expedition from Potomac Creek to, Dec. 30-31, 1862.—Skirmish at, Sept. 26, 1863.

RICHMOND, Reconnoissance from Bottom's Bridge toward, May 23, 1862.—Expedition from Yorktown against, Feb. 6-8, 1864.—Union expedition against, Feb. 28-March 4, 1864.—Siege of, June 19, 1864-April 3, 1865.—Occupation of, April 3, 1865.—Evacuation of, April 9, 1865.

RICHMOND CAMPAIGN, June 13, 1864-April 3, 1865.

RICHMOND AND DANVILLE RAILROAD, Union raid against, May 12-17, 1864.

RICHMOND AND FREDERICKSBURG RAILROAD BRIDGE (South Anna River), Destruction of, May 29, 1862.

RICHMOND COUNTY, Operations in, Feb. 10-16, 1863.

RICHMOND FORTIFICATIONS, Combat at, May 12, 1864.

RICHMOND ROAD, Reconnoissances from Westover on, July 16, 1862.

RIDDELL'S SHOP, Skirmish at, June 13, 1864.

RIXEY'S FORD, Affair near, Sept. 2, 1863.

RIXEYVILLE, Skirmish at, Nov. 8, 1863.

RIXEYVILLE FORD, Skirmish near, Aug. 5, 1863.

ROANOKE RIVER, Capture of Union torpedo party at the mouth of, July 6, 1864.—Naval reconnoissance of, Oct. 22-24, 1864.

VIRGINIA.

ROANOKE STATION, Skirmish at, June 25, 1864.
ROBERTSON'S FORD, Skirmishes at, Sept. 15, 23, 1863.
ROBERTSON'S RIVER, Capture of Union pickets on, Oct. 1, 1863.—Skirmishes along, Oct. 8, 1863.
ROBERTSON'S TAVERN, Skirmishes at, Nov. 27, 1863.
ROBINSON'S PLANTATION, King and Queen County.—Expedition from West Point to, May 15, 1863.
ROCKFISH GAP, Skirmish at, Sept. 28, 1864.
ROWANTY CREEK, Battle of, Feb. 5-7, 1865.
RUDE'S HILL, Skirmishes at, April 17, 1862; May 14-15, 1864; March 7, 1865.—Action at, Nov. 22, 1864.
RUSSELL'S FORD, Robertson's River, Skirmish at, Oct. 10, 1863.
SAILOR'S CREEK, Engagement at, April 6, 1865.
SAINT GEORGE'S ISLAND, Potomac River, Joint expedition to, Nov. 22-23, 1863.
SAINT MARY'S CHURCH, Reconnoissance from Harrison's Landing to, July 29, 1862.—Engagement at, June 24, 1864.
SAINT PETER'S CHURCH, Combat at, June 21, 1864.
SAINT STEPHEN'S CHURCH, Skirmish at, Oct. 14, 1863.
SALEM, Skirmishes at, April 1, Nov. 4, 1862; Oct. 4, 1864.—Descent upon, Dec. 16, 1863.—Scout to, March 19, 1864.—Skirmishes at and near, Aug. 27, 1862; June 21, 1864.—Operations about, March 3-8, 1865.
SALEM CHURCH, near Fredericksburg, Battle of, May 3, 1863.—Near Totopotomoy, Combat at, May 27, 1864.
SALEM HEIGHTS, Battle of, May 3, 1863.
SALIENT, THE, Combat at, May 12, 1864.
SALT PONDS (or Salt Pond Mountains), Skirmish at, May 12-13, 1864.
SALTVILLE, Action at, Oct. 1-2, 1864.—Capture and destruction of salt-works at, Dec. 20-21, 1864.
SANGSTER'S STATION, Skirmishes at, March 9, 1862; Dec. 15, 17, 1863.—Affair near, Nov. 25, 1863.
SAPPONY CHURCH, Engagements at, June 28-29, 1864.
SATELLITE, U. S. Gunboat, Capture of, near mouth of Rappahannock River, Aug. 23, 1863.—Expedition against and destruction of, at Port Conway, Sept. 1-3, 1863.
SAVAGE STATION, Richmond and York River Railroad, Battle of, June 29, 1862.
SCOTT COUNTY, Affair in, Oct. 26, 1864.
SCOTT'S, Skirmish at, Dec. 19, 1863.
SCOTT'S CROSS ROADS, Action at, April 2, 1865.
SCUPPERNONG RIVER, Naval action in, Sept. 29, 1864.
SEABOARD AND ROANOKE RAILROAD, Operations on, May 12-26, 1863.
SECOND MANASSAS, Battle of, Aug. 30, 1863.
SEDGWICK, FORT, Skirmish in front of, Oct. 27, 1864.
SEIVERS' FORD, Opequon Creek, Skirmish at, Sept. 15, 1864.
SELECMAN'S FORD, Affair at, March 22, 1863.

VIRGINIA.

SEVEN DAYS' BATTLES, June 25-July 1, 1862.
SEVEN PINES, Reconnoissances to and skirmishes, May 24-27, 1862.—Skirmishes near, May 29, June 15, 1862.—Battle of, May 31-June 1, 1862.—Reconnoissance beyond, June 1-2, 1862.
SEWELL'S POINT, Engagement at, May 18-19, 1861.—Naval demonstration on, May 8, 1862.—Capture of, May 9, 1862.
SEXTON'S STATION, Combat at, May 27, 1864.
SHADY GROVE, Combat at, May 30-June 1, 1864.
SHALLOW CREEK, Combat at, May 31, 1864.
SHANNON'S CROSS ROADS, Skirmish at, May 4, 1863.
SHAWSHEEN, U. S. Gunboat, Capture of, at Turkey Island, May 7, 1864.
SHELTON'S CREEK, Rappahannock River, Naval reconnoissance to, June 30, 1864.
SHENANDOAH COUNTY, Scout in, Dec. 7-11, 1863.
SHENANDOAH RIVER, Accident at Berry's Ferry on, April 15, 1862.—Skirmish on the South Fork of, April 19, 1862.
SHERIDAN'S EXPEDITION from Todd's Tavern to the James River, May 9-24, 1864.
SHIRLY, Capture of arms at, by the Confederates, July 4, 1862.—Attack on Union camps and shipping near, July 31-Aug. 1, 1862.
SLASH CHURCH, Skirmish at, May 27, 1862.
SLATERSVILLE, Skirmish at, May 9, 1862.
SLAUGHTER'S HOUSE, Skirmish near, Aug. 8, 1862.
SLAUGHTER'S MOUNTAIN, Battle of, Aug. 9, 1862.
SMITH BRIGGS, U. S. S., Destruction of, Feb. 1, 1864.
SMITHFIELD, Affair at, Aug. 23, 1862.—Skirmishes at, Sept. 16, 1863; Jan. 31-Feb. 1, 1864.—Skirmish near, April 14, 1864.—Capture of the tugboat Lizzie Freeman near, Dec. 5, 1864.—Expedition from Bermuda Hundred to, Feb. 11-15, 1865.
SMITH'S PLANTATION, Expedition from Yorktown to, April 1, 1863.
SMITH'S STORE, Skirmish near, June 15, 1864.
SMYTH COUNTY, Skirmish in, Sept. 14, 1863.
SNICKER'S FERRY, Reconnoissance from Chantilly to, Nov. 28-30, 1862, and skirmishes.—Skirmish at, April 13, 1863.—Scout from, May 12-14, 1863.—Engagement at, July 17-18, 1864.
SNICKER'S GAP, Skirmishes at, Oct. 27, Nov. 3, 1862; June 1, July 17, 1863; Sept. 16-17, Nov. 30, 1864.—Skirmishes near, Nov. 2, 1862; July 23, 1863.—Reconnoissance toward, March 16-18, 1864.—Operations about, Oct. 28-29, 1864.
SNICKERSVILLE, Skirmishes at, Oct. 31, 1862; March 6, 1864.—Operations about, Oct. 13, 1862.—Skirmish near, Oct. 21, 1862.—Affair near, Nov. 8, 1862.
SOMERTON ROAD, Skirmish on, April 13, 1863.
SOMERVILLE, Skirmish near, Feb. 9, 1863.

VIRGINIA.

SOMERVILLE FORD, Skirmish at, Sept. 14, 1863.
SOMERVILLE HEIGHTS, Action at, May 7, 1862.
SOUTH ANNA BRIDGE, Skirmishes at, May 3, July 4, 1863; March 14, 1865.—Expedition from Yorktown to, June 23-28, 1863, and skirmish.
SOUTH ANNA RIVER, Destruction of the Virginia Central Railroad Bridge on, May 28, 1862.—Destruction of the Richmond and Fredericksburg Railroad Bridge on, May 29, 1862.—Expedition from White House to, July 1-7, 1863.
SOUTH BOSTON, Expedition from Burkeville and Petersburg to, April 23-29, 1865.
SOUTH FORK, Shenandoah River, Skirmish on, April 19, 1862.
SOUTH QUAY, Scout from Benvard's Mills to, Jan. 2, 1865—Skirmish at, March 10, 1865.
SOUTH QUAY BRIDGE, Skirmish at, May 1, 1863.
SOUTH QUAY ROAD, Skirmish on, April 11, 1863.
SOUTH SIDE RAILROAD, Expedition against, June 22-July 2, 1864.—Engagement at, April 2, 1865.
SOUTHWEST VIRGINIA, Raids from Kentucky and East Tennessee into, Sept. 20-Oct. 7, 1864.—Expedition from East Tennessee into, Dec. 10-29, 1864.—Stoneman's Raid in, March 21-April 25, 1865.
SPARTA, Occupation of, April 19, 1862.
SPERRYVILLE, Scout to, Jan. 10, 1864.—Reconnoissance to, March 17-18, 1864.
SPOTSYLVANIA COURT HOUSE, Skirmish near, April 30, 1863.—Operations about, May 8-21, 1864.
SPRIGG'S FORD, Skirmish near, Feb. 28, 1864.
SPRINGFIELD STATION, Skirmishes at, Oct. 2, 3, 1861.—Scout to the vicinity of, Jan. 17, 1862.
SQUIRREL LEVEL ROAD, Reconnoissance on, Oct. 8, 1864.
STAFFORD COURT HOUSE, Skirmish at, Aug. 22, 1863.
STANARD'S MILL, Combat at, May 21, 1864.
STANARDSVILLE, Skirmish at, Feb. 29, 1864.—Skirmish near, March 1, 1864.
STANTON RIVER BRIDGE, Skirmish at, June 25, 1864
STAUNTON, Occupation of, June 6, 1864, and March 2, 1865.—Expedition from Richmond to, May 6-14, 1865.
STEDMAN, FORT, Assault on, March 25, 1865.
STEPHENSON'S DEPOT, Engagement at, July 20, 1864.—Skirmish near, Sept. 5, 1864.
STEPHENSON'S STATION, Skirmish at, March 11, 1862.
STEVENSBURG, Skirmishes at, Aug. 20, 1862; June 9, Sept. 13, Oct. 11, Nov. 8, 1863.—Skirmish near, April 29, 1863.
STICKLEYVILLE, Skirmish near, Dec. 13, 1863.
STONE CHAPEL, Skirmish near, Aug. 10, 1864.
STONEMAN'S RAIDS, April 29-May 7, 1863; March 21-April 25, 1865.
STONY CREEK, Skirmish at, April 2, 1862.—Engagements **at,** June 28-29, 1864.—Reconnoissance toward, Nov. 7, 1864.

VIRGINIA.

STONY CREEK STATION, Skirmish at, May 7, 1864.—Scouts toward, Oct. 11-12 and Nov. 28, 1864.—Expedition to and skirmish, Dec. 1, 1864.
STRASBURG, Skirmishes at, March 19, May 24, June 2, Dec. 21, 1862; June 2, 1863; Sept. 20, 21, Oct. 14, 1864.—Affairs at, Sept. 19, 1863; May 12, 1864.—Skirmishes near, Feb. 24, Dec. 13, 1863; Feb. 2, Aug. 13-15, Oct. 7, 1864.—Reconnoissance from Winchester toward, April 20, 1863.
STRAWBERRY HILL, Combat at, May 12, 1864.
STRAWBERRY PLAINS, Engagement at, July 27-29, 1864.
STUART'S, Affair at, Oct. 17, 1863.
STUART'S EXPEDITION, Oct. 9-12, 1862.
STUART'S RAID, June 13-15, 1862.
STUART'S CHRISTMAS RAID, Dec. 27-29, 1862.
STUMP'S TANNERY, Expedition from Winchester to, April 17-18, 1863.
SUFFOLK, Expedition from, Sept. 2-3, 1862.—Operations about, Nov. 12-14, 1862.—Skirmishes near, Dec. 28, 1862; June 11, 1863; March 9, 1864.—Engagement near, Jan. 30, 1863.—Reconnoissance from, March 7-9, 1863.—Siege of, April 11-May 4, 1863.—Naval engagement near, April 14, 1863.—Expedition from, to the Blackwater, June 12-18, 1863.—Evacuation of, by Union forces, July 3, 1863.—Raid on, Nov. 11, 1863.
SULPHUR SPRINGS, Actions at and near, Aug. 23-24, Nov. 15, 1862; Oct. 12, 1863.—Skirmishes at and near, Aug. 25-26, Nov. 13-14, 1862; Oct. 11 and Nov. 8, 1863.—Operations about, March 3-8, 1865.
SURRY COUNTY, Expedition from City Point into, Oct. 16-18, 1864.
SUTHERLAND'S STATION, South Side Railroad, Engagement at, April 2, 1865.
SWIFT CREEK, Engagement at, May 9, 1864.
SWOOPE'S DEPOT, Affair at, March 2, 1865.
SYCAMORE CHURCH, Reconnoissance from Coggins' Point beyond, Aug. 4-5, 1862.—Affair near, Aug. 9, 1864.—Skirmish near, Sept. 3, 1864.—Reconnoissance to, Sept. 5-6, 1864.
TABERNACLE CHURCH, Skirmish at, April 4, 1865.
TAPPAHANNOCK, Naval action at, May 30, 1863.
TAYLORSVILLE, Skirmish near, Feb. 29, 1864.
TAYLORTOWN, Skirmish at, Dec. 24, 1864.
THOMPSON'S CROSS ROADS, Skirmish at, May 5, 1863.
THORNBURG, Skirmish at, Aug. 5, 1862.—Action at, Aug. 6, 1862.
THORNTON'S MILLS, Reconnoissance from Dranesville to, Oct. 20, 1861.
THORNTON STATION, Reconnoissance to, Oct. 21, 1861.
THOROUGHFARE GAP, Engagement at, Aug. 28, 1862.—Reconnoissance toward, Sept. 16, 1862.—Expedition to and skirmish at, Oct. 17-18, 1862.—Skirmish at, June 17, 1863.—

VIRGINIA.

Skirmishes at and about, June 21-25, 1863.—Expedition from Bealton toward, Nov. 21, 1863.
THOROUGHFARE MOUNTAIN, Reconnoissance to, Aug. 9, 1862.—Affair near, Jan. 27, 1864.
TIMBERVILLE, Skirmish at, Sept. 24, 1864.
TODD'S TAVERN, Combats at, May 5, 7, and 8, 1864.—Expedition from, to the James River, May 9-24, 1864.
TOLL-GATE, near White Post, Action at, Aug. 11, 1864.
TOM'S BROOK, Skirmishes at, June 3, 1862; Oct. 8, 1864.—Engagement at, Oct. 9, 1864.
TORPEDO STATION, James River, Destruction of, May 10, 1864.
TOTOPOTOMOY CREEK, Operations on, May 22-June 1, 1864.
TREVILLIAN RAID, June 7-24, 1864.
TREVILLIAN STATION, Combat at, June 11, 1864.
TREVILLIAN'S DEPOT, Skirmish at, May 2, 1862.
TUNSTALL'S STATION, Operations about, June 28, 1862.—Skirmish at, May 4, 1863.—Combat at, June 21, 1864.
TURKEY BEND, Naval affair at, July 5, 1864.
TURKEY BRIDGE, Engagement at, June 30, 1862.—Destruction of, July 2, 1862.
TURKEY CREEK, Affair near, Jan. 16, 1864.—Skirmish at, July 12, 1864.—Attack on the U. S. sanitary steamer Brooks at, Aug. 4, 1864.
TURKEY ISLAND, James River, Capture of U. S. gunboat Shawsheen at, May 7, 1864.
TURKEY ISLAND CREEK BRIDGE, Reconnoissance from Bottom's Bridge to, May 23, 1862.
TURNER'S FARM, Combat at, May 31, 1864.
TURNER'S MILLS, Skirmish at, Jan. 30, 1863.
TWELVE MILE ORDINARY, Skirmishes at, April 27-29, 1864.
TYSON'S CROSS ROADS, Skirmish at, Nov. 14, 1863.
UNION, Skirmishes at, Nov. 2-3, 1862.
UNION MILLS, Affair near, Feb. 14, 1863.
UNITED STATES FORD, Affair at, Nov. 16, 1862.
UPPER POTOMAC RIVER, Operations on, Sept. 21, 1862-Jan. 25, 1863.
UPPERVILLE, Skirmishes near, Oct. 29, Nov. 3, 1862; Sept. 25, 1863.—Skirmishes at, May 13, June 2, Dec. 16, 1863; Feb. 20, Oct. 29, 1864.—Engagement at, June 21, 1863.—Scout from Vienna toward, April 28-May 1, 1864.
URBANA, Naval operations near, June 12, 1863; April 21, May 12-13, 1864.
UTZ'S FORD, Affair at, Oct. 7, 1863.
VANDERBURG'S HOUSE, Munson's Hill, Affair near, Sept. 28, 1861.

VIRGINIA.

VAUGHAN ROAD, Reconnoissance on, Oct. 8, 1864.—Skirmishes on, Aug. 22, 1864; March 29, 1865.—Action on, Aug. 24, 1864.—Combats on, Sept. 29, Oct. 2, 1864.—Battle of, Feb. 5-7, 1865.
VERDON, Skirmish at, July 22, 1862.
VIA'S HOUSE, Skirmish near, June 3, 1864.
VIENNA, Action near, June 17, 1861.—Skirmish at, July 17, 1861.—Skirmish near, Nov. 26, 1861.—Expedition to, Feb. 22, 1862.—Scout from, to Gum Springs, Oct. 12-13, 1863.—Reconnoissance from, toward Blue Ridge Mountains, Nov. 18-23, 1863.—Scout from, to Middleburg, Dec. 18-20, 1863.—Scout from, to Leesburg, Dec. 25-29, 1863, and skirmish.—Scout from, toward Upperville, April 28-May 1, 1864.—Scout from, into Loudoun County, April 8-10, 1865.
VINE TREE SIGNAL STATION, Capture of, Aug. 14, 1863.
VIOLETT'S, MRS., Affair at, March 22, 1863.
VIRGINIA, C. S. S. (See Hampton Roads, March 8-9, 1862).—Destruction of, by the Confederates, May 11, 1862.
VIRGINIA AND TENNESSEE RAILROAD, Raid on, Dec. 8-25, 1863.—Expedition against, May 2-19, 1864.
VIRGINIA CENTRAL RAILROAD, Raid on, at Jackson's River Depot, May 20, 1862.
WALKERTON, Expedition from Yorktown to, June 4-5, 1863.—Skirmish near, March 2, 1864.
WAPPING HEIGHTS, Action at, July 23, 1863.
WARD'S BLUFF (See Drewry's Bluff, May 15, 1862).
WARE BOTTOM CHURCH, Skirmish at, May 9, 1864.—Action at, May 20, 1864.
WARE RIVER, Joint expeditions into, March 31-April 1, and April 7-9, 1863.
WARE'S POINT, Attack on Union gunboats at, Feb. 21, 1863.
WARRENTON, Scout to, Aug. 29, 1862.—Expedition from Centreville to, Sept. 29, 1862.—Skirmishes near, Nov. 5, 8, Dec. 25, 1862; May 31, Sept. 22, Oct. 13, 1863.—Reconnoissance from Potomac Creek Bridge toward, Dec. 21-22, 1862.—Expedition from Falmouth to, Dec. 30-31, 1862.—Skirmishes at, May 6, 11, 23, 1863; Jan. 7, 1864.—Capture of Union pickets near, Nov. 7, 1863.—Scout from, Feb. 17-18, 1864.—Operations about, March 3-8, 1865.
WARRENTON JUNCTION, Reconnoissance to, March 29, 1862.—Expedition from Centreville to, Sept. 25-28, 1862.—Skirmish near, Oct. 10, 1862.—Skirmish at, May 3, 1863.
WARRENTON SPRINGS, Actions at, Aug. 23-24, Nov. 15, 1862; Oct. 12, 1863.—Skirmishes at, Aug. 25-26, 1862; Nov. 8, 1863.—Skirmish near, Oct. 11, 1863.
WARSAW, Skirmish near, March 12, 1865.
WARWICK ROAD, Skirmish near, April 5, 1862.
WARWICK SWAMP, Skirmish at, July 12, 1864.
WATERFORD, Skirmishes at, Aug. 27, Dec. 14, 1862; Aug. 8, 1863.—Skirmish near, May 17, 1864.

VIRGINIA.

WATERLOO, Skirmish at, Nov. 14, 1862.
WATERLOO BRIDGE, Actions at, Aug. 24-25, 1862.—Skirmishes at, Aug. 30, Nov. 7, 1862.
WATKINS' BLUFF, Naval action at, June 20, 1862.
WATKINS' HOUSE, Action at, March 25, 1865.
WAYNESBOROUGH, Skirmishes at, June 10, Sept. 29, 1864.—Engagement at, March 2, 1865.
WEAVERVILLE, Skirmish at, Aug. 27, 1863.—Affair near, Oct. 31, 1863.
WELDON RAILROAD, Battle of, Aug. 18-21, 1864.—Reconnoissance on, Sept. 2, 1864.
WELFORD'S FORD, Skirmish near, Aug. 9, 1863.
WEST BRANCH, Engagement at the mouth of, April 14, 1863.
WESTMORELAND COUNTY, Expedition to, Dec. 1-4, 1862.—Operations in, Feb. 10-16, 1863.—Expedition from Belle Plain into, March 25-29, 1863.—Expedition from Point Lookout, Md., to, April 12-14, 1864.—Expedition from Fort Monroe into, March 11-13, 1865.
WESTOVER, Skirmish at, July 4, 1862.—Affair near, July 22, 1862.
WEST POINT, Engagement at, May 7, 1862.—Expeditions from Yorktown to, Jan. 7-9, 13, 1863; Feb. 23-24, 1865.—Affair near, April 16, 1863.—Occupation of, by Union forces, May 7, 1863.—Naval reconnoissance from Yorktown to, May 4, 1862.—Firing on Union mail-boat at, May 23, 1863.—Joint operations at, May 5, 1864.—Evacuation of, by Union forces, May 31-June 1, 1863.
WEYER'S CAVE, Skirmishes at, Sept. 26, 27, 1864.
WHITE HOUSE, Affairs at, June 13-15, 1862.—Naval expedition from, to Bassett's Landing, May 17, 1862.—Destruction of stores, etc., at, June 28, 1862.—Expedition from Yorktown to, Jan. 7-9, 1863.—Expeditions from, to South Anna River and Bottom's Bridge, July 1-7, 1863.—Capture of Confederate steamer near, Sept. 25, 1863.—Skirmishes at, June 12 and 20, 1864.—Naval operations near, June 20-23, 1864.—Combat at, June 21, 1864.
WHITE HOUSE FORD, Reconnoissance from Luray to, July 22, 1862.
WHITE OAK RIDGE, Engagement at, March 31, 1865.
WHITE OAK ROAD, Engagement at, March 31, 1865.—Skirmish at, April 1, 1865.
WHITE OAK RUN, Operations at, April 29-May 2, 1863.
WHITE OAKS, Skirmish at, May 27, 1862.
WHITE OAK SWAMP, Reconnoissance to the left of, June 22-23, 1862.—Skirmish at, June 13, 1864.
WHITE OAK SWAMP BRIDGE, Engagement at, June 30, 1862.—Reconnoissance to, and skirmish at, Aug. 4, 1862.
WHITE PLAINS, Operations about, March 29-31, 1862.—Skirmish at, Sept. 12, 1863.—Scouts from Vienna to, Dec. 28-31, 1863, and skirmish.—Skirmish near, Oct. 11, 1864.

VIRGINIA.

WHITE POST, Skirmish at, June 13, 1863.—Action near, Aug. 11, 1864.
WHITE'S BRIDGE, Skirmish at, May 8, 1864.
WHITE'S FORD, Skirmishes at, Sept. 21-22, 1863.
WHITE'S TAVERN, Combat at, Aug. 16, 1864.
WIGGENTON'S MILLS, Aquia Creek, Skirmish at, Feb. 6, 1863.
WILCOX'S LANDING, Action near, Aug. 3, 1864.
WILDERNESS, Battles of, May 5-7, 1864.
WILDERNESS CHURCH, Capture of wagon-train near, Nov. 27, 1863.
WILLIAMSBURG, Skirmishes near, May 4, 1862.—Battle of, May 5, 1862.—Skirmishes at, Sept. 9, 1862; March 29, April 11, 1863.—Reconnoissance from, Nov. 22, 1862.—Scouts from, Jan. 19, 1863; Jan. 19-24, 1864.—Expedition from, to Bottom's Bridge, Aug. 26-29, 1863, and skirmishes.—Expedition from, toward New Kent Court House, Nov. 9-10, 1863.—Expedition from, to Charles City Court House, Dec. 12-14, 1863, and skirmish.—Expedition from, April 27-29, 1864.—Affair at, Feb. 11, 1865.
WILLIAMSBURG ROAD, Skirmish on, June 29, 1862.
WILLIS' CHURCH, Skirmish near, June 29, 1862.—Battle of, June 30, 1862.
WILMINGTON AND WELDON RAILROAD, Raid on, July 3-7, 1863.—Expedition against, June 20-25, 1864.
WILSON'S WHARF, Action at, May 24, 1864.—Capture of Confederate signal station at, May 6, 1864.
WINCHESTER, Skirmishes near, March 7, June 18, 19, Nov. 22, 1862; Feb. 25, 26, March 19, April 8, Nov. 13, 1863; Aug. 11, Sept. 7, 13, 24, 1864.—Skirmish at, April 8, 1864.—Battles of, March 23, 1862; Sept. 19, 1864.—Engagements at, May 25, 1862; June 13-15, 1863.—Affairs at, Feb. 5, April 26, 1864.—Action at, Aug. 17, 1864.—Evacuation of, by Confederate forces, March 11, 1862; by Union forces, Sept. 2, 1862.—Occupation of, by Union forces, March 12, 1862; by Confederate forces, Sept. 3, 1862.—Capture of train near, Aug. 23, 1862.—Scout from Strasburg to, June 22-30, 1862.—Reconnoissance from Bolivar Heights to, Dec. 2-6, 1862.—Scout to, Aug. 14, 1863.—Reconnoissance from Charlestown, W. Va., to, Jan. 3, 1864, and skirmish.—Reconnoissance from, up Cedar Creek Valley, April 12-13, 1863.—Reconnoissance from, toward Wardensville and Strasburg, April 20, 1863, and skirmishes.—Expedition from, to Stump's Tannery, April 17-18, 1863.—Expedition from, into Fauquier and Loudoun Counties, Nov. 28-Dec. 3, 1864.—Expedition from, to near Gordonsville, Dec. 19-28, 1864.—Expedition from, to Moorefield, W. Va., Feb. 4-6, 1865.—Expedition from Camp Russell near, to Edenburg and Little Fort Valley, Feb. 13-17, 1865, and skirmishes.—Expedition from Camp Averill near, into Loudoun County, Feb. 18-19, 1865.—Expedition

VIRGINIA.

from, to the front of Petersburg, Feb. 27-March 28, 1865.—Scout from, into Hampshire County, May 4-9, 1863.—Scout from near, to Front Royal, March 16, 1865.—Scouts from, to Edenburg, March 17-19, and March 20-21, 1865.—Scout from, to Woodstock, March 27-29, 1865.—Scout from, to Timber Ridge, April 11-12, 1865.

WINDSOR, Skirmishes near, Dec. 22, 1862; March 9, 1863.

WOLFTOWN, Skirmish at, Aug. 7, 1862.

WOOD GROVE, Skirmish at, July 16, 1864.

WOODSTOCK, Advance of Union forces from Strasburg to, April 1-2, 1862.—Skirmishes at, May 18, 21, June 2, 1862; Nov. 16, 1863; Sept. 23, 1864; March 14, 1865.—Skirmish near, Feb. 26, 1863.—Scout from Charlestown, W. Va., to, Jan. 23-25, 1864.—Scout from Winchester to, March 27-29, 1865.

WOODVILLE, Skirmish at, Sept. 30, 1863.—Skirmish near, Nov. 24, 1863.—Reconnoissance to, Dec. 6, 1863.

WORMLEY'S FERRY, Pamunkey River, Skirmish at, June 2, 1862.

WYATT'S FARM, Combats at, Sept. 29, Oct. 2, 1864.

WYERMAN'S MILLS, Skirmish at, Feb. 22, 1864.

WYTHEVILLE, Expedition from Fayetteville, W. Va., to, July 13-25, 1863.—Engagement near, May 10, 1864.—Capture of, Dec. 16, 1864.—Action at, April 6, 1865.

YANKEE, U. S. S., Exchange of shots between the, and the batteries at Gloucester Point, May 9, 1861.

YELLOW HOUSE, Combats at, May 18-21, 1864.

YELLOW TAVERN, Combat at, May 11, 1864.—Reconnoissance beyond, Sept. 2, 1864.

YEOCOMICO RIVER, Naval action at, Sept. 16, 1864.

YORKTOWN, Siege of, April 5-May 4, 1862.—Shelling of, by Union naval forces, May 1, 1862.—Naval reconnoissance from, to West Point, May 4, 1862.—Occupation of, by Union forces, May 4, 1862.—Skirmish near, April 11, 1862.—Reconnoissance from, to Gloucester, Mathews, King and Queen, and Middlesex Counties, Dec. 11-15, 1862.—Expeditions from, to Mathews County, Oct. 4-9, Nov. 16-19, 1863.—Expedition from, to West Point and White House, Jan. 7-9, 1863.—Expedition from, to West Point, Feb. 23-24, 1865.—Expedition from, to Smith's and Byrd's Plantation, Ware River, April 1, 1863.—Expedition from, to Walkerton and Aylett's, June 4-5, 1863.—Expedition from, to South Anna Bridge, June 23-28, 1863, and skirmish.—Expedition from, against Richmond, Feb. 6-8, 1864.

YORKTOWN ROAD, Skirmish near, April 5, 1862.

YOUNG'S BRANCH (See Bull Run, July 21, 1861).

YOUNG'S MILL, near Newport News, Engagement at, Oct. 21, 1861.

ZOAR CHURCH, Skirmish at, March 30, 1863.

WASHINGTON—WEST VIRGINIA.

ZUNI, Skirmishes near, May 30, Oct. 25, 1862.—Affair near, Oct. 3, 1862.—Skirmish at, Nov. 14, 1862.—Skirmishes at and about, Dec. 8-12, 1862.

WASHINGTON.

COLUMBIA RIVER, Affair on the, near the Kootenay River, March 18, 1861.
GRANDE RONDE PRAIRIE, Expedition from Fort Walla Walla to the, Aug. 10-22, 1862.—Affair on the, Aug. 14, 1862.
KOOTENAY RIVER, Affair on the Columbia River near the, March 18, 1861.
SNAKE RIVER, Expedition from Fort Walla Walla to, Feb. 16-23, 1864.
WALLA WALLA, FORT, Scouts from, to the Umatilla River and to Willow and Butter Creeks, Ore., Feb. 5-17, 1861.—Expedition from, to the Grande Ronde Prairie, Aug. 10-22, 1862.—Expedition from, to Snake River, Feb. 16-23, 1864.—Expeditions from, to Southeastern Oregon, April 20-Oct. 26, 1864, and skirmishes.

WEST VIRGINIA.

ADDISON, Expedition from Summerville (Nicholas Court House) to, April 17-21, 1862.
ALDERSON'S FERRY, Skirmish at, July —; 1862.
ALLEGHANY, CAMP, Engagement at, Dec. 13, 1861.
ARMSTRONG'S CREEK, Skirmish at, Sept. 11, 1862.
ARNOLDSBURG, Skirmish at, May 6, 1862.
AVERILL'S RAID IN WEST VIRGINIA, Aug. 5-31, 1863.
BACK CREEK BRIDGE, Skirmish at, July 27, 1864.
BALL'S MILLS, Skirmish at, Aug. 27, 1863.
BALTIMORE AND OHIO RAILROAD, Confederate raids on, April 21 to May 21, 1863; Feb. 11, 1864, and May 5, 1864.
BARBOURSVILLE, Skirmish at, July 16, 1861.
BATH, Skirmishes at, Jan. 3-4, 1862.—Skirmish at, Sept. 7, 1863.
BECKLEY (Raleigh Court House), Occupation of, by Union forces, Dec. 28, 1861.
BEECH CREEK, Skirmish at, Aug. 6, 1862.
BEECH FORK, Calhoun County, Skirmish at, Sept. 8, 1863.
BELINGTON, Skirmishes at, July 7-12, 1861.
BELLER'S MILL, near Harper's Ferry, Skirmish at, Sept. 2, 1861.
BEVERLY, Occupation of, by Union forces, July 12, 1861.—Skirmish at, April 24, 1863.—Confederate expedition to, June 29-July 4, 1863.—Action at, Oct. 29, 1864.—Capture of Union forces at, Jan. 11, 1865.
BIG BEND, Skirmish at, June 4, 1862.—Skirmish at, June 7, 1862.

WEST VIRGINIA.

BIG BIRCH, Skirmish at, Oct. 6, 1862.
BIG CACAPON BRIDGE, Skirmish at, July 6, 1864.
BIG COAL RIVER, Scout from Camp Piatt on, June 18-19, 1863.
BIG SANDY REGION, Operations in, Aug. 1, 1861-March 17, 1862.
BIG SANDY RIVER, Capture of U. S. S. Barnum and Fawn on, Nov. 5, 1864.
BIG SEWELL, Skirmish at, Dec. 11, 1863.
BLACKFORD'S FORD, Skirmish at, Sept. 19, 1862. (Shepherdstown or Boteler's Ford.)
BLAKE'S FARM, Cotton Hill, Skirmishes at, Nov. 10-11, 1861.
BLOOMERY GAP, Affair at, Feb. 14, 1862.—Affair at, March 28, 1864.
BLOOMINGTON, Raid on the Baltimore and Ohio Railroad near, May 5, 1864.
BLUE CREEK, Skirmish at, Sept. 1, 1861.
BLUE'S GAP (or Hanging Rock), Operations at, Oct. 2-4, 1862.
BLUE'S HOUSE, Skirmish at, Aug. 26, 1861.
BLUE STONE, Skirmish at mouth of the, Feb. 8, 1862.—Skirmishes at, Aug. 13-14, 1862.
BLUE SULPHUR ROAD, Skirmish on, near Meadow Bluff, Dec. 14, 1863.
BOLIVAR HEIGHTS, near Harper's Ferry, Skirmish at, Oct. 16, 1861.—Action on, Sept. 13-14, 1862.
BOONE COUNTY, Scout from Camp Piatt through, March 12-16, 1863.
BOONE COURT HOUSE, Skirmish at, Sept. 1, 1861.—Scout from Charleston to, Oct. 21-22, 1863.
BOOTHSVILLE, Marion County, Raid from Fairmount to, April 12, 1862.
BOTELER'S FORD, Skirmish at, Sept. 19, 1862. (Shepherdstown or Blackford's Ford).
BOWMAN'S PLACE, Cheat River, Skirmish at, June 29, 1861.
BRAXTON COUNTY, Skirmishes in, Dec. 29-30, 1861.—Scout from Beverly through, May 15-30, 1864.
BRAXTON COURT HOUSE (See Suttonville, Dec. 29, 1861).
BRIDGEPORT, Skirmish at, April 30, 1863.
BUCKHANNON, Occupation of, by Union forces, June 30, 1861.—Skirmish at, Aug. 30, 1862.—Skirmishes at, Sept. 27-28, 1864.
BUFFALO, Expedition from Point Pleasant to, Sept. 26-27, 1862, and skirmish.
BULLTOWN, Skirmish at, Oct. 13, 1863.—Raid on, May 3, 1864.—Skirmish at, Aug. 20, 1864.
BUNKER HILL, Skirmish near, July 15, 1861.—Skirmish at, March 5, 1862.—Skirmish at, Sept. 4, 1862.—Reconnoissance from North Mountain to, Dec. 12, 1862.—Skirmish at, June

WASHINGTON.

13, 1863.—Affair at, Jan. 1, 1864.—Skirmish at, July 19, 1864.—Skirmish at, July 25, 1864.—Action at, Sept. 2, 1864.—Action at, Sept. 3, 1864.—Skirmish at, Sept. 13, 1864.

BURLINGTON, Skirmish at, Sept. 1, 1861.—Skirmishes near, April 6-7, 1863.—Skirmish at, April 26, 1863.—Skirmish at, Aug. 4, 1863.—Skirmish at, Oct. 13, 1863.—Skirmish near, Nov. 16, 1863.

CABELL COUNTY, Expedition from Camp Piatt through, April 3-6, 1863.—Scout in, March 16-18, 1864.

CACAPON MOUNTAIN, Skirmish at, Aug. 6, 1863.

CACKLEYTOWN, Skirmish near, Nov. 4, 1863.

CAIRO STATION, Affair at, May 7, 1863.

CALHOUN COUNTY, Scout from Parkersburg into, May 15-22, 1863.—Skirmish at Beech Fork in, Sept. 8, 1863.

CAMP CREEK, Skirmish on, in the Stone River Valley, May 1, 1862.

CANNELTON, Skirmish near, Sept. 11, 1862.

CARNIFEX FERRY, Gauley River, Engagement at, Sept. 10, 1861.

CARRICK'S (or Corrick's) FORD, Action at, July 13, 1861.—Scout from Philippi to, March 14-16, 1865.

CASSVILLE, Skirmish at, Sept. 23, 1861.

CENTREVILLE, Skirmish near, Sept. 14, 1864.

CHAPMANSVILLE, Skirmish at, April 18, 1862.

CHARLESTON, Action at, Sept. 13, 1862.

CHARLESTOWN, Skirmish at, July 21, 1861.—Skirmish at, May 28, 1862.—Reconnoissance from Harper's Ferry to, Sept. 3-4, 1862.—Reconnoissance from Harper's Ferry toward, Sept. 27, 1862.—Reconnoissance from Bolivar Heights toward, Oct. 6, 1862.—Reconnoissance from Harper's Ferry to, Oct. 16-17, 1862, and skirmish.—Skirmish at, Nov. 10, 1862.—Reconnoissance from Bolivar Heights to, Nov. 26, 1862.—Skirmish at, Dec. 2, 1862.—Reconnoissance from Martinsburg to, Dec. 25, 1862.—Skirmish near, Feb. 12, 1863.—Skirmish at, May 16, 1863.—Skirmish at, Oct. 7, 1863.—Attack on, Oct. 18, 1863.—Skirmish near, March 10, 1864.—Skirmish near, May 24, 1864.—Skirmish at, June 29, 1864.—Skirmish at, July 19, 1864.—Skirmish near, Aug. 15, 1864.—Skirmish at Welch's (or Flowing) Spring near, Aug. 21, 1864.—Skirmish at, Aug. 22, 1864.—Skirmish near, Aug. 26, 1864.—Skirmish at, Aug. 29, 1864.—Skirmish at, Nov. 29, 1864.—Skirmish near, March 13, 1865.—Affair near, April 6, 1865.

CHEAT MOUNTAIN, Operations in, Sept. 11-17, 1861.

CHEAT MOUNTAIN PASS, Action at, Sept. 12, 1861.—Skirmish at, Sept. 14, 1863.

CHEAT RIVER, Skirmish on Dry Fork of, Jan. 8, 1862.—Skirmish at Seneca Trace Crossing on, Sept. 25, 1863.—Skirmish at, Dec. 6, 1863.

CHEAT SUMMIT, Action at, Sept. 12, 1861.

WEST VIRGINIA.

CHERRY RUN, Skirmish at, Dec. 25, 1861.
CLARK'S HOLLOW, Skirmish at, May 1, 1862.
CLAY COUNTY, Skirmishes in, Dec. 29-30, 1861.—Scout in, May 8-21, 1862.
COAL RIVER, Skirmish near, Sept. 12, 1861.
COALSMOUTH, Skirmish at, Sept. 30, 1864.
COCKRALL'S MILLS, Skirmish at, Nov. 26, 1862.
COLD KNOB MOUNTAIN, Expedition from Summerville to, Nov. 24-30, 1862.
COLD SPRING GAP, Skirmish at, Aug. 5, 1863.
COLUMBIAN IRON WORKS, Destruction of, Dec. —, 1863.
CORRICK'S (or Carrick's) FORD, Action at, July 13, 1861.—Scout from Philippi to, March 14-16, 1865.
COTTON HILL, Skirmish at, Oct. 13, 1861.—Skirmish at, Sept. 11, 1862.
COVE GAP, Skirmish at, June 23, 1864.
CROSS LANES, near Summerville, Action at, Aug. 26, 1861.
DARKESVILLE, Skirmish at, Sept. 7, 1862.—Skirmish at, Dec. 11, 1862.—Skirmish at, July 3, 1864.—Skirmish at, July 19, 1864.—Skirmish at, Sept. 2, 1864.—Skirmish at, Sept. 10, 1864.
DROOP MOUNTAIN, Engagement at, Nov. 6, 1863.
DUFFIELD'S STATION, Skirmish at, June 29, 1864.—Skirmish at, Aug. 27, 1864.—Affair at, Oct. 14, 1864.
ELIZABETH, Skirmish at Sandy River near, Oct. 27, 1863.
ELIZABETH COURT HOUSE, Skirmish at, May 16, 1863.
ELK MOUNTAIN, Skirmish at, March 19, 1862.—Skirmish on, near Hillsborough, Nov. 10, 1863.
ELK RIVER, Skirmish on, Aug. 27, 1863.
ELK WATER, Action at, Sept. 11, 1861.
FAIRMOUNT, Skirmish at, April 29, 1863.
FALLING WATERS (or Hoke's Run), Engagement at, July 2, 1861.—Skirmish at, July 24, 1864.—Skirmish at, July 26, 1864.
FAYETTEVILLE, Skirmish near, Nov. 14, 1861.—Action at, Sept. 10, 1862.—Skirmishes at and about, May 18-20, 1863.—Skirmish near, June 3, 1863.—Skirmish at, July 4, 1863.—Skirmish at, July 28, 1863.—Scout from Camp Piatt at, Sept. 11-13, 1863.
FLAT TOP MOUNTAIN, Skirmish at, July 27, 1862.
FLOWING (or Welch's) SPRING, near Charlestown, Skirmish at, Aug. 21, 1864.
FRANKFORT, Skirmish at, June 26, 1861.
FRANKLIN, Skirmish at, May 5, 1862.—Skirmishes near, May 10-12, 1862.—Skirmish near, May 26, 1862.—Scout from Beverly to, April 11-18, 1863.—Destruction of saltpetre-works near, Aug. 19, 1863.—Destruction of saltpetre works near, March 3, 1864.—Skirmish at, Aug. 19, 1864.—Scout from New Creek through, Jan. 11-15, 1865.
GARNETT, CAMP, near Rich Mountain, Skirmish at, July 10, 1861.—Engagement at, July 11, 1861.

WEST VIRGINIA.

GARRETT'S MILL, Skirmish at, April 27, 1862.
GATEWOOD'S, Skirmish at, Dec. 12, 1863.
GAULEY, Skirmish at, Oct. 23, 1861.
GAULEY BRIDGE (or Cotton Hill), Skirmishes near, Nov. 1-3, 1861.
GAULEY (or Miller's) FERRY, Skirmish at, Sept. 11, 1862.
GAULEY RIVER, Engagement at Carnifix Ferry, on, Sept. 10, 1861.
GILES COURT HOUSE, Occupation of, by Union forces, May 7, 1862.—Action at, May 10, 1862.
GILMER COUNTY, Skirmish in, April 24, 1863.
GLENVILLE, Skirmish at, July 7, 1861.—Skirmish at, Sept. 1, 1862.—Skirmish near, Sept. 30, 1862.—Skirmish near, Aug. 21, 1863.—Skirmish near, Aug. 27, 1863.
GOING'S FORD, Skirmishes near, April 6-7, 1863.
GORDONSVILLE AND KEEZLETOWN CROSS ROADS, Skirmish at, April 26, 1862.
GRAFTON, Advance upon and occupation of, by Union forces, May 26-30, 1861.—Skirmish near, Aug. 25, 1861.
GRASS LICK, Skirmish at, April 23, 1862.
GREAT CACAPON BRIDGE, Skirmish at, Jan. 4, 1862.
GREENBRIER, Skirmish at, Oct. 31, 1861.
GREENBRIER BRIDGE, Skirmish at, Sept. 24, 1863.
GREENBRIER COUNTY, Expedition into, Nov. 9-11, 1862.
GREENBRIER RIVER, Engagement at, Oct. 3, 1861.—Skirmish at, Dec. 12, 1861.—Scout from Meadow Bluff to, Aug. 2-5, 1862.—Skirmish at, Dec. 12, 1863.
GREENLAND GAP, Skirmish at, April 25, 1863.—Scout from New Creek through, Jan. 11-15, 1865.
GREEN SPRING RUN, Skirmish at, March 7, 1863.—Skirmish at, Aug. 2, 1864.—Affair at, Nov. 1, 1864.
GUYANDOTTE, Affair at, Nov. 10, 1861.—Skirmish on the, Nov. 15, 1862.
GUYANDOTTE VALLEY, Expedition to the, Jan. 12-23, 1862.
HALLTOWN, Skirmish near, Nov. 22, 1862.—Skirmish near, Dec. 20, 1862.—Skirmish at, July 15, 1863.—Affair at, May 8, 1864.—Skirmishes at, Aug. 24-25, 1864.—Action at, Aug. 26, 1864.
HAMPSHIRE COUNTY, Operations in, Oct. 2-4, 1862.—Scout from Winchester, Va., into, May 4-9, 1863.—Scout in, Dec. 7-11, 1863.—Operations in, Dec. 31, 1863-Jan. 5, 1864.—Operations in, Jan. 27, Feb. 7, 1864.
HANGING ROCK (or Blue Gap), Operations at, Oct. 2-4, 1862.
HANGING ROCK PASS, Affair at, Sept. —, 1861.—Skirmish at, Jan. 7, 1862. (Blue's Gap.)
HARDY COUNTY, Scout in, Dec. 7-11, 1862.—Operations in, Dec. 31, 1863-Jan. 5, 1864.—Operations in, Jan. 27-Feb. 7, 1864.

WEST VIRGINIA.

HARPER'S FERRY, U. S. Armory at, abandoned and burned by U. S. forces, April 18, 1861.—Evacuation of, by Confederate forces, June 15, 1861.—Skirmish at, July 4, 1861.—Skirmish near, Sept. 17, 1861.—Skirmish at, Oct. 11, 1861.—Operations about, May 24-30, 1862.—Capture of train near, Aug. 23, 1862.—Siege of, Sept. 12-15, 1862.—Capture of, by Confederate forces, Sept. 15, 1862.—Operations about, Sept. 21, 1862-Jan. 25, 1863.—Evacuation of, by Union forces, June 15, 1863.—Skirmish at, July 7, 1863.—Skirmish near, July 14, 1863.—Skirmish near, Oct. 1, 1863.—Operations about, July 4-7, 1864.—Affair near, Feb. 3, 1865.

HARPER'S FERRY AND SHENANDOAH VALLEY Campaign, July 2-25, 1861.

HARRISVILLE, Affair at, May 7, 1863. (Ritchie Court House.)

HAWK'S NEST, Kanawha Valley, Skirmish at, Aug. 20, 1861.—Skirmish near, Sept. 2, 1861.

HEDGESVILLE, Skirmish at, Oct. 20, 1862.—Skirmishes at and near, July 18-19, 1863.—Skirmish near, Oct. 15, 1863.

HOKE'S RUN (or Falling Waters), Engagement at, July 2, 1861.

HUNTERSVILLE, Descent upon and skirmish at, Jan. 3, 1862.—Skirmish at, Aug. 22, 1863.

HURRICANE BRIDGE, Skirmish at, Sept. 12, 1862.—Skirmish at, March 28, 1863.—Affair at, Dec. 13, 1863.—Affair near, Feb. 20, 1864.

HUTTONSVILLE, Skirmish at, Aug. 18, 1862.—Skirmish at, July 4, 1863.—Skirmish at, Aug. 5, 1864.—Affair at, Aug. 24, 1864.

IMBODEN'S (Confederate) operations in West Virginia, April 20, May 9, 1863.

INDEPENDENCE, Affair at, April 27, 1863.

JANELEW, Skirmish at, May 5, 1863.

JOHNSTOWN, Harrison County, Affair near, April 18, 1863.

KABLETOWN, Skirmish at, March 10, 1864.—Skirmish near, June 10, 1864.—Affair at, July 18, 1864.—Skirmish at, July 19, 1864.—Skirmish at, Nov. 18, 1864.—Skirmish at, Nov. 20, 1864.—Skirmish at, Nov. 30, 1864.—Scout from Summit Point through, March 16-17, 1865.—Scout to, March 20, 1865.

KANAWHA GAP, near Chapmanville, Action at, Sept. 25, 1861.

KANAWHA REGION, Operations in, Oct. 19-Nov. 16, 1861.

KANAWHA RIVER, Skirmish near Falls of the, Oct. 31, 1862.

KANAWHA VALLEY, Operations in, June —, Sept. 25, 1861.—Reconnoissance in, Oct. 23-27, 1861.—Campaign in, Sept. 6-16, 1862. (See Virginia and Tennessee Railroad, etc., Dec. 8-25, 1863.)—Nounan's expedition into the, Sept. 23-Oct. 1, 1864.—Witcher's operations in the, Nov. 5-12, 1864.

KEARNEYSVILLE, Skirmishes near, Oct. 16-17, 1862.—Skirmish at, Aug. 23, 1864.—Action near, Aug. 25, 1864.

WEST VIRGINIA.

KEEZLETOWN AND GORDONSVILLE CROSS ROADS. (See Gordonsville and Keezletown Cross Roads, April 26, 1862.)

LAUREL CREEK, Cotton Hill, Fayette County, Skirmish at, Nov. 12, 1861.

LAUREL CREEK, Wayne County, Skirmish at, Feb. 15, 1864.

LAUREL FORK CREEK, Skirmish at, Aug. 20, 1861.

LAUREL HILL, Skirmishes at, July 7-12, 1861.

LEETOWN, Skirmish at, July 3, 1864.—Skirmish at, Aug. 28, 1864.

LEWISBURG, Skirmish at, May 12, 1862.—Action at, May 23, 1862.—Skirmish at, May 30, 1862.—Skirmish near, May 2, 1863.—Expeditions from Beverly and Charleston against, Nov. 1-17, 1863.—Skirmish at, Dec. 12, 1863.

LEWIS'S MILL, on Sinking Creek, Skirmish at, Nov. 26, 1862.

LITTLE CACAPON BRIDGE, Capture of Union forces at, Oct. 4, 1862.

LITTLE CACAPON RIVER, Skirmish near mouth of the, Nov. 30, 1861.

LITTLE COAL RIVER, Scout from Camp Piatt on the, June 18-19, 1863.

LITTLE SEWELL MOUNTAIN, Skirmish at, Nov. 6, 1863.

LOGAN COUNTY, Scout from Camp Piatt through, March 12-16, 1863.—Expedition from Camp Piatt through, April 3-6, 1863.

LOGAN COURT HOUSE, Expedition to, Jan. 12-23, 1862.—Expedition toward, Dec. 1-10, 1862.

LOST RIVER GAP, Skirmish at, May 10, 1864.

LOUP CREEK, Skirmish at, June 26, 1863.

McCOY'S MILL, Skirmish at, Nov. 14, 1861.

McDONALD, CAMP, Skirmish at, May 6, 1862.

MARLING'S BOTTOM, Affair at, April 19, 1864.

MARLING'S BOTTOM BRIDGE, Skirmish at, Dec. 11, 1863.

MARTINSBURG, Occupation of, by Union forces, July 3, 1861.—Skirmish at, March 3, 1862.—Skirmish near, Sept. 3, 1862.—Skirmish near, Sept. 11, 1862.—Evacuation of, by Union forces, Sept. 12, 1862.—Reconnoissance from Sharpsburg, Md., to, Oct. 1, 1862, and skirmishes.—Skirmish at, Nov. 6, 1862.—Skirmish at, June 14, 1863.—Skirmishes at and near, July 18-19, 1863.—Expeditions from, Sept. 2-23, 1863.—Scout from, Nov. 14-18, 1863.—Skirmish at, July 3, 1864.—Skirmish at, July 25, 1864.—Skirmish at, Aug. 31, 1864.—Action near, Sept. 18, 1864.

MEADOW BLUFF, Expedition to, Dec. 15-21, 1861.—Skirmish at, Dec. 4, 1863.—Skirmish at, Dec. 11, 1863.—Skirmish on Blue Sulphur Road near, Dec. 14, 1863.

MECHANICSBURG GAP, Affair at, Sept. —, 1861.

MEDLEY, Capture of Union wagon train at, Jan. 30, 1864.

MIDDLE FORK BRIDGE, Skirmishes at, July 6-7, 1861.

MIDDLEWAY, Skirmish at, Aug. 21, 1864.

WEST VIRGINIA.

MILLER'S (or Gauley) FERRY, Skirmish at, Sept. 11, 1862.
MILL POINT, Skirmish at, Nov. 5, 1863.
MOOREFIELD, Skirmish at, Feb. 12, 1862.—Skirmish at, April 3, 1862.—Scout from Strasburg to, June 22-30, 1862.—Skirmish at, Aug. 23, 1862.—Skirmish at, Dec. 3, 1862.—Expedition to, Jan. 2-5, 1863.—Skirmish at, Aug. 6, 1863.—Skirmish near, Aug. 26, 1863.—Skirmish at, Sept. 4, 1863.—Affair at, Sept. 11, 1863.—Affair at, Sept. 21, 1863.—Skirmish at, Dec. 28, 1863.—Skirmish at, Feb. 4, 1864.—Scout from New Creek to, Feb. 21-22, 1864.—Skirmish near, June 6, 1864.—Engagement at Oldfields near, Aug. 7, 1864.—Expedition from New Creek to, Nov. 6-8, 1864, and skirmish.—Skirmishes at, Nov. 27-28, 1864.—Expedition from Kernstown to, Nov. 28-Dec. 2, 1864.—Expedition from Winchester, Va., to, Feb. 4-6, 1865.—Scout from New Creek to, March 14-17, 1865.
MOOREFIELD JUNCTION, Skirmish at, Jan. 8, 1864.
MORGANTOWN, Affair at, April 27, 1863.
MORRIS'S MILLS, Skirmish at, July 31, 1863.
MUDDY CREEK, Skirmish at, June 8, 1862.—Skirmish near, Nov. 7, 1863.
MUD RIVER, Skirmish at, April 5, 1863.
MUNGO FLATS, Skirmish at, June 25, 1862.
MYERS'S FORD, Scout to, March 20, 1865.
MYERSTOWN, Scout from Summit Point through, March 16-17, 1865.—Scout to, March 20, 1865.
NEW CREEK, Skirmish at, June 19, 1861.—Scout from Strasburg to, June 22-30, 1862.—Action at, Aug. 4, 1864.—Affair at, Nov. 28, 1864.
NEW RIVER, Skirmishes on, Oct. 19-21, 1861.
NORTH MOUNTAIN, Skirmish at, July 3, 1864.
NORTH MOUNTAIN STATION, Skirmish near, July 17, 1863.
NORTH RIVER MILLS, Skirmish at, July 3, 1864.
NOUNAN'S EXPEDITION into the Kanawha Valley, Sept. 23-Oct. 1, 1864.
NUTTER'S HILL, Skirmish at, Aug. 27, 1864.
OILTOWN, Destruction of oil works at, May 9, 1863.
OLDFIELDS, near Moorefield, Engagement at, Aug. 7, 1864.
OPEQUON CREEK, Engagement at Smithfield Crossing of, Aug. 29, 1864.—Skirmish at, Sept. 1, 1864.
PACK'S FERRY, New River, Skirmish at, Aug. 6, 1862.
PANTHER GAP, Skirmish at, June 4, 1864.
PATTERSON'S CREEK, Skirmish on, June 26, 1861.—Skirmish at, Feb. 2, 1864.—Affair near, March 30, 1865.
PATTERSON'S CREEK BRIDGE, Skirmish at, July 4, 1864.
PATTERSON'S CREEK STATION, Skirmish near, March 22, 1865.
PAW PAW TUNNEL, Capture of Union forces at, Oct. 4, 1862.
PEARSBURG (See Giles Court House).
PENDLETON COUNTY, Operations in, Nov. 5-14, 1862.—Expedition through, June 1-13, 1865.

WEST VIRGINIA.

PETERSBURG, Skirmish at, Sept. 12, 1861.—Skirmish near, Oct. 29, 1862.—Expedition to, Jan. 2-5, 1863.—Skirmish at, Sept. 6, 1863.—Skirmish at, Jan. 10, 1864.—Skirmish near, Jan. 15, 1864.—Expedition to, Feb. 29-March 5, 1864.—Affair near, June 19, 1864.—Skirmish near, Oct. 11, 1864.
PETERSBURG GAP, Skirmish at, Sept. 4, 1863.
PEYTONA, Skirmish at, Sept. 12, 1861.
PHILIPPI, Action at, June 3, 1861.—Skirmish at, March 20, 1862.
PIATT, CAMP (Fayetteville), Scout from, Sept. 11-13, 1863.
PIEDMONT, Raid on the Baltimore and Ohio Railroad near, May 5, 1864.—Skirmish at, Nov. 28, 1864.
PIGGOT'S MILL, Skirmish near, Aug. 25, 1861.
POCAHONTAS COUNTY, Operations in, Nov. 5-14, 1862.—Skirmish in, Jan. 22, 1863.—Expedition from Beverly into, Feb. 10-12, 1863.—Scout from Beverly through, May 15-30, 1864.—Scout through, April 15-23, 1865.—Expedition through, June 1-13, 1865.
POINT MOUNTAIN TURNPIKE, Skirmishes at, Sept. 11-12, 1861.
POINT PLEASANT, Skirmish at, Sept. 20, 1862.—Skirmish at, March 30, 1863.—Skirmish at, April 22, 1863.
PORTLAND, Skirmish at, April 26, 1863.
POTOMAC, UPPER, Operations on the, Sept. 21, 1862-Jan. 25, 1863.
PRINCETON, Action at, Sept. 16, 1861.—Skirmish at, May 5, 1862.—Skirmish at, May 11, 1862.—Actions at, May 16-17, 1862.—Skirmish at, May 6, 1864.
PURGITSVILLE, Skirmishes at, April 6-7, 1863.
RALEIGH COURT HOUSE (Beckley), Occupation of, by Union forces, Dec. 28, 1861.
RANDOLPH COUNTY, Scout through, April 15-23, 1865.
RAVENSWOOD, Skirmish at, May 15, 1862.—Skirmish at, Sept. 3, 1862—Skirmish at, May 16, 1863,—Skirmish at, Oct. 26, 1863.
RED HOUSE, near Barboursville, Skirmish at, July 13, 1861.
RED HOUSE LANDING, Skirmish at, Feb. 3, 1864.
RICH MOUNTAIN, Skirmish at, July 10, 1861.—Engagement at, July 11, 1861.
RIGHTER, Skirmish at, June 23, 1861.
RIPPON, Reconnoissance from Bolivar Heights to, Nov. 9, 1862.
RITCHIE COURT HOUSE (See Harrisville, May 7, 1863).
ROANE COUNTY, Affair in, Dec. 15, 1861.—Scout in, May 8-21, 1862.—Skirmish in, Sept. 12, 1863.
ROCKY GAP, near White Sulphur Springs, Engagement at, Aug. 26-27, 1863.
ROMNEY, Descent of Union forces upon, June 13, 1861.—Descent upon, Sept. 23-25, 1861.—Action at, Oct. 26, 1861.—Skirmish near, Nov. 13, 1861.—Skirmish near, Dec. 8, 1861.—Evacuation of, by Union forces, Jan. 10, 1862.—Reoccupation of, by Union forces, Feb. 7, 1862.—Skirmish at, Dec. 1, 1862.—Affair near, Feb. 16, 1863.

WEST VIRGINIA.

ROWELL'S RUN, Skirmish at, Sept. 6, 1861.
ROWLESBURG, Skirmish at, April 26, 1863.
SAINT GEORGE, Tucker County, Capture of, by Confederate forces, Nov. 9, 1862.
SALT LICK BRIDGE, Skirmish at, Oct. 11, 1863.—Skirmish at, Oct. 14, 1863.
SANDY RIVER, Skirmish at, near Elizabeth, Oct. 27, 1863.
SCAREY CREEK, Action at, July 17, 1861.
SECOND CREEK, Skirmish at, on the road to Union, Nov. 8, 1863.
SENECA TRACE CROSSING, Cheat River, Skirmish at, Sept. 25, 1863.
SHANGHAI, Skirmish at, July 16, 1863.
SHAVER MOUNTAIN, Affair on, Sept. 20, 1863.
SHAVER'S RIVER, Raid to, May 30, 1862.
SHENANDOAH FERRY, Scout from Summit Point to, March 16-17, 1865.
SHEPHERDSTOWN, Skirmish at, Sept. 9, 1861.—Action near, Sept. 20, 1862.—Reconnoissance from, Sept. 25, 1862.—Reconnoissance from Sharpsburg, Md., to, Oct. 1, 1862, and skirmishes.—Skirmishes near, Oct. 16-17, 1862.—Expedition from Sharpsburg, Md., to, Nov. 24-25, 1862, and skirmishes.—Skirmish near, July 15, 1863.—Skirmish at, July 16, 1863.—Skirmish near, July 30, 1864.—Action near, Aug. 25, 1864.
SHEPHERDSTOWN (Blackford's or Boteler's) FORD, Skirmish at, Sept. 19, 1862.
SIMPSON'S CREEK, Skirmish near, April 30, 1863.
SIR JOHN'S RUN, Skirmish at, Jan. 4, 1862.—Skirmish at, July 6, 1864.
SLANE'S CROSS ROADS, Skirmish at, Jan. 4, 1862.
SMITHFIELD, Reconnoissance from Sharpsburg, Md., to, Oct. 16-17, 1862.—Skirmish near, Feb. 12, 1863.—Affair at, Sept. 15, 1863.—Skirmish at, Aug. 28, 1864.—Skirmish near, Aug. 30, 1864.—Scout from Stephenson's Depot, Va., to, March 29, 1865.
SMITHFIELD CROSSING, of the Opequon, Engagement at, Aug. 29, 1864.
SOUTH BRANCH BRIDGE, Skirmish at, Oct. 26, 1861.—Skirmish at, July 4, 1864.
SOUTH FORK, Potomac River, Skirmish on, Nov. 9, 1862.
SPENCER COURT HOUSE, Roane County, Surrender of, by Union forces, Sept. 2, 1862.
SPRINGFIELD, Skirmish at, Aug. 23, 1861.—Skirmish near, Oct. 26, 1861.—Skirmish at, June 26, 1864.
STANDING STONE, Skirmish at, Sept. 28, 1862.
SUMMERVILLE, Affair at, July 25, 1862.—Skirmish near, May 12, 1863.
SUMMIT POINT, Skirmish at, Oct. 7, 1863.—Skirmish near, Aug. 21, 1864.

WEST VIRGINIA.

SUTTON, Skirmish near, Aug. 26, 1863.—Skirmish at, Sept. 8, 1863.—Skirmish at, Aug. 24, 1864.
SUTTONVILLE (Braxton Court House), Capture of, by Confederate forces, Dec. 29, 1861.
SWEET SULPHUR SPRINGS, Skirmish at, June 23, 1864.
TIMBER RIDGE, Scout from Winchester, Va., to, April 11-12, 1865.
TOWNSEND'S FERRY, New River, Operations at, Nov. 6-15, 1861.
TUCKER COUNTY, Expedition from Hardy into, Nov. 8-14, 1862.
UPPER POTOMAC, Operations on the, Sept. 21, 1862-Jan. 25, 1863.
VALLEY RIVER, Raid from Fairmount to, April 12, 1862.
VIRGINIA AND TENNESSEE RAILROAD, Raid on the, and demonstrations up the Shenandoah Valley and from the Kanawha Valley, Dec. 8-25, 1863.
WARDENSVILLE, Skirmishes at and near, May 7, 1862.—Skirmish near, May 29, 1862.—Skirmish at, Dec. 16, 1862.—Skirmish at, Dec. 22, 1862.—Reconnoissance from Winchester toward, April 20, 1863, and skirmish.
WARM SPRINGS, Skirmish near, Aug. 24, 1863.
WAYNE COUNTY, Scout in, March 16-18, 1864.
WAYNE COURT HOUSE, Skirmishes at, Aug. 26-27, 1861.—Skirmish near, Jan. 27, 1864.
WEBSTER COUNTY, Skirmishes in, Dec. 29-30, 1861.—Scout from Beverly through, May 15-30, 1864.
WELCH'S (or Flowing) SPRING, near Charlestown, Skirmish at, Aug. 21, 1864.
WEST CREEK, Skirmish at, May 23, 1863.
WEST FORK, Skirmish at mouth of, June 10, 1862.
WESTON, Capture of, by Confederate forces, Aug. 31, 1862.—Skirmish at, Sept. 3, 1862.
WEST UNION, Skirmish at, May 6, 1863.
WEST VIRGINIA CAMPAIGN, July 6-17, 1861.
WHITE SULPHUR SPRINGS, Engagement at Rocky Gap near, Aug. 26-27, 1863.
WINFIELD, Skirmish at, Oct. 26, 1864.
WIRE BRIDGE, Skirmish at, June 26, 1864.
WITCHER'S EXPEDITION into West Virginia, Sept. 17-28, 1864.
WITCHER'S OPERATIONS in the Kanawha Valley, Nov. 5-12, 1864.
WOLF CREEK, Action at, May 15, 1862.
WORTHINGTON, Skirmish at, Sept. 2, 1861.
WYOMING COUNTY, Scout in, July 24-26, 1862.—Scout from Camp Piatt into, Feb. 5-8, 1863.—Scout from Camp Piatt through, March 12-16, 1863.
WYOMING COURT HOUSE, Operations about, Aug. 2-8, 1862.

ARMY CORPS.

ARMY CORPS.

First Army Corps, Army of the Potomac.

Created by Order of the President, March 8, 1862. Announced March 13, 1862, General Order, No. 101, Army of the Potomac, to consist of Franklin's, McCall's, and King's Divisions. Merged into the Department of the Rappahannock, April 4, 1862, by Order of the President. Recreated, Sept. 12, 1862, General Order No. 129, Adjutant-General's Office, by changing the designation of the Third Army Corps, Army of Virginia. Transferred to the Fifth Army Corps, by General Order, No. 115, Adjutant-General's Office, March 23, 1864.

COMMANDERS.

Major-General IRVIN McDOWELL, March 14, 1862.
Major-General JOHN F. REYNOLDS, Sept. 29, 1862.
Brigadier-General J. S. WADSWORTH, Jan. 2, 1863.
Major-General JOHN F. REYNOLDS, Jan. 4, 1863.
Brigadier-General J. S. WADSWORTH, Feb. 27, 1863.
Major-General JOHN F. REYNOLDS, March 8, 1863.
Major-General JOHN NEWTON, July 2, 1863.

First Army Corps, Army of Virginia.

Organized by Order of the President, June 26, 1862, from troops in the Mountain Department. Designated the Eleventh Army Corps, Army of the Potomac, by General Order, No. 129, Adjutant-General's Office, Sept. 12, 1862.

COMMANDER.

Major-General F. SIGEL, June 29, 1862.

First Veteran Army Corps (Hancock's).

Created by General Orders, No. 287, Adjutant-General's Office, Nov. 28, 1864, to consist of men who had served not less than two years. Discontinued, July 11, 1866.

COMMANDER.

Major-General W. S. HANCOCK, Nov. 28, 1864.

Second Army Corps, Army of the Potomac.

Created by Order of the President, March 8, 1862. Announced, March 13, 1862, General Orders, No. 101, Army of the Potomac, to consist of Richardson's, Blenker's, and Sedgwick's Divisions. Discontinued by General Orders, No. 35, Army of the Potomac, June 28, 1865.

ARMY CORPS.

COMMANDERS.

Brigadier-General E. V. SUMNER, March 13, 1862.
Major-General D. N. COUCH, Oct. 7, 1862.
Major-General JOHN SEDGWICK, Dec. 26, 1862.
Major-General O. O. HOWARD, Jan. 26, 1863.
Major-General D. N. COUCH, Feb. 7, 1863.
Major-General W. S. HANCOCK, May 22, 1863.
Brigadier-General WILLIAM HAYS, July 3, 1863.
Major-General G. K. WARREN, Aug. 16, 1863.
Brigadier-General J. C. CALDWELL, Dec. 16, 1863.
Major-General W. S. HANCOCK, Dec. 29, 1863.
Major-General G. K. WARREN, Jan. 9, 1864.
Brigadier-General J. C. CALDWELL, Jan. 27, 1864.
Major-General G. K. WARREN, Feb. 6, 1864.
Major-General W. S. HANCOCK, March 24, 1864.
Major-General A. A. HUMPHREYS, Nov. 26, 1864.
Brevet Major-General F. C. BARLOW, April 22, 1865.
Major-General A. A. HUMPHREYS, May 5, 1865.
Brevet Major-General G. MOTT, June 9, 1865.
Major-General A. A. HUMPHREYS, June 20, 1865.

Second Army Corps, Army of Virginia.

Created by Order of the President, June 26, 1862, to consist of troops in the Department of the Shenandoah. Designated the Twelfth Army Corps, Army of the Potomac, by General Orders, No. 129, Adjutant-General's Office.

COMMANDERS.

Major-General N. P. BANKS, June 26, 1862.
Brigadier-General A. S. WILLIAMS, Sept. 3, 1862.
Major-General J. K. F. MANSFIELD, Sept. 15, 1862.
Brigadier-General A. S. WILLIAMS, Sept. 17, 1862.

Third Army Corps, Army of the Potomac.

Created by Order of the President, March 8, 1862. Announced, March 13, 1862, General Orders, No. 101, Army of the Potomac, to consist of Porter's, Hooker's, and Hamilton's Divisions. Discontinued, March 24, 1864, General Orders, No. 115, Adjutant-General's Office, March 23, 1864. First and Second Divisions transferred to the Second Army Corps, and the Third Division to the Sixth Army Corps.

COMMANDERS.

Brigadier-General S. P. HEINTZELMAN, March 16, 1862.
Brigadier-General GEORGE STONEMAN, Oct. 30, 1862.
Major-General D. E. SICKLES, Feb. 8, 1863.
Major-General D. B. BIRNEY, May 29, 1863.

ARMY CORPS.

Major-General D. E. SICKLES, June —, 1863.
Major-General WILLIAM H. FRENCH, July 7, 1863.
Major General D. B. BIRNEY, Jan. 28, 1864.
Major-General WILLIAM H. FRENCH, Feb. 17, 1864.

Third Army Corps, Army of Virginia.

Created by Order of the President, June 26, 1862, to consist of the troops under McDowell, except those within the fortifications and City of Washington. Designation changed to the First Army Corps, Army of the Potomac, by General Orders, No. 129, Adjutant-General's Office.

COMMANDERS.

Major-General IRVIN McDOWELL, June 26, 1862.
Major-General JOSEPH HOOKER, Sept. 7, 1862.
Major-General GEORGE G. MEADE, Sept. 17, 1862.

Fourth Army Corps, Army of the Potomac, until Aug., 1862, Department of Virginia until Aug. 1, 1863.

Created by Order of the President, March 8, 1862. Announced, March 13, 1862, General Orders, No. 101, Army of the Potomac, to consist of Couch's, Smith's, and Casey's Divisions. Discontinued, Aug. 1, 1863, General Orders, No. 262, Adjutant-General's Office, the troops having been distributed to other Corps.

COMMANDER.

Brigadier-General E. D. KEYES, March 13, 1862.

Fourth Army Corps, Army of the Cumberland.

Created, Sept. 28, 1863, General Orders, No. 322, Adjutant-General's Office. Order carried into effect, Oct. 9, 1863, by the consolidation of the Twentieth and Twenty-first Army Corps, Army of the Cumberland. Discontinued, General Orders, No. 131, Adjutant-General's Office, Aug. 1, 1865.

COMMANDERS.

Major-General GORDON GRANGER, Oct. 10, 1863.
Major-General O. O. HOWARD, April 10, 1864.
Major-General D. S. STANLEY, July 27, 1864.
Brigadier-General T. J. WOOD, Dec. 1, 1864.
Major-General D. S. STANLEY, Jan. 30, 1865.

Fifth Army Corps, Army of the Potomac.

Created by Order of the President, March 8, 1862, to consist of Banks's and Shields's Divisions. Dincontinued, General Orders, No. 34, Adjutant-General's Office, April 4, 1862. Merged

ARMY CORPS.

into the Department of the Shenandoah. The divisions commanded by Generals F. J. Porter and George Sykes were designated the Fifth Provisional Army Corps, Army of the Potomac, by General Orders, No. 125, Army of the Potomac, May 18, 1862. Confirmed by General Orders, No. 84, Adjutant-General's Office, July 22, 1862. Discontinued, General Orders, No. 35, Army of the Potomac, June 28, 1865.

COMMANDERS.

Major-General N. P. BANKS, March 20, 1862.
Brigadier-General F. J. PORTER, May 18, 1862.
Major-General JOSEPH HOOKER, Nov. 10, 1862.
Brigadier-General D. BUTTERFIELD, Nov. 16, 1862.
Major-General GEORGE G. MEADE, Dec. 25, 1862.
Major-General GEORGE SYKES, Jan. —, 1863.
Major-General GEORGE G. MEADE, Feb. 5, 1863.
Major-General GEORGE SYKES, June 28, 1863.
Major-General G. K. WARREN, March 23, 1864.
Brevet Major-General S. W. CRAWFORD, Jan. 2, 1865.
Major-General G. K. WARREN, Jan. 27, 1865.
Brevet Major-General CHARLES GRIFFIN, April 1, 1865.

Sixth Army Corps, Army of the Potomac.

Created by General Orders, No. 125, Army of the Potomac, May 18, 1862, to consist of Franklin's and Smith's Divisions. Confirmed by General Orders, No. 84, Adjutant-General's Office, July 22, 1862. Discontinued by General Orders, No. 35, Army of the Potomac, June 28, 1865.

COMMANDERS.

Major-General WILLIAM B. FRANKLIN, May 18, 1862.
Major-General WILLIAM F. SMITH, Nov. 16, 1862.
Major-General JOHN SEDGWICK, Feb. 4, 1863.
Major-General H. G. WRIGHT, May 9, 1864.
Brevet Major-General GEORGE W. GETTY, Jan. 17, 1865.
Major-General H. G. WRIGHT, Feb. 11, 1865.

Seventh Army Corps, Department of Virginia.

Created by General Orders, No. 84, Adjutant-General's Office, July 22, 1862, to consist of the forces under Major-General Dix. Discontinued by General Orders, No. 262, Adjutant-General's Office, Aug. 1, 1863, and the troops transferred to the Eighteenth Army Corps, Department of Virginia and North Carolina.

COMMANDERS.

Major-General JOHN A. DIX, July 22, 1862.
Brigadier-General H. M. NAGLEE, July 25, 1863.

ARMY CORPS.

Seventh Army Corps, Department of Arkansas.

Created by General Orders, No. 14, Adjutant-General's Office, Jan. 6, 1864, to consist of the troops in the Department of Arkansas. Discontinued by General Orders, No. 131, Adjutant-General's Office, Aug. 1, 1865.

COMMANDERS.

Major-General FREDERICK STEELE, Jan. 20, 1864.
Major-General J. J. REYNOLDS, Dec. 22, 1864.

Eighth Army Corps, Middle Department.

The troops in the Middle Department, under Major-General Wool, were designated the Eighth Army Corps, by General Orders, No. 84, Adjutant-General's Office, July 22, 1862. Discontinued by General Orders, Nc. 131, Adjutant-General's Office, Aug. 1, 1865.

COMMANDERS.

Major-General JOHN E. WOOL, July 22, 1862.
Major-General ROBERT C. SCHENCK, Dec. 22, 1862.
Brevet Brigadier-General WILLIAM W. MORRIS, Aug. 10, 1863.
Major-General ROBERT C. SCHENCK, Aug. 31, 1863.
Brigadier-General ERASTUS B. TYLER, Sept. 28, 1863.
Major-General ROBERT C. SCHENCK, Oct. 10, 1863.
Brigadier-General HENRY H. LOCKWOOD, Dec. 5, 1863.
Major-General LEW WALLACE, March 22, 1864.
Brevet Brigadier-General WILLIAM W. MORRIS, Feb. 1, 1865.
Major-General LEW WALLACE, April 19, 1865.

Ninth Army Corps.

Created by General Orders, No. 84, Adjutant-General's Office, July 22, 1862, to consist of the troops under Major-General Burnside, belonging to the Department of North Carolina. Discontinued by General Orders, No. 131, Adjutant-General's Office, Aug. 1, 1865. (The Ninth Army Corps served in the Department of North Carolina until Aug. —, 1862; Army of the Potomac until Feb. —, 1863; Department of Virginia until March —, 1863; Department of the Ohio until June —, 1863; Department of the Tennessee until Aug. —, 1863; Department of the Ohio until March, 1864; under the direct orders of General Grant until May, 1864; Army of the Potomac until April, 1865; and in the Department of Washington until July, 1865.)

COMMANDERS.

Major-General A. E. BURNSIDE, July 22, 1862.
Major-General J. L. RENO, Sept. 3, 1862.

ARMY CORPS.

Brigadier-General J. D. COX, Sept. 14, 1862.
Brigadier-General O. B. WILLCOX, Oct. 8, 1862.
Major-General JOHN SEDGWICK, Jan. 16, 1863.
Major-General WILLIAM F. SMITH, Feb. 5, 1863.
Major-General A. E. BURNSIDE, March 17, 1863.
Major-General J. G. PARKE, March 19, 1863.
Brigadier-General O. B. WILLCOX, April 4, 1863.
Major-General J. G. PARKE, June 5, 1863.
Brigadier-General R. B. POTTER, Aug. 21, 1863.
Brigadier-General O. B. WILLCOX, Jan. 18, 1864.
Major-General J. G. PARKE, Jan. 26, 1864.
Brigadier-General O. B. WILLCOX, March 16, 1864.
Major-General A. E. BURNSIDE, April 13, 1864.
Major-General J. G. PARKE, Aug. 15, 1864.
Brigadier-General O. B. WILLCOX, Dec. 31, 1864.
Major-General J. G. PARKE, Jan. 12, 1865.
Brevet Major-General O. B. WILLCOX, Jan. 24, 1865.
Major-General J. G. PARKE, Feb. 2, 1865.
Brevet Major-General O. B. WILLCOX, June 17, 1865.
Major-General J. G. PARKE, July 2, 1865.

Tenth Army Corps.

Created by General Orders, No. 123, Adjutant-General's Office, Sept. 3, 1862, to consist of the forces in the Department of the South. Reorganized, April 28, 1864. Discontinued, by General Orders, No. 297, Adjutant-General's Office, Dec. 3, 1864. White troops transferred to the Twenty-fourth Army Corps, and the colored troops to the Twenty-fifth Army Corps. Reorganized, by General Orders, No. 49, Adjutant-General's Office, March 27, 1865, to consist of all troops in North Carolina not belonging to General Sherman's army. Discontinued by General Orders, No. 131, Adjutant-General's Office, Aug. 1, 1865. (The Tenth Army Corps served in the Department of the South until May, 1864, and in the Department of Virginia and North Carolina until Dec. 3, 1864. The reorganized corps served in the Department of North Carolina.)

COMMANDERS.

Major-General O. M. MITCHEL, Sept. 15, 1862.
Brigadier-General J. M. BRANNAN, Oct. 27, 1862.
Major-General DAVID HUNTER, Jan. 20, 1863.
Major-General Q. A. GILLMORE, June 12, 1863.
Brigadier-General A. H. TERRY, June 15, 1864.
Brigadier-General W. T. H. BROOKS, June 19, 1864.
Brigadier-General A. H. TERRY, July 18, 1864.
Major-General D. B. BIRNEY, July 23, 1864.
Brigadier-General A. H. TERRY, Oct. 11, 1864.

ARMY CORPS.

Major-General A. H. TERRY, March 27, 1865. (Reorganized corps.)
Brigadier-General A. AMES, May 12, 1865.

Eleventh Army Corps, Army of the Potomac, until Sept. 25, 1863, and Department of the Cumberland until April 18, 1864.

Created by General Ordres, No. 129, Adjutant-General's Office, Sept. 12, 1862, by changing the designation of the First Army Corps, Army of Virginia. Merged into the Twentieth Army Corps, Army of the Cumberland, by General Orders, No. 144, Adjutant-General's Office, April 4, 1864.

COMMANDERS.

Major-General F. SIGEL, Sept. 12, 1862.
Brigadier-General J. STAHEL, Dec. 9, 1862.
Major-General F. SIGEL, Feb. 5, 1863.
Brigadier-General A. VON STEINWEHR, Feb. 23, 1863.
Major-General C. SCHURZ, March 29, 1863.
Major-General O. O. HOWARD, April 2, 1863.
Major-General C. SCHURZ, Jan. 21, 1864.
Major-General O. O. HOWARD, Feb. 25, 1864.

Twelfth Army Corps, Army of the Potomac, until Sept. 23, 1863, and Department of the Cumberland until April 18, 1864.

Created by General Orders, No. 129, Adjutant-General's Office, Sept. 12, 1862, by changing the designation of the Second Army Corps, Army of Virginia. Merged into the Twentieth Army Corps, Army of the Cumberland, by General Orders, No. 144, Adjutant-General's Office, April 4, 1864.

COMMANDERS.

Brigadier-General A. S. WILLIAMS, Sept. 18, 1862.
Major-General H. W. SLOCUM, Oct. 20, 1862.
Brigadier-General A. S. WILLIAMS, Aug. 31, 1863.
Major-General H. W. SLOCUM, Sept. 13, 1863.

Thirteenth Army Corps, Department of the Tennessee, until Aug. 7, 1863, and Department of the Gulf until June 11, 1864.

Created by General Orders, No. 168, Adjutant-General's Office, Oct. 24, 1862, to consist of the troops under the command of General Grant (Department of the Tennessee). Reorganized by General Orders, No. 210, Adjutant-General's Office, Dec. 18, 1862. Discontinued by General Orders, No. 210, Adjutant-General's Office, June 11, 1864.

ARMY CORPS.

COMMANDERS.

Major-General U. S. GRANT, Oct. 25, 1862.
Major-General J. A. McCLERNAND, Jan. 31, 1863.
Major-General E. O. C. ORD, June 19, 1863.
Major-General C. C. WASHBURNE, Aug. 7, 1863.
Major-General E. O. C. ORD, Sept. 15, 1863.
Major-General C. C. WASHBURNE, Oct. 20, 1863.
Major-General N. J. T. DANA, Oct. 26, 1863.
Major-General E. O. C. ORD, Jan. 9, 1864.
Major-General J. A. McCLERNAND, Feb. 23, 1864.
Brigadier-General W. P. BENTON, June 1, 1864.

Thirteenth Army Corps, Military Division, West Mississippi.

Created by General Orders, No. 20, Military Division of West Mississippi, Feb. 18, 1865, to consist of the reserve of that military division. Confirmed by General Orders, No. 28, Adjutant-General's Office, Feb. 26, 1865. Discontinued by General Orders, No. 124, Adjutant-General's Office, July 20, 1865.

COMMANDER.

Major-General GORDON GRANGER, Feb. 18, 1865.

Fourteenth Army Corps, Department of the Cumberland.

Created by General Orders, No. 168, Adjutant-General's Office, Oct. 24, 1862, to consist of the troops under Major-General Rosecrans (Department of the Cumberland). Reorganized by General Orders, No. 9, Adjutant-General's Office, Jan. 9, 1863. Discontinued by General Orders, No. 131, Adjutant-General's Office, Aug. 1, 1865.

COMMANDERS.

Major-General W. S. ROSECRANS, Oct. 27, 1862.
Major-General GEORGE H. THOMAS, Jan. 9, 1863.
Major-General J. M. PALMER, Oct. 28, 1863.
Brigadier-General R. W. JOHNSON, Aug. 6, 1864.
Brevet Major-General J. C. DAVIS, Aug. 9, 1864.

Fifteenth Army Corps, Department of the Tennessee.

Created by General Orders, No. 210, Adjutant-General's Office, Dec. 18, 1862, consisting of troops in the Department of the Tennessee and Department of the Missouri, operating on the Mississippi River. Discontinued by General Orders, No. 131, Adjutant-General's Office, Aug. 1, 1865.

ARMY CORPS.

COMMANDERS.

Major-General T. W. SHERMAN, Jan. 5, 1863.
Major-General F. P. BLAIR, JR., Oct. 29, 1863.
Major-General JOHN A. LOGAN, Dec. 11, 1863.
Major-General P. J. OSTERHAUS, Sept. 23, 1864.
Major-General JOHN A. LOGAN, Jan. 2, 1865.
Major-General W. B. HAZEN, May 23, 1865.

Sixteenth Army Corps, Department of the Tennessee.

Created by General Orders, No. 210, Adjutant-General's Office, Dec. 18, 1862, consisting of troops in the Department of the Tennessee and Department of the Missouri, operating on the Mississippi River. Discontinued by General Orders, No. 277, Adjutant-General's Office, Nov. 7, 1864.

COMMANDERS.

Major-General S. A. HURLBUT, Feb. 5, 1863, to April 17, 1864. (Corps had no commander from April 17 to Oct. 15, 1864.)
Major-General N. J. T. DANA, Oct. 15, 1864.

Sixteenth Army Corps, Military Division of West Mississippi.

Organized by General Orders, No. 20, Military Division of West Mississippi, Feb. 18, 1865, to consist of the infantry divisions from the Army of the Cumberland. Confirmed by General Orders, No. 28, Adjutant-General's Office, Feb. 26, 1865. Discontinued by General Orders, No. 124, Adjutant-General's Office, July 20, 1865.

COMMANDER.

Major-General A. J. SMITH, Feb. 18, 1865.

Seventeenth Army Corps, Department of the Tennessee.

Created by General Orders, No. 210, Adjutant-General's Office, Dec. 18, 1862, to consist of troops in the Department of the Tennessee and Department of the Missouri, operating on the Mississippi River. Discontinued by General Orders, No. 131, Adjutant-General's Office, Aug. 1, 1865.

COMMANDERS.

Major-General J. B. McPHERSON, Jan. 11, 1863.
Major-General F. P. BLAIR, JR., May 4, 1864.
Brigadier-General T. E. G. RANSOM, Sept. 22, 1864.
Brigadier-General M. D. LEGGETT, Oct. 10, 1864.
Major-General J. A. MOWER, Oct. 24, 1864.
Major-General F. P. BLAIR, JR., Oct. 31, 1864.
Brigadier-General W. W. BELKNAP, July 19, 1865.

ARMY CORPS.

Eighteenth Army Corps, Department of North Carolina, until Aug. —, 1863, and Department of Virginia and North Carolina (Army of the James), to Dec. 3, 1864.

Created by General Orders, No. 214, Adjutant-General's Office, Dec. 24, 1862, to consist of troops in North Carolina. Reorganized, April 28, 1864. Discontinued by General Orders, No. 297, Adjutant-General's Office, Dec. 3, 1864. White troops transferred to the Twenty-fourth Army Corps, and the colored troops to the Twenty-fifth Army Corps.

COMMANDERS.

Major-General J. G. FOSTER, Dec. 24, 1862.
Brigadier-General I. N. PALMER, July 2, 1863.
Major-General J. G. FOSTER, Aug. 8, 1863.
Major-General B. F. BUTLER, Oct. 28, 1863.
Major-General W. F. SMITH, May 2, 1864.
Brigadier-General J. H. MARTINDALE, July 19, 1864.
Major-General E. O. C. ORD, July 21, 1864.
Major-General JOHN GIBBON, Sept. 4, 1864.
Major-General E. O. C. ORD, Sept. 22, 1864.
Brevet Major-General G. WEITZEL, Oct. 1, 1864.

Nineteenth Army Corps, Department of the Gulf, until July —, 1864, and Middle Military Division until March —, 1865.

Created by General Orders, No. 5, Adjutant-General's Office, Jan. 5, 1863, to consist of the troops in the Department of the Gulf, to date from Dec. 14, 1862. Discontinued by General Orders, No. 4, Adjutant-General's Office, March 20, 1865.

COMMANDERS.

Major-General N. P. BANKS, Dec. 16, 1862.
Major-General WILLIAM B. FRANKLIN, Aug. 20, 1863.
Brigadier-General WILLIAM H. EMORY, May 2, 1864.
Brigadier-General B. S. ROBERTS, July 2, 1864.
Brigadier-General M. K. LAWLER, July 6, 1864.
Major-General J. J. REYNOLDS, July 7, 1864.
Brevet Major-General WILLIAM H. EMORY, Nov. 7, 1864.
Brigadier-General C. GROVER, Dec. 10, 1864.
Brevet Major-General WILLIAM H. EMORY, Dec. 28, 1864.

Twentieth Army Corps, Department of the Cumberland.

Created by General Orders, No. 9, Adjutant-General's Office, Jan. 9, 1863, to consist of troops in the Army of the Cumberland. Discontinued, Oct. 9, 1863, in compliance with General Orders, No. 322, Adjutant-General's Office, Sept. 28, 1863.

ARMY CORPS.

Merged into the Fourth Army Corps, Army of the Cumberland. Reorganized by General Orders, No. 144, Adjutant-General's Office, April 4, 1864, by the consolidation of the Eleventh and Twelfth Army Corps, Army of the Cumberland. Discontinued, June 1, 1865, by General Orders, No. 131, Adjutant-General's Office, July 28, 1865.

COMMANDERS.

Major-General A. McD. McCOOK, Jan. 9, 1863.
Major-General JOSEPH HOOKER, April 4, 1864.
Brigadier-General A. S. WILLIAMS, July 27, 1864.
Major-General H. W. SLOCUM, Aug. 27, 1864.
Brigadier-General A. S. WILLIAMS, Nov. 11, 1864.
Major-General J. A. MOWER, April 1, 1865.

Twenty-first Army Corps, Department of the Cumberland.

Created by General Orders, No. 9, Adjutant-General's Office, Jan. 9, 1863, to consist of troops in the Army of the Cumberland. Merged into the Fourth Army Corps, Army of the Cumberland, Oct. 9, 1863, in compliance with General Orders, No. 322, Adjutant-General's Office, Sept. 28, 1863.

COMMANDERS.

Major-General T. L. CRITTENDEN, Jan. 9, 1863.
Brigadier-General T. J. WOOD, Feb. 18, 1863.
Major-General T. L. CRITTENDEN, March 4, 1863.
Major-General J. M. PALMER, July 18, 1863.
Major-General T. L. CRITTENDEN, Aug. 11, 1863.

Twenty-second Army Corps, Department of Washington.

Created by General Orders, No. 26, Adjutant-General's Office, Feb. 2, 1863, to consist of troops in the Department of Washington. Discontinued, June 11, 1866.

COMMANDERS.

Major-General S. P. HEINTZELMAN, Feb. 7, 1863.
Major-General C. C. AUGUR, Oct. 13, 1863.
Major-General J. G. PARKE, June 7, 1865.
Major-General C. C. AUGUR, June 26, 1865.

Twenty-third Army Corps, Department of the Ohio, until Jan. —, 1865, and Department of North Carolina until Aug., 1865.

Created by General Orders, No. 103, Adjutant-General's Office, April 27, 1863, to consist of the troops in Kentucky, not belonging to the Ninth Army Corps. Reorganized by Special Orders, No. 101, Department of the Ohio, April 10, 1864. Discontinued by General Orders, No. 131, Adjutant-General's Office, Aug. 1, 1865.

ARMY CORPS.

COMMANDERS.

Major-General G. L. HARTSUFF, May 28, 1863.
Brigadier-General M. D. MANSON, Sept. 24, 1863.
Brigadier-General J. D. COX, Dec. 8, 1863.
Major-General GEORGE STONEMAN, Jan. 28, 1864.
Major-General J. M. SCHOFIELD, April 4, 1864.
Major-General J. D. COX, April 2, 1865.
Brigadier-General S. P. CARTER, June 8, 1865.

Twenty-fourth Army Corps, Department of Virginia.

Created by General Orders, No. 297, Adjutant-General's Office, Dec. 3, 1864, to consist of the white troops of the Tenth and Eighteenth Army Corps. Discontinued by General Orders, No. 131, Adjutant-General's Office, Aug. 1, 1865.

COMMANDERS.

Major-General E. O. C. ORD, Dec. 3, 1864.
Brevet Major-General A. H. TERRY, Dec. 8, 1864.
Brigadier-General C. DEVENS, Jan. 2, 1865.
Major-General JOHN GIBBON, Jan. 15, 1865.
Brevet Major-General J. W. TURNER, July 1, 1865.

Twenty-fifth Army Corps, Department of Virginia, until June, 1865, and Department of Texas until Jan., 1866.

Created by General Orders, No. 297, Adjutant-General's Office, Dec. 3, 1864, to consist of the colored troops of the Tenth and Eighteenth Army Corps. Discontinued by General Orders, No. 2, Adjutant-General's Office, Jan. 8, 1866.

COMMANDERS.

Major-General G. WEITZEL, Dec. 4, 1864.
Brigadier-General C. A. HECKMAN, Jan. 12, 1865.
Major-General G. WEITZEL, Feb. 17, 1865.

Cavalry Corps, Army of the Potomac.

Created by General Orders, No. 6, Army of the Potomac, Feb. 5, 1863, to consist of the cavalry of the Army of the Potomac. Discontinued, June 28, 1865.

COMMANDERS.

Brigadier-General GEORGE STONEMAN, Feb. 7, 1863.
Brigadier-General ALFRED PLEASONTON, June 7, 1863.
Brigadier-General D. McM. GREGG, March 26, 1864.
Major-General P. H. SHERIDAN, April 6, 1864.
Brevet Major-General D. McM. GREGG, Aug. 4, 1864.
Major-General P. H. SHERIDAN, March 28, 1865.

NAVAL SQUADRONS.

NAVAL SQUADRONS.

Atlantic Blockading Squadron.

Captain SILAS H. STRINGHAM, May 4, 1861, to Sept. 23, 1861.
Captain LOUIS M. GOLDSBOROUGH, Sept. 23, 1861, to Oct. 29, 1861.
  (Squadron divided into the North and South Atlantic Blockading Squadrons, Oct. 29, 1861.)
  (Squadron recreated June 17, 1865, by the consolidation of the North and South Atlantic Blockading Squadrons.)
Commodore WILLIAM RADFORD, June 17, 1865, to Oct. 10, 1865, when he was succeeded by Commodore JOSEPH LANMAN.

Brazil Squadron.

Captain JOSHUA R. SANDS, until June 20, 1861.
Lieutenant WILLIAM H. MACOMB, Senior Naval Officer on Station, from June 20, 1861.
Re-established, and Commodore SYLVANUS W. GODON appointed to command, March 28, 1868.

East Gulf Blockading Squadron.

Created Feb. 21, 1862.

Captain WILLIAM W. McKEAN, Feb. 21, 1862, to June 4, 1862.
Captain JAMES L. LARDNER, June 4, 1862, to Dec. 11, 1862.
Commodore THEODORUS BAILEY, Dec. 11, 1862, to Aug. 7, 1864.
Captain THEODORE P. GREENE, Aug. 7, 1864, to Oct. 12, 1864.
Commodore CORNELIUS K. STRIBLING, Oct. 12, 1864, to July 17, 1865.
  (Squadron consolidated with West Gulf Blockading Squadron, July 17, 1865, forming the Gulf Squadron, which see.)

East India Squadron.

Captain CORNELIUS K. STRIBLING, until July 8, 1861.
Captain FREDERICK ENGLE, July 8, 1861, to July 31, 1865.
Commodore HENRY H. BELL, appointed to command, July 31, 1865.

European Squadron.

Rear-Admiral LOUIS M. GOLDSBOROUGH, appointed to command, June 3, 1865.

NAVAL SQUADRONS.

Flying Squadron.
(See West India Squadron.)

Gulf Squadron.

Captain WILLIAM MERVINE, until Sept. 13, 1861.
Captain WILLIAM W. McKEAN, Sept. 13, 1861, to Feb. 21, 1862.
(Squadron divided into East and West Gulf Blockading Squadrons, Feb. 21, 1862.)
(Squadron recreated, July 17, 1865, by consolidation of East and West Gulf Blockading Squadrons.)
Commodore HENRY K. THATCHER, commanding.

Home Squadron.

Captain GARRETT J. PENDERGRAST, Oct. 10, 1860, to May 17, 1861.

James and York River Flotilla.

Captain CHARLES WILKES, July 6 to Aug. 31, 1862.
(Afterwards vessels operating in these rivers, and in the Sounds of North Carolina, became divisions of the North Atlantic Blockading Squadron.)

Mediterranean Squadron.

Captain CHARLES H. BELL, commanding in 1861.

Mississippi Flotilla (or Western Flotilla).
Captain ANDREW H. FOOTE, Sept. 6, 1861, to May 9, 1862.
Captain CHARLES H. DAVIS, May 9, 1862, to Oct. 15, 1862.
Commander DAVID D. PORTER, Oct. 15, 1862, to Sept. 28, 1864.
Captain ALEXANDER M. PENNOCK (temporarily), Sept. 28 to Nov. 1, 1864.
Captain S. PHILLIPS LEE, Nov. 1, 1864, to Aug. 14, 1865.
(Squadron discontinued, Aug. 14, 1865.)

North Atlantic Blockading Squadron.
Created Sept. 23, 1861.

Captain LOUIS M. GOLDSBOROUGH, Sept. 23, 1861, to Sept. 5, 1862.
Captain S. PHILLIPS LEE, Sept. 5, 1862, to Oct. 12, 1864.
Rear-Admiral DAVID D. PORTER, Oct. 12, 1864, to April 28, 1865.
Commodore WILLIAM RADFORD, April 28 to June 17, 1865.
(Squadron consolidated with the South Atlantic Squadron, June 17, 1865, forming the Atlantic Squadron.)

NAVAL SQUADRONS.

Pacific Squadron.

Captain JOHN B. MONTGOMERY, until Jan. 2, 1862.
Captain CHARLES H. BELL, Jan. 2, 1862, to Oct. 25, 1864.
Commodore GEORGE F. PEARSON, Oct. 25, 1864, to close of the war.

Potomac Flotilla.

Commander JAMES H. WARD, May 16, 1861, to June 27, 1861.
Commander STEPHEN C. ROWAN, June 27, 1861, to July 6, 1861.
Commander T. T. CRAVEN, July 6, 1861, to Dec. 2, 1861.
Lieutenant A. D. HARRELL, Dec. 2-6, 1861.
Lieutenant ROBERT H. WYMAN, Dec. 6, 1861, to July 12, 1862.
Lieutenant SAMUEL MAGAW, July 12 to Aug. 30, 1862.
Commodore CHARLES WILKES, Aug. 30, 1862, to Sept. 10, 1862.
Commodore ANDREW A. HARWOOD, Sept. 10, 1862, to Dec. 31, 1863.
Commander FOXHALL A. PARKER, Dec. 31, 1863, to July 31, 1865.
(Flotilla disbanded, July 31, 1865.)

South Atlantic Blockading Squadron.

Created Sept. 23, 1861.

Captain SAMUEL F. DU PONT, Sept. 23, 1861, to July 6, 1863.
Rear-Admiral JOHN A. DAHLGREN, July 6, 1863, to July 17, 1865.
Commodore STEPHEN C. ROWAN (temporarily), Feb. 23 to May 4, 1864.
(Squadron consolidated with the North Atlantic Blockading Squadron, June 17, 1865, forming the Atlantic Squadron.)

Special Squadron.

Commodore JOHN RODGERS, commanding; sailed from Hampton Roads, Va., for San Francisco, Cal., Nov. 2, 1865.

West India Squadron.

Captain GARRETT J. PENDERGRAST, May 17 to Sept. 7, 1861. (There was no West India Squadron between Sept., 1861, and Sept. 8, 1862.)
Commodore CHARLES WILKES, Sept. 8, 1862, to June 20, 1863.
Commodore JAMES L. LARDNER, June 20, 1863, to Oct. 3, 1864.
(Squadron ceased to exist, Oct. 3, 1864.)

NAVAL SQUADRONS.

Western Flotilla.

(See Mississippi Flotilla.)

West Gulf Blockading Squadron.

Captain DAVID G. FARRAGUT, Jan. 20, 1862, to Aug. 5, 1863.
Commodore HENRY H. BELL, Aug. 5, 1863, to Jan. 18, 1864.
Rear-Admiral DAVID G. FARRAGUT, Jan. 18 to Sept. 5, 1864.
Commodore JAMES S. PALMER, Sept. 5, 1864, to Feb. 28, 1865.
Commodore HENRY K. THATCHER, Feb. 28, 1865, to July 17, 1865.

(Squadron consolidated with East Gulf Bockading Squadron, July 17, 1865, forming the Gulf Squadron.)

www.ingramcontent.com/pod-product-compliance
Lightning Source LLC
Chambersburg PA
CBHW022018220426
43663CB00007B/1119